Lieve Gies
Editor

Trial by Media

Participatory Justice in a Networked World

palgrave
macmillan

Editor
Lieve Gies
Department of Media
and Communication
University of Leicester
Leicester, UK

ISSN 2946-3912 ISSN 2946-3920 (electronic)
Palgrave Studies in Crime, Media and Culture
ISBN 978-3-031-80592-9 ISBN 978-3-031-80593-6 (eBook)
https://doi.org/10.1007/978-3-031-80593-6

Cover illustration: the_burtons/Gettyimages

This Palgrave Macmillan imprint is published by the registered company Springer Nature Switzerland AG
The registered company address is: Gewerbestrasse 11, 6330 Cham, Switzerland

Foreword

Unfortunately I could not participate in the 'New Perspectives on Trial by Media' conference that was held in June 2023. Then Lieve got in contact noting that there were quite a few references to my work with Chris Greer and kindly suggesting that it might be appropriate to write a Preface. Before discussing the issues raised by this fascinating collection I want to briefly explain the working theory of Trial by Media that we are continuing to develop (Greer & McLaughlin, 2023).

As criminologists our starting point was trying to make sense of the rapidly transforming crime news environment in the UK. Crime has always been and will always be newsworthy, and therefore profitable as a 'it bleeds so it leads' media commodity.

Crime news works across the highly emotional registers of moral righteousness, fear, anger, and fascination (Katz, 1987). Criminologists have long complained about how media reporting routinely misrepresents and distorts the nature of the crime problem, public perceptions of who is and who is not a perpetrator and victim and the functioning of the criminal justice system (Greer, 2009). Sensational and violent crimes headline and saturate news reporting, stimulating fear of and anger about crime, and generating 'moral panics' (Cohen, 2002). Crime and criminal justice also provide the storylines for a lucrative global crime infotainment industry, including of course 'True Crime' podcasts. In many respects we continue to be culturally obsessed with crime and criminal justice (O'Brien, 2024).

Our initial research noted how within an increasingly chaotic information milieu, news organisations were attempting to capture and retain audiences through publishing/broadcasting increasingly adversarial content. This 'adversarial turn' was one response to social media's 'free news on demand' disruption of the stranglehold of the mainstream or 'legacy' media (Davies, 2015; Rusbridger, 2018; Lawrence & Napoli, 2023). It also fed off and reflected a range of broader cultural shifts such as the decline of deference to authority and increasing public distrust in/mistrust of establishment institutions and elites (Illouz & Sicron, 2023; Jones, 2015; Mishra, 2018; Norris & Ingelhart, 2019; O'Brien, 2024). Energised by tabloidisation and digitalisation, adversarialism was/is reconstituting the nature of news in the UK. One of the most notable expressions of this 'adversarial turn' is the extraordinary surfacing of Trial by Media' (TbM).

The dictum 'justice must seen to be done' creates a tricky balancing act between (a) the right of the news media to report freely and proactively (b) the citizen's right to a fair and unimpeded trial and (c) the integrity of the rule of law. The US constitution facilitates a relatively permissive approach to the news coverage of court cases. Reporting is authorised to continue after a defendant has been charged. Advocates for both the prosecution and defence can 'try' high-profile cases simultaneously in both the law courts and the court of public opinion. The melodrama generated by the O. J. Simpson trial has stood the test of time as an example of an exceptionally polarising TbM that fixated the American public. An estimated 95 million people watched the live TV coverage of O. J. Simpson's 90-minute-long attempt to evade the police in a white Ford Bronco. America subsequently tuned in to watch the trial that made celebrities out of all involved (Toobin, 2015; Bailey, 2021).

More recently, live-streaming court proceedings involving cases of public interest encourages and reinforces frenzied media reporting. And of course the infamous 'perp walk' of the hand-cuffed accused being paraded in front of the camera is a defining image of US criminal justice. 'Walking the perp' also conjures up pre-modern spectacles of public humiliation of the accused and condemned (Wringe, 2016; Haberman, 2018).

In the UK there are stringent restrictions on the media reporting of criminal cases and routine warnings are issued about the risks posed by 'TbM' in its various forms.

In the 1960s the judiciary focused on the deleterious effects of 'Trial by Television'. In 1973 Lord Denning stated: "We must not allow 'trial by newspaper' or 'trial by television' or trial by any medium other than the courts of law" (*Financial Times*, 19 February 1973, p. 4).

Lord Hailsham, the Lord Chancellor, warned journalists in 1987 that criticism of the judiciary should be "well informed, well researched and temperately expressed or there will be trial by media" (Graves, 1987, p. 5).

Contempt of court legislation imposes restrictions to ensure that jurors deliberate in a media-free bubble, reaching verdicts on the basis of the evidence presented in court, free from the baleful influence of prejudicial news reporting. There are also curbs on: naming suspects, what can be reported after an arrest is made and what can be reported during judicial proceedings (Nicol et al., 2009). The police and Crown Prosecution Service routinely remind the media and the public that in active criminal cases there should be no reporting, commentary or sharing information online which could in any way prejudice proceedings. Unlike in the US, UK court proceedings are, for the most part, also camera-free (Ministry of Justice, 2012). These restrictions are now being tested to the limit in the clickbait news environment.

Two other legal impediments facing news media organisations are defamation and privacy laws. They must avoid both making defamatory statements which could trigger expensive libel cases and/or publishing/broadcasting embarrassing or humiliating details about someone's private life (Mitchell, 2005). The wealthy and the powerful can resort to 'lawfare' in the form of SLAPPs - Strategic Lawsuits Against Public Participation (SLAPPs) where a plaintiff threatens to or launches defamation proceedings against an individual or an organisation in order to suppress investigation, discussion or debate on matters of public interest (Dawson, 2024).

TbM is a market driven form of interactive populist justice in which individuals and institutions are judged and sentenced in an inter-mediatised 'court of public opinion' that operates across multiple platforms and formats. This 'court' can be constructed and attended by a worldwide audience. Anyone with internet access can participate in the online trial proceedings. In this court no-one is objective or impartial, there is no right to anonymity and nothing can be ruled out. The allegations driving TbM range across four overlapping categories of infraction: criminality, immorality, negligence and/or incompetence. The disruptive power of TbM resides in its capacity to trigger an extreme emotional public reaction—shock, anger, outcry, contempt—that can re-define cultural, political, and policy agendas and leave an indelible imprint on the collective conscience.

The nature and targets of TbM are diverse, and include: naming and shaming public figures and institutions accused of: acting as if they are above the law; violating an assumed moral consensus; failing to deliver on obligations and responsibilities; pre-judging the outcome of criminal investigations involving 'knowns' and 'unknowns'; 'retrying' individuals considered to have evaded justice and/or proportionate punishment. Active public participation—which may vary from posting accusations and/or salacious and sensational speculation to web sleuthing for evidence, assessing the truth/untruth of evidence, trolling and weaving evidential webs, to sharing in collective judgement on the guilt or innocence of the accused—is integral to the immersive feeding frenzy.

Through viral interactivity, TbM reclaims aspects of 'justice' from the law courts and returns them to a digital court of public opinion. The extra-legal investigation practices that form a core part of TbM may uncover sufficient evidence to activate or reinforce legal due process. TbM thus has the power to initiate formal legal proceedings that otherwise may not otherwise have occurred. But it can also swing the other way not only challenging but undermining due process. Inverting a defining principle of due process, TbM cases are premised on a presumption of 'guilty until proven innocent'. 'Presumed guilty' precipitates a frantic search for irrefutable 'gotcha' evidence of any kind that can reinforce the case against the accused as 'guilty as charged'. While opinion and hearsay are generally regarded as inadmissible in a court of law, 'evidence' in TbM ranges from that which might be legally admissible to head-spinning conjecture, insinuation and conspiracy theorising. The accused can find themselves being used as a 'flypaper' being hung out with the hope of attracting other accusations and indeed other names.

Attempting to exercise the 'right to silence' or 'lawyering up' in the face of accusation is viewed as a tacit admission of guilt. Those who publicly declare their innocence or display recalcitrance, including contempt for the court of public opinion, will be subjected to relentless scrutiny aimed at uncovering 'Gotcha' proof of their irrefutable guilt. In desperation the accused may be tempted to subject themselves to a TbM in an attempt to tell their side of the story. Anyone daring to defend the accused runs the risk of investigation & mobbing. The 'gotcha' moment is critical to energising the feeding frenzy. Through the public naming of alleged 'wrongdoers', TbM orchestrates both 'guilt-scrolling' and shaming ceremonies that (a) dramatise community norms and moral boundaries and (b) transform the public identity of individual and institutional actors. A public confession of guilt, particularly if it has to be dragged out of the accused, and/or self-abasement can exacerbate the trial. Of course, counter TbMs can be triggered that ensnare accusers are also possible.

TbM is capable of providing an alternative forum for delivering 'justice' to victims. Punishment of the 'guilty' ranges from varying degrees of devastating status degradation (mockery, humiliation, vilification and demonisation) to criminal sanction, the introduction of new laws and regulatory frameworks, the transformation of institutional practice, and the rewriting of collective memory. Those judged to be innocent or who manage to see off their accusers never really recover from a fully-fledged media trial. In a 'no right to be forgotten' social media context, 'no smoke, without fire' suspicions will always linger, pariah status persist and the media trial can be revived, including in the form of fictional entertainment. For some of the accused the only choice is to embrace and exploit their notoriety.

TbM has also played a key role in the reinvigoration of investigative journalism as part of news organisations' attempts to establish market distinction and demonstrate their sense of relevance and power. Campaigning across a range of issues has emboldened UK news organisations to claim to be acting as the 'voice for the voiceless' and extending their traditional agenda setting role to one of overt advocacy and activism. For example, through high-profile campaigning, different news organisations are pressurising the state to take responsibility for a succession of institutional failures perpetrated by a dysfunctional criminal justice system, namely: conviction of the innocent; allowing the guilty to walk free; permitting dangerous offenders to remain at liberty; and incompetent/corrupt criminal justice leadership. The development of TbM, often working through victim-centred campaigns, has allowed news organisations to test the legal limits and public appeal of the exposure of individual wrongdoing, institutional failures and co-ordinated cover-ups. All UK news organisations, including serious newspapers such as the *Financial Times*, are now aggressively engaged in individual and institutional scandal-hunting premised on the activation and amplification of a full-blown media trial.

This interdisciplinary, international collection of chapters put together by Lieve and her collaborators expands existing theorising and research through interrogation of different constructions, manifestations and anatomies of media trials as well as the myriad effects. Collectively the chapters raise an important set of questions that require further research. An over arching issue addressed in all the chapters is whether TbM should be conceived of as a progressive or dangerously reactionary development. The chapters also pose important questions concerning: the distinctiveness of TbM; the parameters of TbM; the significance of TbM; why and how TbM activates, unfolds and recedes; the stakeholders in TbM; the impact, effects and legacies of TbM; what counts as an effective TbM; the nature of 'justice' TbM offers and delivers; the broader socio-political context that cultivates and sustains TbM; and how TbM vary historically and comparatively. Developing methodological rigour in this still emergent field requires accounting for how exactly we select TbM cases for research purposes. There are sound reasons to focus on high-profile TbMs but what about the TbMs that fail to ignite or that fizzle out or that are successfully blocked by 'lawfare'? Then there are the critical social issues that should be subjected to TbM but are not. In addition, researchers now need to employ methodologies that are capable of capturing the automated, algorithmic logics and dynamics of social media trials. Future research should also include the lived experience of those who find themselves embroiled in a TbM.

Eugene McLaughlin
City St George's
University of London
London, UK

References

Bailey, F. L. (2021). *The truth about the O.J. Simpson trial*. Skyhorse Publishing.
Cohen, S. (2002). *Folk devils and moral panics* (3rd ed.). Routledge.
Davies, N. (2015). *Hack attack*. Vintage Books.
Dawson, J. (2024). *SLAPPs: Strategic litigation against public participation: Research briefing number 9962*, House of Commons.
Financial Times. (1973, February 17). Lord Denning on freedom of press to make fair comment. *Financial Times*, p. 4.
Graves, D. (1987, April 16). Hailsham urges press to avoid trial by media. *Daily Telegraph*, p.5.
Greer, C. (2009). *Crime and media: A reader*. Routledge.
Greer, C., & McLaughlin, E. (2023). Crime news, trial by media, and scandal hunting. In A. Liebling, S. Maruna, & L. McAra (Eds.), *The Oxford handbook of criminology* (7th ed.). Oxford University Press.
Haberman, C. (2018, December 2). For shame: A brief history of the perp walk. *New York Times*.
Jones, O. (2015). *The establishment: And how they get away with it*. Penguin Books.
Illouz, E., & Sicron, A. (2023). *The emotional life of populism*. Polity Books.
Katz, J. (1987). What makes crime 'news'? *Media, Culture and Society, 9*(1), 47-75.
Lawrence, R. G., & Napoli, P. M. (Eds.). (2023). *News quality in the digital age*. Routledge.

Ministry of Justice. (2012). *Proposals to allow the broadcasting, filming, and recording of selected court proceedings.* Ministry of Justice.

Mishra, P. (2018). *Age of anger: A history of the present.* Penguin Books.

Mitchell, P. (2005). *The making of the modern law of defamation.* Hart Publishing.

Norris, P., & Inglehart, R. (2019). *Cultural backlash.* Cambridge University Press.

Nicol, A., QC, Millar, G., & Sharland, A. (2009). *Media law & human Rights.* Oxford University Press.

O'Brien, G. (2024, February 8). A craving for crime. *The New York Review.*

O'Brien, J. (2024). *How they broke Britain.* W.H. Allen.

Pilger, J. (2005). *Tell me no lies.* Vintage Books.

Rusbridger, A. (2018). *Breaking news: The remaking of journalism and why it matters now.* Canongate Books.

Toobin, J. (2015). *The run of his life: The people v. O. J. Simpson.* Random House Books.

Wringe, B. (2016). *An expressive theory of punishment.* Palgrave Macmillan.

Eugene McLaughlin is Professor of Criminology in the School of Policy and Global Affairs at City St. George's, University of London. His current research centres on understanding institutional corruption, 'trial by media' and contemporary cults. He has also written extensively on the crisis of policing, the managerialisation of criminal justice and criminological theory. Recent books are Cults (with Stephanie Baker and Chris Rojek, forthcoming 2024), the Sage Dictionary of Criminology (with John Muncie, 4th Edition, 2019) and Understanding Deviance (with David Downes and Paul Rock, 7th Edition, 2016).

Acknowledgements

This book is the product of the online workshop 'New Perspectives on Trial by Media' held in June 2023 at the University of Leicester (UK) in cooperation with the Centre for Europeanisation and Internationalisation (CELI). I gratefully acknowledge CELI for the financial support provided and for creating the interdisciplinary research environment from which this project has benefited. I am especially thankful to its directors Rossana Deplano and Katja Ziegler for their support and encouragement. I would also like to thank the workshop participants for their invaluable input. Finally, I would like to thank Didier Meert for his IT support in dealing with the little gremlins that invariably appear when working with a set of documents that have been authored by different people.

Contents

Notes on Contributors

Katrina Clifford is an Associate Professor in Communication in the Faculty of Arts and Education at Deakin University (Australia). She is a specialist in media criminology and media framing analysis. Her research focuses on the complex and shifting intersections between law, justice and journalism in the contemporary mediascape. Katrina is the author of *Policing, Mental Illness and Media: The Framing of Mental Health Crisis Encounters and Police Use of Force* (Palgrave Macmillan, 2021) and co-author of *Media and Crime: Content, Context and Consequence* (OUP, 2017).

Lieve Gies is Associate Professor in the School of Arts, Media and Communication, and convenor of the Law, Media and Communication Research Group at the University of Leicester (UK). Her specialism is media representations of the law and the legal system. She is the author of *Law and the Media: The Future of an Uneasy Relationship* (Routledge, 2008) and *Mediating Human Rights: Media, Culture and Human Rights*

Law (Routledge, 2014), and co-editor of *Transmedia Crime Stories: The Trial of Amanda Knox and Raffaele Sollecito in the Globalised Media Sphere* (Palgrave, 2016).

Tanya Horeck is Professor of Film and Feminist Media Studies at Anglia Ruskin University where she is also Research Lead for the Cambridge School of Creative Industries. She has published widely on sexual and gender-based violence. Her books include *Public Rape: Representing Violation in Fiction and Film* and *Justice on Demand: True Crime in the Digital Streaming Era*. More recently, she has worked on the projects: 'The Role of the Intimacy Coordinator: New Depictions of Sex and Consent in UK Television Culture' (with Susan Berridge) and Young People's Experiences of Technology-Facilitated Gender-Based Violence During Covid-19 (with Jessica Ringrose and Kaitlynn Mendes).

Deborah Jermyn is Associate Professor in Film at the University of Roehampton where she specialises in feminist film and media studies. She has written widely on media representations of crime and is author and editor of 11 books, including *Crime Watching: Investigating Real Crime TV* (2006) and the BFI TV Classic *Prime Suspect* (2010). Currently she continues to work too on what she has termed 'the menopausal turn'—in which a new era of pronounced attention to menopause has become evident across multiple cultural sites—including articles in the *Journal of Aging Studies* and the *European Journal of Cultural Studies*.

Bethan Jones is a Research Fellow in the Faculty of Business and Creative Industries at the University of South Wales. She has written extensively on anti-fandom, media tourism and participatory culture and her more recent work explores engagement with true crime. Bethan is co-editor of *Popular Communication* as well as co-chair of the SCMS Fan and Audience Studies Scholarly Interest Group. She is co-editor of the journal *Popular Communication* and co-editor of *Crowdfunding the*

Future: Media Industries, Ethics, and Digital Society (Peter Lang, 2015) and *Participatory Culture Wars: Controversy, Conflict and Complicity in Fandom* (Iowa University Press, 2025).

Azi Lev-On is a Professor and a Faculty Member in the School of Communication in Ariel University. His research focuses on the social and political uses and impact of the Internet and social media, and particularly on their affordances for and usage by citizens in terms of speech and action, and the corresponding institutional responses. His latest book is *The murder of Tair Rada and the Roman Zdorov affair: Establishment, justice, citizens and social media* (Yedioth Books, 2023).

Stefan Machura is Professor of Criminology and Criminal Justice at Bangor University. He has studied sociology and political science at the Ruhr–Universität Bochum (Germany), where he got his PhD. In his second dissertation (*Habilitation*, Universität der Bundeswehr München in 2000) he researched the cooperation of lay and professional judges at criminal courts. Publications include *Law and Film* (co-edited with Peter Robson, 2001, Blackwell), *Recht im Film* (co-edited with Stefan Ulbrich, 2002, Nomos), *Krieg im Film* (co-edited with Rüdiger Voigt, 2005, Lit) and *Law and War in Popular Culture* (editor, Nomos, in print).

Steff El Madawi is an independent scholar and visiting academic at the University of Southampton (UK). Her specialisms are literary testimony and modes of witnessing, with additional research interests in auto/biography, documentary and nonfiction.

Belinda Middleweek is a Senior Lecturer in the School of Communication at the University of Technology Sydney (Australia). Her research investigates the ways in which engagements with technology are embodied (sensory, emotional, and intellectual) and deeply rooted in social, cultural, and affective practices. She has published widely on the Chamberlain case, examining the emotional dynamics of social media platforms, trial by media processes and media portrayals of criminally implicated women. She is the author of *Feral Media? The Chamberlain* *case, 40 years on* (ASP, 2021), and co-author of *Real Sex Films: The New Intimacy and Risk in Cinema* (OUP, 2017).

Anat Peleg is a Lecturer in the School of Communications at Tel-Aviv University and in the Faculty of law at Bar Ilan University. Anat served as the Senior Legal Reporter at the National Israeli Radio for 17 years. Her research focuses on the effects of trial by both social media and mainstream media on the legal community and on the judicial process in Israel.

Maria Rae is a Senior Lecturer in Politics and Policy at Deakin University in Australia and previously worked as a newspaper journalist. Her research focuses on political communication, media, justice and digital journalism. Specifically, her work explores how marginalised and fringe communities use media to contest dominant narratives. More recently, she is working on the sound of politics through voice, power and audio technology. Her work has been published in *New Media and Society*, *Continuum, International Journal of Communication* and *Media, Culture and Society*.

Simon Statham is Senior Lecturer in English Language and Linguistics at Queen's University Belfast, where he researches and teaches in Critical Discourse Analysis, Stylistics and related fields of study. He is author of *Redefining Trial by Media* (Benjamins, 2016) and *Critical Discourse Analysis* (Routledge, 2022) and co-author of *Language and Power* (Routledge, 2018). His current project examines the linguistic constructions of and strategies in the Irish abortion debate.

Maria Stoyanova is an Analyst in the Law Program of the Center for the Study of Democracy and a Ph.D. candidate in European Political Science at Sofia University 'St. Kliment Ohridski'. Her research focuses on the role of media in criminal justice, enhancing media freedom, and investigating online hatred and other malign activities in the digital environment. She is the author of The Presumption of Innocence and the Media Coverage of Criminal Cases: Case Studies Analysis (Center for the Study of Democracy, 2021) and Disclosing Information on Criminal

Cases: Guidebook for Criminal Justice and Media Professionals (Center for the Study of Democracy, 2022).

Paolo Vargiu is Associate Professor at Leicester Law School, University of Leicester (UK), where he teaches international law, jurisprudence, and law and religion. He holds degrees from the Universities of Cagliari (JD), Nottingham (LL.M. and Ph.D.) and Leicester (PGCHE) and is a Fellow of the Higher Education Academy. His research interests lie primarily on matters of public international law, international dispute settlement and human rights law.

List of Figures

List of Tables

1

Introduction: Understanding Trial by Media and Participatory Justice in a Networked World

Lieve Gies

What Is Trial by Media?

A woman in her forties goes missing on a cold winter's day, triggering a media feeding frenzy which sees TikTok influencers descend on the location to solve a crime that never was. Convinced that the person in prison for the murder of a schoolgirl is innocent, supporters-turned-sleuths point the finger of blame at the schoolgirl's friends, marking the start of a prolonged campaign of online defamation and harassment. A piece of investigative journalism proves a catalyst for bringing a Serbian war criminal to justice. An award-winning podcast is widely credited for the breakthrough in a cold case and results in a murder conviction. A student hazing with fatal consequences triggers social media-led protests against the non-custodial sentences which members of the elite and predominantly white student fraternity received for their involvement in the death of the young minority-ethnic student. An American

L. Gies (✉)
University of Leicester, Leicester, UK
e-mail: lg149@leicester.ac.uk

L. Gies (ed.), *Trial by Media*, Palgrave Studies in Crime, Media and Culture,
https://doi.org/10.1007/978-3-031-80593-6_1

woman who was convicted and subsequently exonerated in Italy for the murder of her flatmate is still struggling to escape the narrative of guilt thrust upon her by the media more than a decade on from the tragic events. A bitter legal feud on both sides of the Atlantic between a famous Hollywood couple generates hours of real-time infotainment and acres of media commentary, most of which is very hostile towards the woman at the centre of the case. The arrest of HIV-positive sex workers leads to a widespread campaign of media naming and shaming, with tragic consequences when one of the accused takes her own life. A television drama about the wrongful conviction of 900 postal workers for computer fraud triggers such a tremendous public response that the government moves to introduce new legislation to accelerate the process of legally exonerating the many victims of the miscarriage of justice.

Nicola Bulley, Tair Rada, Captain Dragan Vasiljković, Lynette Dawson, Sanda Dia, Depp v Heard, Amanda Knox, HIV-positive sex workers in Greece, *Mr Bates vs The Post Office*: all of these are discussed in this volume as exemplars of trial by media. Each case comes with pseudo-judicial acts performed by media participants across a variety of channels and platforms, but what exactly constitutes 'trial by media'? What typifies these cases? What are their common traits? How do they differ? How can we explain the dynamics, trajectories, processes and affordances of trial by media? Why does a particular sequence of events become the focus of a media trial while other cases barely get a mention? Is trial by media always harmful or does it hold out the promise of democratising justice? These are some of the questions that formed the inspiration for this book which grew out of the online workshop 'New Perspectives on Trial by Media' held in June 2023 at the University of Leicester (UK).

The first thing to note is that, even though the trope of trial by media has strong emotive appeal, evoking the pitchfork and witch-hunt mentality of a less enlightened age, academic research in this area remains relatively limited. The term 'trial by media' is used in a small range of sources to describe media practices and processes which potentially interfere with justice as administered through the court system and pose a threat to fundamental rights, including the presumption of innocence. 'Trial by media' is commonly understood to be the very opposite of 'trial by law', negating the safeguards of a process which in a democratic society is conducted in strict adherence with the rule of law. Greer and McLaughlin, whose work is widely quoted in this volume, characterise trial by media 'as a dynamic, impact-driven, news media-led process by which individuals—who may or may not be publicly known—are tried and sentenced in the "court of public opinion"' (Greer & McLaughlin, 2010, p. 27) and as 'a market-driven form of multi-dimensional, interactive, populist justice in which individuals are exposed, tried, judged and sentenced in the "court of public opinion"' (Greer & McLaughlin, 2012, p. 397). At the same time, they hint at a potential benefit of trial by media in that it 'can lead to prosecutions that otherwise would not have occurred and in that sense its democratic potential should not be overlooked' (ibid.).

Trial by Media as the New Normal

A key concern in the literature is that, if left unchecked, media justice may supplant or eclipse procedural legal justice. Judges have been particularly critical of any media activity that has the capacity to compromise fundamental rights and negatively affect the integrity of the judicial process (e.g. Sunday Times v UK 1979; Attorney General v English 1983). In a dissenting opinion in the recent European Court of Human Rights case of Mesić v Croatia (No. 2), one of the judges was emphatic that 'no one (...) can be left to the mercy of trial (let alone conviction) by media. No one. Never. Under no circumstances' (p. 27). Doctrinal analysis typically frames trial by media as a risk to be managed with the aid of reporting restrictions (Fielder, 2023; Phillipson, 2008). England and Wales, in common with other common law countries, have strict contempt of court laws to deter pre-trial media publicity that is harmful to criminal trials (Contempt of Court Act, 1981), but such rules would be ill-suited to other legal systems (Lochs, 2019). While the European Court of Human Rights has recently expressed concern about the threat posed by social media to the right to a fair hearing, a slightly different assessment was made by the UK Government stating that the problem was 'not unmanageable' and could be addressed using existing law, with the aid of some additional measures such as the cooperation of social media platforms to remove potentially harmful content (Attorney General's Office, 2019).

However, as this book shows, media trials do not always unfold in the shadow of courts. A good example is the disappearance of Nicola Bulley in January 2023: ultimately there was no crime and therefore no legal case to answer. Contemporaneous or impending court proceedings represent only one facet of trial by media. There can be trial by media without any related proceedings in court. This may be because no legal wrong was committed or because judicial redress is unavailable, for example, because the suspect is deceased or because of the expiring of legal time limits. So pervasive is the phenomenon of trial by media that it routinely involves issues that are not even remotely legal or criminal in nature. Media commentators, users and audiences pass judgement and seek to apportion blame on an almost daily basis, seemingly in the most random cases. When Catherine, Princess of Wales, released her own family photograph to mark Mother's Day in 2024, news agencies promptly issued an alert over its authenticity. With the story immediately going viral, the suspicion that the image had been extensively photoshopped followed a familiar trial by media pattern. Minute, forensic-like scrutiny of the image and intense global speculation about its origins and significance forced an admission from the Princess that 'like many amateur photographers, I do occasionally experiment with editing' (Harrison & Coughlan, 2024). Trial by media has seemingly become the new normal. As Jermyn and Horeck argue in Chapter 6, even the menopause, a natural stage in a woman's life, can become the focus of forensic media scrutiny. As several contributors in this book argue, the potential harms of trial by media encompass more than just a detrimental impact on legal procedure and the right to a fair trial, with reputational damage and an invasion of privacy among its potentially most pervasive and most enduring effects which can occur regardless of any court proceedings.

Another dimension of trial by media highlighted in this book is that intense media publicity may support rather than hamper the cause of justice. Strictly speaking, if we adhere to the doctrine that trial by media is never acceptable, media campaigns aimed at influencing the prospect and outcome of an appeal process—the typical wrongful conviction or miscarriage of justice scenario—should also be resisted. Similarly, media lobbying in favour of prosecuting a particular crime, which usually involves promoting a strong narrative of guilt ahead of any legal action, would need to be treated as unacceptable. However, to do so would be to ignore the 'democratic potential' of trial by media alluded to by Greer and McLaughlin, as well as denying the media's watchdog role which legitimises the critical probing of the workings of the criminal justice system frequently on display in highly mediatised cases. This book features an analysis of the ground-breaking television drama *Mr Bates vs The Post Office* (ITV, 2024) which brought to fruition the long and previously little-known legal fight against the 'largest miscarriage of justice ever' in English legal history (see Machura in Chapter 3). While proposed legislation to expedite the quashing of convictions in this case was widely welcomed, lawyers also voiced concerns about the implications of this highly unusual move for the constitutional principle of separation of power between government and judiciary and, by extension, about the role of the media and public opinion in this matter (Boffey, 2024). When it comes to weighing up harms and benefits, it is worth noting that the situation is not always clear-cut: one person's trial by media may deliver long-awaited justice to another. Whereas defence lawyers may denounce intense media scrutiny as trial by media, victims and their supporters may embrace it as integral to their campaign for justice. In other scenarios, a media trial may bolster the defence case but be less favourable to the victim. Trial by media is not a black-and-white phenomenon, but it is riven with ambivalence and tension.

The Dynamics of Participatory Justice

If we accept that that trial by media is ubiquitous and impacts parties in different ways, the question arises as to how wide its contours should be drawn. When does a particular media narrative become a trial by media? The notion of a 'court of public opinion' provides a useful starting point as it foregrounds the public's stake in media trials which derive their power from their ability to mobilise and appeal to audiences' moral judgement. On the other hand, public opinion is a notoriously nebulous concept: trial by media may not be representative of public opinion, but only resonate with a limited group of people. This is especially so in today's hybrid and highly fragmented media landscape. Social media sleuths who take it upon themselves to investigate and solve crimes cannot automatically count on widespread public support but, on the contrary, may provoke disapproval in other media. Yet, in other cases, social media campaigns may go viral to attract broad public support: the #Metoo campaign is one such example. Nevertheless, ever since the advent of Web 2.0, it appears that citizens increasingly desire to be more than mere passive witnesses or bystanders in the administration of justice. The old adage that 'justice must be seen to be done' has morphed into 'seeing to it that justice is done'. The inexorable rise in amateur sleuths online seems to provide clear evidence of the transformation of a public which implicitly trusts the criminal justice system to solve and prosecute criminality into a public which appropriates the role of various authorities to become investigators, prosecutors and judges. A clear manifestation is digital vigilantism (Trottier, 2020), one prominent example of 'citizen-led' policing being 'paedophile hunters' who use basic technology to entrap child sexual abusers online, often with little regard for due process (Purshouse, 2020).

Yet, citizen involvement in justice is nothing new: open justice constitutes the cornerstone of a transparent and democratically accountable criminal justice system, with the public gallery as its proud emblem. The concept of 'participatory justice' highlights the continuum between contemporary, digitally enabled forms of citizen involvement and the long-standing tradition of citizen participation in justice. Greer and McLaughlin (2012, p. 397) point to this connection when they argue that 'Trial by media reclaims "justice" from the courts and returns it to a networked citizenry'. Media discourses inviting public discussion, opinion and judgement of criminal justice issues are an embodiment of participatory justice and the presumptive power of public opinion. In the pre-digital age, the public's deliberations and adjudications remained to a large extent undetected and undocumented, save for the occasional vox pop in television interviews and letters to the editor. However, as ethnographic studies have shown (Livingstone, 2015), traditional media audiences are most certainly active participants who endow media texts with their own meaning, often in defiance of the 'preferred' meaning pre-construed by the original creators of a text. While the concept of 'participatory media' was coined more recently to capture the active voices of digital media users (Deuze, 2006), mass media, contrary to what some earlier theories may have suggested, have always been a site of audience resistance. 'Audiences have never been docile recipients of true crime infotainment, passively absorbing the content they consumed', Yardley et al. (2018, p. 86) remind us. As Middleweek shows in Chapter 2, long before the Internet, the Lindy Chamberlain case was the subject of a very active miscarriage of justice campaign in the 1980s producing pamphlets and booklets which defied the guilty narrative promoted in mainstream media.

The idea of participatory justice acknowledges the active participation by a public simultaneously performing the role of audiences and citizens. Whereas the notion of trial by media predominantly focuses on the outcome of intense media publicity, participatory justice is concerned with processes which may or may not generate the deleterious effects commonly attributed to trial by media. The concept therefore represents a more nuanced assessment of trial by media—traditionally burdened with very negative connotations—by exploring the idea that citizen participation can cause harm but also make a positive contribution to justice. Participatory justice, in other words, is not seen as inherently incompatible with the public good; however, that does not mean that it should go unchecked, as Clifford explains in Chapter 9.

Hybridity and Trial by Media

The affordances of digital media in enabling participatory justice may be unparalleled, but to understand trial by media better we need to be cognisant of its pre-digital histories. Statham argues in Chapter 12 that trial by media is traditionally deeply entrenched in common law jury trials where it manifests itself through the influence which media have on courtroom actors. The example he uses is the way in which defence lawyers strategically deploy rape myths circulating in mainstream media discourse to influence juries. While there is only a limited body of literature which utilises the terminology of trial by media, the topic already exercised scholars before the domestication of the Internet. A prominent example involves the growing popularity of court TV (named after the US television network Courtroom Television Network) in the US in the 1990s. The 1994 trial of O. J. Simpson, which attracted 'gavel-to-gavel coverage' (Nasheri, 2002, p. 33) and which was back in the headlines recently when news of Simpson's death broke, became synonymous with trials as a form of infotainment. Although not unprecedented in US legal history, the presence of television cameras in court in the Simpson case gave rise to widespread concerns about its adverse impact on the rights of the defence and its potential influence on jurors and other courtroom actors who, it was feared, would be tempted to perform for the camera (Neubauer, 2023). Media coverage no longer served the function of traditional court reporting, which is to inform citizens and aid overall transparency, but instead it adopted a style, form and tone which turned justice into a 'media circus'. Cameras in court remain a controversial issue, but the televising—or nowadays livestreaming—of court proceedings was always about much more than just the intrusive presence of a specific technology. Ultimately, the camera symbolises the dramatisation of trials and their capacity to be transformed into 'mega-spectacles' (Neubauer, 2023).

O. J. Simpson and other highly mediatised trials may be seen as the distinct product of the American legal and media systems—and indeed they may have set back the case for allowing cameras in courts in other jurisdictions (Stepniak, 2013)—but it is important to bear in mind that in the UK and elsewhere in Europe pre-digital television formats similarly sought to provoke an affective response through re-enactments, photo montages and other visual techniques cultivating close audience engagement. Much discussed in the criminological literature is the television programme *Crimewatch* which, as Schlesinger and Tumber (1993) explain, was imported from Germany where it had been running since 1967. In this instance, it was another crucial and controversial form of camera technology, namely CCTV, which acted as the narrative centrepiece and co-opted audiences as direct witnesses (Jermyn, 2013; McCahill, 2013). Crime appeal programmes were a stepping stone towards the form of participatory justice which we today associate with a digital culture in which users, having evidence at their disposal online which was previously not readily available to the public, take it upon themselves to actively investigate, debate and in some instances punish deviant behaviour.

Mass media precursors of contemporary participatory justice have not disappeared but they acquired a new lease of life in the digital era. The dichotomy between 'old' and 'new' media and the prediction that pre-digital media would inevitably become extinct have been replaced with the vision of a hybrid media system in which mass media have successfully evolved by embracing and appropriating digital technology. Broadcasting has morphed into on-demand streaming, but live TV still endures; newspapers exist in both paper and digital formats; journalism has branched out on platforms such as Twitter (now 'X') without abandoning its traditional outlets; and so forth. Chadwick (2017, p. 5) refers to this straddling of boundaries as follows: 'The hybrid media system is built upon interactions among older and newer media logics—where logics are defined as technologies, genres, norms, behaviors, and organizational forms (...)'. The interaction and fusion between older and newer media forms have invigorated participatory justice, as Yardley et al. (2018, p. 86) explain: 'Audiences now have considerably more participatory opportunities when it comes to [real crime] infotainment—they can post a comment on an online news article, tweet about a television programme using a hashtag or join one of the multiple online communities established to discuss and debate particular cases'. True crime forms part of the staple diet of streaming platforms, podcasting and other hybrids. The current offering on Netflix—one of the most successful streaming platforms—even includes a series entitled 'Trial By Media' (Netflix, 2020) which examines the media's influence on trials, a form of 'media meta-commentary' (Jacobs & Townsley, 2018) in which media reflexively critique media, setting in train a potentially endless feedback loop enabled by digital transmediation. True crime podcasts that are spinoffs of traditional investigative journalism, as Clifford explores in Chapter 9, allow the written press to reach new audiences and thus contribute to its survival in the digital age. Crime stories accumulating huge numbers of shares and likes across a variety of platforms in a very short space of time become the object of 'viral justice', engendering a hyperconnected digital court of public opinion which is 'a product of media convergence, defined variously as the blending of different media forms, as well as the increasing flow of content across different media platforms' (Wood et al, 2019, p. 382).

The Risks and Opportunities of Participatory Justice

Despite the fact that legacy media have become largely interwoven with digital media, the resulting media ecology is anything but harmonious. The contemporary media space is notoriously fragmented and divided. Its transmedial qualities make it easy for topics and discussions to go viral and become the focal point of (global) conversation, but it also creates echo chambers which do not allow any space for opposing viewpoints. Conspiracy theories thrive easily in this environment, which is not helped by the fact that mainstream media in the post-truth era are viewed with suspicion by many social media users who prefer to seek their own 'truth' rather than trust the information provided by professional reporters or other authoritative sources. This conspiracy mentality affects many different areas of public life, including, as we saw during the COVID-19 pandemic, public health. Similar distrust is directed at legacy media's reporting of criminal justice. Peleg in Chapter 4 writes about the decline in the professional standing of court reporters in Israel and the levels of hostility they experience from social media users who accuse them of being biased and untrustworthy. This book contains several case studies documenting the extremes to which some social media users go to investigate and solve crime, trusting their own faculties over second-hand media reports. The Nicola Bulley case, which Jermyn and Horeck in Chapter 6 describe as 'a cultural moment' of the TikTok era, showed how participatory justice was taken to an entirely new level with the emergence of 'true crime tourism' which competed and interfered with the official police investigation. Online sleuths in this case, as Jones and El Madawi argue in Chapter 7, were not content to witness and comment from a distance but they wanted to become part of the story through their own physical proximity to the unfolding events.

Digital technology may furnish the tools, but websleuthing, true crime tourism, vigilantism and other practices are potentially motivated by a myriad of factors which have yet to be fully investigated. One such factor is a lack of public trust in authorities' ability and willingness to effectively police crime (Trottier, 2020) which, as I explain in Chapter 10, may find its roots in past failures of the criminal justice system. Another potential driver is the sense of belonging and community which users derive from tackling wrongdoing with other like-minded individuals. There may also be a commercial factor at play: the adage that 'crime sells' holds true in a media ecology which remunerates clicks, likes and shares. Yet, in other cases, an overwhelming sense of injustice moving ordinary citizens to fight wrongs will provide a more selfless motive, even if such efforts are at times deeply misguided (Yardley et al., 2018). A burning desire to know, or what Jones and El Madawi in this book term 'epistephilia', is a further reason why audiences are drawn to true crime genres which, in keeping with the idea of crime as entertainment, cultivate suspense and intrigue through techniques such as dramatisation and serialisation. 'A reconfigured sense of control (…) over the "story"' (Glitsos & Deuze, 2024, p. 3) is another possible motivation for users' desire to co-create true crime narratives in the digital realm.

When we consider the many different forms that participatory justice can take on in a networked world and the wide range of reasons why citizens may decide to get involved in justice seeking, the potential impact of mediated campaigns and interventions equally needs to be thought of as varied in scope and depth. Some of the adverse impacts of trial by media appear almost self-explanatory: platform-to-platform coverage insinuating that an individual is guilty of a crime—the 'guilty until proven innocent' narrative which Greer and McLaughlin (2010, p. 27) refer to—jeopardises the presumption of innocence, as Stoyanova demonstrates in Chapter 11. Even a formal acquittal may not be enough to restore a person's innocence in the eyes of fellow citizens. Conceptualising the harm to reputation, Lev-On in Chapter 5 describes a hierarchy of defamation which is governed by the degree of exposure which individuals receive, or alternatively actively seek, through the media. A loss of privacy is another form of additional punishment which may be very difficult to reverse in a media environment in which it is hard to contain or control flows of information. A more insidious impact may occur when media stereotypes permeate the courtroom and are used to discredit defendants and witnesses: as Statham argues in Chapter 12, in rape cases, victims may experience something that is tantamount to media-made sexual assault in court.

The benefits of participatory justice in individual cases may be more ambiguous and more difficult to measure. Clifford in Chapter 9 discusses the impact of the award-winning podcast which seemingly contributed to the successful resolution of the Lynette Dawson cold case, resulting in a murder conviction. However, the podcast was also criticised by the trial judge for being extremely prejudicial. A temporary stay of proceedings was imposed to allow for the impact of the pre-trial publicity to subside. For victims, by contrast, prolonged or renewed media attention may deliver long-awaited justice. Investigative journalism contributed to the extradition and eventual conviction of a Serbian war criminal, bringing justice to victims, as Rae discusses in Chapter 8. She notes that: 'Although highly problematic, a trial by media has the potential to address injustice when the public or victims perceive the legal system to be failing or constrained in certain functions'. Miscarriages of justice campaigns which are largely conducted in the media spotlight may similarly right a wrong and even bring freedom to those who were wrongly convicted of a crime. While it is perfectly possible that the end result would have been the same if the legal process had been allowed to run its natural, if much slower, course, the acceleration of justice will bring tangible benefits in terms of less time spent incarcerated and quicker access to compensation for victims of miscarriages of justice. When justice has failed, when it is being denied or when it is simply unavailable, close media scrutiny may provide an alternative pathway to justice. There is a wider discussion to be had about the reasons why it requires the intervention of the media to achieve progress or a breakthrough in some crime cases. Although this debate is largely beyond the scope of the book, some chapters hint at factors such as institutional biases against victims and/or defendants, vested interests and inadequate resources for the criminal justice system.

The system-wide effects of mediated participatory justice, i.e. those that transcend the costs and benefits to individuals, are also discussed in this book. While empirical evidence is very limited, a common fear is that trial by media has the potential to undermine procedural safeguards and significantly disrupt the administration of justice. Prejudicial media publicity presents a particular challenge for public confidence in the jury system. Even the mere possibility of trial by media may make it difficult to preserve the right to a fair trial if jurors have been exposed to widespread pre-trial media coverage insinuating guilt or innocence. The type of TikTok sleuthing observed in the Bulley case may interfere with the police investigation and compromise a crime scene, reducing the chances of a successful prosecution. In many legal systems, the pre-trial phase is protected by confidentiality, but this, as Stoyanova argues, creates an information vacuum which news media but also increasingly online sleuths will try to fill with their own speculative version of events. The cumulative effect of media narratives painting criminal justice in a persistently negative light may weaken public confidence, especially when there is also a significant degree of misinformation and public misunderstanding. On the other hand, it is also seen as axiomatic that the media by exercising free speech rights contribute to an effective scrutiny of the entire system of justice in a democratic society. Vargiu in Chapter 13 deplores the lack of media interest in international courts which are consistently under-reported, despite the global significance of their rulings. Less scope for participatory justice in this area also means limited public awareness of how international legal disputes are resolved and reduced opportunities for improving audiences' knowledge of international law. Social justice is another potential beneficiary of trial by media: this book contains several examples of how an online public can be instrumental in denouncing structural inequalities in the wake of high-publicised cases, with race and gender constituting prominent examples. In some cases, trial by media meets its own reckoning and stimulates the emergence of counterpublics strongly opposing dominant media narratives and sparking a wider social debate about the unfavourable representation of under-privileged groups.

How do we then negotiate these various risks and opportunities? Is it possible to harness the benefits of participatory justice and minimise the drawbacks of trial by media? When it comes to content produced by professional actors, most prominently by journalists, media ethics and regulation provide a central reference point in the delicate balancing exercise between a legitimate exercise of media freedom and countervailing interests, including the presumption of innocence. Incentivising media users and platform owners to be more responsible in a digital realm that is notoriously difficult to regulate is a much harder challenge, but the hope remains that it is possible to arrive at a more robust ethical framework to promote values of fairness and equity in online forums. Differences between legal systems also need to be factored in. As I argue in Chapter 10, debates on trial by media are predominantly focused on adversarial legal systems, but the issue does not necessarily present itself in the same way elsewhere. Similarly, national media systems vary greatly: if trial by media is often associated with 'tabloid justice', how does it play out in countries where there are no tabloid media? These questions call for much more research into the dynamics of participatory justice and its potential to engender trial by media. Our ambition with this book is to contribute to this emerging field by presenting a broad range of case studies, each of which approaches trial by media from a different perspective and exemplifies its extraordinary complexity.

Structure of the Book

The first part of the book reflects on the role which legacy media have played and continue to play in stimulating public engagement with criminal justice. In Chapter 2, Middleweek finds remarkable continuity between 'old' and 'new' media in her study of the Australian case of Lindy Chamberlain who was wrongly convicted in 1982 for killing her baby daughter in what is globally known as the 'Dingo Baby case'. Whereas the origins of amateur sleuthing are often associated with the rise of social media and are thus directly attributed to the digital age, Middleweek demonstrates that this kind of active public participation in justice already occurred before the Internet. Using archival research, she examines how Chamberlain's supporters were actively scrutinising and debating the evidence through the relatively low-tech medium of pamphlets and booklets. Their activities displayed several of the hallmarks of amateur sleuthing: the group would analyse and present forensic evidence in different forums, develop narratives challenging the judicial outcome and undertake coordinated action to have Chamberlain's conviction overturned. This makes the case a striking example of participatory justice from the pre-Internet era which, perhaps unsurprisingly given the cultural significance of the Chamberlain case, continues to be debated in pockets of social media. These findings serve as a reminder that more research into the pre-digital origins of amateur sleuthing is required to place the public's fascination with true crime in its proper historical context.

Machura in Chapter 3 discusses 'trial by film', outlining the role which the 'old' media of film and television continue to play in popular legal culture. He highlights the significance of fictional portrayals in shaping perceptions of the law, an influence which continues to manifest itself in the blend of fact and fiction that characterises true crime. Machura draws on classic sociology to provide an explanation for audiences' enduring fascination with the law: a violation of norms commands public attention and continues to do so until it is decisively addressed through a finding of guilt or innocence. While scripts writers are described as 'conservative' in that they are reluctant to depart from familiar plotlines, drama is also capable of breaking the mould by acting as a catalyst for change and justice. This is something which Machura illustrates with the example of the ground-breaking UK television drama *Mr Bates vs The Post Office* broadcast by ITV in January 2024. Almost overnight this fictionalised account of the wrongful conviction of 900 Post Office workers for fraud, which was in fact caused by accounting errors triggered by a faulty computer system, galvanised public opinion and spurred the Government on to fast-track the appeals process and compensate the many victims of this large-scale miscarriage of justice.

In Chapter 4, Peleg discusses how court reporters, another stalwart among legacy media, are struggling to preserve their professional standing in the digital era. Findings from her longitudinal study in Israel suggest a decline in public esteem for court reporters who have received some fierce criticism for violating the presumption of innocence by overstating the case for the prosecution. They are frequently attacked in social media and have their profession routinely questioned, ironically despite adapting their practices to stay relevant in the contemporary media landscape, for example, by focusing more on high-profile court cases involving celebrities and politicians. Their 'epistemic authority', the power to provide authoritative information and act as gatekeepers of knowledge, has been diluted in a media infrastructure in which every user has the tools to generate and disseminate information. Using the concept of 'boundary work', Peleg explains that what is at issue for professional journalists is who can legitimately claim to be a 'journalist' in the contemporary media space. This leads Peleg to ask whether the decline in court reporting represents a form of democratisation and a victory for participatory justice, or, by contrast, whether it will deprive the public of reliable, professionally verified, information and increase the risks of trial by media.

The second part of the book turns its attention to trial by social media. The case of Roman Zadarov is the focus of Lev-On's analysis in Chapter 5. Zadorov was convicted for the murder of the schoolgirl Tair Rada but was eventually acquitted after a retrial. Fighting to establish his innocence, Zadarov's supporters conducted a vigorous social media campaign which descended into a campaign of harassment and defamation targeting friends of the victim whom they blamed for her death. Lev-On points to the fine line between truth and justice seeking, on the one hand, and harassment and other harms, on the other, in online forums. Trial by social media is therefore much more complex than public scrutiny and commentary on ongoing legal proceedings: it carries the risk of violence and additional punishment. Lev-On's study of the dynamics of the campaign demonstrates the importance of anonymity to protect those who are (wrongly) accused of serious crime from the negative effects of trial by media. His principal finding is that the level of media exposure which individuals receive or seek themselves, for example, because of their pre-existing online presence, is positively associated with the level of harassment and defamation which they experience, evidencing a 'hierarchy of defamation' involving varying degrees of harm to an individual's reputation.

The theme of trial by media beyond legal trials is also taken up Jermyn and Horeck in Chapter 6 in their analysis of the Nicola Bulley case. With the victim's fate unknown for several weeks, the information vacuum was filled by intense (online) media speculation which centred around the familiar 'missing white woman' trope and generated what the authors call 'a gendered media spectacle'. What made this case extraordinary was not just the feverish social media activity and the outlandish theories to which it gave rise, but also the way in which it triggered widespread criticism of the police's handling of the case. This extended most infamously to their suggestion that the victim's disappearance was somehow related to the menopause, perpetuating deeply entrenched gender stereotypes. Online discourse in this case revealed that there was not just one but several interlocking trials by media triggering a chain reaction across the entire media space. The case showcased some of the worst excesses of trial by media and demonstrated that even topics that are not legal or justiciable can be the subject of media judgement. However, there were also some redeeming features, such as attempts by social media users to engage in a positive form of participatory justice by calling out police misogyny.

Jones and El Madawi in Chapter 7 zoom in on the extraordinary role played by online sleuths in the Bulley case, exploring the links between forensic fandom, a mode of address which invites users to a deeper engagement with a true crime story, and digital witnessing enabling users to bear witness in a direct fashion with the aid of easily accessible digital technology. The police appeal in the Bulley case was interpreted by many online as an invitation to not only actively pursue a true crime narrative but to become part of the story themselves and direct the narrative, with TikTok influencers visiting the scene of the disappearance to gather, film and evaluate their own 'evidence'. Their presence was deemed to have interfered with the police investigation and descended in the harassment of innocent parties. Once again, we see how social media users' participation challenged the role of journalists who traditionally have been the eyes and ears of the public by being present at the crime scene. Significantly, online sleuths were pursuing a true crime narrative that ultimately did not exist, as the death of Nicola Bulley was subsequently ruled to have been purely accidental. The case raises important questions about the need for a stronger ethical framework to guide and regulate online sleuthing.

The chapters in the third part of the book examine the fine line between legitimate democratic scrutiny and respect for individual rights in media campaigns which aim to expose failings in the criminal justice system. Rae in Chapter 8 outlines the media's potential role as an alternative space for justice in respect of war crimes which have proved very difficult to prosecute in Australian courts and which are often neglected in the media space because they are often regarded as the domain of international courts and tribunals. Rae discusses an exception to the rule, the case of the Serbian commander Dragan Vasiljković who was leading an anonymous life in Australia until he was tracked down by *The Australian* newspaper in 2005 and exposed as a war criminal, triggering an extradition request from Croatia. While fighting his extradition, Vasiljković brought a defamation case against *The Australian* which he lost. The outcome arguably amounted to a trial by media as media discourse insinuated guilt in the absence of a criminal trial. However, at the same time, Rae argues, the case demonstrates the potential of investigative journalism to expose and compensate for the inertia of the domestic court system in bringing suspected war criminals to justice. Reporting which is defamatory but which is ultimately truthful or has a public interest dimension may therefore provide a compelling justification for trial by media. Rae suggests that online sleuths may have a similar justification, provided they are willing to commit to the ethical principles of investigative journalism.

Staying with the theme of investigative journalism, Clifford in Chapter 9 examines the award-winning Australian podcast which resulted in a decisive breakthrough in the cold case involving the unsolved murder of Lynette Dawson in 1982. Podcasts produced by professional journalists are a good example of how legacy media have risen to the challenge of digital media by embracing hybridity and the opportunity to diversify their reach. While Clifford agrees that true crime podcasts, which compared to traditional reporting offer audiences a more immersive experience, can be a highly effective way of exposing shortcomings in the criminal justice system, she also cautions that the publicity they generate can be extremely prejudicial and jeopardise the prospect of a fair trial. In the Dawson case, the podcast came close to obstructing justice, with the defence citing the pre-trial publicity it generated as a ground for requesting a permanent stay of proceedings. Granting a temporary stay, the trial judge had to strike a difficult balance between society's interest in seeing justice being done and protecting the defendant's right to a fair trial. Observing that these issues are likely to become more commonplace in the digital age, Clifford calls for a stronger ethical and regulatory framework to foster a more responsible form of true crime journalism.

In Chapter 10, I also reflect on the difficult balancing exercise between the media's freedom to report and the public's right to know, on the one hand, and individual rights, including the right to a fair trial, on the other. Exploring the case of the minority-ethnic Belgian student Sanda Dia who lost his life during a brutal hazing organised by an elite and predominantly white student fraternity, I argue that trial by media should be evaluated with sufficient regard to the local media and institutional context. In this instance, the potentially detrimental impact of the intense media publicity generated by the case was offset by the fact that the accused's anonymity—with the exception of some notable breaches in social media—was preserved by mainstream media and the fact that the defendants were tried by a panel of professional judges, meaning that there was no risk of the media coverage biasing a jury. Furthermore, accusations of an institutional cover-up in favour of the accused, some of whom were related to members of the judiciary, along with accusations of racial and class bias by criminal justice authorities, deserved to be robustly probed in the interest of public confidence, especially considering the historical failings of the Belgian criminal justice system.

The fourth and final part of the book is an opportunity to delve deeper into the impact of trial by media. Stoyanova in Chapter 11 develops the idea that negative publicity can amount to a form of extra punishment. Through a set of case studies drawn from four different European countries, the chapter provides an insight into the type of media practices that can have detrimental consequences for those accused of crime, but also cause collateral harm to those close to them. Stoyanova highlights how media reporting can impact society at large by creating expectations about the legal outcome of a case that cannot be met, but also by promoting division and prejudice. These impacts occur despite existing legal frameworks regulating media publicity before and during a trial. The use of derogatory language, disregarding suspects' right to anonymity, violating their privacy and speculating on guilt prior to the legal verdict are among the problematic features of media conduct observed in the case studies. To protect the individual right to a fair trial more effectively and avoid the wider harms associated with prejudicial media coverage, Stoyanova's analysis echoes the call for tighter ethical standards for journalists made by several other contributors in this book.

Adopting a critical forensic-linguistic perspective, Statham in Chapter 12 is not so much focused on negative media influences outside of the judicial process as on those occurring inside the courtroom. He argues that in common law jurisdictions trial by media inside court itself is the norm rather than the exception. He elaborates the 'Spectrum of Trial by Media', a model consisting of three interrelated dimensions which are rooted in the idea that not just jurors but legal professionals too routinely bring media-made preconceptions to court. The different dimensions refer to the way in which the forensic-linguistic structure of court trials promote 'direct trial by media', 'enhanced trial by media' and 'reinforced trial by media'. Applying this model, Statham examines how this third dimension manifests itself in sexual assault trials in a context in which convictions for rape remain stubbornly low. He describes how defence lawyers use a strategy to deliberately activate media-sourced rape myths against victims in the knowledge that jurors have been primed to be receptive to such prejudices through previous media exposure. While in common with other contributors Statham calls for a stronger media ethics to change the overall representation of rape victims, he is also rather pessimistic about the prospect of this coming to fruition in the contemporary media landscape.

In the final chapter, Vargiu strikes a distinctly optimistic note about the potential of trial by media to improve public awareness and accountability in the arena of international law. Echoing Rae's observation about the neglect of international human rights abuses in domestic media, Vargiu notes that trial by media is usually reserved for domestic legal issues. He argues that the scant publicity given to international courts represents a missed opportunity to capitalise on the public's moral investment in legal issues and increase awareness of the paramount importance of the international legal order. He shows that there is no lack of media appetite to elevate specific domestic court cases to global spectacles, citing the recent cases of Heard v Depp and Amanda Knox. By contrast, international law appears often too distant and too abstract to be relevant to wider audiences. Its procedural and structural complexities, along with negative perceptions of its efficacy, further compound the problem. While Vargiu is not advocating that the excesses of trial by media be brought to bear on international courts and tribunals, he explores the benefits that a livelier media debate would bring, including greater public literacy of the way in which international law works and increased public pressure for change in areas where it is falling short.

References

Attorney-General v English [1983] 1 AC 116.

Attorney-General's Office. (2019). *Response to call for evidence on the impact of social media on the administration of justice.* https://assets.publishing.service.gov.uk/media/5c7e846ce5274a3f8b91a3f6/Call_For_Evidence_05.03.2019_v2.pdf

Boffey, D. (2024, January 10). No precedent: Why commons approach to Post Office scandal has lawyers nervous. *The Guardian*. https://www.theguardian.com/uk-news/2024/jan/10/no-precedent-why-commons-approach-to-post-office-scandal-has-lawyers-nervous

Chadwick, A. (2017). *The hybrid media system: Politics and power*. Oxford University Press.

Contempt of Court Act 1981.

Deuze, M. (2006). Participation, remediation, bricolage: Considering the principal components of a digital culture. *The Information Society, 22*(2), 63–75.

Fielder, S. (2023). Trial by media: Where fact and fiction co-exist in high-profile cases. *Lincon Memorial University Law Review, 10*(2), 81–111.

Glitsos, L., & Deuze, M. (2024) Serial killers and the production of the uncanny in digital participatory culture. *New Media and Society*, 1–19.

Greer, C., & McLaughlin, E. (2010). Trial by media': Policing the 24–7 news media sphere and the 'politics of outrage. *Theoretical Criminology, 15*(1), 23–46.

Greer, C., & McLaughlin, E. (2012). Media justice: Madeleine McCann, intermediatization and 'trial by media' in the British Press. *Theoretical Criminology, 16*(4), 395–416.

Harrison, E., & Coughlan, S. (2024, March 11). Kate photo: Princess of Wales seen after saying she edited Mother's Day picture. *BBC News*. https://www.bbc.co.uk/news/uk-68534359

ITV (2024) *Mr Bates vs The Post Office.*

Jacobs, R. N., & Townsley, E. (2018). Media meta-commentary and the performance of expertise. *European Journal of Social Theory, 21*(3), 340–356.

Jermyn, D. (2013). Photo stories and family albums: Imagining criminals and victims on *Crimewatch UK*. In P. Mason (Ed.), *Criminal Visions: Media Representations of Crime and Justice* (pp. 175–191). Routledge.

Livingstone, S. (2015). Active audiences? The debate progresses but is far from resolved. *Communication Theory, 25*(4), 439–446.

Lochs, M. (2019). *Contempt of court: Een meerwaarde voor de goede strafrechtspleging in Nederland?* Leiden University. https://hdl.handle.net/1887/82076

McCahill, M. (2013). Media representations of visual surveillance. In P. Mason (Ed.), *Criminal visions: Media representations of crime and justice* (pp. 192–213). Routledge.

Mesić v Croatia (No. 2). https://hudoc.echr.coe.int/eng?i=001-224963

Nasheri, H. (2002). *Crime and justice in the age of court TV*. LFB Scholarly Publishing.

Netflix (2020) *Trial by Media.*

Neubauer, T. (2023). *The mediatization of O. J. Simpson case: From reality television to filmic adaptation.* Open Library Medienwissenschaft.

Phillipson, G. (2008). Trial by media: The betrayal of the first amendment's purpose. *Law and Contemporary Problems, 71*(4), 15–29.

Purshouse, J. (2020). 'Paedophile hunters', criminal procedure, and fundamental human rights. *Journal of Law and Society, 47*(3), 384–411.

Schlesinger, P., & Tumber, H. (1993). Fighting the war against crime. Television, police, and audience. *British Journal of Criminology, 33*(1), 19–32.

Stepniak, D. (2013). British justice: Not suitable for public viewing? In P. Mason (Ed.), *Criminal visions: Media representations of crime and justice* (pp. 254–277). Routledge.

Sunday Times v UK (1979) 2 EHRR 245.

Trottier, D. (2020). Denunciation and doxing: Towards a conceptual model of digital vigilantism. *Global Crime, 21*(3–4), 196–212.

Wood, M., Rose, E., & Thompson, C. (2019). Viral justice? Online justice-seeking, intimate partner violence and affective contagion. *Theoretical Criminology, 23*(3), 375–393. https://doi.org/10.1177/1362480617750507

Yardley, E., Lynes, A. G. T., Wilson, D., & Kelly, E. (2018). What's the deal with 'websleuthing'? News media representations of amateur detectives in networked spaces. *Crime, Media, Culture, 14*(1), 81–109. https://doi.org/10.1177/1741659016674045

Part I

Legacy Media and the Court of Public Opinion

2

Websleuthing Before the Web? Pre-digital Sleuthing in Public Writing About Australia's Dingo Baby Case

Belinda Middleweek

Introduction

In the subreddit TodayILearned (TIL), users of the social media site Reddit comment on 'interesting and specific facts' they've just discovered. One user expressed disbelief over the wrongful imprisonment of an Australian mother for the murder of her baby daughter, who was later discovered to have been taken by a dingo in August 1980. The post garnered 3.8k replies and 55k votes among Reddit users responding with theories, facts, speculations, commentary and analyses of the case evidence. This was 41 years after the dingo attack and is one of many discussion threads in online fora that continue to debate Australia's infamous 'dingo baby case'.

Public investigation of true crime has attracted increasing attention in recent years in media and scholarly research. Social media sites Reddit,

B. Middleweek (✉)
University of Technology Sydney, Ultimo, NSW, Australia
e-mail: belinda.middleweek@uts.edu.au

L. Gies (ed.), *Trial by Media*, Palgrave Studies in Crime, Media and Culture,
https://doi.org/10.1007/978-3-031-80593-6_2

TikTok and YouTube among others provide a platform for 'digital detectives' (Elphick et al., 2021) and 'websleuths' (Yardley et al., 2018) to pour over the details of a crime, such as the victim or perpetrator's whereabouts, and sift, sort, share and theorise evidence, discussing the minutiae of each case in real time. Reddit was one of the initial hubs for websleuths investigating the 2013 Boston Marathon bombing and has since been closely associated with the practice (see Lally, 2017; Myles et al., 2020; Nhhn et al., 2017), along with Websleuths.com—a pioneering platform in online detection that has been active since 2004 (Diggins, 2022).

Several high-profile cases in the United States and England have also contributed to increased interest in websleuthing. The 2021 murder of aspiring social media influencer, Gabby Petito, 22, while on a road trip with her fiancé, and the 2023 disappearance of financial advisor, Nicola Bulley, 45, while walking her dog are two examples. Users of social media platforms played a major role in search efforts for Petito, sometimes assisting, at other times, hindering official police investigations (Rosman, 2021). In the case of Bulley, police were forced to issue a dispersal order after crowds attempted to join the official search for her body (Vinter, 2023). News headlines have since lamented the 'disturbing rise' (Diggins, 2022) and 'serious problem of internet sleuths' and 'true crime addict[s]' (Dean, 2016), while the practices, perceptions, media representations (Yardley et al., 2018) and ethics of websleuthing (Jones, 2022) continue to be debated in crime media research.

The terms '*web*sleuth' and '*digital* detective' would suggest the phenomenon is relatively new or at least distinguishable from historical, non-digital instances of public participation in true crime by several key features or characteristics. The latter is true in much of the literature on websleuthing where the practice is tied to twenty-first-century advancements in digital technologies that have enabled interested publics to, among other defining features, produce their own critical or counter representations of crime with little formal training, actively witness events unfold in real time (Yardley et al., 2018, p. 86), and interact across multiple media platforms, eliciting emotional reactions and responses in their encounters (Horeck, 2019). But does websleuthing have pre-digital origins? Can historical evidence be found for the practices, interactions and engagements that define digitally mediated publics in true crime cases within a low-tech, analogue context? These are some of the questions this chapter seeks to answer through analysis of an archive of public writing in the 1980s about Australia's infamous dingo baby case involving the disappearance of Azaria Chamberlain. The archive at the State Library of New South Wales (SLNSW) in Australia comprises material related to the convictions of Lindy Chamberlain for the murder of her daughter, Azaria, and her then-husband, the late Michael Chamberlain, as an accessory after the fact—findings that were subsequently overturned, resulting in their exoneration. The writings were penned by Chamberlain supporters who were mobilised in their efforts, wrote regularly and for a public audience including politicians and public figures who could champion the Chamberlain cause (Middleweek, 2017, 2021). While I was the first to publish findings on the SLNSW archive in my research of trial by media claims about the reporting of the case in the 1980s (see Middleweek, 2007, 2017, 2021), this study focuses on the writers's investigative practices—their analysis of scientific evidence, theorising of judicial outcomes, accusations, speculations and attempts to seek redress for a woman they believed law enforcement agencies had wrongly convicted of the murder of her infant daughter. Beginning with a brief background on the Chamberlain case, I then review current definitions, practices and characteristics of websleuthing along with arguments about its origins. Thereafter, I outline the procedure for analysis of the archival material, examine public participation in the Chamberlain case as demonstrated in the writing of supporters and consider the case as a pre-digital example of the amateur sleuthing and detective practices prevalent in contemporary online discussions of crime.

The Dingo Baby Case

On 17 August 1980, Lindy Chamberlain claimed her nine-and-a-half-week-old baby daughter, Azaria, was taken by a dingo while on a family camping trip at Ayers Rock (now Uluru) in the central Australian desert. She was convicted of the murder, sentenced to life imprisonment, released after three and a half years following the discovery of a crucial piece of exonerating evidence, and had her conviction quashed. It was not until 32 years later that a court finally declared Lindy and Michael innocent and for a fatal dingo attack to be recorded on Azaria's death certificate. The Chamberlain case continues to resonate in Australian cultural history with Azaria's disappearance the subject of 17 books including my own *Feral Media* (Middleweek, 2021), a television mini-series, a Hollywood movie, an opera, a theatre production and a permanent exhibition at the National Museum of Australia. The legal case was one of the longest running in Australia's history and from 1980 to 2012 spanned four coronial inquests, a trial, two appeals and a Royal Commission of Inquiry. Since the 1980s, Lindy Chamberlain has been frequently cited as the benchmark of injustice, and the historical yard-stick against which other cases of wrongful persecution are measured. In turn, the 'Lindy' moniker is invoked by defendants, criminal lawyers and public commentators alike often in unrelated circumstances including, for example, in the 2005 trial of Bali drug trafficker Schapelle Corby, in the 2018 historical child sex abuse case of Catholic Cardinal George Pell, in rape allegations brought against Australia's Attorney-General Christian Porter in 2021, and in discussions around the 2023 unconditional pardon of Kathleen Folbigg for the murder of her infant children. Though Lindy is positioned as the victim exemplar of trial by media processes, elsewhere I have argued that the SLNSW archive of pro-Chamberlain writing challenges this perception, as authors interacted with, and sometimes relied upon, news media coverage of the case to advocate for the Chamberlains' innocence (Middleweek, 2017). In this chapter, I revisit the archive to test whether its writing exemplifies the kind of sleuthing prevalent on social media today, starting with a review of the definitions and practices that constitute online amateur detective work.

Defining Websleuthing and Its Origins

Websleuthing is defined as the 'investigative efforts within digital communities to solve a crime case or identify a suspect' (Wästerfors et al., 2024). It involves the engagement of internet users in crime governance which may lead to the pursuit of alternative forms of justice for victims (Loveluck, 2020, p. 213; Myles et al., 2020, p. IV), and sometimes, the identification of a wrongful conviction. The range of practices that constitute websleuthing include 'searching for information, uploading documents, images and videos, commenting, debating, theorising, analysing, identifying suspects, and attempting to engage with law enforcement and other organisations and individuals connected to the cases' (Yardley et al., 2018). While 'websleuthing' is a catch-all term more commonly used to describe these online investigative efforts (Yardley et al., 2018), within criminological and media studies critiques, 'digital detective' (Elphick et al., 2021), 'digilante', a portmanteau of 'digital' and 'vigilante' (Nhan et al., 2017; for 'retributive vigilantism' see Myles et al., 2020), 'citizen police' (Huey et al., 2013, p. 85), 'desktop detective' and 'internet sleuth' (Horeck, 2019, pp. 6–7), are also used. However, some of these naming strategies have been criticised for limiting the scope of activities of websleuths or failing to differentiate between the motivations, behaviours and practices of individuals within the crowd. For example, 'digilante' would imply that contemporary engagements with true crime are intended to be crusading with the crowd a mob of activists seeking redress for a perceived failure of law enforcement agencies to deal with criminal activity (Yardley et al., 2018). Others have argued that such terms impose a moral judgement on the actions of websleuths for constituting a form of 'weaponised visibility' in public acts of shaming an alleged offender (Trottier, 2016, p. 1 in Yardley et al., 2018). For these reasons, the broader terms 'websleuth' and 'digital detective', will be used interchangeably throughout this discussion in reference to the modern phenomenon.

The digital setting has become so entwined with the investigative efforts of contemporary true crime audiences that their activities have been described in cyborgian terms as a 'human flesh search engine' (Gao & Stanyer, 2014), 'cyber crowdsourcing' (Chang & Poon, 2016), 'crowdsourced policing online' (Huey et al., 2013; Nhan et al., 2017), 'crowdsourcing for justice' (see Smallridge et al., 2016) and 'online detective work' (Wikhamn et al., 2019). Indeed, the frequent classification of websleuthing as a form of crowdsourcing—when an individual or 'crowdsourcer' uses the internet to issue an open call to a crowd of people with instructions for the performance of a specific task that carries a mutual reward or benefit (Estellés-Arolas, 2022, pp. 692–693)—further underscores its connection to digital culture. However, not all websleuthing involves crowdsourcing given that some individuals choose to websleuth as a solo activity (Yardley et al., 2018, p. 91). In all, the varying terms used to describe amateur sleuthing underscore the role of digital technologies in enabling the participatory behaviours of true crime audiences. Taken together, they signal that amateur sleuthing is a web-based phenomenon tied to contemporary digital, networked culture. Amateur sleuthing is argued to epitomise the principles of participatory media in changing audience/producer relationships, while their practices, interactions and engagements follow the logics of time and space in the digital world (Yardley et al., 2018, p. 82). Thus, the websleuth stands as a figure of contemporary digital culture, participating in criminal investigations in real time with a wider geographical reach than ever before, through online activities that carry tangible, real-world consequences (Yardley et al., 2018, p. 82). One often cited example of those tangible, real-world consequences is the National Public Radio (NPR) podcast *Serial*, which debuted in October 2015 and followed the 1999 murder of high school student Hae Min Lee in Baltimore and the conviction of her boyfriend Adnan Syed. The podcast invited new opportunities for public participation in the case such as the Reddit community that formed in response to the production, giving audiences a platform to reverse the findings of the criminal justice system and operate as co-producers of knowledge and truth (see Stratton, 2019, p. 183).

Increased opportunities for networking, content creation and sharing, coupled with the acceleration in the speed of these processes has, no doubt, amplified the reach and impact of amateur investigations of crime. However, locating these practices in digital media overlooks the ways in which people interact, mobilise and share resources across multiple media—old and new—creating communities of interest in their investigation of a crime, as well as the discursive practices within those communities and the meanings attributed to them. Those closest to this line of thinking acknowledge the interactions of pre-digital audiences of true crime across media platforms in a 'multidirectional communication flow' (Yardley et al., 2018, p. 102; see also Horeck, 2019). For example, Yardley et al. (2018) argue websleuthing involves remediation, in which older forms of media are refashioned, represented and repurposed in newer formats. They trace the widespread popularity of 'true crime infotainment'—the blending of fact and fiction presented in a highly stylised and entertaining manner—in a range of historical and contemporary cultural artefacts: from the seventeenth-century true crime accounts in the *Newgate Calendar* and Truman Capote's non-fiction novel *In Cold Blood* (1965), to the true crime television programmes BBC's *Crimewatch* (1984), *America's Most Wanted*, *Police Camera Action!* and, more recently, true crime podcasts such as *Serial.* In doing so, they chart a history of public participation in mediated discourses of crime across traditional and new media platforms. What sets contemporary websleuths apart, they argue, is their capacity to act in ways that have real-world consequences for both society and the individual; to produce 'critical or counter representations' with little formal media production training; and to enact a new form of 'embodied *witnessing*' in those representations (Yardley et al., 2018, p. 86). Rather than 'public actors', Yardley et al. (2018, p. 86) call for websleuths to be re-framed as 'active meaning-makers' who, in turn, influence and are influenced by the social and cultural conditions that shape the construction and mediation of crime.

While acknowledging the potential to enact social change, Horeck (2019, p. 33) argues the distinguishing feature of the contemporary true crime genre is its affective mode of engaging audiences across new platforms, interfaces and protocols. Through emotionally charged narratives that provide plot twists, tags and directly address the viewer/listener the affective responses of audiences are imagined, elicited and managed in a multimodal entertainment experience that is commodified (Horeck, 2019). Horeck is sceptical about the new forms of civic engagement afforded by contemporary true crime media, instead arguing they fuel public interest, keeping the audience binged and hooked. The chief characteristics that distinguish websleuths from their pre-digital counterparts—affective, active and embodied participation in mediated discourse about crime, the navigation of multiple media platforms in multidirectional communication flows, and the production of critical or counter representations from people with little formal media training—will be considered in a qualitative content analysis of the SLNSW Chamberlain archive.

Analysing the SLNSW Chamberlain Archive

While there are various entries in the SLNSW catalogue in a Boolean search of 'Azaria' or 'Lindy Chamberlain', the SLNSW Chamberlain archive I refer to here comprises original and rare printed material that is only accessible through the library's special collections and cannot be taken off site. In that collection are fifteen loose-leaf issues of the Azaria Newsletter and five supplements containing (among other excerpts) parliamentary speeches, court transcripts, correspondence, book reviews and appeals for financial support, as well as four booklets, most of which are self-published. It is modest in size compared to other collections of writing about the Chamberlain case such as the 20,000 private letters and cards, mostly addressed to Lindy, and penned by ordinary Australians, which are now archived in boxes labelled The Chamberlain Papers (MS9180) held by the National Library of Australia (see Cunningham, 1997; Howe, 2005). By contrast, the SLNSW archive presents a more organised and coordinated response to the dingo baby case, as the material was written for a public audience and distributed through wider, multimodal channels (see Middleweek, 2017).

The fifteen issues and five supplements of the Azaria Newsletter held in the SLNSW archive were published between April 1984 and October 1989 by a support group known as the Chamberlain Information Service. Although they followed a serial format, the publications were ad hoc in their length and timing: some issues were as short as half a page and others numbered forty-eight pages, while the majority were released in 1984 ($n = 5$) and 1985 ($n = 5$) in response to significant legal developments in the case, including the uncovering of new evidence and Lindy's release from prison. The SLNSW collection also contains four booklets written by Chamberlain supporters Veronica M. Flanigan, George W. Rollo, Glenn Rosendahl and Terrence O'Keeffe. I refer to these publications as 'booklets' because they typically feature paper covering (with the exception of one enclosed in a plastic sleeve), originate locally, and were mostly distributed as self-published titles, with a singular focus on the Chamberlain case. The booklets were published between April and August 1984 with the exception of O'Keeffe's booklet that is undated (though references situate its publication in 1984), and were available for purchase through the Azaria Newsletter. They too vary in length, with the shortest at 16 pages (O'Keeffe, c.1984) and the longest at 192 pages (Rosendahl, 1984). Due to their susceptibility to degradation and restrictions on accessing the material on site, the material was coded by hand at the SLNSW using a qualitative content analysis. Content analysis was chosen as the most appropriate method given its usefulness for measuring the frequency and scale of messages and drawing meaningful inferences from their occurrence (Krippendorff, 2004). The protocol for analysis consisted of identifying legalistic keywords and phrases that reflected the investigative nature of the authors' activities. These included terms such as 'evidence', 'testimony', 'judgement', 'logic', 'scientific' and 'witness'. How the authors engaged their audience through rhetorical and affective appeals, personal observation and calls to action were also recorded. Finally, the ways in which authors interacted with diverse sources such as mainstream news media, by extracting quotes or utilising news reports to support their arguments, were also noted. These participatory practices were analysed in the context of behaviours typically exhibited by contemporary websleuths and outlined earlier (e.g., Horeck, 2019; Yardley et al., 2018).

'To Think – and To Act'

The authors represented in the SLNSW archive implored their readers to take action using the tools at their disposal to agitate for a judicial review of the case. In one issue of the Azaria Newsletter, the editor declared 'We call upon the Government to take immediate steps in granting a judicial inquiry'. Readers were urged to write to their state and federal parliament representatives with 'facts' about the case that disputed the official legal finding of guilt. Readers were also directed to share and purchase resources from the Chamberlain Information Service including VHS and BETA recordings about Azaria's disappearance, academic journal articles and books about the case. Authors repeatedly called upon their readers 'to think—and to act' (Rosendahl, 1984, rear-cover) and, by virtue of their access to 'the facts', to set themselves apart from 'the masses who swallowed [untruths]' (Rollo, 1984, p. 6). They addressed their audience as 'reasonable persons', the 'thinking public' (Flanigan, 1984, pp. 1, 23) and 'thinking men and women' dissatisfied with the Chamberlain guilty verdict (Rollo, 1984, p. 1). It is for them that fundamental principles of the Australian criminal justice system were explained, such as the presumption of innocence, the burden of proof and trial advocacy. Despite the authors' diverse backgrounds—a doctor, businessman and pastor among them—they drew on legal, philosophical and scientific principles such as 'reason', 'logic', 'ethics', 'the scientific method' and 'justice' to argue the case for the Chamberlains' innocence.

The authors' calls to action were complemented by efforts to theorise, investigate and discuss crucial pieces of evidence in the case. Their arguments were organised around disputed 'facts' (Flanigan, 1984), common 'myths' (O'Keeffe, c.1984) or errors of judgement made in the various legal proceedings to determine Azaria's cause of death (Rosendahl, 1984). Veronica Flanigan's 40-page booklet 'The Azaria Evidence: Fact or Fiction' (1984), unfolded by addressing uncontested and so-called facts about the case such as 'Fact' No.1: 'Mrs Chamberlain was the only person, apart from the two boys, who had opportunity to kill the baby'. Her reply was partially underlined for emphasis, as follows: 'Mrs Chamberlain had <u>no</u> opportunity to kill the baby <u>in the car</u>, as the Crown assumed' (Flanigan, 1984, p. 2). In a similar style, Terrence O'Keeffe's booklet was structured around the disputation of key myths about the case that appear in boxed text such as 'Myth 1: Lindy was cold and unemotional during the tragedy' (O'Keeffe, c.1984, p. 3) or 'Myth 4: Azaria means "sacrifice in the wilderness" and Adventists kill every third child' (O'Keeffe, c.1984, p. 10). Each issue of The Azaria Newsletter contained a report and appraisal of the ongoing investigation into Azaria's disappearance. Some offered breaking news and case updates with 'stop press' and 'exclusives' for the reader reminiscent of the layout of popular newspapers at the time. The updates for readers included findings from the (re)examination of case evidence, comments from prominent individuals (e.g., politicians) questioning the sanctity of the guilty verdict, recent dingo attacks, changes to the Chamberlains' legal team, avenues of appeal of the guilty verdict, public opinion polls and updates on the welfare of the Chamberlains, especially Lindy who until 1986 was languishing in prison. These were accompanied by continuing pleas for financial support and reader action.

While their investigations were grounded in scientific fact, reason and logic, the authors also leveraged embodied, personal observations to evoke an emotional response from readers. In his role as a Seventh-day Adventist pastor and a family friend of Lindy's, Rollo provided a descriptive account of his observations, dispelling any notion of her capacity for murder: 'In all my close association and careful observation of Lindy Chamberlain I have not seen the slightest trace of emotional instability but on the contrary an exceptionally healthy and outstandingly successful mother' (Rollo, 1984, p. 6). Although Rosendahl wrote in his capacity as a medical practitioner and did not claim to have any personal relationship with the Chamberlains, his reflections nonetheless revealed his emotional state: 'As a medical practitioner, I am more than a little angry with the misunderstanding evident in the judges' argument. Bloody noses and lacerated scalps can bleed profusely—indeed, death by exsanguination is one of the real hazards of uncontrolled epistaxis, and although less common, is by no means impossible from an extensive scalp laceration' (Rosendahl, 1984, p. 57). As well as establishing his own expertise for interpreting the case evidence, the author encouraged his readers to draw on their personal experience of, for example, treating a head wound ('as any good first-aid practitioner knows') and watching fluid spill in a moving car ('as any lay person knows fluids rarely fall vertically') (Rosendahl, 1984, p. 57). Similarly, Flanigan offered personal commentary on key pieces of evidence such as the testimony of a scientist she portrayed as '…curiouser and curiouser!' (Flanigan, 1984, p. 31), staging the scene for a plot twist not unlike the narrative devices often used by contemporary websleuths (Horeck, 2019). Her remarks also highlighted the kind of emotional work that participation in amateur sleuthing entails.

The booklet authors used a range of literary techniques to connect with and persuade readers. Rollo repeatedly positioned himself as a representative voice by posing questions he assumed the public wanted answered, e.g., 'Can a mother kill?', 'Is infanticide probable?', 'Was the death intended?', 'Did she destroy the child because of a ritual?' (Rollo, 1984, pp. 1, 2 and 4). For Rosendahl, literary allusions were designed to move his reader and forment outrage. In the frontispiece of his booklet, he recounted Russian literary giant Fyodor Dostoevsky's (misspelt as 'Feodor Dostoievsky') story about a seven-year-old girl libelled in court to obtain the acquittal of her father on the charge of child abuse. Rosendahl drew comparisons between that child and Lindy against whom a 'cruel libel' was levelled by the Superintendent of Police when he stated 'to the citizens of Australia' that the name Azaria meant 'sacrifice in the wilderness', an error which contributed to the climate of suspicion around the Chamberlains (Rosendahl, 1984, no page ref). The booklet also referenced the 'bitter humour' of Aleksander Solzhenitzyn in The Gulag Archipelago on the case of 'persons being punished for offenses [sic] with which they were not charged' (Rosendahl, 1984, p. 48). Common rhetorical devices used among the booklet authors were anaphora in the repetition of the phrase 'It is highly improbable…' to reinforce the contestability of claims about the couple's guilt (Rollo, 1984, p. 7), as well as capital letters and underlined text to emphasise the importance of the argument, e.g., 'Let judges and assessors never forget that this baby cry, heard by separate independent witnesses was from a LIVE child who had just been put to sleep in a tent and left there… QUITE ALIVE AND BREATHING' (Rollo, 1984, p. 8) and 'IF THE BLOOD IN THE CAR WAS NOT FOETAL BLOOD…' (Rosendahl, 1984, p. 42). Deploying these rhetorical and literary techniques is an example of amateur sleuths mobilising affective reaction and response to attract readers and establish a collective sense of outrage about the guilty verdict.

Media-Public Dialogue

The writing in the SLNSW Chamberlain archive exemplifies the ways in which authors derived 'impetus' and 'momentum' for their cause from news media coverage of the Chamberlain case (Azaria Newsletter, August 1984, p. 1). In one issue of The Azaria Newsletter published in 1985, readers were advised of a 'recent change of tone in [media] reporting' of the case with Lindy now portrayed as a 'wrongfully convicted woman' (August 1984, p. 1). Contributor Bronwyn Reid argued that 'informed sections of the media' were leveraging exonerating evidence and directing their persuasive efforts towards advocating for Lindy's release. The newsletter named publications and journalists sympathetic to the Chamberlain cause, including the magazines *Woman's Day* and *New Idea*, which had significantly contributed to the momentum towards total exoneration (Azaria Newsletter, August 1984, p. 1). Ita Buttrose, editor of *New Idea* magazine, was singled out for her comprehensive and perceptive report on the personal aspects of the Chamberlains' plight, which garnered cross-platform appeal and made front-page headlines in *The Sun* newspaper and other major syndicated papers. Other 'responsible journalists' (Flanigan, 1984) and media coverage that was 'sensitive and perceptive' had provided 'new impetus' for the Chamberlains' cause (Azaria Newsletter August, 1984, p. 1). The 'new impetus' advocates derived from the case's media coverage is clear in the volume of news articles cited in the Azaria Newsletter. One so-called significant comment is extracted from a Sydney Morning Herald editorial published in April 1984: 'The Chamberlain case needs to be reviewed. It is quite clear that the High Court decision supporting the jury's verdict of guilty, is not accepted by a substantial, growing and well-informed section of the community' (Azaria Newsletter, June 1984, p. 4). Azaria Newsletter editor Nonie Hodgson argued that sections of the media were instrumental in publicising the free Lindy cause: 'The media appears to be running riot with new evidence. Not a day passes without at least one new story breaking in our favour' (Azaria Newsletter, April 1984).

Similarly, the booklet authors drew on contemporary and historical news coverage to substantiate their claims the Chamberlains were innocent. Rollo established a historical precedent of dingoes attacking humans by referring to the 1891 Victorian publication The Boort Standard which carried a story with the headline 'Eaten Alive by Dingoes' (Rollo, 1984, p. 10). O'Keeffe based 'the case for Lindy Chamberlain' on evidence he had extracted from a news article of the same name (The Australian, June 16, 1984 in O'Keeffe, c.1984), while Rosendahl described in the introduction to his booklet that the publication 'arises from a study of various media sources' among other documents relevant to the case (Rosendahl, 1984). The timing of these media reports is significant, as just two months earlier, the Chamberlains' appeal to the High Court had failed, and by all accounts, the case was considered 'closed', with Lindy expected to remain in prison for her daughter's murder. As the newsletter and booklets demonstrate, news media coverage of the case had a rallying effect on Chamberlain supporters, who used favourable reports and sympathetic journalists to buttress their cause.

Interactivity Across Multiple Media Platforms

While they were without social media tags, likes and follows, there is evidence in the SLNSW Chamberlain archive of authors soliciting audience interactivity across multiple media platforms, echoing the remediation practices of digital detectives who borrow, refashion and transform elements from older media in their online discussion of crime (Yardley et al., 2018, p. 103; also Horeck, 2019). As part of their investigations, authors in the SLNSW Chamberlain archive cited the content of television programmes, newspapers, books and documentaries on VCR and BETA tapes in their newsletters, booklets and petitions. They encouraged fellow supporters to share those tape recordings with prominent and influential people in their network. Together, they enabled supporters to widen their distribution channels, reach a bigger audience and contest official crime narratives. The Channel 10 television programme *Azaria: A Question of Evidence* (1984), hosted by journalist Kevin Hitchcock, played a pivotal role in the pro-Chamberlain movement and is further evidence of the media-public dialogue. For booklet authors and contributors to the Azaria Newsletter, the television documentary substantiated claims the Chamberlains were innocent. Readers were encouraged to purchase and distribute the programme, while the Azaria Newsletter provided instructions on maximising its audience and impact: 'There is no end of creative ways this documentary can be used, e.g., lending it to prominent people, inviting groups of people to view it in private homes. Local TV stations can be requested to run this documentary as it was seen on the 0/10 network' (Azaria Newsletter, April 1984, p. 2). The programme was regarded as a crucial piece of 'evidence' that readers could send to parliamentarians and other influential figures, with distribution efforts coordinated by advocacy groups like the Concerned Citizens Groups of Parramatta (Azaria Newsletter, June, 1984, p. 3). Readers positioned to approach senators around Australia and provide them the opportunity to view the documentary were praised for their contributions to the cause (Azaria Newsletter, August 1984, p. 2). Artist Guy Boyd and author of the book 'Justice in Jeopardy: Twelve Witnesses Speak Out' (1984), described the programme as 'an accurate record of eyewitnesses and experts' evidence, and of many of the significant human responses to the injustice of this case', and even included the programme transcript in the early part of his book (Azaria Newsletter, October 31, 1984, p. 5). The programme was responsible for shifting public perceptions and had a rallying effect on Chamberlain support groups by directing the tone and focus of their protests. Instructing supporters to use and share mainstream media productions, such as Hitchcock's television documentary, in alternate contexts and applauding them for their efforts is an example of the authors soliciting audience interactivity, as well as the flow of information between amateur detectives and mainstream media.

A Pre-digital Case Study of Websleuthing

In their investigation of the dingo baby case, the authors represented in the SLNSW Chamberlain archive exemplify some of the traits of modern digital detectives. They searched for information, investigated, commented, shared, debated and theorised the case evidence to push for the couple's exoneration (Wästerfors et al., 2024). They also attempted to engage with legal and political agencies such as the courts, legal representatives and ministers of parliament to call for a judicial review into the case. The following focuses on four characteristics in crime media research that distinguish digital detectives from their historical counterparts and I use the SLNSW Chamberlain archive to suggest these websleuthing practices had echoes in a pre-digital context.

Active, Embodied Participation in Mediated Discourse About Crime

Websleuthing practices occur in online and offline spaces (Yardley et al., 2018), extending beyond the internet to places of interaction that exist in the physical world. Digital detectives immersed in the Nicola Bulley disappearance exemplified this interweaving of spheres in their joining of the official police search for her body. The investigations of the SLNSW Chamberlain authors also extended beyond the printed word, even though they lacked the affordances of the virtual realm such as the immediacy of interaction and opportunities for content creation and sharing. The authors urged their readers to stage private viewings of the Hitchcock documentary at their home (Azaria Newsletter, April 1984, p. 2), contact government officials and other prominent people, join street protests, sign petitions, write to Michael and Lindy, give donations to the Chamberlain support groups, purchase books about the case and share court transcripts (see Young, 1989). Their amateur investigations, inscribed in pages of newsletters and booklets, and performed in face-to-face interactions on the streets and even recorded in documents presented to the Northern Territory Government, demonstrated their embodied ways of being and acting in opposition to the guilty verdict.

Affective Engagement with True Crime

One of the hallmarks of contemporary websleuthing is an affective engagement with online crime discussions, enabling digital detectives to maintain and establish a sense of collective identity (Hannerz et al., 2023; Horeck, 2019). It is ordinary people sharing affective reactions and judgements on matters of justice, and through their participation in online crime discussion, capturing and managing audience attention (Horeck, 2019). While the Chamberlain case unfolded in a pre-digital era before the emergence of participatory media technologies, the ways in which the authors represented in the SLNSW archive construct a collective identity among Chamberlain supporters, appeal to and interpelate readers bear similarities to the genre's contemporary modes of audience engagement. The authors' embodied capacities for observation on aspects of the Chamberlain case (e.g., 'I am more than a little angry', Rosendahl, 1984, 57), appeals to the reader to take action, and attempts to persuade through rhetorical devices and other literary techniques, capture their incredulity and outrage at the Chamberlain verdict as well as the affective labour of bearing witness to a miscarriage of justice. The authors directly communicated with their readers using modes of address such as 'reasonable persons' (Flanigan, 1984, pp. 1, 23), and 'thinking men and women' (Rollo, 1984, p. 1) and even acknowledged their participation—the cultural work—they performed. In an issue of The Azaria Newsletter those 'in a position to make personal approaches to the Senators around Australia, giving them opportunity to view the video of the documentary, 'Azaria, A Question of Evidence' were applauded for their 'most valuable' efforts (August, 1984, p. 2). Though their affective reactions and judgements lacked the speed, reach and logic of the digital realm, they were shared in and across media platforms and are a testament to the ways in which amateur detectives subjectively engaged with the case and established a sense of collective identity with their audience.

Production of Critical or Counter Representations

Amateur investigators and concerned citizens have long been involved in mediated discourse about crime. While analogue communities engaged in true crime discussion may have lacked the synchronous, hypermediated communication of their digital counterparts, they used the media at their disposal to participate in and create representations that opposed official narratives. As the Chamberlain example shows, the SLNSW authors used a variety of media including newsletters, booklets, petitions, news clippings, phone calls, VHS and BETA recordings to dialogue, connect, persuade and engage audiences. The authors' appeals to attention and action through multimodal communication, integrating old and new media forms, shows the capacity for pre-digital publics to actively participate in and shape mediated discourse about crime.

In addition, news coverage of the case gave momentum to Chamberlain supporters and elsewhere I have argued that their interactions constituted a dialogic connection between mainstream media and Chamberlain counter-publics (see Middleweek, 2017, p. 14). I described them as 'counter-publics' because their contributions opposed the dominant view about the couple's guilt and gave rise to novel modes of discourse about the Chamberlain case (Fraser, 1993, pp. 13–15). Consistent with the function of counter-publics the discursive spaces they opened up incited 'agitational activities directed toward wider publics' (Fraser, 1990, p. 68) and their critical and counter representations of the event were taken up by traditional media outlets.

Multidirectional Communication Flows

Contemporary engagements with true crime are characterised by 'multidirectional communication flows between websleuths and mainstream media' (Yardley et al., 2018, p. 102). These flows are characteristic of contemporary media environments in which widespread and instantaneous communication is facilitated across diverse networks and platforms. Websleuths copying links to media reports and posting extracts from news stories in websleuthing spaces are one example (Yardley et al., 2018). So too the writing in the SLNSW archive evidences the multidirectional communication flows among amateur sleuths investigating the Chamberlain case who cited mainstream media coverage of the case to substantiate claims the Chamberlains were innocent and counter official juridico-legal narratives. At times they even mirrored the language, format and tone of mainstream news publications with 'stop press' and 'exclusives' to engage audiences through familiar news tropes.

In the digital context, these 'multidirectional communication flows' operate in reverse with news outlets publishing content circulated in websleuthing communities, often taking the form of photographs and other social media posts (Yardley et al., 2018, p. 102). A pre-digital corollary of those social media posts is the publication of evidence collected by amateur investigators in traditional news media. One issue of the Azaria Newsletter describes news media reporting of Chamberlain supporters who, in 1985, presented to the Northern Territory Government a 'positive and full "package"' of exonerating evidence spanning forty pages (Azaria Newsletter, August 1984, p. 5). Though the government later rejected the package, the evidence contained therein '[had] been taken up by the media' (Azaria Newsletter August, 1984, p. 5). Whereas the SLNSW Chamberlain authors were without the enhanced opportunities for interaction with mainstream news media that are afforded websleuths today, their contributions opened up information flows and spaces for public participation in mediated crime discourse.

Conclusion

It is a commonplace in crime media research that websleuthing practices are so entwined with digital technologies that the phenomenon is widely understood to be a 'manifestation of the norms and values of digital culture' (Yardley et al., 2018, p. 105; also Trottier, 2016). No doubt, digital communications technologies have enabled instant, widespread and diverse forms of communication, transforming the speed and nature of information exchange. However, characterising websleuthing as a digitally driven phenomenon, overlooks the common factors underlying amateur detective work in digital and analogue communities. As this study has shown, the contributions of pre-digital amateur detectives to mediated discourse about crime bear some of the characteristics of contemporary counterparts: their engagements can be active, embodied and affective, characterised by 'multidirectional communication flows' (Yardley et al., 2018, p. 102), and lead to critical or counter representations of a crime that oppose official juridico-legal narratives.

Acknowledging historical actors such as those writing about Australia's dingo baby case in the 1980s, contributes to our understanding of the public's enduring fascination with crime, attempts to seek redress where official judicial processes are perceived to have failed, and the use of media technologies to connect with others in communities of interest. The SLNSW archive is a testament to the enduring ways in which people interacted, mobilised and shared resources across multiple media—old and new—creating communities of interest in their investigation of Azaria's disappearance and its aftermath. For researchers, such a body of writing can be rich ground for tracing material and discursive practices that have real-world and embodied impacts. Future research that explores historical antecedents to contemporary websleuthing in the Chamberlain case could draw on additional archives of public writing such as the letters and ephemera stored in boxes at the National Library of Australia (see Cunningham, 1997). Other high-profile cases involving prolonged public engagement in true crime discussion within a pre-digital context may also provide fertile ground for analysis. In all, the writing in the SLNSW Chamberlain archive contributes to our understanding of online sleuthing, the cultural importance of the Chamberlain case and the role of historical public participation in shaping justice outcomes.

Competing Interests The author has no conflicts of interest to declare that are relevant to the content of this chapter.

References

Azaria Newsletter (The). (1984, April to 1989, October). nos. 1–15. Chamberlain Information Service, Cooranbong, New South Wales.

Boyd, G. (Ed.). (1984). *Justice in jeopardy: Twelve witnesses speak out*. Self-Published.

Chang, L. Y. C., & Poon, R. (2016). Internet vigilantism: Attitudes and experiences of university students toward cyber crowdsourcing in Hong Kong. *International Journal of Offender Therapy and Comparative Criminology, 61*(16), 1912–1932. https://doi.org/10.1177/0306624x16639037

Cunningham, A. (1997). Icons, symbolism and recordkeeping: The Lindy Chamberlain and Eddie Mabo Papers in the National Library of Australia.

Australian Academic & Research Libraries, 28(2), 103–110. https://doi.org/10.1080/00048623.1997.10755002

Dean, M. (2016, June 23). 'True crime addict' and the serious problem of Internet Sleuths. *The New Yorker*. https://www.newyorker.com/books/page-turner/true-crime-addict-and-the-problem-of-internet-sleuths

Diggins, A. (2022, June 14). The disturbing rise of amateur internet detectives. *The Telegraph*. https://www.telegraph.co.uk/tv/0/sleuthing-can-take-really-dark-path-disturbing-rise-amateur/

Elphick, C., Philpot, R., Zhang, M., Stuart, A., Pike, G., Strathie, A., Havard, C., Walkington, Z., Frumkin, L. A., Levine, M., Price, B. A., Bandara, A. K., & Nuseibeh, B. (2021). Digital detectives: Websleuthing reduces eyewitness identification accuracy in Police Lineups. *Frontiers in Psychology*, 12. https://doi.org/10.3389/fpsyg.2021.640513

Estellés-Arolas, E. (2022). Using crowdsourcing for a safer society: When the crowd rules. *European Journal of Criminology, 19*(4), 692–711. https://doi.org/10.1177/1477370820916439

Flanigan, V. M. (1984). *The Azaria Evidence: Fact or fiction?* Self-Published.

Fraser, N. (1993). Rethinking the public sphere: A contribution to the critique of actually existing democracy. In B. Robbins (Ed.), *The Phantom public sphere*. University of Minnesota Press.

Fraser, N. (1990). Rethinking the public sphere: A contribution to the critique of actually existing democracy. *Social Text, 25*(26), 56–80.

Gao, L., & Stanyer, J. (2014). Hunting corrupt officials online. Human flesh search engines and the search for justice in China. *Information Communication and Society, 17*(7), 814–829

Hannerz, E., Burcar Alm, V., & Wästerfors, D. (2023). Accomplishing reality media: The affective lure of online crime discussions. *Cultural Sociology, 17*(4), 476–492. https://doi.org/10.1177/17499755221113944

Horeck, T (2019). *Justice on demand: True crime in the digital streaming era.* Wayne State University Press.

Howe, A. (Ed.). (2005). *Lindy Chamberlain 'revisited': A 25th anniversary retrospective*. Southwood Press.

Huey, L., Nhan, J., & Broll, R. (2013). 'Uppity civilians' and 'cyber-vigilantes': The role of the general public in policing cyber-crime. *Criminology & Criminal Justice, 13*(1), 81–97.

Jones, B. (2022). Websleuthing, participatory culture and the ethics of true crime content. *Ethical Space: The International Journal of Communication Ethics, 19*(3/4), 52.

Krippendorff, K. (2004). *Content analysis: An introduction to its methodology* (2nd ed.). Sage.
Lally, N. (2017). Crowdsourced surveillance and networked data. *Security Dialogue, 48*(1), 63–77.
Loveluck, B. (2020). The many shades of digital vigilantism. A typology of online self-justice. *Global Crime, 21*(3–4), 213–241. https://doi.org/10.1080/17440572.2019.1614444
Middleweek, B. (2021) *Feral media? The Chamberlain case, 40 years on.* Australian Scholarly Publishing.
Middleweek, B. (2017). Dingo media? The persistence of the 'trial by media' frame in popular, media, and academic evaluations of the Azaria Chamberlain case. *Feminist Media Studies, 17*(3), 392–411.
Middleweek, B. (2007). *Dingo media? The Chamberlain case as model for an Australian media event* (PhD thesis, University of Sydney).
Myles, D., Benoit-Barné, C., & Millerand, F. (2020). 'Not your personal army!' Investigating the organizing property of retributive vigilantism in a Reddit collective of websleuths. *Information, Communication & Society, 23*(3), 317–336. https://doi.org/10.1080/1369118X.2018.1502336
Nhan, J., Huey, L., & Broll, R. (2017). Digilantism: An analysis of crowdsourcing and the Boston Marathon bombings. *The British Journal of Criminology, 57*(2), 341–361.
O'Keeffe, T. (c.1984). *The Dingo Shakes its head*. Self-Published.
Rollo, G. (1984). *Azaria Mystery: A reason to kill*. Dixie Print, Penrith, New South Wales.
Rosendahl, G. (1984). *The dark side of the law*. Self-published. Weston Creek.
Rosman, K. (2021, September 20). How the Case of Gabrielle Petito Galvanized the Internet. *The New York Times*. https://www.nytimes.com/2021/09/20/style/gabby-petito-case-tiktok-social-media.html
Smallridge, J., Wagner, P., & Crowl, J. N. (2016). Understanding cyber-vigilantism: A conceptual framework. *Journal of Theoretical & Philosophical Criminology, 8*, 57. https://search.proquest.com/docview/1787752058?accountid=10134
Stratton, G. (2019). Wrongful conviction, pop culture, and achieving justice in the digital age. In D. Akrivos & A. K. Antoniou (Eds.), *Crime, deviance and popular culture* (pp. 177–201). Palgrave Studies in Crime, Media and Culture. https://doi.org/10.1007/978-3-030-04912-6_8
Ten Network. (1984, April 4). Azaria: A question of evidence. Television Program.

Trottier, D. (2016). Digital vigilantism as weaponisation of visibility. *Philosophy & Technology*, 1–18.

Vinter, R. (2023, February 10). Nicola Bulley: Police issue dispersal notices after social media speculation. *The Guardian*. https://www.theguardian.com/uk-news/2023/feb/09/nicola-bulley-police-issue-dispersal-notices-after-social-media-speculation

Wästerfors, D., Burcar Alm, V., & Hannerz, E. (2024). The bumpy paths of online sleuthing: Exploring the interactional accomplishment of familiarity, evidence, and authority in online crime discussions. *New Media & Society, 26*(11), 6289–6306. https://doi.org/10.1177/14614448221149909

Wikhamn Remneland, B., Ljungberg, J., Rolandsson, B., et al. (2019). Given enough eyeballs, all crimes are shallow: The organizing of citizen collaboration to solve an online detective story. *Journal of Technology Management & Innovation, 14*(2), 59–67.

Yardley, E., Lynes, A. G. T., Wilson, D., & Kelly, E. (2018). What's the deal with 'websleuthing'? News media representations of amateur detectives in networked spaces. *Crime, Media, Culture, 14*(1), 81–109. https://doi.org/10.1177/1741659016674045

Young, N. H. (1989). *Innocence regained: The fight to free Lindy Chamberlain.* Federation Press.

3

Trial by Film: Cases and Causes in Popular Legal Culture

Stefan Machura

> … how big is the part of our direct experience?
> We know most from books or television.
>
> (Niklas Luhmann, 1997, author's translation)

The Pervasive Influence of Popular Legal Culture

Views on the law are deeply influenced by people's media consumption. Film in all its forms that today include TV shows, frequently depict the law, its agents and institutions. So much so that often, concern has been raised by legal practitioners and legal scholars alike (e.g. Gies, 2008; Rapping, 2003). For example, after analysing films, Michael Asimow

S. Machura (✉)
Bangor University, Bangor, UK
e-mail: s.machura@bangor.ac.uk

L. Gies (ed.), *Trial by Media*, Palgrave Studies in Crime, Media and Culture,
https://doi.org/10.1007/978-3-031-80593-6_3

(2000, p. 269) stated that U.S. law students are being told they must be 'Rambo with a briefcase'. The law 'goes pop' is a formulation by Richard K. Sherwin (2000). Yet, others suggest that watching films can have a positive effect. For example, it helps law students to prepare for future appearances in court. After all, lawyers are storytellers themselves (Meyer, 2014). In the following, it will be shown that moving pictures based on real cases have a variety of effects which do not necessarily have to be seen negatively.

Lay and sometimes professional people think they are influenced by fictional portrayals of the law. In a recent survey of university students in London and Wales, about 30% clearly indicated that their views on the police were influenced by 'films, TV shows and novels on police'. Moreover, this proved to be a significant factor in explaining their trust in the police (Machura & O'Riordan, 2023). In an earlier study, German school student's inclination to advise a female friend to report a sexual harassment, so that the case can be discussed in court, was researched. Positive views on lawyers and the number of classical Hollywood courtroom dramas consumed coincided with a higher likelihood (Machura & Kammertöns, 2010). A serving police officer told the author that his colleagues seek out documentaries about historic crimes for learning purposes. And in a study on Welsh police officer's ability to recognise cases of modern slavery, the majority of responding officers indicated to be influenced by 'film, TV and novels on crime' (Machura et al., 2019, p. 215). Those informed by these sources were marginally significantly less accurate in identifying cases of modern slavery (Machura et al., 2019, p. 213). Other studies include, for example, the effect of frequently watching the television show *Judge Judy* on American jurors (Podlas, 2001). Anecdotical evidence points to, for example, films influencing judges (e.g. Bergman & Asimow, 1996, p. 51; Fortes, 2017, p. 64; Kuzina, 2000, p. 315). There is thus growing evidence that people's viewing behaviour matters when it comes to law.

Leaving aside the thorny question of effect on actual behaviour, the study of law in film is important as it speaks to the ideal of law prevalent in society (Greenfield et al., 2001, p. 27). From film and other products of popular culture, the expectations of the public can be understood. Furthermore, the point of comparison for law as portrayed in a film should not primarily, as Greenfield, Osborn and Robson argue (2001, p. 27), be real law, real trials, real lawyer behaviour, but the idealistic assumptions of the audience: 'the cinematic myth of law'. Indeed, films dealing with historic or contemporary cases, suggest such as comparison to the audience. They aim at a trial of fictionalised facts in the court of public opinion.

In academic terms, such studies fall into the research area of 'popular legal culture'. Here, academics are concerned more with what the average citizen thinks than how lawyers perceive the depiction of things legal (Friedman, 1985, p. 191). Popular legal culture is important for a range of reasons, including because voting behaviour and public opinion frame political and administrative decisions. The views of the public may even influence how judges decide cases. Professional magistrates, for example, in Shari S. Diamond's (1990) study in London, felt under public pressure to sentence defendants more harshly than lay magistrates who saw themselves as representatives of the public and could be more lenient if necessary. Opinion on the law, the legal personnel and institutions will, as indicated above, influence how much people trust and consequently use the legal system. A very negative image may even deter talented students to go to law school and university graduates to embark on a legal career.

Of special interest are fictional stories based on real cases and claiming to portray historic events. As much as 'believability' is a prerequisite for films to be taken seriously by the audience (Black, 1999, p. 142), it may also add to the influence those pop cultural products have on the citizenry. Films portraying historic cases command the viewer's attention and appeal to take them seriously. A similar case can be made for television series which in recent years have become more high-value and socially significant. They can go into much more detail and are potentially more likely to do justice to complicated and long drawn-out cases. Believability is, indeed, a general concern for fictional representations of the law (Machura, 2017, pp. 4, 7–8).

In the following, the content of films and television series will be discussed to understand their potential to inform viewers on the law, the personnel of the law and the legal system. Content analyses are a key element in media studies (Machura, 2007), especially when it comes to their capacity to influence the public. Methodologically, researchers are on firmer ground when they gather experience in film-and-law analyses by comparing products from different times and several countries. A regular check with others' perception helps grounding the analysis. The author teaches a 'law in film'/'crime in the media' module almost every year since 1995 (see Machura, 2016). Full-length films made for cinema and television series episodes were shown to and discussed with classes in Finland, Germany and Wales. In addition, the following draws on a range of academic publications dealing with popular fiction based on real cases.

In this chapter, it will be shown why audiences are interested in films based on real trials. Then the vital link between character development and message of a film will be explained. The penultimate part looks at messages from a different angle, namely how much films based on real cases suggest changes and reforms to the law. Several film examples will be cited but the main example is the television mini-series *Mr Bates v The Post Office* broadcasted in January 2024 which sparked a UK-wide debate about a large-scale miscarriage of justice and an avalanche of political and legal activity to remedy it. The conclusion highlights the wider function of such productions for society, justice and the concept of trial by media.

Why Are People so Interested?

Most of the time, films and television series on actual trials deal with events that lie in the past. As an example of a production that was contemporaneous to the real legal proceedings, *Mr Bates v The Post Office* can be cited. The knowledge of the real existence of the story at some point in time lures in rather than turns away audiences. If necessary, advertisements and press or internet coverage can remind them about the show's roots in historic events.

Conflicts make good entertainment (Machura, 2017, pp. 4–5). There are then two parties, and the viewer can wonder which wins as sociologist Niklas Luhmann (2000, p. 28) argued for news coverage. Winners and losers are mostly clear in fictional depictions of real trials, if not always in less prominent ones. And still, if they are known, we can add, the issue also is what tactics influenced the case and was the outcome deserved? Luhmann (2000, pp. 29–31) additionally pointed out that norm violations are making good news stories, especially the graver they are. In entertainment, the same applies. Those stories which become part of popular legal culture are typically about heinous crimes, or terrible offences in the realm of private and public law. Few would see them differently. Two further news values which Luhmann (2000, p. 31) discusses are that individual contributions to a situation can be determined by readers and they can pass value-judgements on people and their actions. These are also elements making good entertainment (Machura, 2017, pp. 4–5). In a production based on real trials, both requirements, pertaining to individual contributions and moral judgement, are fulfilled. Not only in the Hollywood cinema but much more widely, storytelling commonly utilises characters which 'live' through the unfolding chain of actions. Their alleged or actual behaviour is assessed in the fictionalised account and then again by the audience. Committing crime is a moral choice according to the Situational Action Theory of Crime, when people inclined to illicit action find themselves in a situation conducive to crime (Wikström, 2010). Crime invites and involves moral judgement in real live as in fiction.

'Topicality'—that the audience has known about a story before, that the current reporting is part of a chain—forms another of Niklas Luhmann's (2000, pp. 33) criteria of newsworthiness. Similarly, fictional formats dealing with law-related actual events typically pick up on previous exposure by audiences. They have heard, read, seen some form of precursor. Maybe a newspaper report, or a feature on television. On balance, the claim to a degree of veracity only serves to reinforce the seriousness of the events depicted and the sense that time is well spent consuming the new product.

A large part of the explanation why audiences are drawn to fictional portrayals of justice lies in Emile Durkheim's sociological theory. According to the French theorist, all people have a stake in society's functioning, eagerly observe if social norms are upheld and want to see transgressions sanctioned (Durkheim, 2013). The failure of a trial to unambiguously apportion blame and adequately punish criminal behaviour sends an alarming message. The guilty may go free and the innocent may be convicted. Crime pays, or, in the realm of civil justice, norm breaking goes on unchecked. Popular legal culture in its various guises draws on this main societal concern (Machura, 2017, pp. 3–4). The audience is only the more worried if the story told is based on a real trial. The norm violation has happened, so it may happen again.

It is in the eye of the beholder how long back their concern for the upholding of norms goes. In France, the miscarriage of justice suffered by Captain Alfred Dreyfus at the turn of the nineteenth to the twentieth century and the ensuing violent political debate that antagonised political left and right for decades to come, is still profoundly meaningful to many. There were films made for cinema and a high production value mini television series on the Dreyfus case. The latter (*L'Affaire Dreyfus*, France 1995) is long enough to expand on the political background and ramifications of the case as well as the flaws of the secret service investigation and the trials. The real traitor who gave away construction details of a new cannon to the Germans, was known and protected by the military investigators, and compromising material forged. In an extraordinary scene, a uniformed messenger enters the deliberation room of the officer judges and conveys the order to read a secret piece of 'evidence'. Even if a case may have slipped in public memory completely, or may have been confined to the school curriculum, new films or television series may rekindle public interest.

In Germany, how courts dealt with the Nazi legacy in the post-war years, forms a topic of much criticism up until today. An example is the guilt to be accepted by artists like filmmakers for their involvement. As his personal pet project, Minister of Propaganda Joseph Goebbels had promoted the anti-Semitic film *Jud Süß* (Germany 1940). The show piece of National Socialist ideology extremely but artfully distorted the facts of a case in the eighteenth-century Duchy of Wurttemberg that had led to the execution of the defendant. Jud Süß was screened throughout Germany and occupied Europe and aroused anti-Jewish hatred (Ecke, 2001, pp. 66–68). The film's director, Veit Harlan, faced a court trial after the war and was acquitted, claiming that he had been blackmailed by Goebbels to cooperate. This trial was the subject of a 2001 German film *Jud Süß – Ein Film als Verbrechen?*, discussing if a film can be a crime and Harlan's responsibility. The final judgement is left to the viewer.

At least for historically interested Germans, such films dealing with the aftermath of the Third Reich are important to watch.

Some cases will have been recent and had created a lingering crisis of confidence in major institutions. In the UK, the post offices and their personnel are held in affection by many. Sub-postmasters are typically private contractors who run another business side-by-side with their post duties (Mackintosh, 2024). In rural areas, the local post offices are one of the last signs of life in villages which have long lost almost all their social infrastructure. Against this background, the Horizon scandal broke out. Postmasters had to use Fujitsu's Horizon computer programme 'for tasks such as transactions, accounting and stocktaking' (Peachey, 2022). Though, it produced false deficits in hundreds of post offices, driving many to desperation. The Post Office stubbornly denied that there was a fault to the system, demanded paybacks, sent its inspectors, closed post offices, drove postmasters into ruin and dragged them to civil and criminal courts. The Mirror newspaper wrote:

> 736 blameless individuals were prosecuted by the Post Office between the years 2000 and 2014 (…) More than 230 sub-postmasters and sub-postmistresses were jailed after 700 had been prosecuted for theft, fraud and false accounting and four killed themselves. (Nozari, 2024)

Many suffered bankruptcy, even imprisonment, and were socially ostracised (Peachey, 2022). The four-part mini-series *Mr Bates vs The Post Office* (2024) by the private broadcaster ITV, deemed 'highly accurate' and not sensationalised by Post Minister Kevin Hollingrake (BBC Radio 4, 2024), picked up the story. Meanwhile, the courts and even the Post Office, the latter reluctantly and dragging its feet, had accepted the truth and a programme had started to recompensate the victims. Criminal courts began quashing convictions. Yet, new controversies ensued about the clunky and painfully slow procedures. This all will have made sure that the television audience had heard something about the case and was ready to watch an account of the legal conflict in which three UK institutions, the Post Office, the government, owning the enterprise, and the legal system, do not look good. The UK government fully owns the

Post Office (Clark & Booth, 2021, p. 4). State-owned enterprises should be properly regulated and controlled (Machura, 1993).

Where not indicated differently, the following account is based on the portrayal in the mini-series. It contained some fictionalisation. Especially the actions and responsibility of film characters do not necessarily provide a reliable account of historic events. Here, the focus is on the film's narrative and how the actors are depicted.

Mr Bates vs The Post Office—*Trial by TV Series*

In *Mr Bates vs The Post Office* and countless other products of popular legal culture, the story is personalised. As unique quality of drama, the show's script writer Gwynedd Hughes described:

> [I]n drama, you're right there during this terrible event, experiencing it through the eyes of the person who went through it, and, in the hands of a brilliant actor, that just can grab your heart and grab your attention like nothing else. (cited in Collier, 2024)

The Alan Bates character, played by Toby Jones, states in episode 1: 'I am not letting the Post Office getting away with this'. He starts campaigning systematically and founds the 'Justice for Postmasters Alliance'. Here and in other pop cultural products, the events are told through the suffering of and resistance by individuals. This key technique and its function to transport the message of a film or television series depends on the juxtaposition of heroes and villains. Audiences relish following both their moves, and this is part of attractive entertainment (Machura, 2017, pp. 6). Nicole Rafter (2006, p. 136) wrote about 'justice figures' and 'injustice figures'. The former strive for a just resolution and the latter try to stop this from happening. In *Mr Bates vs The Post Office*, various managers and investigators of the Post Office appear as harbingers of injustice. In the television series, Post Office director Angela van den Bogerd uses any trick against the postmasters to protect her employer. She even feigns personal sympathy with victims to manipulate them. The antagonist detailed the most in the mini-series, is that of General Manager Paula Vennels. A middle-aged career woman, she is painted as putting aside moments of scruples and following a hard-nosed policy to prosecute, shut down, delay and silence where she can. Surprisingly, she also doubles as an Anglican priest, and the series shows her preaching in church. A stronger contrast à la Jekyll and Hyde is hardly imaginable. What then, is her motivation and that of the Post Office, the main corporate culprit in this saga? Eventually, in episode 3, Vennels and her lieutenant van den Bogerd have to appear in front of a parliamentary select committee. Here they are sharply interrogated by a member of parliament. The former minister Nadhim Zahawi is giving a cameo appearance as interrogating MP, which is only adding to an appearance of 'authenticity'. They should answer 'Yes' or 'No' if they will make all evidence henceforth available. The MP summarises Vennels' prevarication with: 'I take it as a No'. Finally, it bursts out of Vennels: the reputation of the Post Office is at stake!

Vennels' mistake in *Mr Bates* is ultimately that she thinks such a big scandal can be kept under wraps—and through this, she surely destroys her company's reputation. Too many people are involved as well as taking an interest, and their actions cannot be foreseen. They become the small heroes of the story apart from the active sub-postmasters themselves. A member of parliament is involved early on and uses political channels to find out what is happening. There is the independent accountant employed by the Post Office who is moved to tears by the victims' fate and starts to investigate properly. He can be dismissed and ordered to hand over all his files. But as the case is more widely reported, lawyer James Hardley hears about the contracts on the radio, invites Bates and declares the sub-postmaster contracts contradicted the law from the start and should therefore be void. Importantly, a Fujitsu employee calls Bates and not only says the software bug was known but that after the sub-postmasters had closed their shops, a Fujitsu team used to access their computers to try to correct miscalculations. When they were unable to do so, the sub-postmasters had to take the blame. By the end of episode three, there is hope for the suffering victims.

Hardley helps preparing a class action lawsuit which finally forces the Post Office to accept that Horizon was unsafe. In the trial, the Post Office's position became untenable after the Fujitsu whistle blower testifies. As money runs out, the sub-postmasters are forced to accept a settlement which after legal costs and fees are deducted, leaves the victims with a compensation much below their actual losses. But, after it was established that Fujitsu could interfere with the sub-postmaster's account, any criminal conviction was 'unsafe' and had to be revoked. Popular legal culture at its best not only appeals to a common concern for justice but draws in the widest possible number of people. Aspects that make good entertainment are largely identical with properties of good news stories. The claim to veracity especially invites the audience to pass moral judgement. Having established what makes the attraction, how about popular culture's influence on the viewing public? Is it possible that 'Trial by Media' can have 'positive' effects by mobilising the public for a worthy cause and forcing the hand of decision-makers slow to act?

Character Trajectory and Message

'The character is the story', Dunne (2017, p. xvii) advises script writers. Overwhelmingly, law-related fictional stories show how selected characters are dealing with challenging situations involving law and crime. 'Crime clings to certain characters', it is 'personalised', wrote Brunt (2021, p. 82, p. 85) on opera and this also applies to film and television. Furthermore, given the issues commonly at stake, Good and Bad are recognisable, the audience is typically able to sympathise and maybe even identify with characters.

How films or television series balance heroes and anti-heroes determines the message. In the story, the protagonists take a moral stance. In this way, the audience is invited to pass a moral judgement. In addition, individuals may be depicted as consumed by a legal conflict or crime. They are undergoing a profound change of character, maybe to their detriment, maybe to ultimately become a better person, lawyer or judge.

When 'justice figures' key to a story are committing serious crimes, the message to the audience can be even more compelling. Smaller offences can be easily explained and forgiven by the audience. Sometimes, law is broken for the sake of a higher good. In the Dutch film *Lucia de B.* (aka *Accused* 2014), assistant public prosecutor Judith Jansen sneaks in and searches the Chief Prosecutor's office for evidence that will help exonerating Lucia. In popular culture, such behaviour may even demonstrate the highest commitment to finding the truth and delivering justice. It is then interesting to see how far 'justice figures' go. Viewers may start to worry if they overstep the mark and are becoming criminals.

A devastating message is sent if the main (somehow good) character of a story is destroyed, suffers from adverse consequences, or even causes these for others. In the acclaimed drama *I Want to Live!* (USA 1958) based on the real character of Barbara Graham, a young mother characterised by Bergman and Asimow (1996, p. 10) as 'happy-go-lucky party girl', is made the scapegoat for a murder committed by someone else and eventually executed. The audience is left in no doubt about the injustice of the death penalty certainly in this case and most likely as a form of punishment in general. *Lucia de B.* not only traces the historic mistrial of nurse Lucia de Berk, mistakenly convicted of killing babies on her ward, but also shows how a young prosecutor erroneously misdirected the machinery of justice. When she learns about the mistake, a devastated assistant prosecutor Judith Jansen visits Lucia in prison and confesses.

In very many fictional portrays, some form of justice is achieved in the end. A few examples from productions based on real cases suffice. *Lucia de B.* is finally publicly exonerated. The figure of ex-judge Ernst Janning in *Judgement at Nuremberg* (U.S.A. 1961) who served the Nazis, has to confront his responsibility as he should have known better. The film is loosely based on one of the trials against major Nazi war criminals (Bergman & Asimow, 1996: 25). Dr Samuel Mudd in *The Prisoner of Shark Island* (U.S.A. 1936), falsely convicted as co-conspirator in the assassination of U.S. President Abraham Lincoln in 1865, is pardoned for his self-less care for wardens and prisoners alike.

Law films typically suggest that the law can be a good instrument, if only in the hands of the right people. This is quite clear for lawyer heroes (Greenfield et al., 2001, p. 27) but applies much wider. The subpostmasters in *Mr Bates vs The Post Office* (2024) develop a sense of solidarity and, especially the title figure, Alan Bates, the tenacity, and leadership qualities allowing to persevere for many long years. They show that while hard, organised resistance to injustice is possible. In many other fictional stories, the main heroes are good lawyers. Yet, things are complicated in films or television series based on real cases as these cases are remembered for something that was amiss. There may still be a lingering suspicion that justice was not served on the occasion or that something is not right with the system. The cases are not yet settled in the court of public opinion and that is part of why the viewing public is attracted (Machura & Böhnke, 2016, p. 11). A closer look is required on the messages those films send about law.

Conservativism and Change in Popular Legal Culture

Popular legal culture has long been accused of being structurally conservative. Several reasons why films and television series appear conservative can be cited. State, church and industry self-censorship had a role at various times (e.g. Machura & Böhnke, 2016, pp. 15–17; Springhall, 1998). Famous is the Hollywood Production Code demanding a sympathetic treatment of law: illicit behaviour does not pay and law should not be 'ridiculed' (Motion Picture Association of America, 1930, sections 2. I and II)! But more fundamentally, stories need to be widely understandable. Otherwise, the products would not reach an audience. They need to cater to the demand. Some films or television series may aim at a niche viewership, in this case they must talk to this differently defined target group. To be not off-putting for the desired audience, stories should not deviate too much from people's experiences and from existing cultural patterns. (Or patterns familiar to and accepted by the niche audience.) Thus, even producers wishing to challenge the public need to consider existing views.

Another factor that results in a conservative streak in popular legal culture arises more from the supply side. Films often aim at if not high art, then at the kind of recognition which comes with following in the footsteps of other artists. Producers are not keen to give an absolutely accurate description of laws in effect in a certain country at a specific time, or how exactly trials are run (which would be tedious indeed!). They often employ lawyers as advisors, but filming is a team effort and other crafts also contribute. The most admired on an international scale are leading and acclaimed U.S. films and television series. As they bring versions of American justice to the screens, the tendency of producers in other countries to borrow ideas from them leads to an Americanisation of how things legal are portrayed (Machura & Ulbrich, 2001). For example, elements of the American version of the adversarial procedure complete with stereotypical lawyer behaviour appear in films set in Germany or France. How much an individual film or television broadcast is Americanised varies, though. The result appears as a conservative influence because a decades-old, predominant pattern is set for how trials and other legal actions are represented. But qualification as conservative depends on the context. In countries without an independent judiciary, where lawyers are much reduced in their function and the powerful are unaccountable completely, Hollywood dramas open a window into a different world.

As much as popular legal culture is a conservative influence, reinstating tried- and tested formulas, re-enforcing ways of thinking, there is also an in-built mechanism for perpetual incremental change. Namely, a simple repetition of the old would not be entertaining. The audience expects an intelligent variation. Therefore, producers of popular legal culture must come up with new ideas to enrich their products. For example, a cross-over of different genres is attempted. A classic courtroom drama can be combined with elements of a classic anti-war film as in the Australian production *Breaker Morant* (1980). It deals with the historic case of three Australian lieutenants serving in a special unit created by the British Army during the Boer War. The 'Bushveldt Carbineers' answered the unconventional warfare of the Boer guerrillas with equally gruesome methods. Key to the film's story is a policy by the commanding British General Herbert Kitchener, delivered down the chain of command by spoken word only, not to take prisoners. During the campaign, the title figure, Lieutenant Harry Harbord 'The Breaker' Morant, had taken command of the 'Carbineers', enraged by the mutilation and killing of the unit's captain by guerrillas. Later, to prepare the ground for an international peace conference, General Kitchener convened and manipulated a trial of the *Bushveldt Carbineers*. The film depicts the defendants as scapegoats and how war changes ordinary men (Kershen, 2006). The masterpiece contains still another variation in addition to combining courtroom drama and anti-war film. Where court martial films often depict how innocent soldiers pay with their lives for the machinations and failure of others higher up in the command chain (Machura, 2017, p. 16), in *Breaker Morant*, the audience is left in no doubt that two of the three defendants are without doubt guilty of murder. The youngest one, Lieutenant Witton, reluctantly relayed Morant's order to execute a group of Boer prisoners but immediately returned to plead with him not to go ahead. The defence lawyer declares in court that Witton's only 'crime' has been to shoot a Boer in self-defence and the scene is shown in a flashback. Unlike the Australian lieutenants, more senior officers, including Kitchener himself, were protected and escaped punishment for their involvement altogether. To this day, there is controversy about the historic Breaker Morant case in Australia and South Africa (Asimow, 2024) and the film will have contributed by not only questioning how the trial was conducted and decided but also by questioning the nature of war. The example shows that what might have been a run-of-the-mill court martial film gains extra significance.

As a result of the in-built mechanism for innovation that characterises ambitious products of popular culture, the audience is presented with the possibility of a different reality. What if post-war German courts had been stricter with Nazi criminals? What if military courts are more independent? What if police and the public prosecution investigated and checked cases more carefully before they bring them to court? These are examples of questions which the audience is invited to ponder.

Quite regularly, the audience is prompted to think about and sometimes even contribute to legal reforms by films and television series based on real cases. *I want to live!* appealed to Americans to help abolishing the death penalty. Or, in one case (*Cry for Help: The Tracey Thurman Story*, U.S.A. 1989), a film made for television based on an actual crime has influenced the law and police training (Neuhaus, 2005, p. 39). *Mr Bates vs The Post Office* points to an issue with the legal system of England and Wales. Since centuries, Royal Mail was allowed to investigate cases without involvement of the police as an independent authority, using the legal instrument of private prosecution. As a solicitor explains to her client in episode 1: Royal Mail can prosecute cases up to the level of the High Court. The lack of qualified third-party involvement such as normally provided by police and Crown Prosecution Service before defendants go to court was a disaster in waiting and something that needed changing.

The screening of a story can itself prompt actions. *Mr Bates vs the Post Office* immediately revived media and public interest in the underlying chain of events. For years, the Post Office had been able to limit damages. According to Nokes, Moorhead and Day (2024),

> It has fought exposure of the truth with such approaches as non-disclosure agreements, threats of litigation against journalists, selective reporting of investigations and litigation methods that have elicited strong criticism from the judges involved.

The television drama series, watched by 9 million viewers, finally took the scandal to the top of the political agenda, as Stephen Barber (2024) wrote:

> [t]he story was broken by Computer Weekly 14 years ago. It has been the subject of an in-depth BBC podcast helmed by Nick Wallis, and has received regular attention in the magazine Private Eye. It has been raised multiple times in parliament, and there is even an official inquiry slowly working its way through what happened.

The facts of the case were known for years but what has missed and what the mini-series has finally provided, in the view of Computer Weekly's Chief Reporter Karl Flinders was 'public anger' (BBC One, 2024). After and during the screening of the mini-series, more victims came forward and felt encouraged to contact lawyers. Questions were asked about the role of politicians serving at the time. The Chancellor of the Exchequer had to confirm the government's commitment to reimburse the sub-postmasters and the Prime Minister Rishi Sunak himself had already stated that 'almost £150 mn had been paid out to over 2,500 people' (Uddin, 2024). Under public pressure, with 'over a million people' demanding it in a petition (Mason, 2024), ex-Director Vennels gave up her honorary title as Commander of the Order of the British Empire (Slow, 2024) that she had once received 'for services to the Post Office and to charity' (Mitchell & Devlin, 2024). London's Metropolitan

Police announced 'a fraud inquiry would build on investigations into perjury and instances where Post Office officials may have perverted the course of justice' (Uddin, 2024). The leader of the opposition demanded that the Post Office should not prosecute cases in court and the chair of the advisory group overseeing compensation to the victims a law which rehabilitates those convicted of a crime (BBC News, 2024a, 2024b). Shortly after, the Prime Minister announced to introduce a law to exonerate and compensate quickly the affected sub-postmasters (Grunewald, 2024). Not to underestimate in all of this is the public rehabilitation of the affected sub-postmasters. Reactions also occurred to other products of popular culture before (examples in e.g. Bergman & Asimow, 1996; Kuzina, 2000). They testify to the power of 'trial by film'.

When dealing with scandalous events, films and television shows based on real cases can become part of the strong tradition of social issue dramas described by Kuzina (2001). In these, the suffering of protagonists is vividly depicted to alert the public to what goes wrong in society and what needs to be done. 'When it comes to problem-oriented courtroom dramas (social issue courtroom dramas), a single legal case is at the centre which is of general social significance' (Kuzina, 2000, p. 217, author's translation). Kuzina (2000, p. 217) goes so far as to say that most of the U.S. social issue courtroom dramas are after actual cases. A good example is the drama *I Want to Live!* already introduced. Others include the acclaimed AIDS drama *Philadelphia* (USA 1993) (Kuzina, 2000, pp. 234–235). Andrew Beckett, a top lawyer working in a law firm, is dismissed because senior partners get wind of his illness and sexual orientation. A fight back through the court system begins which turns into a race against death as Beckett's health deteriorates rapidly. The film is based on an actual AIDS antidiscrimination case (Bergman & Asimow, 1996, p. 136) and is often said to have profoundly influenced public opinion.

An altogether different trajectory is found in *Schindler's List* (USA 1993). Oskar Schindler was a Nazi party member and ran a factory with Jewish slave labourers. However, he then changed and started to employ as many persecuted Jews as possible to save them from certain death. The film shows how his connections to leading officials who believe him to be one of their ilk and the factory production supposedly important for the German war effort, help him in his endeavour. The film finishes with the release of the survivors who have become Schindler's friends. Thirty years after its first screening, the impressive film still appeals to a worldwide audience. When visiting Krakow and the Auschwitz concentration camp with a group of university students in 2019, a guided tour of Schindler's factory was part of the standard programme for tourists. The building, turned into an exhibition about the Holocaust and the fate of Poland in World War II, proved absolutely packed with people of all ages and from faraway countries. Didactically, visitors were picked up by their knowledge of the film. And copies were on sale. 'Dark tourism' (Lennon, 2017), often inspired by films, television series or novels, has become another manifestation of popular culture. This again testifies for the power of film and television, how they invite audiences to think about law-related behaviours, judge the characters involved and convey a certain meaning to them.

Conclusion

Characters make a story and they let the audience experience legal conflict/crime. This proves to be a powerful influence on audiences, what they think about the law, lawyers and other servants of the law, as well as the legal institutions. Many of the best products of popular legal culture are based on real cases: the suffering and often eventual triumph of individual heroes. Reality-based stories pick up cases not settled in the court of public opinion. Something seems amiss in how the events unfolded or they still tell audiences about the state of the world they live in.

Overall, films and TV series suggest that the law will be helpful, if only in the hands of the right people. How can this be reconciled with those stories that contain strong villains and in which injustice prevails? 'Where there is law, there is injustice', those words spoken by Platon Karataev in Tolstoy's 1869 novel *War and Peace* (Tolstoy, n.d., book 12, chapter XII) come to mind. Yet, a different audience reaction is more likely, one that is less radical, more pragmatic and more affirmative of modern life. People cannot afford legal nihilism as it would leave them defenceless against others who use law to their disadvantage. Certainly, some people may systematically turn to films or TV series with a bleak outlook. But for most, their consumption of popular legal culture will be mix of everything with positive portrayals paramount.

Popular legal culture suggests a classic liberal view: The rule of law is a good thing. It is much to be preferred above what has been called the 'rule of men'. But there need to be checks and balances, and no blind trust. Even the best laws can be abused, the best courts can get things wrong and the best trained lawyers may serve the wrong client or just simply may serve their clients wrongly. It needs proper legal procedures, including the chance to appeal against decisions, and in an extension to earlier forms of liberalism, a system that supports the economically or otherwise weaker party in defending their rights. Popular legal culture continuously contributes ideas and challenges to the public debate and in this way may serve the regeneration and maybe even reform of a society's law. 'Trial by film' based on real cases is one of the most powerful ways to achieve this.

Competing Interests The author has no conflicts of interest to declare that are relevant to the content of this chapter.

References

Asimow, M. (2000). Bad lawyers in the movies. *Nova Law Review, 24*(2), 533–591.

Asimow, M. (2024). All's fair in love and war: Military justice in the movies. In S. Machura (Ed.), *Law and war in popular culture* (pp. 51–69). Nomos.

Barber, S. (2024, January 12). Post Office scandal: What the lack of action tells you about Britain's polarised politics. *The Conversation*. https://theconversation.com/post-office-scandal-what-the-lack-of-action-tells-you-about-britains-polarised-politics-220958?

BBC News. (2024a, January 8). Parliament should pass act overturning convictions—Justice professor. https://www.bbc.co.uk/news/live/uk-politics-67910908

BBC News. (2024b, January 8). Starmer: All Post Office convictions should be revisited. https://www.bbc.co.uk/news/live/uk-politics-67910908

BBC One. (2024, January 13). Breakfast. Television broadcast, 6:00–9:00.
BBC Radio 4 (2024, January 13). Any questions? Radio broadcast, 13–14:00.
Bergman, P., & Asimow, M. (1996). *Reel justice. The courtroom goes to the movies*. Andrews and McMeel.
Black, D. A. (1999). *Law in film*. University of Illinois Press.
Brunt, L. (2021). Crime at the opera house. In D. Siegel & F. Bovenkerk (Eds.), *Crime and music* (pp. 73–86). Springer.
Clark, H., & Booth, L. (2021). *The Post Office*. Commons Library. https://researchbriefings.files.parliament.uk/documents/CBP-7550/CBP-7550.pdf
Collier, K. (2024, January 14). ITV Post Office drama: Gwyneth Hughes told it wouldn't be success. *North Wales Chronicle*. https://www.northwaleschronicle.co.uk/news/national/uk-today/24048446.itv-post-office-drama-gwyneth-hughes-told-wouldnt-success/
Diamond, S. S. (1990). Revising images of public punitiveness: Sentencing by lay and professional English magistrates. *Law and Social Inquiry, 15*(2), 191–221.
Dunne, W. (2017). *The dramatic writer's companion* (2nd ed.). University of Chicago Press.
Durkheim, E. (2013). *The division of labour in society* (W. D. Halls, Trans., 2nd ed.). Palgrave Macmillan (Original work published 1893).
Ecke, F. (2001). Braune Leinwand. Antisemitische Rechtspropaganda im Film des Dritten Reiches. In S. Machura & S. Ulbrich (Eds.), *Recht im Film* (pp. 54–69). Nomos.
Fortes, P. R. B. (2017). Lights, camera, affirmative action: Does Hollywood protect minorities? *Journal of the Oxford Centre for Socio-Legal Studies, 2*, 60–75. Retrieved January 14, 2024 from https://joxcsls.files.wordpress.com/2017/07/pedro_changed.pdf
Friedman, L. (1985). Transformations in American legal culture 1800 1985. *Zeitschrift Für Rechtssoziologie, 6*(2), 191–205.
Gies, L. (2008). *Law and the media: The future of an uneasy relationship*. Routledge-Cavendish.
Greenfield, S., Osborn, G., & Robson, P. (2001). *Film and the law*. Cavendish.
Grunewald, Z. (2024, January 11). Post Office scandal: How will the new law to exonerate victims of Horizon work? *The Guardian*. https://www.independent.co.uk/news/uk/politics/post-office-scandal-new-law-b2476352.html
Kershen, D. L. (2006). Breaker Morant (1979). In R. Strickland et al. (Eds.), *Screening justice—The cinema of law* (pp. 353–371). Hein.
Kuzina, M. (2000). *Der amerikanische Gerichtsfilm. Justiz, Ideologie, Dramatik*. Vandenhoeck und Ruprecht.

Kuzina, M. (2001). The social issue courtroom drama as an expression of American popular culture. *Journal of Law and Society, 28*(1), 79–96.

Lennon, J. (2017). Dark Tourism. In N. Rafter & M. Brown (Eds.), *The Oxford Encyclopedia of Crime, Media, and Popular Culture* (pp. 547–563). Oxford University Press.

Luhmann, N. (1997). Interview mit Niklas Luhmann: Das Internet ist kein Massenmedium? Interviewed by S. Laurin. Retrieved January 3, 2024, from https://www.ruhrbarone.de/niklas-luhmann-%E2%80%9Edas-internet-ist-kein-massenmedium%E2%80%9C/1109/

Luhmann, N. (2000). *The reality of the mass media* (K. Cross, Trans.). Polity Press (Original work published 1995).

Machura, S. (1993). The regulation of state-owned enterprises. *Annals of Public and Cooperative Economics, 64*(4), 605–616.

Machura, S. (2007). An analysis scheme for law films. *University of Baltimore Law Review, 36*(3), 329–345.

Machura, S. (2016). Recht im Film—Themen und Formen des Unterrichts. *Zeitschrift Für Didaktik der Rechtswissenschaft, 3*(4), 363–381.

Machura, S. (2017). Representations of law, rights and criminal justice. In *Oxford Research Encyclopedia of Criminology.* https://doi.org/10.1093/acrefore/9780190264079.013.201

Machura, S., & Böhnke, M. (2016). The legal system in German popular culture. In *Oxford Research Encyclopedia of Criminology.* https://doi.org/10.1093/acrefore/9780190264079.013.198

Machura, S., & Kammertöns, A. (2010). Deterred from going to court? A survey at German schools on media influences. *Entertainment and Sports Law Journal, 8*(2). https://www.entsportslawjournal.com/article/id/798/

Machura, S., & O'Riordan, C. (2023). *Effects of national media coverage on local trust in the police.* Report for the All-Wales Policing Academic Collaboration, Bangor University.

Machura, S., Short, F., Hill, V. M., Suddaby, C. R., Goddard, F. E., Jones, S. E., Lloyd-Astbury, E. L., Richardson, L., & Rouse, C. A. (2019). Recognising modern slavery. *Journal of Human Trafficking, 5*(3), 201–219.

Machura, S., & Ulbrich, S. (2001). Globalizing the Hollywood Courtroom Drama. *Journal of Law and Society, 28*(1), 117–132.

Mackintosh, T. (2024, January 8). Explained—The role of a postmaster and sub-postmaster. *BBC News.* https://www.bbc.co.uk/news/live/uk-politics-67910908

Mason, P. (2024, January 9). A TV drama may help deliver change for sub-postmasters. *BBC News.* https://www.bbc.co.uk/news/uk-politics-67920145

Meyer, P. N. (2014). *Storytelling for lawyers*. Oxford University Press.

Mitchell, A., & Devlin, K. (2024, January 4). Ex-Post Office boss Paula Vennells should hand back CBE over scandal, says Tory minister. *The Independent*. https://www.independent.co.uk/news/uk/politics/post-office-scandal-paula-vennells-tory-b2472540.html

Motion Picture Association of America. (1930). Motion picture production code of 1930. Reprinted in T. Doherty, *Pre-Code Hollywood. Sex, immorality, and insurrection in American cinema, 1930–1934* (pp. 347–359). Columbia University Press (1999).

Neuhaus, K.-J. (2005). Jura Im Pantoffelkino. *JUSTUF, 20*(1), 30–42.

Nokes, K., Moorhead, R., & Day, S. (2024, January 13). Post Office scandal: why thousands of victims are yet to see justice. *The Conversation*. https://theconversation.com/post-office-scandal-why-thousands-of-victims-are-yet-to-see-justice-220881?

Nozari, A. (2024, Januar 3). ITV Mr Bates vs The Post Office humiliates BBC's The Tourist in TV ratings war. *Mirror*. https://www.mirror.co.uk/3am/celebrity-news/itv-mr-bates-vs-post-31796703?int_source=amp_continue_reading&int_medium=amp&int_campaign=continue_reading_button#amp-readmore-target

Peachey, K. (2022). Post Office scandal: What the Horizon saga is all about. *BBC news*. Retrieved January 2, 2024, from https://www.bbc.co.uk/news/business-56718036

Rafter, N. (2006). *Shots in the mirror. Crime films and society* (2nd ed.). Oxford University Press.

Podlas, K. (2001). Please adjust your signal: How television's syndicated courtrooms bias our juror citizenry. *American Business Law Journal, 39*(1), 1–24.

Rapping, E. (2003). *Law and justice as seen on TV*. New York University Press.

Sherwin, R. K. (2000). *When the law goes pop*. University of Chicago Press.

Slow, O. (2024, January 9). Paula Vennells: Ex-Post Office boss handing back CBE over IT scandal. *BBC News*. https://www.bbc.co.uk/news/uk-67925304

Springhall, J. (1998). Censoring Hollywood: Youth moral panic and crime/gangster movies of the 1930s. *Journal of Popular Culture, 32*(3), 135–154.

Tolstoy, L. (n.d.). *War and peace* (L. Maude & A. Maude, Trans.). Project Gutenberg (Original work published 1869). Retrieved July 27, 2023, from https://www.gutenberg.org/files/2600/2600-h/2600-h.htm#link2HCH0055

Uddin, R. (2024, January 6). Police open investigation into 'potential fraud' at UK Post Office. *Financial Times*. https://www.ft.com/content/2069fb3b-c79c-410d-a284-de176f65dfae

Wikström, P.-O.H. (2010). Explaining crime as moral actions. In S. Hitlin & S. Vaysey (Eds.), *Handbook of the sociology of morality* (pp. 211–240). Springer.

4

Between a Rock and a Hard Place: Israel's Courtroom Journalists in the Digital Age

Anat Peleg

Introduction

> In the era of social media, the reporter is already part of the story... Agendas are attributed to them. They themselves are already a target... We are at war now, and you have to choose a side... Like a political discourse... This way it's hard to stay faithful to your journalistic values. (R)[1]

These remarks by R', an esteemed veteran courtroom reporter, shed light both on the changes that are occurring in courtroom journalists' perception of the job and their commitment to journalistic ethics in the

[1] All quotes are from the interviews conducted in 2020. The names of the interviewees have been withheld at their request.

A. Peleg (✉)
Tel Aviv University, Tel Aviv, Israel
e-mail: apeleg@netvision.net.il

L. Gies (ed.), *Trial by Media*, Palgrave Studies in Crime, Media and Culture, https://doi.org/10.1007/978-3-031-80593-6_4

digital era, and on the decline of their professional authority in the eyes of the Israeli public.

This chapter analyses the positions of court reporters, who are the administrators of trial by media, concerning the external and internal-professional factors which they believe have led to a diminution of their journalistic authority in public discourse. The chapter draws upon a qualitative longitudinal study, which compares the findings from in-depth interviews conducted in 2020 with 12 leading courtroom journalists and commentators from all the media in Israel, with the findings of previous studies conducted among 40 courtroom journalists in Israel (2007, 2012).

The analysis of the findings is based on Carlson and Lewis's (2020) model for analysing journalistic authority in the digital age, which draws on the school of boundary work research in sociology. The study sheds light on the unique catch for the court reporters, which stems from a process in which, alongside internal-journalistic changes, the interactions between the judicial system and the established media weaken the standing of both in public discourse. This chapter offers an assessment of the potential demise of courtroom reporting and its traditional bridging function between courts and public opinion. In so doing, it also contributes to the analysis of the complexity of contemporary relations between the established media and the social institutions that it covers.

Studying Journalistic Authority

Among the types of authority that have been identified in sociological research, the most relevant to this study is epistemic authority (Gieryn, 1999), which is the authority of the knowledgeable to create information and disseminate it in society. In the research literature journalists have claimed that the basis for their cultural authority to produce knowledge and exercise the public's right to know is precisely their professionalism, which draws upon norms, working routines, connections with authorized sources of information, and a certain level of institutionalization (Carlson, 2017). However, in the digital era ordinary citizens can disseminate information in immediate fashion, with a corresponding decline in the recognition of journalists' professionalism and their exclusive authority to mediate information to the public (Carlson, 2017; Reich, 2018).

Chris Anderson and Michael Schudson (2020) point out that methodologically there has been a renewed convergence between study of the media and the study of professions in sociology for the purpose of examining journalism's loss of authority in the digital era. They look into the journalism profession's areas of responsibility in the digital environment and ascertain the link between journalists' ethical and practical conduct and the erosion of their professional authority in the public discourse.

Hence, media scholars have returned to the theory of boundary work developed by sociologist Thomas F. Gieryn (1999). According to Gieryn, communities of knowledge seek to justify their authority and to defend their professional autonomy by expanding the scope of their occupation and by distancing unworthy players and practices beyond the boundaries of the profession. Matthew Carlson and Seth Lewis (2020), who study the boundaries of the profession of journalism in the digital era, draw upon the theory of boundary work, viewing journalism as a process of negotiation between diverse actors that are competing over the definition of 'journalist'. They emphasize that beyond examining the internal-journalistic factors that shape the authority of journalists, such as their values and working routines, it is necessary to look at journalists' online struggle over their authority in external discourse, the meta-journalistic discourse being conducted on social media (Hanitzsch & Vos, 2017), where journalists are having to contend with harsh public criticism of their conduct by citizens, politicians, and interested parties. Table 4.1 presents the correspondences between Carlson & Lewis and the theory of boundary work for the purpose of analysing journalistic authority in our time.

In recent decades, the changes in the values of the profession of journalism and in the working routines practised in it have been extensively studied, as well as how they relate to the decline of journalistic authority in the digital age. This linkage will be demonstrated in Table 4.2 at the end of the Findings section and in the Discussion and Conclusions section.

Table 4.1 Model of Journalists' Boundary Work in the Digital Era (Carlson & Lewis, 2020)

	Expanding the profession	Excluding from the profession	Defending the profession's independence
Participants	Players are accepted to the profession of journalism	Players are excluded from the profession of journalism	External players are presented as a threat to journalism
Working routines	Recognition of journalistic working routines as professional	Rejection of journalistic working routines and their depiction as unprofessional	Grasping working routines outside the journalistic community as a threat to journalism
Fundamental positions	Professional norms are grasped as customary in the profession of journalism	Professional norms are grasped as not customary in the profession of journalism	Professional norms are grasped as a threat to the profession of journalism

Changes in the Normative Conception of the Journalist's Role

Even though the definition of journalistic professionalism is not fixed or universal, and one's conception of the journalistic role is affected by national and cultural context (Hanitzsch & Voss, 2017), the study of Western journalism has identified certain common components in the conception of that role: independence, objectivity, a search for truth, monitoring the centres of power, giving voice to citizens, and providing a platform for public debate (Kovach & Rosenstiel, 2014).

In the research literature, the following obstacles to the actual realization of the principle of objectivity in contemporary journalistic work have been identified: the rise in the public standing of bloggers and citizen journalists, who are amateur journalists, reporting on newsworthy events despite having no experience or training in the field of journalistic ethics; organizational pressures on journalists to achieve higher

Table 4.2 Differences between the interviewees' positions at three research time points in the light of Carlson and Lewis' (2020) model

	Interviews 2007	Discussion group 2012	Interviews 2020	Analysis of findings in the light of Carlson & Lewis' model (2020)
Positions toward participants in judicial reporting	Political reporters perceived as responsible for decline in quality of judicial reporting	Resignation regarding the involvement of political reporters in coverage	Alternative commentators perceived as a threat to journalistic authority	Entry of additional players to the judicial reporting field, including such perceived as a threat to the court reporters' professional authority

(continued)

Table 4.2 (continued)

	Interviews 2007	Discussion group 2012	Interviews 2020	Analysis of findings in the light of Carlson & Lewis' model (2020)
Positions toward working routines in judicial reporting	Fieldwork and extended coverage of judicial proceedings; rejection of reliance on PR consultants	Fieldwork and extended coverage of judicial proceedings; rise in dependency on PR consultants	Broader coverage of VIP investigations; reduction in fieldwork and extent of judicial coverage; complete dependency on PR consultants; politicization of courtroom reporting	Departure from traditional reporting routines and adoption of working routines formerly perceived as a threat to journalistic autonomy
Fundamental positions toward the judicial system	Confidence in the judicial system; caution exercised in criticizing the courts; call for requiring journalists to defend the values of a fair trial	Confidence in the judicial system; criticism of the judicial system perceived as a measure of professionalism	Decline in confidence in the judicial system; denial of responsibility to defend the values of a fair trial; rallying to the defence of the judicial system from populistic attacks	Departure from fundamental values and change in perception of the courtroom reporter's journalistic role

ratings due to declining profits in the established media; journalists' own conception of reality and political bias; and journalistic language, which has a penchant for highly charged words that nullify the objectivity of the reportage (Anderson & Schudson, 2020; Boudana, 2016).

Anderson and Schudson (2020) point to a process of blurring of the boundaries between professional journalists and bloggers and citizen journalists, who in the past were considered non-professional. They argue that the declining numbers of professional journalists in news organizations have led to the inclusion of materials produced by these amateur journalists in the news broadcasts, and their style has sparked a conceptual change, which is manifested by the inclusion of personal opinion in factual news reporting, something viewed as necessary to achieve higher ratings (Montgomery, 2006).

The study of the partisan press has revealed a variety of reporting and editing methods that are contrary to the value of journalistic objectivity, including: employing a biased tone in reportage, providing an extended platform for speakers from a certain side of the political spectrum, and even the suppression of inconvenient facts or their relegation to a remote spot on the news agenda (Panievsky, 2021). It has also been argued that in the digital era, under the influence of the blogosphere, a predilection has developed for emotive writing and the production of 'emotional' news, due to a belief that it arouses involvement, interest, and consumption on the part of the addressees (Wahl-Jorgensen, 2019). In place of the concept of objectivity, some scholars (Boudana, 2016; Ryfe, 2013) have therefore suggested alternative professional norms such as transparency, balance, fairness, and compassion. Over the years broader models of the journalist's role have been conceptualized, which depart from the imperative of objectivity or neutrality in reportage and argue that the journalist's job is to provide context and a broad picture of reality (Fink & Schudson, 2014). The models that are relevant to this article, which is about court reporters, include the 'investigative journalist', and the 'lawyer/defence attorney journalist'.

The investigative journalist uses the facts as a basis for analysing a broad social issue. Under this model, the journalist's job is to gather facts in order to challenge institutional authority and protect the citizens from an abuse of power. The lawyer/defence attorney journalist model is an umbrella concept for subjective forms of reportage and stressing the journalist's personal opinion for the sake of advancing social goals. Ginosar and Reich (2020) argue that in the post-truth era, which is characterized by frequent attacks on journalistic expertise, journalists are looking for a way to prove their contribution to society. This has given rise to another mode of activity, of the 'obsessive journalist'—the social activist, who covers social injustices and seeks solutions to them out of full and long-term personal commitment.

Other researchers have found that due to the financial problems in the media industry in the social media era, the owners have reached an understanding that meeting the audience's needs is the key to journalistic survival. Therefore journalists feel a personal responsibility also for marketing the journalistic product that they have created (Tandoc & Vos, 2015). The changes in the current conception of the journalist's role and ethical norms, alongside developments in communication technologies, contribute to the change in journalistic working routines.

Ramifications of the Use of New Technologies for Journalistic Working Routines in the Era of Social Networking

A rich research literature deals with the effects of new communication technologies on journalistic working routines and on the quality of the journalistic product. An Israeli study conducted over 16 years (Reich, 2018) found that the use of interpersonal interactions in the creation of news items has declined, to be replaced by communications in writing, email, and WhatsApp between reporters and their sources, as well as reliance on documents. In Reich's opinion, this 'textual turn' contributes to the reduction of inaccuracies when citing interviewees and to the transparency of the information. Nonetheless, communication in writing enables PR consultants (spokespersons of the legal system and media advisers to lawyers and defendants who develop media strategies to improve the image of their clients in the public discourse) to disseminate biased information and influence the media framing. Such information is of lesser quality than information obtained through interpersonal interaction between journalist and source, in the course of which the journalist can pose challenging questions and better assess the interviewee's reliability (Guirdham, 2015).

The flourishing of social media has sparked changes in the established media, the consequences of which are dividing researchers' opinions. Some argue that social media are an arena for locating socially significant stories of critique of the establishment and giving voice to weak populations that have not had a platform in the past (Tandoc & Vos, 2015). Graves (2016) even points to a rise in the insistence on accuracy in the established press, through the adoption of fact-checking techniques, in response to the publication of 'fake news' on the internet. By contrast, it has been argued that journalists echo false information that is spread over social media, making it harder to correct erroneous conceptions that are harmful to the public (Tsfati et al., 2020). Tandoc and Vos (2015) believe that journalists' very participation in the discourse on the web, mainly for the purpose of personal branding, is contrary to the distance that the classical journalistic ethos demands should be maintained between journalistic and commercial considerations.

Nonetheless, it should be noted that in the expanding research literature on the changes to journalists' working routines and ethical norms in the digital era, very little research has been done as regards court reporters.

Studies on Court Reporters' Relations with Their Sources

Researchers of the discourse between law and the media are also divided in their opinions on two fundamental issues. First, which of the sides is leading the discourse, the legal community or the media? And second, what are the consequences of the evolving discourse between the legal professionals and journalists for the standing of law in society?

Postmodernist theoreticians (Fiske & Glynn, 1995; Garapon, 1996) have warned that the anticipated danger posed by the media depictions of law to the very essence of judicial proceedings stems from the proliferation of media representations of courts and the relocation of adjudication from the institutional space to the popular space. Other researchers maintain that the influence of media discourse on the judicial sphere is miniscule, because the latter is exclusively under the control of the judicial system (Haltom, 1998). Still other researchers have argued that in the discourse between law and the media, there are lines of similarity and common social goals, the most important of which are achieving social order and determining public policy (Ericson, 1996). Researchers of the influence of Internet discourse on law are concerned about the damage the Internet does to the presumption of innocence regarding suspects and their right to due process, but they are also aware of the advantages of the democratization of legal discourse, exposing the public to counter-narratives that compete with establishment narratives (Gies & Bortoluzzi, 2014).

The routines of courtroom coverage in the Western press have been studied very narrowly. In studies conducted in the period 1974–1998 (Davis, 1994; Haltom, 1998; Jones, 1974), researchers viewed law as a field of low news value, and court reporters as lazy and subject to manipulation by their sources, having internalized the values of the judicial system without critiquing or challenging them. Later researchers have identified a rise in the commercial and news value of judicial reporting in the media and a change in the approach of court reporters who have become more competitive and more critical of the judicial system (Bogoch & Holtzman-Gazit, 2020; Gies, 2008). By contrast, studies conducted in the 2000s have pointed to a drop in the quality of courtroom reportage in the established media, due to the diminishing number of journalists in response to economic pressures, their reduced presence in courthouses, and their reliance on processed legal documents provided by spokespersons in the judicial system and PR consultants in the private sector (Simons & Bosland, 2020). Studies in the United States have also pointed to the politicization of judicial reporting, due to the wider platform that is afforded to politicians and other interested parties to express their opinion on the functioning of the Supreme Court (Sullivan & Carmody-Tilley, 2020).

Researchers of judicial reporting in the Israeli media found that until the year 2000 the Israeli media engaged in a low level of critique and helped to legitimise the power of the Supreme Court (Bogoch & Holtzman-Gazit, 2008). A study by Zvi Reich et al. (2016) found a high level of confidence in the judicial system, which contrasts with a low level of confidence in political institutions.

Research Structure

The present research draws upon three qualitative studies in which 52 court reporters were interviewed at three different points in time:

1. In-depth interviews were conducted in 2007 with 30 court reporters from all the media (15 former journalists and 15 active journalists). The professional experience of the former journalists in legal reporting ranged from eight to 50 years, during the period 1950–2000, and three of them had legal training. The experience of the still-active journalists ranged from three to 30 years, and half of them had legal training.
2. An interview with a group of active reporters that convened at the end of 2012 to discuss changes in the reporting of judicial affairs, following the layoff of journalists in all media channels because of the economic crisis in the media. The group consisted of ten courtroom journalists and commentators from the print media, radio and television, and internet sites of the print media. Their professional experience ranged from four to 30 years, and six of them had legal training. The group included six reporters who were also interviewed in 2007.
3. In-depth interviews conducted between January and September 2020 with 12 leading court reporters and commentators from the best-rated television and radio stations and daily newspapers. Journalists who work for ultra-right media channels were interviewed too. Their professional experience ranged from ten to 30 years of reporting, and eight of them had legal training. Eight interviewees also participated in the previous two studies.

This methodology is familiar from longitudinal qualitative research for the purpose of understanding long-term social and cultural processes and their consequences for the individual (Thomson, 2007).

The key research question of this study is:

1. Regarding the decline of public trust in the mainstream media in Israel (Shwarts Altshuler, 2018), what are the court reporters' opinions on the external and internal-professional factors that have caused a decline in their journalistic authority in public discourse?

To answer this question, the findings were analysed in four stages. In the first stage, for the purpose of comparison, data from interviews at previous points in time, which had already been analysed, were collated on four topics which were also discussed by the participants in the current study: court reporters' area of responsibility in the news departments; their working routines and professional norms; reporters' relations with their sources; and reporters' positions vis-à-vis the meta-discourse that is critical of their relationship with the judicial system. In the second stage, the findings of this study were compared to the findings of the two previous studies on court reporters that I conducted in 2007 and 2012. In the third stage, the findings were re-analysed on second reading, based on Carlson and Lewis's (2020) model of the decline of journalistic authority. In the fourth stage, the unique predicament for court reporters was identified: it was found to stem from internal-professional changes and from interactions between reporters and the judicial system in public discourse, which are damaging to the authority of both reporters and judges.

Findings

Court Reporters' Positions Regarding Internal-professional Changes that are Damaging Their Professional Authority

As in the previous studies, so too in 2020 the court reporters point to the high news value of the legal field in the media, as indicated by its positioning at the top of the news agenda in Israel and the senior standing of court reporters in news organizations. However, the interviewees' remarks make it clear that the court reporters' area of responsibility has changed over the years. They point to three new changes that in their view have led to a decline in the scope of courtroom reporting and its growing shallowness:

1. A rise in the news value of the criminal investigation phase and decline in the news value of all the judicial procedural stages prior to rendering a verdict.
2. A decline in the news value of socially important judicial proceedings, at the centre of which stand unknown figures, due to increased coverage of trials of public officials and celebrities.
3. A rise in the news value of legal topics that are discussed on social media.

Changes in Court Reporters' Area of Responsibility in the Mainstream Press in the Digital Era

It appears that in recent years the courtroom reporter's field of coverage has been extended to stages of the police investigation, which in the past would have come under the responsibility of the police reporter. However, this extension, which stems from rating considerations, in effect renders the legal coverage shallow. A says:

> There are many subjects which I think ought to be dealt with, but I don't deal with them, because I simply don't have the ability or the resources... I find myself writing 70% of the time only about the investigations in the cases of Prime Minister Benjamin Netanyahu, and that means that certain legal issues take over the agenda and push aside all the other subjects.

N adds that in consideration of ratings, the newspapers adjust themselves to the news agenda of social media, downgrading the news value of law and economics, which used to be central to news coverage in the past. B argues that there is a turning away from social issues in courtroom reporting. Unlike in the past, she says, courtroom reporting has stopped reporting proceedings involving an anonymous defendant or civilian plaintiff, personal stories that have the potential to expose social injustices, or precedents in judgement on matters important to the daily lives of citizens. This is because the editors in the newsrooms believe that the coverage of trials of public officials and celebrities is more attractive to the audience and increases the ratings.

The reporters' positions reflect on the one hand a critical self-observation of the reduction in the scope of the legal information that they disseminate in public, but on the other hand also an indifference in the face of the news bureaus' commercially inclined editorial considerations. We find a similar mix of responses—critique of professional transformations, coupled with an apathy towards their social consequences—also in regard to the changes which interviewees identify in their professional norms in the digital era.

Changes in Working Routines and Norms of Courtroom Reporting in the Social Networking Era

Participants in the present research pointed to two changes in the digital era: in their working routines and in the norms of courtroom reporting:

1. Changes in working routines: a reduction in fieldwork, increasing dependency on PR consultants, and less time devoted to journalistic work due to the activity expected of court reporters on social media.
2. Changes in the norms of reporting: greater drama and affectation in the style of coverage, and a drawing away from the rules of journalistic ethics.

Changes in Working Routines

In the present study, journalists for the first time attested to their diminishing presence in the courthouse, which in the past was the core of their fieldwork in this field. R believes that the court reporters' absence from the courthouse is detrimental to their ability to broaden the circle of their informants:

> In the Watergate affair, when reporters came to a detention proceeding, they understood that lawyers from the Republican Party were there and understood the connection to Nixon. I had the same thing… I was at a detention proceeding, and somebody approached me with dynamite recordings on a corruption scandal in one of the parties… The material was a bombshell. If I hadn't been there physically, I wouldn't have received that material.

In the group interview that was conducted in 2012, the journalists noted that media advisers of legal counsels and defendants, who are present in court during the legal proceedings of their clients and supply the journalists that are unable to be in court—due to the growing work pressures on fewer court reporters—with legal documents, had therefore become prominent players in the legal arena, much to the detriment of the journalists' standing as the agenda-setters of the legal news. In the present study, the journalists claimed there has been an entire 'textual turn' (Reich, 2018), i.e., there are more textual exchanges between journalists and sources and more textual materials than auditory information behind the news, which even further intensifies their dependency on legal documents and on biased information provided by PR consultants:

> PR consultants are usually the suppliers of the initial information, they are the conduit… The discrepancy between the reality and that presented by the PR person is a growing discrepancy, therefore the initial news will often be biased, they set the agenda. (A)

The courtroom journalists explain their inability to fight PR consultants' manipulations—their attempts to circulate biased interpretations of the legal documents that they possess and to put words in journalists' mouths—as being due to the pressures of the speedy reporting required on online platforms. B explains:

> Whereas once it was possible to be without Twitter, today there is no such thing. You've got to respond a lot. My need to balance checking the information against the speed of response is becoming more and more difficult because the speed is growing.

Changes in the Norms of Reportage and Vulgarization of the Writing Style

The retired courtroom journalists who were interviewed in 2007 attested that they were cautious when writing about the courts and even practised self-censorship to avoid any disrespect of the judicial institution. In the study conducted in 2012, however, the journalists already pointed to a rise in the level of criticism in their writing and a tendency to express an opinion in favour of one or the other side at trial. In the present study, the participants expressed discontent with the adoption of the extremely outspoken style, which characterizes online discourse, in reporting on legal issues in the established media.

According to L, this combative and unnuanced writing style is detrimental to the journalistic skills and to the credibility of the courtroom journalist: 'Something in us journalists has been grinded down. This style has both overwhelmed attention and eroded sensitivity'. According to him, the belligerent writing style in writing about the courts is the cause of polarization and factionalism within the journalistic community and of a tribalistic perception of court reporters among the general public. T emphasizes that arguments between reporters on social media are contrary to journalistic ethics and detrimental to their public authority:

> They are fighting wars that seem inappropriate to me. The goal of court reporters is to promote themselves on Twitter. They refer in harsh words to the Justice Minister, afterward they cover him, and then you think anyone will believe you? They do not have a neutral visibility.

The court reporters employ a defensive rhetoric, which places the blame for superficializing the media discourse on the work routines in a digital environment and on marketing pressures. Similar defensive rhetoric has been found also in their positions regarding external elements that are affecting their professional authority.

Reporters' Positions Regarding External Elements Impacting Their Professional Authority

The court reporters who participated in the present study pointed to three external factors, which they consider to be accelerating the decline in their professional authority in the online era:

1. Involvement of external players in reporting on judicial affairs;
2. Flaws in the judicial system's conduct vis-à-vis the media;
3. An accusatory populistic discourse, which claims there is a symbiosis between the judicial system and the journalists.

Involvement of External Players in Reporting on Judicial Affairs

In 2007 the court reporters maintained that the more political reporters joined the coverage of trials of public officials, the more their professional reputation as neutral reporters was damaged as the style of political reporting leached into the legal reporting and led to a rise in the level of cynicism in the coverage and to a superficial 'winners and losers' and 'horse racing' framing (Haltom, 1998) that is customary in sports reporting. In the present study the court reporters argued that for the first time their authority in the public discourse is being diminished due to incorrect legal interpretations by political reporters and by social media influencers, who have no legal training or experience in courtroom reporting. They are being forced to invest time, they say, to refute the claims of such actors before their own editors and before the public, which attributes importance to what recognizable figures say. O explains:

> I am shocked. When they talk about legal rulings, about the Supreme Court, and express their learned opinion. At best maybe they talked with somebody. Mostly they in my opinion are [like] the fan in the stands who says what he thinks of the referee who blew the whistle when the ball went right or left. That is the level of analysis of judicial decisions, and that is what I have to refute in the eyes of my editors.

According to the interviewees, over the years the perception of the courtroom reporter's journalistic role has changed due to changes in the reporters' fundamental positions vis-à-vis the judicial system. The court reporters in the legacy media have become more critical of the judiciary, more aware of its failings, and more concerned about instances of injustice.

Pointing to Flaws in the Judicial System's Conduct vis-à-vis the Media

In the previous studies that I conducted, in 2007 and 2012, the journalists did not express any lack of confidence in the judicial system. In the present study, we find a mixed bag of positions, which reflects a decline in the interviewees' confidence in the judicial system as well as opposition to their past commitment to avoid publishing anything that might be detrimental to a fair trial. They also admit, for the first time, that due to the populistic attacks by Netanyahu and his political allies on the justice system, contending that it is corrupt and that the charges against him are trumped-up, they fear the collapse of the rule of law and have rallied to its defence.

The court reporters pointed to a decline in their confidence in the judicial system. R accuses the heads of the office of state attorney in the ministry of justice of personal motives in conflicts that are ostensibly legal: 'These are people with weaknesses. The more they acknowledge their weaknesses and know how to deal with them… they will know how to contend outward and rebut more attacks'. T says that he has lost confidence in the system because of the lack of transparency and complains that the courts accede to police requests to conceal information, thereby blocking freedom of the press:

> The judges issue nondisclosure orders automatically. The police ask and are given straightaway. The judges don't take into consideration the public interest in disclosure. And there is no equality either – requests for nondisclosure orders by highfaluting suspects, [with] big and powerful lawyers, are immediately granted.

Alongside the harsh criticism of the judicial system, mixed positions were also heard regarding a social responsibility to defend the values of law. G feels free of any need to be cautious in disclosing information from investigations:

> I had an argument about it with another journalist. He'd received news that he didn't disclose, [about] an investigation that had been opened, because he knew it would be detrimental to the investigation. I did report… It's not my job as a courtroom reporter to protect the judicial system.

By contrast, O is worried about the media's influence on the fairness of judicial proceedings and feels a civil commitment to defend the presumption of innocence regarding defendants and not impair the fairness of a trial. O says: 'I'm old school, who believes not only in the presumption of innocence, but that no opinion should be expressed after a trial has begun'.

Despite the criticism of judicial conduct and the disagreement among the journalists regarding their social responsibility to defend the values of a fair process, there appears to be support for a professional and civil commitment on the part of the court reporters to defending the judicial system from political attacks and from a belligerent online public discourse.

Reporters' Positions Regarding Alleged Symbiosis Between Them and the Judicial System

Most of the court reporters justified, conceptually and practically, a broad view of the courtroom reporter's role that includes defending the judicial system from populism. This view leads to self-censorship in courtroom reporting. H explains: 'I see myself as an emissary of the principle of separation of powers in the belief that it is a more trustworthy system. I really restrain my criticism. Once I used to write criticism when I felt it was my job to help the defendants, today I am cautious in my criticism'.

Accordingly, most of the court reporters admit that there is a symbiosis with the judicial system. Some of them contend that this reciprocity increases the flow of authorized and trustworthy judicial information to the public. Others see this relationship as reflecting the weakness of legal journalism in Israel. C contends that the lack of formal legal training among a minority of reporters causes them to adopt the prosecution's narrative, depriving the public of its right to hear the arguments of the defence:

> This synergy yields dividends for both extremes. …The judicial authorities enjoy and deepen this synergy. If they want to give prominence to white-collar criminals, they will choose journalists to whom the prosecution narrative is dear, and who feel that they are part of the war on corruption on the ideological level… I think that due to their lack of legal training reporters do not examine issues in depth. Arguments of the 'reasonable doubt' and 'selective enforcement' type are not echoed.

According to C, the relationship between court reporters and their sources in the judicial system is damaging to journalistic independence and to journalists' public standing, as well as to the conduct of the judicial system:

> In my view it was also very damaging to the prestige of the court reporters. The price that the reporter pays is that he entirely loses his journalistic freedom, that he cannot criticize his sources… It is also damaging to the police. When there are many cases and prioritization among them is necessary, more investigative resources will be channelled to cases that capture the headlines.

The reporters in 2020 seem to have adopted for themselves the professional identity of 'anti-corruption fighters' who feel obliged to refute the populistic accusations that the judiciary in Israel is corrupt. This ideological fervour speaks to the rise of the 'obsessive journalists' model (Ginosar & Reich, 2020), who see themselves as social activists. However, the conduct of the courtroom reporter is essentially different to that of the 'obsessive reporter', because the reporter is fighting on behalf of a very powerful establishment and not on behalf of weak groups in society.

The following comparative table summarizes the findings and the identification of changes in the positions of the court reporters regarding their ethical and practical conduct, between the various time points at which the study was conducted. Carlson and Lewis's (2020) model of boundary work for researching contemporary journalistic authority serves in this table for the purpose of examining the reporters' self-perception of the connection between the external and internal-professional changes and the process of decline in their journalistic authority.

Discussion and Conclusions

This chapter reflects on the enduring significance of legacy media for public perceptions of the law and the disruptive impact associated with digital media as regards fulfilling court reporters' expected role. This study has for the first time comparatively examined the evaluations by court reporters of the internal-professional and external factors which in their view have contributed to the decline in their journalistic authority in public discourse in the digital era.

Analysis of the research findings in the light of Carlson and Lewis' (2020) model allows for a diachronic examination, over time, of the boundary work that court reporters have conducted and are conducting vis-à-vis changing players and diverse interests, both within and outside the profession of journalism, for the purpose of defining their professional authority. Analysis according to this model also allows for a synchronic examination—taking a broad view of the connection between the change in reporters' perceptions of their journalistic role and overall changes in the standing of law and the media in Israeli society. Court reporters are engaged in a boundary defence of the profession of journalism in three ways:

1. Reflexive criticism of changes in working routines and adoption of norms that threaten the independence of journalists.

2. A rhetoric of separation between professional court reporters and alternative commentators on social media platforms.
3. Rallying to the defence of the rule of law and the image of the reporters covering the field.

An analysis of the findings applying Carlson and Lewis' model shows that over the years court reporters have adopted working routines and professional norms which they rejected in the past. These in turn have contributed to the decline in their authority. So, we find a combination of journalistic considerations and marketing considerations coming into play in determining the news value of the law and judicial affairs. This blurring of the boundaries has led to broader coverage of the law in the sense of a greater preoccupation with investigations of politicians and celebrities, to the detriment of the public's right to know about important struggles of ordinary citizens against the wheels of justice. The declining revenues of media outlets, which have led to the dismissal of reporters from newspapers, TV, and radio channels, and the importance of speed in reporting have led to a reduced presence of reporters in the courtroom and their greater dependency on PR consultants. This blurring of the boundaries between reporters and PR consultants contributes to bias in the coverage of the legal reporting, as the reporters become committed to aligning with the various interests of the PR consultants who supply them with exclusive legal documents for reporting.

The court reporters' boundary work in defence of their authority is made more complicated by legal discourse conducted on social media where the old boundaries between professional journalists and an opinionated public are breaking down. This blurring of the boundaries influences the conduct of court reporters and arouses an ethical unease in them. The reporters' remarks regarding the vulgarization of the reporting style and a departure from journalistic ethics accord with a phenomenon termed 'the Twitterization of news making' (Revers, 2014), which according to researchers is shaping journalistic rhetoric and weakening the journalist's authority as a reliable source of news. The journalists attested that under the influence of disclosures regarding judicial affairs on social media, they themselves have abandoned the traditional separation between factual reporting and expressing a personal opinion. Thus, the news discourse on judicial affairs in the established press has become politicized, and court reporters have all been labelled politically, which in their view is detrimental to their professional authority. According to the participants in this study, disputes on Twitter between court reporters supporting one or the other party at trial, alongside the exposure of sources of rival reporters, are detrimental to the journalistic code of ethics and the image of the journalists in the eyes of the public.

According to Carlson and Lewis (2020), it is necessary to look at the broader social contexts to analyse the boundary work done by the journalists. Indeed, in an era of populistic attacks worldwide on the judicial system and on the media, which are common also in Israel (Panievsky, 2021), there appears to be a change in the fundamental positions of the interview participants towards the judicial system and towards the conventions of reporting that were traditionally shaped by the relationship between journalists and their sources. Journalists reject reporting norms that were given expression in the journalistic code of ethics before the digital era in accordance with the demands of the judicial system, and view them today as a threat to their professional independence; they have distanced themselves from their responsibility to assist with the fair execution of justice. They also expect a new model of their relations with their sources in the judicial system, which in the past were characterized by a hegemony of the judicial system, and are calling for increased transparency and fairness in the legal system's relations with the media. At the same time, they are being forced by their opponents to confront accusations of the blurring of the boundaries and the connections between them and the judges in the public discourse that are drawn by political figures, who lump them together in their populistic attacks.

The media and the judicial system are mutually dependent on each other, for the media needs independent courts to defend freedom of the press from politicians, and the judicial system needs broad media coverage to assist the law in its role deterring crime (Peleg & Bogoch, 2014). In the meta-journalistic public discourse, which Carlson and Lewis (2020) view as the main public battlefield over journalistic authority in the digital era, three similar aspects can be identified on which populistic criticism of the judicial system and of the mainstream press covering it focuses: overactivity, representability, and concealment.

The courts are accused of judicial activism, the public prosecution of 'baseless and trumped-up indictments' against Prime Minister Benjamin Netanyahu, and the media—of overzealously seeking to frame right-wing politicians' activity as negative and criminal. The accusation of concealment, which has characterized public discourse in recent years, degrades the public standing of both the legal system and the media. Both systems have been accused of concealing their connections with the elites and their political bias. The claim of politicization is the most destructive threat to the authority and independence of each because both the legal system and the media claim to be neutral, expert, and independent. Furthermore, this discourse endangers the rule of law and freedom of the press, which are fundaments of democracy in Israel.

In Israel the basic confidence in the judicial system among legacy media journalists in general is greater than in other countries (Panievsky, 2023; Reich et al., 2016). Perhaps for this reason, despite the legacy media court reporters' professional criticism of the relations between the judicial system and the media, an emotionally charged discourse has developed between these professionals and social media influencers and reporters from ultra-right channels whose criticism is much more far-reaching. Indeed, only in this study in Israel have the participants exhibited a pattern of rallying to the defence of the judicial establishment, to the point of self-censorship and public altercations with social media influencers and reporters from ultra-right media.

In the post-truth era, which is characterized by conspiratorial thinking, some of the Israeli court reporters expressed a willingness to defend the judicial system. This may arouse in some segments of the public, who are influenced by the parallel populistic attacks on the legal system and the legacy media, the feeling that the game is rigged, that it is being manipulated by corrupt elites. Additionally, perhaps due to the disregard of the presumption of innocence in reporting, the wrath of those being put on trial intensifies against the 'inhumane' media and a brutal judicial system, whose leaks are damaging to the 'weak' defendant. The court reporters suggest that the decline in the public's confidence in governmental institutions and in the media leads to a rise in the standing of alternative legal commentators in the social media. These media personas lack professional training, but express the popular rage against both the judicial system and the reporters covering it.

In the journalists' view, according to this study, the blurring in the public's eyes of the boundaries between the journalists' interests and those of the judicial system even further weakens the standing of both systems, the legal system and the media, in the public discourse. In the light of Carlson and Lewis' (2020) model, this study's findings reflect the tension in which the court reporter operates. He or she must navigate the treacherous waters between the expansion of judicial reporting and the rise in court reporters' professional standing in news organizations on the one hand, and the blurring of professional and normative boundaries on the other. This tension stems from changes in activities and norms within and outside the field of journalism, in a way that threatens journalistic independence.

In the light of the current study's findings, follow-up studies are necessary to track the development of this predicament for court reporters—being caught between external changes and internal-professional changes, in countries where populistic attacks on the judicial system and on the media are rampant. I would also suggest researching how both these systems, the courts and the media, are contending with the damage to their image and standing in the public discourse.

In addition, further studies are needed to assess the consequences of the potential demise of courtroom reporting for the process of 'trial by media' in the court of public opinion. Would society benefit from an alternative 'trial by social media' without the coverage of trials in the legacy media? Would the disappearance of court reporters or a decline in their professional authority mark the democratization of the legal discourse in the public sphere? Would the absence of professional courtroom reporters create more significant legal risks, such as libel suits or hate speech suits, for the public who will come to base their opinions and speech on unreliable sources? Will the legal knowledge offered to the public by court reporters be valueless in the future public legal discourse due to the proliferation of participatory justice (Gies, 2024)? Will trial by social media affect the decision-making process the same as trial by the mainstream media? Trial by social media may play a facilitator's role, rather than tilt the scales in favour of one party or another.

The widespread use of social media in the community, together with the prevailing attitude that social media discussions are less 'official' than the traditional press, presents both unique opportunities and intriguing challenges for the twenty-first-century justice system and public sphere.

Competing Interests The author has no conflicts of interest to declare that are relevant to the content of this chapter.

References

Anderson, W., & Schudson, M. (2020). Objectivity, professionalism, and truth seeking. In K. Wahl-Jorgensen & T. Hanitzsch (Eds.), *The handbook of journalism studies* (pp. 136–150). Routledge.

Bogoch, B., & Holzman-Gazit, Y. (2008). Mutual bonds: Media frames and the Israeli High Court of Justice. *Law and Social Inquiry, 33*(1), 53–87. https://www.jstor.org/stable/20108749

Bogoch, B., & Holzman-Gazit, Y. (2020). Critical coverage: How the media criticize supreme courts—Evidence from Israel. *Law & Policy, 43*, 51–72. https://doi.org/10.1111/lapo.12160

Boudana, S. (2016). Impartiality is not fair: Toward an alternative approach to the evaluation of content bias in news stories. *Journalism, 175*, 600–618. https://doi.org/10.1177/1464884915571295

Carlson, M. (2017). *Journalistic authority: Legitimating news in the digital era.* Columbia University Press.

Carlson, M., & Lewis, S. (2020). Boundary work. In K. Wahl-Jorgensen & T. Hanitzsch (Eds.), *The handbook of journalism studies* (pp. 123–135). Routledge.

Davis, R. (1994). *Decisions and images.* Prentice Hall.

Ericson, R. (1996). Why law is like news. In D. Nelken (Ed.), *Law as communication* (pp. 195–230). Dartmouth.

Fink, K., & Schudson, M. (2014). The rise of contextual journalism, 1950s–2000s. *Journalism, 15*(1), 3–20. https://doi.org/10.1177/1464884913479015

Fiske, J., & Glynn, K. (1995). Trials of the postmodern. *Cultural Studies, 9*(3), 501–521. https://doi.org/10.1080/09502389500490541

Garapon, A. (1996). Justice out of court: The dangers of trial by media. In D. Nelken (Ed.), *Law as communication* (pp. 232–245). Dartmouth.
Gieryn, T. (1999). *Cultural boundaries of science: Credibility on the line.* University of Chicago Press.
Gies, L. (2008). *Law and the media: The future of an uneasy relationship.* Routledge Cavendish.
Gies, L., & Bortoluzzi, M. (2014). Purity and contamination in online popular forensics: Amateur-expert readings of the Meredith Kercher murder case. *Continuum: Journal of Media and Cultural Studies, 28*(4), 532–544. https://doi.org/10.1080/10304312.2014.907871
Ginosar, A., & Reich, Z. (2020). Obsessive-activist journalists: A new model of journalism? *Journalism Practice.* https://doi.org/10.1080/17512786.2020.1816488
Graves, L. (2016). *Deciding what's true: The rise of political fact-checking in American journalism.* Columbia University Press.
Guirdham, M. (2015). *Work communication.* Palgrave Macmillan.
Haltom, W. (1998). *Reporting on the courts.* Nelson-Hall.
Hanitzsch, T., & Vos, T. (2017). Journalistic roles and the struggle over institutional identity: The discursive constitution of journalism. *Communication Theory, 27*(2), 115–135. https://doi.org/10.1111/comt.12112
Jones, M. (1974). *Justice and journalism.* Barry Rose.
Kovach, B., & Rosenstiel, T. (2014). *The elements of journalism, revised and updated: What newspeople should know and the public should expect*. Three Rivers.
Montgomery, M. (2006). Broadcast news, the live 'Two-Way' and the case of Andrew Gillian. *Media, Culture and Society, 28*, 233–259. https://doi.org/10.1177/0163443706061683
Panievsky, A. (2021). Covering populist media criticism: When journalists' professional norms turn against them. *International Journal of Communication, 15*, 2136–2155. https://ijoc.org/index.php/ijoc/article/view/15299
Panievsky, A. (2023). Strategic rituals of loyalty: When Israeli journalists face digital hate. *Digital Journalism, 11*(10), 1940–1961. https://doi.org/10.1080/21670811.2022.2118144
Peleg, A., & Bogoch, B., (2014) Mediatization, legal logic and the coverage of Israeli politicians on trial. *Journalism Practice, 8*(3), 311–325. https://doi.org/10.1080/17512786.2014.889449; https://www.tandfonline.com/doi/epdf/10.1080/17512786.2014.889449?needAccess=true&role=button

Reich, Z. (2018). The decline in orally negotiated news: Revisiting (again) the role of technology in reporting. *New Media & Society, 20*(11), 4116–4134. https://doi.org/10.1177/1461444818768064
Reich, Z., Barnoy, A., & Hertzog, L. (2016). Country report: Journalists in Israel. *Worlds of Journalism Study*. https://epub.ub.uni-muenchen.de/31036/1/Reich_Bamoy_Journalists_in_Israel.pdf
Revers, M. (2014). The Twitterization of news making: Transparency and journalistic professionalism. *Journal of Communication, 64*(5), 806–826. https://doi.org/10.1111/jcom.12111
Ryfe, D. (2013). *Can journalism survive?* Polity Press.
Shwartz Altshuler, T. (2018). *Public trust in mass media - Breaking, turning and soaring? The Israeli Democracy Institute*. https://en.idi.org.il/articles/20512
Simons, M., & Bosland, J. (2020). From journal of record to the 24/7 news cycle: Perspectives on the changing nature of court reporting in Australia. In A. Gulyas & D. Baines (Eds.), *The Routledge companion to local media and journalism* (pp. 193–202). Taylor & Francis.
Sullivan, B.& Carmody-Tilley, C. (2020). Supreme court journalism: From law to spectacle. *Washington & Lee Law Review, 77*, 343–453. https://heinonline.org/HOL/LandingPage?handle=hein.journals/waslee77&div=8&id=&page
Tandoc, E., & Vos, T. (2015). The journalist is marketing the news. *Journalism Practice, 10*(8), 1–17. https://doi.org/10.1080/17512786.2015.1087811
Thomson, R. (2007). The qualitative longitudinal case history: Practical, methodological and ethical reflections. *Social Policy and Society, 6*(4), 571–582. https://doi.org/10.1017/S1474746407003909
Tsfati, Y., Boomgaarden, H. G., Strömbäck, J., Vliegenthart, R., Damstra, A., & Lindgren, E. (2020). Causes and consequences of mainstream media dissemination of fake news: Literature review and synthesis. *Annals of the International Communication Association, 44*(2), 157–173. https://doi.org/10.1080/23808985.2020.1759443
Wahl-Jorgensen, K. (2019). Questioning the ideal of the public sphere: The emotional turn. *Social Media + Society, 5*(3), 1–3. https://doi.org/10.1177/2056305119852175

Part II

Social Media and the Perils of Amateur Sleuthing

5

The Complexities of Trial by Social Media: Examining the Connection Between Self-exposure and Harassment

Azi Lev-On

Introduction

Facilitated by the ubiquitous presence of social media platforms, the concept of 'trial by media' has transcended the traditional courtroom to pervade the court of public opinion. This phenomenon, characterized by the media's capacity to influence public perception and affect judicial processes, has morphed with the advent of the Internet into a more decentralized yet equally potent form of public adjudication. Unlike the conventional 'trial by media' that involves mainstream media outlets impacting narratives around legal cases, the digital age introduces a participatory dimension where ordinary people, armed with access to vast amounts of information and the ability to disseminate their views widely, engage in what can be termed 'social media trials.' These trials occur in the absence of formal legal proceedings, where individuals are

A. Lev-On (✉)
Ariel University, Ariel, Israel
e-mail: azilevon@gmail.com

L. Gies (ed.), *Trial by Media*, Palgrave Studies in Crime, Media and Culture,
https://doi.org/10.1007/978-3-031-80593-6_5

judged, vilified, or exonerated in the public domain, often with profound implications for their privacy, reputation, and even mental health.

This study delves into a specific subset of 'trial by media' in the digital realm—during obstruction of justice campaigns—focusing on the intersection of self-exposure on social media and the resultant harassment. By examining the case of Roman Zadorov and the public discourse surrounding his trial and acquittal, we witness how social media platforms become arenas for justice and judgment, sometimes blurring the lines between seeking truth and perpetuating harassment. Here, 'trial by media' is not merely a parallel to legal proceedings but a complex interplay of online activism, public participation, and the amplification of personal narratives. This expanded understanding of 'trial by media' underlines the necessity to reconsider its implications in the digital age, where the dynamics of public engagement, information dissemination, and the quest for justice converge in unprecedented ways.

One concerning consequence of the widespread proliferation of the Internet and social media is the exacerbation of a troubling trend: the amplification of online harassment and violence. Illustratively, a study from 2014 (when the phenomena described later took place) gleaned insights from 1094 students spanning grades 4 to 11. The results unveiled a disquieting reality: 27% of respondents reported having fallen victim to instances of online harassment, and 46% recounted instances where they had borne witness to acts of cyberbullying directed at others (Heiman et al., 2014). Another study conducted by the Sarid Institute (2017), focusing on individuals aged 18 and above, unveiled that a significant 24% acknowledged exposure to manifestations of online violence. This exposure exhibited an upward trajectory as the age of the respondents decreased. Notably, within the 55–64 age demographic, only 14% recounted enduring repeated instances of online violence, whereas an alarming 33% within the 18–24 age bracket reported similar encounters.

Why does the Internet become a 'fertile breeding ground' for violence? Vismonsky (2020) argues that some architectural features of the Internet empower online harassment, surpassing what has traditionally been encountered in the context of physical harassment. (1) The extensive *accessibility* of online platforms facilitates engagement for virtually anyone, (2) the *instantaneous dissemination* of offensive publications, (3) their *viral propagation*, (4) the *cloak of anonymity* that is sometimes offered, (5) Adding to this complexity is the *cumulative* character of online posting, where subsequent contributors may join the initial ones, often competing to create progressively shocking and offensive content. (6) Additionally, the ease of accessing information, often directly tied to the victim's identity, persists on the Internet for extended durations, with limited options for deletion. (7) The *global* character of cyberspace, where advertisers may operate from different countries than the victims, presents challenges in terms of locating, investigating, and attributing culpability. (8) A further challenge arises due to the *intermediation required to access content*, involving interactions with intermediaries like content providers or social media platforms. This makes it difficult to establish accountability, identify content posters, and gather evidence against them.

Moreover, people subjected to online violence tend to display a reduced inclination to report incidents in comparison with victims of physical violence. Consequently, this hesitancy to report renders the identification of online harm considerably more complex for educational and therapeutic organizations, as well as parents (Heirman & Walrave, 2008).

In contrast to the many articles that concentrate on various forms of harassment, my focus here is on the people who are subjected to harassment and, notably, *the connection between their public self-exposure and the harassment they experience.* A central argument presented in the paper is that the magnitude of slanderous activities is associated with the degree of self-exposure individuals exhibit. In essence, the quantity and visibility of visual materials associated with particular people act as critical determinants influencing the severity of the defamation they experience.

In exploring the dynamics of online harassment through the lens of a 'hierarchy of defamation,' it is essential to clarify that this framework does not imply a normative judgment toward individuals based on their visibility in digital and traditional media. The intention behind identifying this hierarchy is to understand the mechanisms through which defamation occurs and its impact on individuals, rather than attributing responsibility or blame to the victims themselves. Recognizing the complexity of online interactions and the multifaceted reasons individuals may have a prominent online presence, this study is committed to a nuanced analysis that seeks to highlight systemic issues rather than individual actions.

The case of Roman Zadorov, which has captivated public interest and sparked extensive online discourse, serves as a compelling context for examining the multifaceted character of 'trial by media' in the social media age. Zadorov's case, marked by a whirlwind of social media activism, public scrutiny, and the subsequent impact on individuals tangentially related to the case, illustrates the profound effects of digital platforms on justice and public perception. This study leverages the Zadorov affair to explore the broader implications of social media's role in shaping narratives around justice, the intersection of self-exposure with harassment, and the emergence of a 'hierarchy of defamation.' By focusing on this case, I aim to shed light on the nuanced challenges and ethical considerations that arise when digital platforms become arenas for public judgment and advocacy.

By setting the Zadorov affair as a backdrop, this article contributes to the critical discourse on digital media's influence on legal and social justice processes, highlighting the urgent need for a balanced approach to digital engagement and the protection of individuals from unwarranted public scrutiny.

Next, I outline the Zadorov affair and its significance in studying 'trial by media.' Then, the article delves into the methodology employed. The core of the article presents my findings on the 'hierarchy of defamation,' providing insights into the varying degrees of vulnerability among individuals based on their online presence. The conclusion synthesizes the analysis, reiterating the importance of refraining from victim-blaming, and suggests directions for future research and policy development aimed at mitigating online harassment while preserving the open discourse essential to democratic societies.

Research Environment: The Online Activism Calling for Justice for Roman Zadorov

On 6 December 2006, the 13-year-old Tair Rada was murdered at her school in Katzrin, Israel. Roman Zadorov, a flooring installer who worked at the school, was arrested six days later, and a week later confessed to the killing—but immediately recanted, and since denied connection to the murder. Zadorov was convicted of murder in 2010 and sentenced to life in prison, and his appeal to the Supreme Court was rejected in 2015.

But the firmness of the court's ruling contradicts public opinion, with polls repeatedly showing that overwhelming majorities thinking Zadorov is innocent. In 2021 the Supreme Court decided to grant Zadorov a retrial, and in March 2023 he was fully acquitted (Lev-On, 2023b).

After the murder, public attention swiftly focused on the affair due to the victim being a young girl murdered within the school premises. Another significant factor that fueled skepticism regarding Roman Zadorov's culpability in the crime was the stance taken by Tair Rada's mother. Shortly following Zadorov's reconstruction of the murder, she publicly expressed doubts about his involvement as the perpetrator. Subsequently, discrepancies in Zadorov's confession and reconstruction further fueled these doubts. Additionally, alternative narratives surfaced regarding the identity of the perpetrator(s), the method of the murder, and the potential motives behind it, all contributing to the atmosphere of uncertainty surrounding the case.

Unlike many other cases, where murder investigations are typically conducted away from the public eye, here the investigation materials were available to a wide audience. These materials were transferred by Zadorov's defense team to the victim's family and activists who supported them. Over time, these materials gradually became accessible to the public, including being disseminated through various online platforms such as Facebook groups. Furthermore, since 2016, they have been available on the website 'Truth Today.'[1] Correspondence, summaries, and documents related to the retrial have continued to be uploaded to this

[1] https://truthtoday.co.il/.

website. There are also a number of YouTube channels with video materials—from the investigations, conversations with police informers, and the reconstruction. Additionally, numerous documentaries and articles on the case can be found online.

Another factor responsible for the overwhelming public interest in the case is the intensive social media activity to promote Zadorov's innocence. Since 2009, many Facebook groups dealing with this affair were established. In 2015, after Zadorov's appeal to the Supreme Court was rejected, the largest of these Facebook groups, entitled *The whole Truth about the Murder of the Late Tair Rada*, became one of the largest in Israel (Ben-Israel, 2016).

Apart from its scope, this social media activity is unique in additional aspects:

1. The context: The activity involves a murder trial and a call for justice for a putative false conviction. By contrast, findings and products of police investigations and legal proceedings are typically far from the public eye.
2. The identity of participants: Typically, participants in public discourse regarding law and justice are 'insiders'—police officers, lawyers, and legal commentators. Here, however, the involvement of 'outsiders' is evident, including activists who were thoroughly familiar with the legal case, who even advised and closely assisted Zadorov's defense in the retrial (Grossman & Lev-On, 2023).
3. The activity is also unique in its significant effects; for example, on public opinion of the functioning of the relevant state institutions and Zadorov's guilt/innocence (Lev-On & Steinfeld, 2024).

In addition, this activism is unique in that it led to the many discoveries by activists—including discoveries that led to the decision to hold a retrial (Lev-On, 2023a). For all these reasons, the social media activity calling for justice for Zadorov represents a fascinating case for examining the characteristics and effects of social media activism.

Method

This study is based on netnographic research. Netnography is a qualitative-interpretive research approach to studying the behavioral and communicative patterns of individuals and groups online (Kozinets, 2010; Rageh & Melewar, 2013). Netnography involves collecting data from online sources such as social networks, chats, petition sites, and more. Researchers can identify communities, observe and join them, and interview participants. The triangulation of participant observation, interviews, and content analysis enables a comprehensive picture of the justice for Zadorov activism. This netnographic study lasted seven years, from 2015 (the rejection of Zadorov's appeal to the Supreme Court and resulting intensification of activism) to 2022.

Participant Observation

Contacts were established with group administrators and leading activists. Conversations with administrators were about content that was published, issues and dilemmas that arose, and activities that occurred.

Content Analysis

I have employed several methods to ensure the inclusion of a maximum number of relevant posts. Firstly, with the assistance of activists, I identified and mapped the active Facebook groups related to Zadorov, subsequently focusing on the five largest groups that attracted the most active participants. Secondly, I utilized the netVizz software initially, and after its discontinuation, I transitioned to using CrowdTangle software to back up all the posts published within these groups. This resulted in a collection of over 10,000 posts and hundreds of thousands of comments. The content analysis was carried out thematically by repeatedly reviewing the texts and identifying recurring themes, which were subsequently categorized.

Interviews

Twenty-five interviews with group administrators were conducted—among other issues, about the truth-value and content of stories posted online, and reactions by admins. The interviews lasted an hour to an hour-and-a-half, and were conducted by four interviewers under the supervision of the lead researcher.

In addition to conducting interviews with group administrators on social media platforms, I also conducted ten interviews with individuals who were teenagers at the time of the murder but who were adults at the time of interviewing them. They have since endured online harassment over the years. While delving into the investigation materials and examining the circulating online rumors regarding the potential involvement of specific people in the murder, I compiled a list of these people and initiated contact.

The interviews were primarily conducted via telephone, except for two cases where face-to-face meetings were arranged. These interviews typically lasted approximately half an hour. Participants were asked about their experiences with harassment, the specific circumstances in which these incidents occurred, and the character of the harassment, online and offline.

Findings: A History of Online Violence and Harassment

The paper traces the origins and development of suspicions and harassment toward the friends of the late Tair Rada as suspects in the murder, the role of social media in this process, and the differential manifestations of harassment according to the degree of self-exposure of the friends.

The origin of suspicions cast upon Tair's friends can be traced back to Ilana Rada, the mother of the victim, and Haim Sadovsky, a former private investigator. Following the murder, Sadovsky reached out to support the Rada family, who harbored intuitive concerns regarding Tair's social circle. These shared suspicions served as the impetus for Sadovsky's conviction. Subsequently, he collaborated with Zadorov's legal team to formulate a hypothesis, with a specific focus on Tair's friends, suggesting their involvement in the murder.

Immediately after Zadorov confessed and reenacted the murder of her daughter, Ilana Rada expressed her disbelief in his guilt. She reiterated multiple times her belief that adolescents might be withholding information possibly related to the murder, and she even considered the possibility that they could have been involved as perpetrators themselves (Lev-On, 2023b). For instance, in a 2016 TV interview (2016) she stated, 'I am convinced that the children are concealing something significant. It seems highly unlikely that an entire school during an activity would fail to notice anything, and that Tair's entire life would be erased from the memory of all the students in a single day.'

As late as 2008, the 'suspicions' directed at specific people from Katsrin were not widely known. This changed with the release of Sharon Gal's documentary titled 'Only Tair Knows.' The documentary included interviews with Tair's friends, L.L., N.B., and S.B. (Gal, 2008). Gal accompanied the friends to the 'Gamla' school, located in a different part of the town, where they were interviewed. Notably, they were placed in a restroom resembling the one where Tair was murdered. There, they were tasked with recalling the sequence of events from that fateful day while being filmed. Their participation in the film was a sincere gesture of support for Tair's grieving family and a way to commemorate her memory.

Upon the documentary's airing in 2008, the participants were surprised by the significant contrast between the intent conveyed during the original interviews and the way they were ultimately presented in the edited version. The editing process included an eerie musical soundtrack reminiscent of horror films. Additionally, snippets depicting the cleaning of restroom walls were intercut with the interviews. This juxtaposition could potentially be interpreted as casting suspicion on the interviewees, implying their involvement in cleaning and concealing evidence.

The people most profoundly impacted by Gal's film were L.L. and N.B., both had testified to the police, along with others, that they had been in the bathroom around the time of Tair's murder. L.L. was interviewed for Gal's (2008) movie, and expressed doubts about Zadorov being the murderer. When asked for her reasons, she replied, 'Because of various reasons, like others that I am aware of,' followed by a brief moment of laughter (Gal, 2008) (L.L. later explained this laughter as an awkward pause, which was subsequently edited in a manner that appeared 'suspicious').

Similarly, N.B. recounted being in the bathroom at the time of the murder and seeing an unfamiliar girl whom she did not encounter again. Notably, N.B.'s interview for Gal's documentary underwent manipulation during editing: eerie music was added, and she was featured in close-up shots, insinuating that she might be 'concealing something.' Following the release of the documentary, both girls found themselves branded as 'primary suspects' in the eyes of numerous people advocating for Zadorov's innocence.

Gal's film aired in 2008. In 2011, a highly defamatory video titled 'Tair Rada's Girlfriends' Connection of Silence' surfaced on YouTube. This video maliciously incorporated 'suspicious' clips from Gal's film, accompanied by false captions that portrayed the female participants in a negative and unfounded light. Figure 5.1 illustrates a screenshot from the video, displaying N.B. where on the right side of the image, the video's editors provided their unfounded interpretations, falsely alleging that she had been in conflict with Tair since elementary school, fabricated her testimony to the police, and falsely claimed she is the daughter of a senior police officer. The video went viral, amassing nearly half a million views as of October 2019.

Another primary source of generating slander is Haim Sadovsky, the former private detective mentioned earlier. Sadovsky strongly held the belief that teenagers were responsible for the murder. Merely three weeks after the murder, he sent a concise fax message to the police commissioner, providing a list of potential suspects. A month following the murder, Sadovsky compiled a comprehensive six-page report. This document juxtaposes, on the one hand, the findings that, in his view, cast doubt on Zadorov's guilt as a criminal, and, on the other hand, outlines his personal hypotheses regarding alternative potential participants (Lev-On, 2023b).

In his report, Sadovsky references various the (arguably) jealousy among Tair's friends, the argument between Tair and her friend who left town the day after the murder, and Tair's invitation to a 'conversation' in

Fig. 5.1 N.B in the video *The Connection of Silence of Tair Rada's Girlfriends*

the bathroom, which ultimately led to her murder. Most of these claims are based on mere speculations.

In his book 'To Stitch up an Innocent Person' (Sadovsky, 2010) Sadovsky also advanced the theory that teenagers were responsible for the murder. Furthermore, in collaboration with Doron Baldinger, Sadovsky produced a film that echoed similar arguments (Lev-On, 2023b). As social media gained prominence, Sadovsky also became active on these platforms. An analysis of his participation in a prominent online group, from its inception to 2016, reveals that he was the second most prolific contributor in terms of visibility. His posts often carried a confrontational tone and included defamatory content (Lev-On, 2023b).

In 2017, a civil lawsuit was filed against Sadovsky for the first time by L.L. The lawsuit encompassed claims of defamation, negligence, harassment, and privacy violation. In the verdict issued on September 10, 2020, the judge confirmed that several publications presented to him constituted defamation, and that Sadovsky played a prominent role in promoting the 'girlfriends theory,' referring to him as the 'living spirit' in this regard (Lev-On, 2023b).

In 2009, the first Facebook group advocating for justice for Zadorov was established (Lev-On, 2023b). Shortly after that, in 2011 a significant derogatory activity toward Tair's friends (some of them mentioned above) *migrated* onto social media platforms. Several key events led to this migration. First and foremost, 2011 marked the year immediately following Zadorov's original conviction, which triggered a surge of online and offline engagement in his support. Simultaneously, Facebook further entrenched itself as a central platform for social engagement, notably among teenagers. Within this online realm, Facebook groups advocating for justice for Zadorov emerged and garnered a substantial following.

At the same time, there was a growing trend of private individuals, mostly teenagers in Tair's age group, establishing Facebook profiles. These profiles, aside from being platforms for sharing personal updates, gradually became hubs for monitoring these adolescents. Consequently, people interested in the Zadorov affair, especially those speculating on any links between the youths and the murder, started following the teenagers' profiles and sending them private messages.

Furthermore, starting from that year, a series of videos began to appear on YouTube, implicating Tair's close friends. In February 2011, a video was uploaded to YouTube, appealing to the public for information about the murder and offering a financial reward. This video featured letters emerging against a black background, accompanied by eerie music. These letters displayed inscriptions found on the door of the teacher's toilets. The video posed a disturbing question: 'Which of them will be the first to crack and cooperate?' Implicitly, the video suggested a link between adolescents like N.B., L.L., and others to the murder (Fig. 5.2).

Concurrently, the video's release coincided with the submission of a petition to the High Court, advocating for the case's re-examination. This juxtaposition underscores the activists' strategic bifurcation: simultaneous pursuit of redress through the judicial apparatus while concurrently maintaining a robust presence and engagement on social media platforms.

Over the course of several years, L.L. endured a series of harassments, prompting her to file multiple complaints with the police. However, it seemed that these complaints did not lead to any substantial investigative

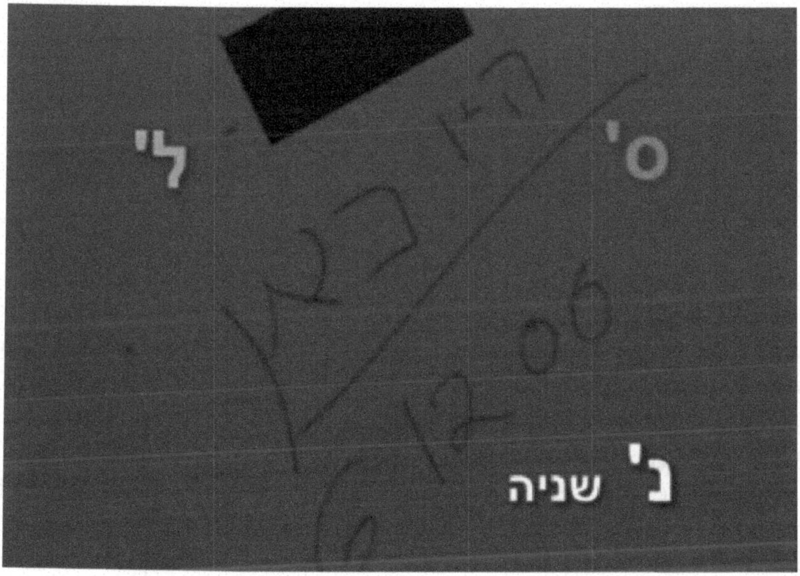

Fig. 5.2 Screenshot from the video *Evidence from the scene of the murder shows the involvement of teenagers*

actions. In 2013, she took her story to the prominent TV program, 'The Magazine,' which was broadcast on Channel 10. The segment shed light on the online harassment targeting L.L. and her friends. In response, the founder and administrator of the prominent Facebook group advocating for justice for Zadorov made the group 'secret' and removed several administrators who had allowed the cyber harassment to escalate (Lev-On, 2023b).

However, changing the group's settings to 'secret' did not lead to significant improvements in the situation. Instead, it created a 'vacuum of slander,' causing disgruntled members who had been blocked from the original group to migrate to new ones, notably the group 'The Whole Truth about the Murder of the Late Tair Rada,' which had opened shortly before. This migration further exacerbated the proliferation of slanderous content to such an alarming extent (Lev-On, 2023b).

The gravity and extent of this phenomenon become evident when we look at a post shared by one of the former group administrators who

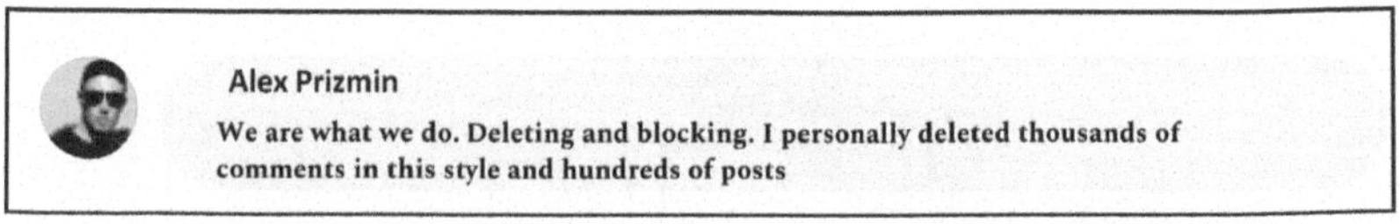

Fig. 5.3 'I deleted thousands of comments and hundreds of posts' (*Source The whole Truth about the Murder of the Late Tair Rada*, 4.2.2016)

claimed to have removed hundreds of posts and thousands of inflammatory comments (Fig. 5.3). Although group administrators make efforts to delete slanderous content, a challenge arises when slanders are embedded within responses to posts that don't necessitate administrator approval for publication. Consequently, these slanders are more challenging to detect and, even when detected, are often removed belatedly, if at all.

As time goes on, these groups go through a learning process in which both administrators and activists exercise increased caution. For example, while earlier posts may have included full names, current practices tend to use only initials or subtle allusions to prevent clear violations.

Harassment takes various forms, including both textual and visual. For instance, in Fig. 5.4, there is a collage featuring the faces of four individuals who are viewed as the main 'suspects' by certain activists: S.Y., N,B,; S.T., and L.L. In this collage, their mouths are depicted as allegedly mutilated, suggesting that they have 'lost the ability to speak' and are unwilling to share the information they might possess.

In 2016, a group of teenagers who had been significantly harmed by the persistent defamatory content decided to take legal action. As a result, several administrators and members of social media groups received preliminary warning letters before actual litigation, leading to the occasional posting of apologies and regret (Fig. 5.5).

Who is Slandered

Up to this point, I have discussed the identity of the defamers and the tactics they employ for defamation. Moving forward, I will delve into the identities of the vilified youths and the multiple ways in which they are

Fig. 5.4 Silent girls (*Source The whole Truth about the Murder of the Late Tair Rada*, 17.12.2018)

Dear friends... I would like to express my regret for the accusations against Tair's friends in connection with the murder. I never used the word "killer" because I don't believe any of them are directly involved or committed this abominable murder. However, I mistakenly thought they were aware of it and chose not to disclose this information. This belief was fueled by an incorrect interpretation of the investigation materials, and I relied on information that was not accurate at all.

Fig. 5.5 Apologetic post toward Tair's friends (*Source* The friends of the late Tair Rada speak-*Breaking the Silence*, 2016)

subjected to targeting. I start by focusing on those who endure the most significant extent of slander.

S.Y

A notable person who has frequently faced baseless suspicion in relation to the murder case is S.Y., a ninth-grade student at the time of the murder, one year ahead of Tair. In Tair's phone, S.Y. was listed as 'my sister.' Their interactions primarily revolved around school-related activities, including walking home together, sharing moments on the dance floor as members of Katzrin's band, and occasionally meeting on the school grounds.

On the day of the murder, S. and Tair were seated in the pergola just before Tair's murder. Subsequently, Tair proceeded to enter the high school building. As time passed without Tair's return, S. decided to enter the school premises and took a seat on a bench, patiently waiting for her friend. Despite her efforts to locate Tair, she couldn't find her anywhere. S. suspected that Tair might have gone home. At the conclusion of her lesson, S. made her way home.

During the 2015–2016 period, S.Y participated in the seventh season of 'Big Brother' and emerged as the winner, gaining significant public recognition. Before the start of the program, Ilana Rada expressed disapproval of S.Y's participation, alleging that she was leveraging her connection with Tair to gain fame (Boker, 2016). During the program, S.Y. made the following statement: 'Tair and I were inseparable, the best of friends. She was like my little sister… Tair had this radiant smile, and her dancing was unmatched. To this day, I've never seen a girl who danced quite like her.' In response to the question 'Were you at school when it happened?', S. replied, 'I won't talk about that' (Boker, 2016; Walla! Culture, 2016).

Following S.Y's discussion of Tair during the program, albeit briefly, Ilana Rada said on a radio program: 'This girl is a liar; she provided four statements to the police, and she lied seven times' (Walla! Culture, 2016). Subsequently, the North District Prosecutor's Office issued a letter stating, 'We regret the baseless accusations raised in the interview against Shay and her associates, and this is not the first time such allegations have surfaced.'

Today, S.Y is actively engaged in the entertainment industry, participating in TV programs and pursuing a modeling career. In 2019, a theater drama related to the murder case was released, and its creators consulted with S.Y for her insights. However, Ilana responded again, asserting that 'S.Y was never truly Tair's friend, and to be precise, she abandoned Tair. This is not how someone who defines themselves as a 'close friend' should behave. Even the police investigator at the time found something strange and illogical in her conduct.' To support this claim, Ilana included a police memorandum (Fig. 5.6) with a request by the police computer officer to examine S.Y's chat correspondence. Upon examination, it was revealed that there were no ICQ conversations between S. and Tair in the four months before the murder. According to the memorandum's author, 'this doesn't align with her testimony of being a close friend of the deceased.'

Over the years, Facebook group members have made frequent defamatory accusations against S., alleging her involvement in the murder or knowledge of crucial details that she's concealing. At a certain juncture, a poll on this topic even emerged within one of the groups, and the majority of respondents indicated that they believed she was either withholding information or being untruthful in her testimony (Fig. 5.7).

N.B.

N.B.'s name is frequently mentioned in conspiracy theories that connect Tair's classmates and friends to the murder. She was a classmate of Tair's and had attended the same theater class as her—the last class Tair attended. N. testified that during that class, approximately at 1:30 PM (around the estimated time of the murder), she left the theater class and headed toward the restroom. As she approached the bathroom area, she encountered an unfamiliar female figure whom she had neither seen before nor after the murder. N. entered the third stall, which was adjacent to the murder scene. She remained there for an estimated 4–5

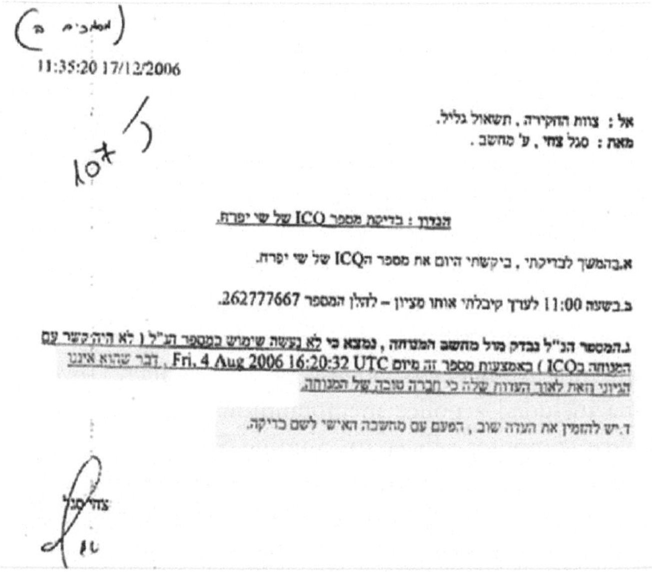

11:35:20 17/12/2006

אל : צוות החקירה , תשאול גליל.
מאת : סגל צחי , ע' מחשב .

הנדון : בדיקת מספר ICQ של שי יפרח.

א.בהמשך לבדיקתי , ביקשתי היום את מספר הICQ של שי יפרח.

ב.בשעה 11:00 לערך קיבלתי אותו מציון – להלן המספר 262777667.

ג.המספר הנ"ל נבדק מול מחשב המנוחה , נמצא כי לא נעשה שימוש במספר הנ"ל (לא היה קשר עם המנוחה בICQ) באמצעות מספר זה מיום Fri, 4 Aug 2006 16:20:32 UTC , דבר שהוא אינו הגיוני ואת לאור העדות שלה כי חברה טובה של המנוחה.

ד.יש להזמין את העדה שוב , הפעם עם מחשבה האישי לשם בדיקה.

Fig. 5.6 A police memorandum uploaded to the Internet (*Source* Ilana Rada's Facebook page, went online on September 5, 2019)

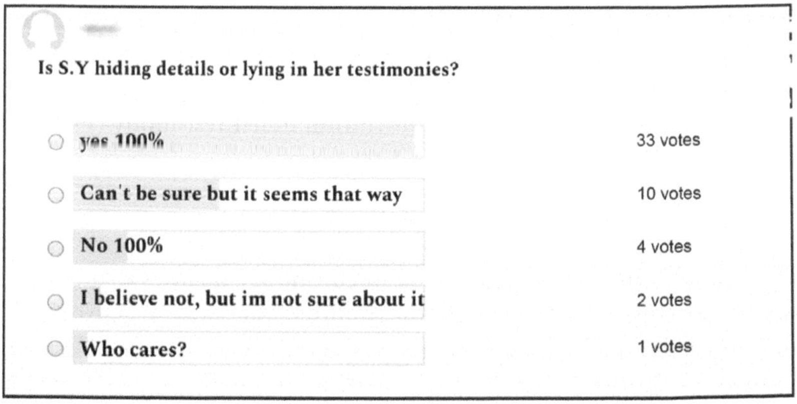

Fig. 5.7 'Is S.Y. hiding details or lying in her testimonies?' (*Source The whole Truth about the Murder of the Late Tair Rada*, 20.8.2016)

minutes. During her time in the stall, N. did not observe any bloodstains or anything else suspicious. When she turned to leave, she heard the girl exiting the bathroom.

Over time, N. became the primary subject of suspicion among those who subscribe to the conspiracy theory implicating Tair's friends in the murder. According to N., the scrutiny intensified after she appeared in Sharon Gal's documentary film 'Only Tair Knows' (Gal, 2008). In a conversation with her, N. said, 'I believe one of our missteps was participating in interviews with the best of intentions, only for it to turn against us. Perhaps, if we had declined those interviews, people might have eventually forgotten about us, and our names wouldn't have become so widely circulated on the internet today.'

Once branded as connected to the murder, N.'s name continued to surface periodically on the Internet. In 2014, Haim Sadovsky created a documentary where he traversed Katsrin with a video camera, retracing the supposed route of the 'murderer' from school to her home. N. has been the subject of several interviews addressing the online harassment she faced. In 2016, she participated in an interview for the 'Shadow of Truth' series.

Within the relevant social media groups, one can find repeated slanderous allegations closely tied to the case's details. For instance, false claims suggest that her father, a retired police officer at the time of the murder, had interfered with the investigation and attempted to conceal evidence. It was also falsely asserted that she was sent to the central region of the country for a week after the murder to allow her supposed wounds, incurred during the alleged murder of Tair, to heal.

L.L.

L.L. was Tair's closest friend, they spent a lot of time together and maintained frequent phone and chat communications in the months before the murder. On the day of the murder, L. was with Tair in the theater class- the last class Tair attended. Just before the end of the school day, L., along with S.T., visited the restroom together. During her subsequent testimony, S. recalled hearing the sound of toilet paper being torn and a voice saying 'occupy' from one of the restroom stalls. They decide to go instead to the teachers' restroom which was located opposite the department where the homicide occurred. There, they inscribed their names and the date of that day (6.12.2006) on one of the doors (see Fig. 5.2).

At the conclusion of the school day, the two friends proceeded to S.'s residence. Around 4:00 p.m., just prior to the scheduled commencement of the dance class attended by S. and Tair, S.'s father transported them back to Katsrin. As the dance class commenced, Ilana Rada reached out to the community center to confirm Tair's attendance. In response to Ilana's inquiry, S. exited the dance class to engage in a conversation with her. Subsequent to their discussion, instead of returning to the class, she left and participated in the search efforts. L. also became involved in the search after being informed of Tair's disappearance.

S. transferred to the school in the year of the murder and formed a close friendship with Tair. On the day of the tragedy, S. had multiple interactions with Tair. Tair even borrowed her MP4 player, which was later found with her body.

The last two hours of school were dedicated to various enrichment classes. Among these, Tair, L., N.B, and others participated in the theater class held in the high school building. In contrast, S.'s enrichment class centered on jewelry making and took place in the junior division building. After her class ended, S. stayed at the school, waiting for L. to finish her theater class and join her on the bus. Before the theater class concluded, S. encountered L. in the bathroom.

One of the questions raised by the activists is why S., who was attending a jewelry class in another building, arrived at the building where the theater class was held and found time to accompany L. to the bathroom before the class ended. Additionally, it is claimed that every Wednesday, instead of leaving Katsrin and returning for the dance class, S. came to Tair, and they went to the class together. However, on the day of the murder, S. decided to invite L. to her home at the end of the school day. Critics saw this change in her regular routine as an attempt to disrupt the investigation. Still, such conspiratory concerns have straightforward explanations (Fig. 5.8).

The harassment against L. began after the release of Sharon Gal's film in 2008 and intensified with increased social media activity. Her name

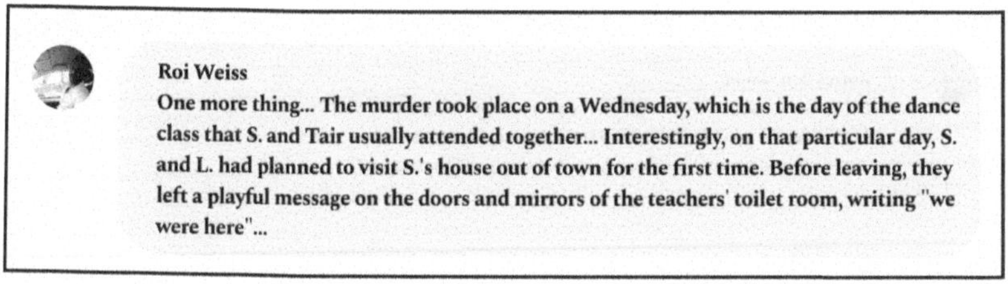

Fig. 5.8 The group administrator slanders S.T. (*Source The whole Truth about the Murder of the Late Tair* Rada, 2016)

appears prominently in various groups, far more often than S.T's, even though they were together at the time of the murder. One might assume they would have similar public recognition. However, L. has frequently featured in the media, leaving a significant online footprint. In contrast, S. avoided media exposure almost entirely and largely remaining in relative obscurity.

Additional 'Suspicious' Youngsters

In addition to Tair's friends and classmates, who are often subjected to harassment in connection with the murder, the names of other youngsters (at the time of the murder) occasionally resurface on social media, although less frequently. One such individual is D.Z., a 9th-grade student at the time of the murder. The teacher expelled him from the Bible class he attended, and as he exited the building, he encountered Tair, who gave him a kiss on the cheek before proceeding upstairs toward the restrooms. Following this encounter, he continued on his way home.

In 2010, D.Z. posted a cryptic Facebook status that served as a cautionary message: 'the one who understands will understand and stay away from Katsrin.' This statement was made in response to underage drinking at parties where he was a DJ. Almost every mention of D.'s name on social media is invariably connected to this post. Activists have construed this status as a potential threat to teenagers who may possess information about the murder, suggesting that they should remain silent to avoid possible repercussions. For instance, Rotem Ben Simon,

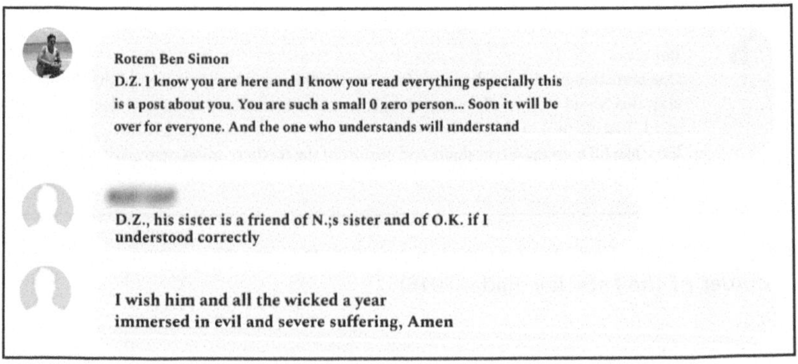

Fig. 5.9 Activists attacking D.Z. (*Source The whole Truth about the Murder of the Late Tair Rada*, September 26, 2016)

a manager of 'The Whole Truth…' group, commented on the post (see Fig. 5.9), contributing to the baseless speculation surrounding his (non-existing) connection to the murder.

Another person subjected to slander and harassment is S.E, a close friend of Tair's. However, a few weeks before the murder, Tair and S. had a falling out, leading to a temporary break in their friendship. This estrangement persisted until a week before the murder when they resumed communication.

Activists' suspicion regarding S. was significantly heightened by a specific incident on the morning of the murder. While S. and Tair were attending a lecture in the school's auditorium, S. sent her an SMS that read: 'Did it/he ring?' S. explained that he sent this message after noticing Tair glancing at her phone and then at him. He interpreted her look as an indication that she believed he had called her, prompting him to check if her phone had indeed rung.

However, some activists operating under the assumption that Tair was being harassed by someone, interpret the statement as an inquiry into whether this harasser called her. Some even speculate that this same harasser might have contacted her to arrange a meeting later in the day, possibly within the restroom. In one post, there's a claim that the individual who was supposed to call her waited for her in the bathroom and

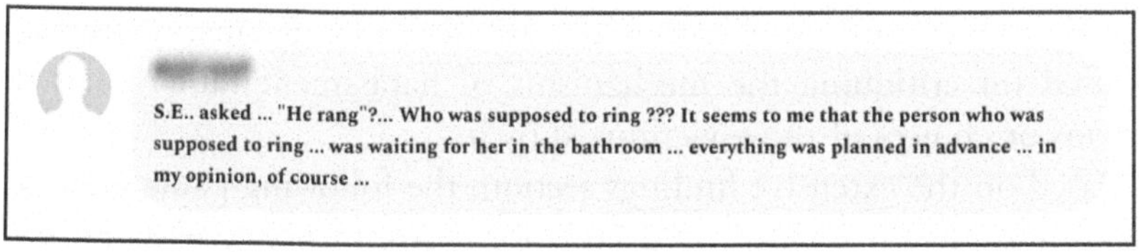

Fig. 5.10 Who was supposed to ring? (*Source The whole Truth about the Murder of the Late Tair Rada*, 29.11.2014)

subsequently committed the murder (Fig. 5.10). Once again, this illustrates how various details from the events of the day of the murder are pieced together to construct a new and misleading interpretation of the events.

'Hierarchy of Defamation': The Extent of Slanders and the Scope of Exposure

Why do some people experience more harassment, while others face less or none at all? The study sheds light on the existence of a 'hierarchy of defamation.' Those who willingly embraced exposure, appeared on television, and had their videos widely circulated on the Internet became the primary targets of widespread vilification. Paradoxically, their extensive media presence provided ample material for 'public judgment,' making them the central focus for those seeking visual content. In contrast, teenagers with limited to no online presence have largely been spared from this form of harassment.

As we delve into the 'hierarchy of defamation,' it is paramount to underscore that the recognition of this hierarchy does not suggest a normative stance toward those who find themselves at different levels of visibility and, consequently, vulnerability to defamation. This segmentation is employed as an analytical tool to better understand the patterns of online harassment, not to imply that victims bear responsibility for the defamation they endure. Individuals' presence on social media and other digital platforms is a reflection of the complex interplay between personal expression and the inherent design of these platforms to encourage sharing. Thus, any examination of visibility and defamation remains focused on critiquing the mechanisms of harassment rather than the actions or choices of those victimized by it.

Based on the extensive findings section, the following paragraphs will delve into the 'hierarchy of defamation,' commencing with individuals who experience the highest levels of harassment and progressing to those who encounter no harassment whatsoever. I will commence with teenagers who willingly place themselves in front of a camera, then proceed to individuals who create content about themselves that the public deems problematic. Subsequently, I will address individuals whose names are recognized by the public due to their inclusion in investigative materials but have not shared additional public content about themselves. Finally, I will conclude with individuals whose names are absent from publicly visible investigative materials. My argument is that the degree of defamation corresponds to the degree of self-exposure.

People Who Chose to Stand in Front of a Camera

Among Tair's friends who garnered the most substantial media attention is L.L., along with N.B. They have made appearances in various media outlets, including Sharon Gal's film, TV items, and documentaries. On the other hand, some of Tair's friends made just one appearance, such as S.T., and subsequently faded from the public eye.

The young people interviewed for various programs are not professional interviewees. During interviews, they may scratch their noses, avoid direct eye contact, provide answers that don't precisely address the questions, and appear uncomfortable in their chairs. Each of these gestures is meticulously scrutinized from every angle for over a decade after the individuals appeared in front of a camera during their teenage years.

In most cases where teenagers appear in video clips, their names are displayed as captions alongside them. However, there are instances where they are not identified by name. For example, in a brief scene in Sharon Gal's film, teenagers are asked about the identity of the killer, and they respond that he is probably a handsome man. The way this section is edited suggests that they may be concealing something, although this is not true in reality. Yet, because their names are not disclosed, the extent of slander and harassment against them has been relatively minor and has gradually faded over the years. In other words, even if visual materials exist online and are accessible, the capacity for slander and harassment diminishes when a name cannot be linked to a face.

People Who Write about Themselves on Social Media

In exceptional cases, individuals voluntarily post 'suspicious' content on their Facebook profiles. Such content may come under scrutiny by members of the public who actively search for information to support their preferred narrative. For example, D.Z., one of the last people to see Tair alive, shared a post that appeared threatening and mysterious, as previously mentioned. In that post, he stated, 'the one who understands and will run away from Katsrin.' It's important to note that it is highly unlikely that those involved in the murder would openly write cryptic comments about it on their Facebook profiles. Nonetheless, D. faced periodic slander stemming from a post he made a decade ago.

A counterexample is S.B., a close friend of Tair who was interviewed for Sharon Gal's film. However, since S. was not present on social media until 2013, she couldn't be subjected to harassment there. Teenagers who don't have social media profiles lack the ability to communicate with their friends on these platforms, but are also spared from harassment.

People Whose Names Came up as a Result of the Investigation but Left no Visual Traces

As previously mentioned, the investigation materials, court hearing transcripts, and legal documents associated with the Zadorov case are accessible to the general public. Consequently, even individuals whose names are referenced within these documents, despite not choosing to make themselves visible on camera—such as S.E.—remain recognizable to advocates championing justice for Zadorov. Interestingly, it becomes evident that while their identities are acknowledged, 'suspicious' textual content tends to elicit fewer reactions compared to 'suspicious' visual content, resulting in a more limited extent of harassment.

People Whose Names Are Unknown

As previously mentioned, the investigation materials, court hearing transcripts, and legal documents associated with the Zadorov case are accessible to the general public. Consequently, even individuals whose names are referenced within these documents, despite not choosing to make themselves visible on camera—such as S.E.—remain recognizable to advocates championing justice for Zadorov. Interestingly, it becomes evident that while their identities are acknowledged, 'suspicious' textual content tends to elicit fewer reactions compared to 'suspicious' visual content, resulting in a more limited extent of harassment.

In some cases, individuals' identities remain undisclosed due to legal restrictions imposed on the publication of investigation materials. Another scenario involves individuals whose names appeared in the investigation materials but were ultimately not submitted to the court. For instance, consider N.A.: during a search conducted immediately after the murder, a wallet was discovered in the boys' bathroom inside the toilet tank. The presence of the wallet in the boys' bathroom, situated directly below the bathroom where the murder occurred, and the fact that Zadorov returned to that bathroom to clean himself up, is an intriguing discovery. This information reached the Rada family, and in their 2007 petition to the High Court, where they demanded that the investigation be reopened, the wallet was mentioned.

It was not until a year after the murder, in November 2007, that the police approached N.A. She testified that the wallet had been stolen a few weeks before the murder. If N.'s name was more widely recognized by the public, it is possible she would have been susceptible to slander and harassment from conspiracy theorists who might have speculated that she had hidden her wallet in the toilet tank after being involved in Tair's murder.

Another example involves a hair stylist named Moriah, who resides in Katsrin and had also been Tair's hairdresser. Moriah made the last call to Tair when she was still alive, which occurred on the evening before the murder at 19:41. According to Moriah, she had intended to call her husband's daughter, who shares the name Tair, but accidentally dialed the wrong Tair. Fortunately for her, this went unnoticed by the general public since her name isn't widely known, and she was spared from unfounded conspiracy theories. For instance, speculations that she called Tair to settle an old account, but Tair did not cooperate, and as a result, the debt had to be settled the next day.

Conclusions

The online environment is characterized by factors that amplify the offensiveness and intensity of harassment, including accessibility, immediacy, viral spread, anonymity, and the retrievability of information. These factors set the stage for a complex interplay of elements that contribute to the intensity and scope of online harassment, making it a pervasive issue in the digital age (Vismonsky, 2020).

This study has shed light on the multifaceted dynamics of online harassment, using the case study of the Tair Rada murder and the Roman Zadorov affair. As mentioned above, the social media activity surrounding the affair is unique due to several key factors. It operates within the context of a murder trial and a call for justice in the case of a putative false conviction, with the participation of both 'outsiders' and knowledgeable activists. This activity has a significant impact on shaping public opinion about the functioning of relevant state institutions and Zadorov's guilt or innocence, while also leading to numerous significant discoveries initiated by these activists.

The key finding is the influence of self-exposure and varying degrees of online presence in shaping the extent of defamation and harassment individuals face, and the emergence of a 'hierarchy of defamation':

1. People who willingly put themselves in the spotlight and have their content widely disseminated are subjected to the most significant defamation. Ironically, their readiness to participate leads to the generation of materials that attract public scrutiny. In cases where the

identity of the photographed teenagers remains concealed, the degree of defamation against them is less severe.

2. Following this hierarchy, we have individuals who take the initiative to share content on their social media profiles that activists perceive as 'suspicious.'
3. Progressing in the hierarchy are individuals whose names appear in legal investigative materials but lack a visual presence. While these individuals may face a certain degree of harassment, textual materials generally evoke milder emotional reactions in comparison with visual content, resulting in less widespread harassment.
4. Occupying the bottom tier of the hierarchy of defamation are individuals whose identities remain hidden due to either publication bans or errors in the investigation materials. This form of pseudo-anonymity serves as a shield, protecting them from the harassment they would otherwise endure if their names were revealed.

Individuals who willingly exposed themselves to the public eye, frequently appeared on television, and had their videos widely disseminated on the Internet found themselves at the epicenter of extensive vilification. Their prominence and availability of visual content made them primary targets for those seeking to perpetuate conspiracy theories and unwarranted accusations.

In contrast, teenagers with minimal online content or presence generally managed to evade the brunt of such unwarranted harassment. This is a testament to the notion that the extent of defamation is directly linked to the depth of one's exposure in the online realm. Those who choose to maintain a low online profile may find themselves less susceptible to widespread vilification.

Moreover, subtle nuances can significantly affect the degree of harassment faced by individuals. Factors like the presence of a caption alongside a person in a video, the correct spelling of their name, or the posting of 'suspicious' content or photos many years after the incident took place can either amplify or mitigate the level of online harassment directed toward them.

In concluding this examination of the 'hierarchy of defamation,' it bears repeating that the framework does not convey a normative judgment toward individuals based on their visibility in the media. The purpose of highlighting this hierarchy is to shed light on the structural and systemic dimensions of online harassment, emphasizing the role of digital platforms and societal norms in facilitating defamation.

The emergence of a 'hierarchy of defamation,' as elucidated through this study, underscores a pivotal link to the broader dynamics of 'trial by media' in the digital age. This hierarchy, propelled by the degree of self-exposure and the character of online presence, vividly illustrates the complex interplay between individual agency in digital self-representation and the collective power of social media as a platform for public adjudication. It is within this context that the traditional understanding of 'trial by media' is expanded, revealing not only how media narratives can pre-empt legal adjudication but also how they can incite and amplify public harassment and defamation absent of formal legal proceedings. This phenomenon attests to a transformative shift in the locus of power from institutional media entities to the dispersed, yet potent, networks of social media users. Herein, the 'trial by media' transcends its conventional boundaries, manifesting through the prisms of visibility and exposure that individuals navigate within the digital sphere.

This study's key finding—that the extent of defamation and harassment one faces is significantly shaped by their self-exposure and online presence—casts a critical light on the responsibilities borne by digital platforms and their users in the context of 'trial by media.' It calls into question the ethical dimensions of digital engagement, urging a reevaluation of the ways in which digital discourse contributes to, and at times undermines, the principles of justice and fairness. The findings from this study not only contribute to our understanding of 'trial by media' in the digital era but also implore stakeholders to foster environments where the pursuit of justice does not devolve into platforms for harassment.

This study is rooted in a netnographic research approach, which delves into the digital facets of ethnographic research. Future research endeavors in this domain may benefit from employing a combination of methods, including experiments, to delve even deeper into the factors that determine whether online information about specific individuals encourages or mitigates the extent of harm directed toward them on the internet.

Research Ethics Statement Approval for this study was granted by the Ethics Committee of Ariel University (AU-COM-ALO-20230829). Informed consent was obtained from individual participants.

Written consent to publish identifying details of individual participants, as well as identifiable images or data, has been obtained from these individuals.

Competing Interests The author has no conflict of interests to declare that are relevant to the content of this chapter.

References

Ben-Israel, D. (2016). 'The Tube' celebrates 900K and Ynet is hysterical: Facebook page Ranking. *Mizbala*. http://mizbala.com/digital/social-media/109150

Boker, R. (2016, January 7). Tair Radha's mother to big brother: 'Keep my daughter's honor.' *Ynet*. https://www.ynet.co.il/articles/0,7340,L-4749881,00.html

Gal, S. (Director). (2008). *Only Tair knows* [Film].

Grossman, N., & Lev-On, A. (2023). Social media jurors: Conceptualizing and analyzing online public engagement in reference to legal cases. *Crime Law and Social Change, 79*(3), 223–240.

Heirman, W., & Walrave, M. (2008). Assessing concerns and issues about the mediation of technology in cyberbullying. *Cyberpsychology, 2*.

Heiman, T., Olink-Shemesh, D., & Eden, S. (2014). *Violence and vulnerability on the Internet: Characteristics, patterns, risk factors and protective factors among children and teenagers. Research report for the Ministry of Education.* https://ecat.education.gov.il/Attachment/DownloadFile?downloadId=7736

Interview by Ilana Rada. (2016, February 23). Originally broadcast on Channel 20. 'Everything for quotation' with Lior Dayan—the first and full episode. [Video]. YouTube. https://www.youtube.com/watch?v=JZrsyETkxgw

Kozinets, R. V. (2010). *Netnography: Doing ethnographic research online*. Sage.

Lev-On, A. (2023a). Democratizing the discourse on criminal justice in social media: The activity for justice for Roman Zadorov as a case study. *Humanities and Social Sciences Communications, 10*, Article 770.

Lev-On, A. (2023b) *The murder of Tair Rada and the trial of Roman Zadorov: establishment, justice, citizens and social media*. Yedioth Books.

Lev-On, A., & Steinfeld, N. (2024). The power of the visual Web: Watching online videos influences viewers' opinion about what's in the videos and also about what's not in the videos. *Heliyon*, e27895.

Rageh, A., & Melewar, T. C. (2013). Using netnography research method to reveal the underlying dimensions of the customer/tourist experience. *Qualitative Market Research: An International Journal, 16*(2), 126–149.

Sarid Institute. (2017). *Cyber violence: Research for the Israeli Internet Association.*

Sadovsky, H. (2010). *To sew an innocent person*. Sade.

Vismonsky, H. (2020). Criminalization of online harassment and the test cases of harassment against public servants and minors in the online space. *Law and Business, 23*, 410–345. (Hebrew).

Walla! Culture. (2016, March 20). Ilana Rada, the mother of the late Tair Rada, against her childhood friend, Shai Mika Yifarah from 'Big Brother.' *Walla!*. https://e.walla.co.il/item/2945108

6

A Gendered Media Spectacle for the Digital Era: Nicola Bulley, 'Missing White Woman Syndrome' and Middle-Class, Middle-Aged, Menopausal Womanhood on Trial

Deborah Jermyn and Tanya Horeck

Introduction

Saidatu Jalloh (14, Lambeth). Maureen Gitau (24, Lewisham). Taiwo Balogun (52, Bexley). These names likely won't be familiar to many readers. They are just a few of the Black women and girls reported missing in the UK since 2021, gleaned from a single newspaper article published in *The Voice* newspaper in January 2023 (Mahon, 2023), mere weeks before Nicola Bulley, a 45-year-old mortgage advisor who lived with her partner and two daughters in a village in rural Lancashire in the North of England, went missing. In a news story that transfixed the UK and generated worldwide interest, Bulley disappeared without a trace on the morning of January 27, 2023. Last seen walking her dog

D. Jermyn (✉)
University of Roehampton, London, UK
e-mail: d.jermyn@roehampton.ac.uk

T. Horeck
Anglia Ruskin University, Cambridge, UK
e-mail: Tanya.Horeck@aru.ac.uk

L. Gies (ed.), *Trial by Media*, Palgrave Studies in Crime, Media and Culture,
https://doi.org/10.1007/978-3-031-80593-6_6

by the River Wyre having dropped her children at school, her phone was found on a bench shortly after 9.30am, still connected to a Teams work call. In the weeks that followed, while the police enquiry remained live, an extraordinary public drama unfolded as intense speculation mounted regarding what might have happened to her. Crucially for the purposes of our discussion, unlike the largely unrecognised names we share above, Bulley was white and, furthermore, normatively attractive, the photos of her shared in the public domain capturing snapshots of a well-groomed woman from a seemingly comfortable milieu. Hence in this chapter, we ask how the case came to function as a consummately gendered media spectacle for the digital era, with public discussions about Bulley's possible fate driven by persistent cultural anxieties and fantasies regarding white, middle-class, middle-aged womanhood. Beginning with an analysis of true crime TikTok, where the Nicola Bulley hashtag accrued 270 million views within three weeks of her disappearance (Spring, 2023), we consider the complex entanglement between social media, true crime tourism, and police investigation in the case, arguing that it brought burgeoning concerns over internet sleuthing to a crisis point.

At the same time, we open with the names of these missing Black girls and women, to immediately underline how, while the ubiquitous cultural prioritising of the stories of missing white women like Bulley has become a media standard, reports of missing women of colour recurrently go unmade or unshared in mainstream coverage. We do so too to acknowledge that in what follows, in applying the 'Missing White Women Syndrome' framework to explore the Nicola Bulley case, it might be argued we may ourselves be helping to *propagate* missing white women syndrome. Coined by the African American news journalist and political analyst Gwen Ifill at the Journalists of Color Conference in the USA on August 5, 2004 (Musial, 2024, p. 272) the term enduringly and powerfully captures the media's fixation with stories of missing white girls and women, most particularly 'innocent' ones who form ideal victims, despite it being the case that it is Black people who disproportionately go missing (Purnell, 2021). We thus undertake this work alive to the need to do so in ways that continue to challenge and critically contextualise this status quo, rather than merely reproduce it, and agitate to put the experiences of women of colour on the media agenda. Hence, in the analysis that follows we examine how, as it developed, news coverage of the case went on to appropriate a further, dominant cultural discourse that recurrently centres white women to embed their representation and experience as constituting womanhood itself—namely the pathologisation of menopause. For as conjecture about the case continued to spiral, almost three weeks after Bulley's disappearance a police press conference tantalisingly shared another facet of her case—that she was considered 'high-risk'; before an additional police statement contextualised this status, revealing in a further twist that she had been experiencing 'significant issues with alcohol' prompted by 'ongoing struggles with the menopause' (see, e.g., Tweed, 2023).

Resonating through the implications here lay a whole matrix of deeply symbolic and problematic cultural tropes which we unpack below, in which the Nicola Bulley case became not only the latest instance of missing white woman syndrome but of the representation of menopause as rendering women unstable and erratic, as 'mad, moody or vulnerable' (Perz & Ussher, 2008, p. 293). Indeed, the two paradigms are intricately enmeshed, since both operate as recurrent normative cultural exemplars that centre and spectacularise middle-class white women, in the process devaluing and marginalising the humanity of women of colour. Here, though, we examine not only what the terms of the police statement cited above crystallise about enduringly problematic attitudes to menopause but what can be learned from the angry backlash it provoked, echoed too in the rebukes that met the sexist scrutiny that exploded around the senior woman detective leading the enquiry. In sum, the intense affective responses to this case of 'trial by media' warrant deeper analysis into the tensions it exposed between sleuthing and advocacy, and between empathy and irresponsibility. Through close analysis of coverage of Bulley's disappearance in local and national press and social media, and with instructive comparative reference to other germane national and international cases, our analysis is by necessity informed by a breadth of interdisciplinary approaches and scholarship, including criminology, feminist media studies, and digital humanities. In adopting such a multi-perspectival method, we seek to underline how a breadth of social concerns about violence, justice, and regulation—pertaining to digital media, true crime, contemporary policing, gendered victim blaming, online abuse, and more—came to converge in this case, crystallising a variety of intertwined contemporary cultural preoccupations. It would be too easy to regard the story as merely another perplexing instance of exploitative tabloid journalism and reckless social media gone wild in the digital era. Rather, we argue what the Bulley case ultimately reveals is not only a cultural crisis around internet sleuthing, but an increasingly insistent refusal to tolerate the casual pathologisation of menopausal women, and a growing insistence on calling police misogyny to account.

Missing White Woman Syndrome in the Time of TikTok

To grapple with the complex ways in which Nicola Bulley's disappearance functioned as a gendered media spectacle for the digital era, it is first necessary to explore what led to the media obsession with the case. From the start, Nicola Bulley's disappearance fed into longstanding fantasies of white women as 'idealised citizens' (Musial, 2024, p. 271). In the outpouring of concern, there was grief over an 'aborted white future', which is common to the media representation of missing white women (Musial, 2024, pp. 371–372). Descriptions of Nicola Bulley as a 'loving mum' who 'doted on her children' were prevalent throughout media stories of her disappearance (Baum, 2023; Blake, 2023; Mills, 2023) (Fig. 6.1).

Photos of Bulley also played a significant role in amplifying public interest in the case, corresponding with existing research which suggests that 'news is most remembered when accompanied by photographs and missing white women are more likely to have photographs attached

Fig. 6.1 Photos of Nicola Bulley that circulated in the media

to their stories' (Musial, 2023, p. 277; see also Slakoff, 2020). In the widely reproduced selfies that circulated in the media, Bulley is smiling directly into the camera; in some she is walking the dog, in others she is posing with her partner, Paul Ansell. As Musial has written, 'missing white women are framed around three key themes: their appearance, their family status, and their morality' (2024, p. 273). Certainly, this was the media framing of Bulley: she was presented as a caring friend, a loving daughter and partner, and a wonderful mother.

In the early days of Bulley's disappearance, the public response on social media was one of concern, and predominantly involved sharing her photos and details of the search response in the hopes she would be found. However, the story also immediately activated established true crime tropes of the lost white woman and raised the spectre of violence against women. While the police soon stated their belief that it was a tragic accident and that Bulley had fallen into the water (Robinson & Tingle, 2023), this was met by a seemingly widespread public refusal to accept this narrative. Various theories were asserted regarding what might have happened to her, including abduction and murder, scenarios which activated ideas of defiled 'innocence', another central feature of missing white woman syndrome (Wanzo, 2008, pp. 111–113).

Although, in the aftermath of the case, an independent review criticised the Lancashire police for not communicating clearly enough with the public their valid reasons for thinking it was an accidental death (College of Policing, 2023) (herein CoP), it is nonetheless remarkable how quickly—and deeply—the theory that it was a suspicious death took hold. As discussion of the case spread virally, 'a cacophony of ideas' was 'pitched and skewered by armchair detectives in thousands of posts on Reddit and other websites' including Twitter and TikTok (Bryant, 2023). Such internet sleuthing is part of a wider digital 'culture of detection' (Andrejevic, 2007, 38; Horeck, 2019), which has emerged through social media's solicitation of participatory involvement through the activities of 'liking', commenting, and sharing. While armchair detection is not new, digital networks have undeniably heightened a sense of public involvement in criminal cases. The 'affective publics' (Papacharissi, 2015) that came together in speculation about what might have happened to Bulley, produced what Jodi Dean has called 'feelings of community' if not community itself (2010, p. 22). As Susanna Paasonen et al., write, 'networked affect' coheres through various interfaces and platforms which 'allow us to experience sensations of connectivity, interest, desire, and attachment' (2015, p. 3). These 'sensations of connectivity' are considerably intensified by the fact that missing people in the twenty-first century have Instagram and Facebook accounts (amongst other social media apps), which can be pored over in a bid to piece together the details of their lost lives and to speculate about what might have led to this terrible moment for them. Indeed, internet users scoured Bulley's Facebook account and photos and left random comments on her posts, until the account was shut down (Herbert, 2023).

While the Bulley case bears the trademarks of other missing white woman syndrome cases in the 1990s and 2010s, it is also specific to a cultural moment, occurring just under two years after the emergence of the COVID-19 crisis and the UK's national lockdowns. During this period, true crime media had a dramatic surge in popularity, exemplified by the success of Netflix's streaming true crime docuseries, *Tiger King: Murder, Mayhem and Madness* (2020). The series became a global lockdown hit and spread virally across a range of platforms, including TikTok where the hashtag #carolebaskinkilledherhusband garnered millions of views (Horeck, 2021, p. 48). Further, as a social media app, TikTok rose to cultural prominence during the COVID crisis, and was embraced as the 'perfect medium for the splintered attention spans of lockdown' (Kendall, 2021, p. 41).[1] TikTok was founded by Chinese company Bytedance in 2018 and is an app for creating and watching short-form videos. It now has over 1 billion monthly active users worldwide (Dean, 2024). In contrast to other social media platforms such as Instagram, TikTok's 'virality doesn't stem from having a coherent persona or online identity; instead, users' posts, not their profiles, go viral' (Banet-Weiser & Maddocks, 2024, p. 173). This feature of the app is significant for True Crime TikTok, which, at the time of writing this chapter, has over a billion views. True crime stories are prime material for trending on

[1] TikTok was founded by Chinese company Bytedance in 2018 and is an app for creating and watching short-form videos. It shot to popularity during COVID-19 and now has over 1 billion monthly active users.

the app, and TikTok provides a significant new space for missing white woman syndrome to take hold. The Gabby Petito case in the USA in 2021 is a prime example. Petito was a 22-year-old white woman who was missing over a period of several weeks. Her remains were eventually found at a campground in Wyoming on September 19, 2021, and it was revealed that her fiancée Brian Laundrie had murdered her. During the time she was missing the hashtag #gabbypetito garnered nearly a billion views on TikTok and it was strongly debated whether TikTok helped or hindered the official investigation into her disappearance. In an op-ed for *The Washington Post*, Rachel Monroe notes that the line between internet sleuthing and 'content creation' in the Petito case was virtually impossible to discern as internet 'posters delivered breathless updates on Petito's case, as if…recounting plot twists from the latest prestige drama' (2021; see also Bethan Jones, 2023).

In the UK context, two years later, the Nicola Bulley case was seen to bring this blurring of the lines between content creation and citizen investigation to yet another crisis point.[2] Though in contrast to the Petito case there was no evidence of third-party involvement, true crime TikTok still responded with a flood of content, fuelled by the app's algorithm and its 'For You' page, which amplifies videos based on individual user preference and activity. The TikTok videos on Bulley's disappearance are a complex mixture of breaking news, evidence updates, conspiracy theories, body language analysis; dog behavioural analysis; CCTV analysis; river water analysis and emotional retellings of her disappearance.

Journalists and social media pundits alike suggested that a steady diet of true crime streaming television, podcasts, and films was to blame for why the public latched onto Bulley's disappearance in this way. On Twitter (now X), for example, there was criticism of how the story of Bulley's disappearance functioned as a piece of true crime 'infotainment', with some users citing the influence of Netflix true crime documentaries (see Fig. 6.2).

Meanwhile, the consensus of the British media was that the Bulley case revealed internet sleuthing at its worst, with TikTok being singled out for blame. Media headlines from the time include: 'Nicola Bulley:

[2] On this see Jones & Steff El Madawi in their chapter in this collection.

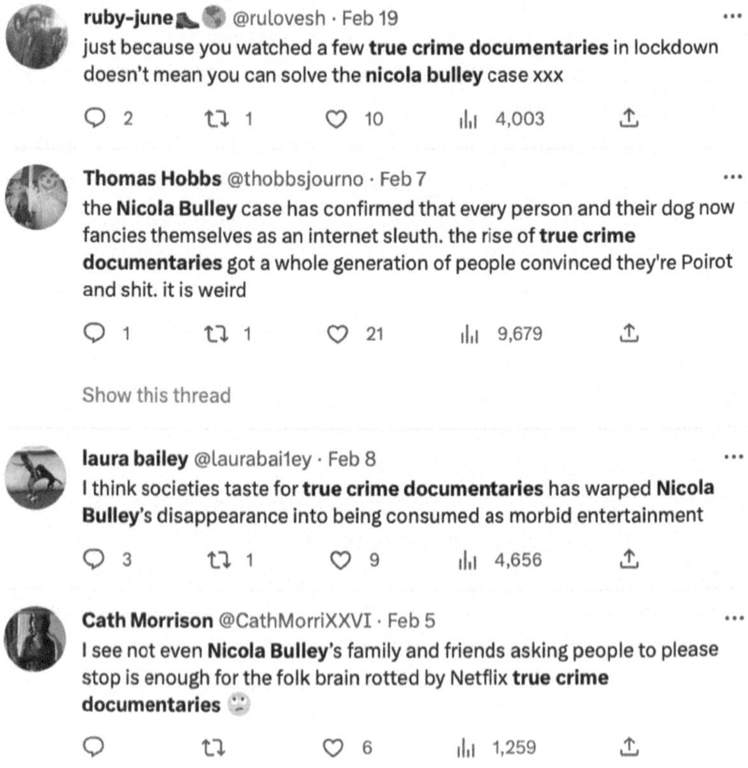

Fig. 6.2 Tweets on the Bulley case as true crime 'infotainment'

How TikTok detectives finally went too far' (Greig, 2023) and 'How TikTok turned hunt for mum Nicola Bulley into "vile circus of cruelty"' (Veljanovski, 2023). However, it is important to note that legacy media relied on that same TikTok content to generate stories, providing yet another example of the increasing journalistic dependency on social media sources in the face of dwindling resources for journalism.[3] Indeed, in the early stages of her disappearance, news media sites used images of

[3] For discussion of how social media platforms such as Twitter changed journalistic practices, see, for example, Broersma and Graham (2013); Moon and Hadley (2014); Lecheler, S. and Kruikemeier (2016).

Bulley obtained from her Facebook account to illustrate and dramatically heighten accounts of her disappearance (see Whelan, 2023). For instance, *BBC News* quoted from the Facebook posts of Bulley's friends (Lazaro, 2023) and *The Independent* referenced Bulley's previous Facebook posts recounting her morning dog walks to embellish discussions of her final known movements (Noyce, 2023). The practice of using material from social media to help construct and dramatise crime stories was first established in the British media treatment of Amanda Knox, the American university student convicted of murdering her roommate Meredith Kercher in Perugia, Italy in 2007. While Knox's conviction was eventually overturned, a study by Atalanta Goulandris and Eugene McLaughlin has shown how British tabloids 'lift[ed] text and images' from Knox's MySpace account, reworking information to produce a sensationalist, and heavily sexualised and criminalised image of the young woman as a killer (2016, p. 20). Although the Bulley case was very different, the British media continued the practice of reworking personal social media material, taking content from Bulley's social media accounts to heighten their presentation of her as beatific partner and mother.

The Entanglement of the Digital and the Non-Digital

The Bulley case brought into sharp relief the extent to which online and offline are now entangled in what theorists refer to as a 'postdigital' culture (Evans & Ringrose, forthcoming 2025). As Adrienne Evans and Jessica Ringrose argue, although there is a tendency for 'institutions, regulations, laws, ethics, and policies' to 'still make distinctions between digital experiences and 'real life'', it is important to recognise that 'life is increasingly an amalgamation of digital and the non-digital' (2025). Indeed, the consequences of this amalgamation are fundamental to the theme of this collection, which invites us to reevaluate the stakes of Trial by Media. As defined by criminologist Elizabeth Yardley et al., internet sleuthing or 'websleuthing' is 'the embodiment of participatory media, where the lines between the producer, consumer and subject are blurred, there are fewer restrictions in relation to time and space and online activities have real world, embodied consequences' (2018, p. 82). The Bulley case revealed the material, real-world consequences of online engagement with police investigations in a way that had not been previously seen in the UK context before, at least not on this scale, for a missing persons investigation that was not suspected to involve a third-party or any criminal activity.[4]

What happened on TikTok did not stay on TikTok—a striking number of people travelled to Bulley's village of St. Michael's on Wyre, which has a recorded population of 3,359, to generate social media content. For some, this consisted of taking a selfie beside the bench where Bulley left her phone; for others, it involved greater interference. As Zoe Williams reported for *The Guardian*, 'YouTuber, Dan Duffy, joined the search just to post a video of himself joining it, and was fined on a public order offence, which he also filmed. One TikTok account, Curtis Cool Stuff, posted a video of a man digging up woodland, and another of him roaming around a derelict house opposite the bank where Bulley was last seen. Another group of men had to be dispersed from the house, having travelled there from Liverpool' (2023). Offline interference and invasion of the village were matched by online harms: Bulley's partner, Paul Ansell, was increasingly targeted on social media, and his Pinterest account was hacked and filled with sexually explicit photos (ibid., 2023). In other words, while the disappearance of Nicola Bulley did not involve violence or criminal activity, the *response* to her disappearance certainly did.

According to digital media theorist Joss Hands there are 'two dialectically opposed tendencies in digital consciousness' (2023). On the one hand, there is the 'digital 'mob' that does not think in any sense beyond reflexive action' (2023). The case of the Boston Marathon bombing in 2013 in which Redditors and 4chan-ers scoured photos and spun theories around who might have committed the murders—ultimately identifying the wrong suspects because of racial stereotyping—exemplifies this mob tendency. On the other hand, there is a more nuanced form

[4] The University of Idaho murders in the US in November 2023 led to similar concerns about internet sleuthing as so-called TikTok detectives descended upon the small town of Moscow, Idaho. See Coppins' 'The Gross Spectacle of Murder Fandom' (2023).

of collective intelligence, 'characterised by networked association, reflection, and mutual recognition – manifesting a form of thinking together, *for* each other rather than merely by each other' (2023). As Hands writes: 'While the former represents the divisive destructive tendencies of the digital, the latter offers hope' (2023). In his book *Gadget Consciousness: Collective Thought, Will and Action in the Age of Social Media* (2019). Hands cites the viral #MeToo movement as an example of a more productive form of collective intelligence gathering in which victim-survivors across the globe have organised through the hashtag, bringing about a heightened awareness of the problem of gender-based violence.

While it might be easier to point to the 'digital mob' in cases such as Bulley, it is important to also reflect on how networked thinking might, to borrow the words of the symposium invitation that preceded this collection, 'provide alternative spaces for justice which are unavailable within the judicial realm' (private corres with Lieve Gies, 2023). There is an important distinction to be drawn here between online 'sleuthing' and activism. At the same time as it can spread conspiracy theories and fake news, an app such as TikTok can also be used as a tool for finding justice in relation to gender-based violence. One striking recent example is the murder of Daisy De La O in Compton, California in 2021. Where the media had virtually ignored De La O's case—with the *LA Times* referring to her in passing as a 'Latina Jane Doe' (Swann, 2022)—De La O's friend Rebecca Fuentes posted on TikTok to humanise her friend and to try to locate the boyfriend who murdered her.[5] Beneath the video posted by Fuentes, TikTok users talked about tagging and commenting on it to strategically boost the algorithm; the post was also reshared on other sites such as Instagram and Twitter to amplify the information. Ultimately, the TikTok videos posted by Fuentes were credited with locating the boyfriend who was subsequently arrested and has since been convicted of De La O's murder. Fuentes' viral TikTok appeal also highlighted—and critically challenged—'missing white woman syndrome' and called out the media tendency as noted above to focus unduly on missing and murdered white women to the detriment of stories of violence against

[5] Fuentes video is available here: https://www.tiktok.com/@barecce/video/6966763757997395205?is_copy_url=1&is_from_webapp=v1

women of colour. The Gabby Petito case similarly led to accounts on TikTok and Instagram asking that indigenous and black women be granted the same concern and attention (see Krishnan, 2021).

However, as Sarah Banet-Weiser and Sophie Maddocks have cautioned, while TikTok circulates feminist activism, it also perpetuates misogyny, with 'networked feminism' and 'networked misogyny' operating in tandem on the platform (2024, p. 371). While TikTok videos critical of missing white woman syndrome are part of a wider feminist TikTok that seeks to inform users about 'critical race theory, white supremacy, capitalism and Indigenous and black feminisms', it is important to note that research also shows it is often 'white TikTok creators within these trends' that 'get the most views' (371). Further, the very design of online spaces tends to perpetuate what Safiya Noble terms 'algorithmic oppression' and produce opportunities for what Banet-Weiser and Maddocks call 'new nodes in the network of misogyny' (372). It is possible to discern this complex intermingling of feminist and misogynist discourses online in the flood of content that both revelled in, and despaired over, the disappearance of Bulley.

'This Will Take Years to Repair'

A crucial context for understanding the public response to the Bulley case is the kidnap, rape, and murder of 33-year-old Sarah Everard by Metropolitan police officer Wayne Couzens during a COVID-19 lockdown in the UK in March 2021. Everard's murder triggered widespread protest and outrage over violence against girls and women, which UN Women labelled the 'shadow pandemic' (UN Women, n.d.). TikTok was a significant site of digital feminist activism over Everard's murder, with a swell of posts by girls and women discussing how it related to wider institutionalised misogyny and violence against women (see Mendes et al., 2021). However, this was accompanied by backlash, as the misogynistic discourses of the manosphere also rose during this period, with research showing the 'increased normalization of men's rights activist (MRA) discourses' during lockdowns for COVID-19 (Horeck et al., 2023, pp. 3, 15).

As London mayor Sadiq Kahn noted on the anniversary of Everard's murder on March 3, 2024, at the time we were writing this chapter: 'Sarah's murder by a serving police officer horrified the entire country and significantly damaged the trust and confidence women and girls have in the police. This will take years to repair' (Anon, 2024). The Nicola Bulley case indicates just how much repair work is required, as the sleuthing and conspiracy theorising arguably revealed the depth of public anxiety and mistrust over how police deal with cases of violence against women. As Claire Birchall and Peter Knight suggest, conspiracy theories 'often reflect genuine and legitimate concerns, even if their factual claims are wide of the mark or draw on troubling registers' (2022, p. 4). In the conjecture over what might have happened to Bulley, there was a general sense that social media had to step in to do the work of the police. Take the example of the subgenre of body language analysis videos on TikTok, in which amateur detectives forensically pored over interview footage of Bulley's partner, Paul Ansell, to detect signs of his possible involvement in her disappearance. Some of these videos compare Ansell's interview footage to that of Chris Watts, the American man who murdered his wife and two children on August 13, 2018, and lied about it in a video clip that went viral. The videos analysing Ansell's body language are wildly problematic and a troubling example of how trial by social media can lead to unevidenced accusations. Yet to varying extents these videos also indicate societal awareness, however misguided, of the realities of violence against women, and the statistics regarding intimate partner homicide, in which 62% of murdered women are killed by a former partner (Femicide Census, n.d.).

Ultimately, the Bulley case exposed serious fractures in the chain of communication between police, traditional media sources, and social media users. As noted in the Independent Review of Lancashire Constabulary, the police 'lost control of the media narrative' at an early stage and were woefully underprepared for dealing with the social media engagement with the case (CoP, 2023). Asked if social media sleuths had hindered the police investigation, Lancashire Police Detective Superintendent Rebecca Smith said, 'Yes, it has significantly distracted the investigation. In 29 years' police service I've never seen anything like it' (see, e.g., Marshall, 2023); this, ironically, shortly before Smith herself, in a further diversion, became subject of sexist and intrusive media debate, as we now explore below.

An Unsuitable Dress for a Woman (Detective)

As the case went on and Bulley remained unaccounted for, and while the wild speculation described above spiralled, Lancashire police held a press conference to try and curb some of this damaging conjecture. On February 15, almost three weeks after Nicola's disappearance, they met with the press, led by Assistant Chief Constable Peter Lawson and Detective Superintendent Rebecca Smith, the senior investigating officer on the case. Fascinatingly, in the days that followed what unravelled was not only a renewed round of intrigue regarding Bulley, which we turn to shortly. Rather, the press conference itself became the site of another gendered media spectacle, when journalist Amanda Platell, from conservative UK daily tabloid the *Daily Mail*, responded to the briefing by indignantly condemning Smith's appearance (see also Wyatt, 2023). Taking to social media to vent her outrage, the morning after the conference Platell tweeted[6] a picture of Smith from the *Daily Mail*'s coverage declaring:

> Detective Superintendent Rebecca Smith at press conference yesterday – skin tight navy dress, stilettos, poker straightened hair – whatever happened to a cop uniform! Or is she auditioning for Love Island for midlifers. Show some respect for a missing mother! (Platell, 2023)[7]

Indeed, this single tweet itself collapses numerous themes we are concerned with in this chapter, regarding appropriateness, gender, age, and 'worthy' or ideal victimhood (Christie, 1986; Greer, 2007; Slakoff, 2020), Smith's outfit is deemed inappropriate not only for the context, but because of who is wearing it: namely another middle-aged woman. Here, Platell disparagingly refers to Smith as a 'midlifer' who looks like

---

[6] Then known as Twitter, this platform subsequently became 'X' in July 2023.

[7] *Love Island* is a hugely popular but somewhat controversial dating game show in the UK, broadcast on ITV since 2015.

she's trying out for a reality TV dating show, with all the connotations that bring of attention-seeking and desperation. Furthermore, such an outfit is disrespectful not only because this is a missing person case but because Bulley is a missing *mother* and therefore seemingly worthy of more reverence, the lingering implication being that non-mothers would warrant less particular regard.

A whole other chapter could easily be written at this juncture, indeed, about what the opinions voiced here suggest regarding prevalent perceptions of policing, professionalism, and gender, in a culture where even the most authoritative working women in all kinds of careers can still expect their attire and appearance to be scrutinised in a manner rarely accorded to their male peers. Women with bare arms appear to be particularly triggering to conservative observers (as seen, for example, in the continued analysis that has long met Michelle Obama whenever she appears at a work-related meeting without sleeves); here, it was fellow *Daily Mail* and *Spectator* writer Petronella Wyatt, like Platell on Twitter, asking in exasperation, 'Who wears a sleeveless dress in February?' and suggesting Smith was using the case 'as a [sic] excuse to showcase her toned physique' (Wyatt, 2023). The story that blew up around Smith's appearance chimes potently with Susan Watson's research into how women working in a variety of 'major public facing occupations' are subject to online abuse 'overwhelmingly underpinned by misogyny and gendered discrimination' (Watson, 2022, pp. 830–831).[8] Within this larger study Watson found that while women politicians and journalists, for example, suffered more 'violent or sexualised' threats, by comparison 'police officers [were] more likely to receive abuse that targets their age or appearance' (2022, p. 841). Condemnation of Platell and the concurring commentators who joined in her judgemental appraisal came swiftly from senior policing figures, however. These included Michelle Skeer, the Chief Constable of Lancashire Constabulary, who rebuked Platell's 'poor journalism' as 'absolutely disgraceful'; and Zoe Billingham, a former HM inspector of constabulary, who speaking on Sky News

[8] While Watson's work on policing was particularly focused on high-ranking women officers active in the online space, and the furore around Smith on social media was prompted by her TV appearance, Watson's findings about the prevalence of disparaging attention to women officers' appearance nevertheless merit reference.

regarding the coverage was moved to ask, 'It is the 21st Century isn't it?' (see Gregory, 2023). Nevertheless, in this post-press conference moment, the case became about publicly judging the actions and respectability of not one but two middle-aged white women and brought a whole other misogynistic thread and mode of symbolic violence to bear in the gendered media spectacle that was already underway.

The New Prime Suspect: Pathologising Menopause

But crucially also in this press conference, Smith shared that Bulley had been deemed a 'high risk' missing person from the onset of the investigation. The officer disclosed that she had "specific vulnerabilities' which had informed their 'working hypothesis' that she had fallen into the River Wyre' (Calderbank, 2023), but declined to detail what those vulnerabilities were. The widespread response to this was in essence that the police update had been pointless. But what it did prompt was intrigue regarding the disclosure that she was considered 'high risk' without specifying *why*; leading to an entirely counter-productive response of generating more speculation rather than quelling it. To address this, in a highly unusual move suggestive of crisis management (as was later confirmed by the College of Policing independent inquiry (2023)) Lancashire police issued a new statement just six hours later that same day, where they fleshed out these 'vulnerabilities'. Nicola, it was now shared, had '*some significant issues with alcohol which were brought on by her ongoing struggles with the menopause*' (our emphasis) (Tweed, 2023; see also Herbert, 2023).

For clarity, and as the UK's National Health Service defines it, menopause refers to 'when your periods stop due to lower hormone levels' (NHS UK, 2022). In what circumstances, then, would it be considered appropriate, or necessary for the good of an investigation, for police to release such information? The overwhelming public and media reaction was that it was not necessary, and a great deal of angry fallout followed, regarding what was widely considered to be an unacceptable breach of privacy (e.g. Anon, 2023b) which furthermore misogynistically framed menopause as a 'vulnerability' that might lead to reckless behaviour. This was expressed everywhere from popular UK daytime TV personalities taking to Twitter—with Fern Britton criticising the implication that Bulley was 'perhaps even 'not in her right mind'. Too easy to write a woman off like this', and actor Tamsin Outhwaite, commenting 'Fuming. Police have no idea so let's point the finger at the victim and talk about our hormones and alcohol… headlines like this are a classic example of misogynistic c**p' (see Marshall, 2023)—through to comments from Members of Parliament and others in the highest political office. Both Prime Minister Rishi Sunak and Home Secretary Suella Braverman shared concerns that such information had been released, with Braverman even taking the controversial step of intervening to ask Lancashire Constabulary for an explanation (Anon, 2023a), thereby potentially raising 'questions over the government's respect for the principle of operational independence in British policing' (Dearden, 2023). Meanwhile, in an article for *The Independent* entitled 'The Nicola Bulley Case is one of the biggest disasters in British policing', former Scotland Yard detective and TV crime consultant Peter Bleksley observed the investigation had, at a time when already 'public trust in the police was plummeting', released 'a calamitously timed revelation' which 'managed to turn a missing person enquiry into arguably the biggest communications disaster ever cobbled together by a British police service' (Bleskley, 2023). Further, as a result of the statement, on February 17 the Information Commissioner's Office (ICO), 'the UK's independent body set up to uphold information rights', requested that Lancashire Police provide an explanation accounting for their disclosure (Anon, 2023b; Keaney, 2023).

Crucially in all this, in sharing that Nicola's 'struggles with menopause' had rendered her 'high-risk', it was not only Bulley's reputation that was perceived to have been sullied or put on trial. Rather, menopausal women as a whole were by implication thrust under suspicion, cast as potentially unstable, as a possible danger to themselves as volatile subjects. As the case unfolded further, then, the stakes shifted in some important ways. Officers who were already 'on trial' among the internet sleuths, were now newly scrutinised, being widely criticised for sexism and information mismanagement in the case, and perhaps a breach of GDPR. As referred to above, this comes at a time when confidence in the British police was, and perhaps remains still, at an all-time low. This has been most particularly in the 2020s in respect of evidence of rampant misogyny in its ranks, as so dreadfully brought home not only by the rape and murder of Sarah Everard by a serving Metropolitan Police officer in 2021 as noted, but by the conviction of serial rapist David Carrick (also a serving Metropolitan Police officer) in 2023, and the appalling police failings regarding the murders of Nicole Smallman and Bibaa Henry in 2020[9] (whose negligently managed disappearance was another signal reminder of missing white women syndrome) (see Anon, 2023b). Indeed, Lancashire Police were accused of having released Bulley's private information as a means of deflecting criticism from themselves, weaponising menopause against Bulley and victim blaming, with Mandu Reid, leader of The Women's Equality Party, observing, 'The police are there to protect people - not to protect their own reputation. It feels like they have protected their own reputation at Nicola's expense… They have betrayed women and over. This is a point on the continuum of that betrayal' (cited in Oppenheim, 2023).

But also on trial now was menopause itself. A woman's menopausal status had been announced in the highest profile news story in the land as a determining factor in assessing her to be a high-risk missing person. Menopause had been publicly identified by safeguarding professionals as a condition that could render one '*vulnerable*'. This kind of pathologisation of menopause of course is far from unusual, having an established history in Western culture. As scholars such as Louise Foxcroft have charted, 'it groans under centuries of cultural baggage' (2009, p. xiii), and chimes with long-held mythologies of women's wombs, menses, and cycles constituting the source of female 'hysteria'. Yet it was unprecedented to see it called on in this fashion in an ongoing, conspicuous police investigation. In this way, we would argue this redirection in the case was a further instance of what has been termed 'the

[9] Sisters Nicole Smallman and Bibaa Henry were murdered in a London park in June 2020. Among other things, the subsequent Independent Office for Police Conduct inquiry into the investigation of their case examined whether police had initially failed to manage and escalate their disappearance sufficiently in part because they were women of colour. Furthermore, two officers were eventually convicted and jailed for sharing photographs of the women taken at the murder scene.

menopausal turn'—the shift in recent years to 'an unprecedented period of pronounced public cultural conversation and promotion around a newly inflected era of menopause awareness' (Jermyn, 2023, p. 1). Importantly, this has most often been popularised and fostered in the UK media by white women celebrities, replacing one kind of predominantly white archetypal representation of menopause (cf an older white lady looking dejectedly into space) with another (an aspirationally positioned, well-groomed middle-aged white lady resisting the previous archetype) (Jermyn, 2023). Against this dominant backdrop, acknowledgement of how women of colour might experience menopause differently both culturally and physically has had to continually push against mainstream representation to be considered, while demographic discrepancies in treatment are such that, as Dr Nighat Arif put it in one *Guardian* article, 'Many think menopause is a white middle class or western phenomenon' (cited in Mills, 2022). Tellingly, this same article, which importantly sought to highlight the need to 'make sure that menopause is not just for posh white women' (Mills, 2022) was illustrated with a photo of two smiling, white, glamorous television stars, TV presenter and fitness guru, Davina McCall, and daytime TV personality/model, Penny Lancaster.

As Belinda Steffan has observed, increasing menopause awareness can be a 'double edged sword' (Steffan, 2022). Hence many commentators have expressed concern that the recent greater amplification of attention to menopause will be used against menopausal women's interests, as a means to frame ageing and older women as problematic, as erratic and risky subjects (McDonagh, 2021; Turner, 2023), adopting a neoliberal discourse also to compel them to manage menopause better though discerning consumption and 'self-care' (Jermyn, 2023) rather than to elicit greater empathy or understanding. It thus paradoxically threatens to disenfranchise them further, rather than buttress support for them, such that Janice Turner, for example, entreated in *The Times* just weeks before Bulley's disappearance, that we must not '[elevate menopause] into this tragic female flaw… it won't help older women - it will become yet another reason to write them off' (2023). In many ways, this 'writing off' Turner conjures would appear to be just what happened as police apparently sought to account for why their controversial and seemingly 'cobbled together' (Bleksley, 2023) investigation had unravelled as it had by signalling Bulley's (implicitly 'poorly'-managed) menopause as the root cause.

Re/solving the Nicola Bulley Case

But we want again to return here to one of the conceptual prompts driving this collection—namely, to look beyond merely condemning the phenomenon of 'trial by media', to instead reflect on the ways in which public interest and investment in crime might be managed or harnessed. Here we might consider what in the aftermath of the press conference can be called the inadvertently constructive outcomes of Lancashire police's deeply troubling statement. Indeed, the fallout from the statement prompted an extraordinary round of resistance to the pathologisation of menopause—a refusal to accept this tired and demeaning trope—as well as a vocal insistence that as a society, we must hold our police to account.

The intensity of the response put the archetype of the erratic menopausal woman needing paternalistic care under the spotlight as one that must be challenged and would not be accepted as an explanation for implications of reckless behaviour. If it was meant as a means of deflection by the police, subconsciously or otherwise, it spectacularly backfired as it turned scrutiny and media attention precisely back on themselves. Dame Vera Baird, the former victims' commissioner for England and Wales, decried the handling of the case as 'as sexist as it comes', observing it had dealt a further blow to trust in the police, and asking, 'Would we have had police officers saying… he's been unfortunately tied down with alcohol because he's been suffering from erectile dysfunction for the last few weeks? I think not' (cited in Anon, 2023a). Still, the ICO investigation concluded the case did not warrant enforcement action (Keaney, 2023). Further, the CoP's independent external review of Lancashire Constabulary's management of the case later elaborated that the press conference had been called in order to try to avert concerning speculation around Bulley's partner which had reached such a level that there was apprehension regarding its 'potential impact on Mr Ansell's safeguarding and welfare' (CoP, 2023, p. 84). Additionally, the decision to state that Bulley's 'vulnerabilities' were related to menopause had been prompted at the suggestion of a family member who was unhappy with the police proposal to describe them as related to 'ongoing mental health' (CoP, 2023, pp. 90–91).[10] Nevertheless, the CoP enquiry concluded that the decision to share Bulley's 'most personal information' was 'in our view [avoidable] and unnecessary' (CoP, 2023, p. 94). The ICO enquiry, furthermore, led them to revisit advice regarding 'Necessity and proportionality' in order 'to share the wider lessons all police can benefit from', formulated in a series of five questions that 'police must ask when considering sharing personal information with the public' (Kearney, 2023). All of this, then, bolstered a new round of deliberation about the UK police's remit, standards, and actions.

There is so much more that might be unpacked here if space allowed, including the nagging sense that the whole post-press conference furore underlined how, despite the progress made in some areas by the menopausal turn, menopause is still something to feel a certain shame about—something still belonging behind closed doors, something not to be spoken about, bordering in some respects on the distasteful. Further, it is important to note that observing Bulley's case underscores the enduring cultural pathologisation of menopause, and that this is principally represented through images and testimonies of middle-class white women, is *not* to say that this means women of colour are somehow mercifully shielded or spared from a disparaging gendered discourse. Rather, it is again an example of exclusionary practice, where their narratives don't count and aren't counted. Alongside missing white women syndrome, the marginalisation of women of colour from the mainstream discourses of the menopausal turn constitute two manifestations of the same process and perspective; i.e. both are cultural paradigms

[10] Strikingly too, given the shocking public scorn around her appearance that Det Superintendent Rebecca Smith was subjected to after the press conference, the external review of the case provides eye-opening background context to how the conference was managed, from which one learns that she had been obliged by a commanding officer to take part under duress. As the Senior Investigating Officer, she had thought it inappropriate to be called on to appear as the 'media talking head'. Further, in what evidently proved to be a highly prescient response, 'They recorded in their daybook notes that they felt vulnerable and exposed by this decision. That day, they raised in the gold group meeting that they felt Lancashire Constabulary had placed them in a vulnerable position' (CoP, 2023, p. 92).

that construct fundamental concerns for understanding the experiences of womanhood/femininity/feminine vulnerability, in which womanhood proper is constructed as white and middle-class. Just as the disappearances of Saidatu Jalloh, Maureen Gitau, and Taiwo Balogun were not made to count in mainstream media narratives, neither have the experiences of women of colour featured in the bulk of the burgeoning recent popular media interest in menopause.

In June 2023, the case was closed when the Inquest ruled that Nicola Bulley had died almost immediately on falling into the river on January 27 and recorded a verdict of accidental death. But in the multiple diversions and contortions we have traced and unpacked in her case throughout this chapter, one sees how instances of trial by media can act to instructively crystallise a huge terrain of social preoccupations. As we have suggested, there is crucial critical insight to be garnered from unpicking the multi-faceted reasons for the global attention this story received, and the various directions it took, from problematic 'sleuthing' to a more productive interrogation of raced and gendered discourses and the pathologisation of menopause. Rather than singling out individual actors, or blaming the operations of one platform, our analysis underscores just how crucial a multiperspectival approach is to interrogate the entanglement of interests at work in contemporary trial by media. Here, this includes not only the cultural stakes of the collective swell of interest in the case; but the welding together of the digital and non-digital affective gathering around the figure of the lost white woman, and the ways in which the responses of legacy media, online media, the police, and the public became interwoven and sustaining of one another, trading in troubling but all too familiarly longstanding raced and gendered tropes. In order to tackle the problem of misogyny in policing, in reporting, and in the wider social media surround that now envelops everything, there is a need to keep attention closely focused on the complex Russian doll processes by which such tropes nest, travel, and evolve across multiple sites and networks.

Competing Interests The author has no conflict of interests to declare that are relevant to the content of this chapter.

References

Andrejevic, M. (2007). *ISpy: Surveillance and power in the interactive era.* University Press of Kansas.

Anon. (2023a, February 17). *Nicola Bulley: Home secretary asks police to explain health disclosures.* BBC Online, https://www.bbc.co.uk/news/uk-england-lancashire-64671261

Anon. (2023b, February 19). The *Observer* view on the mistakes made in the investigation into Nicola Bulley's disappearance. *Observer*, Editorial. https://www.theguardian.com/commentisfree/2023/feb/19/the-observer-view-on-the-mistakes-made-in-the-investigation-into-nicola-bulleys-disappearance

Anon. (2024, March 3). *Sarah Everard: It will take years to repair trust—London mayor.* BBC Online, https://www.bbc.co.uk/news/uk-england-london-68461765

Banet-Weiser, S., & Maddocks, S. (2024). Networked Misogyny on TikTok: A critical conjuncture. In K. Boyle & S. Berridge (Eds.), *The routledge companion to gender, media and violence* (pp. 369–379). Routledge.

Baum, S. (2023, February 12). Nicola Bulley's next-door neighbour speaks for first time since mum disappeared. *Metro.* https://metro.co.uk/2023/02/12/nicola-bulleys-next-door-neighbour-speaks-for-first-time-18269557/

Birchall, C., & Knight, P. (2022). *Conspiracy theories in the time of Covid-19.* Routledge.

Blake, E. (2023, February 3). 'Their hair wasn't right today because that's not how mummy does it': Friend of missing mother Nicola Bulley reveals struggles of her little girls who 'know mummy is missing. *Mail Online.* https://www.dailymail.co.uk/news/article-11709587/Friend-missing-Nicola-Bulley-reveals-struggles-little-girls-know-mummy-missing.html

Bleksley, P. (2023, February 18). The Nicola Bulley case is one of the biggest disasters in British policing. *The Independent.* https://www.independent.co.uk/voices/nicola-bulley-alcohol-issues-lancashire-police-b2284141.html

Broersma, M. J., & Graham, T. S. (2013). Twitter as a news source: How Dutch and British newspapers used tweets in their news coverage, 2007–2011. *Journalism Practice, 7*, 446–464.

Bryant, B. (2023, February 13). "I feel a need to get vindication for the victim": Meet the armchair detectives determined to solve the Nicola Bulley case. *The Independent.* https://www.independent.co.uk/news/uk/crime/nicola-bulley-missing-theories-reddit-b2281369.html

Calderbank, M. (2023, February 15). Nicola Bulley update as Lancashire Police answer questions about missing mum's disappearance. *Lancashire Post*. https://www.lep.co.uk/news/crime/nicola-bulley-update-as-lancashire-police-answer-questions-about-missing-mums-disappearance-4028378

Christie, N. (1986). The ideal victim. In E. A. Fattah (Ed.), *From crime policy to victim policy* (pp. 17–30). Palgrave Macmillan.

College of Policing (CoP). (2023, November). *Independent external review of Lancashire Constabulary's operational response to reported missing person Nicola Bulley*. Retrieved February 27, 2024, from https://www.lancashire-pcc.gov.uk/wp-content/uploads/2023/11/Nicola-Bulley-independent-external-review.pdf

Coppins, M. (2023, June 14). The Gross Spectacle of Murder Fandom. *The Atlantic*. https://www.theatlantic.com/ideas/archive/2023/06/idaho-university-murders-true-crime-frenzy/674384/

Dean, B. (2024). TikTok Statistics You Need to Know. *Backlink,* 15 February. https://backlinko.com/tiktok-users

Dean, J. (2010). Affective networks. *Media Tropes eJournal, 2*(2), 22.

Dearden, L. (2023, February 17). Suella Braverman demands Lancashire Police explain disclosure of private Nicola Bulley information. *The Independent*. https://www.independent.co.uk/news/uk/crime/nicola-bulley-police-alcohol-menopause-braverman-b2283842.html

Evans, A., & Jessica, R. (2025). 'More-than-human, more-than-digital: Post-digital intimacies as a theoretical framework for intimate therapeutics and technology-facilitated sexual violence', forthcoming, *Social Media & Society*.

Femicide census. (n.d.). *Data Matters- Every Woman Matters*. Retrieved March 14, 2024, from https://www.femicidecensus.org/data-matters-every-woman-matters/

Foxcroft, L. (2009). *Hot flushes and cold science: A history of the modern menopause*. Granta.

Goulandris, A., & McLaughlin, E. (2016). What's in a Name? The UK Newspapers' Fabrication and Commodification of Foxy Knoxy. In L. Gies & M. Bortoluzzi (Eds.), *Transmedia Crime Stories*. Palgrave Studies in Crime, Media and Culture, https://doi.org/10.1057/978-1-137-59004-6_2

Greer, C. (2007). News media, victims, and crime. In P. Davies, P. Francis, & C. Greer (Eds.), *Victims, crime and society* (pp. 21–49). SAGE.

Gregory, A. (2023, February 18). Police figures criticise 'disturbing' remarks about Nicola Bulley detective's appearance. *The Independent*. https://www.independent.co.uk/news/uk/home-news/nicola-bulley-lancashire-police-rebecca-smith-b2285009.html

Hands, J. (2019). *Gadget consciousness: Collective thought, will and action in the age of social media.* Pluto Press.

Hands, J. (2023, June 5). *Tech, politics and publicness.* Retrieved March11, 2024, from https://blog.politics.ox.ac.uk/tech-politics-and-publicness/

Herbert, L. (2023, February 16). Nicola Bulley: Facebook account wiped as Lancashire Police examine missing mum-of-two's social media accounts. *The Gazette.* https://www.blackpoolgazette.co.uk/news/crime/nicola-bulley-facebook-account-wiped-as-lancashire-police-examine-missing-mum-of-twos-social-media-accounts-4029935

Horeck, T. (2019). *Justice on demand: True crime in the digital streaming era.* Wayne State University Press.

Horeck, T. (2022). #carolebaskinkilledherhusband: The gender politics of *Tiger King* meme culture. In J. Baron & K. Fuhs (Eds.), *Tiger King: Murder, Mayhem and Madness: A Docalogue*. Routledge.

Horeck, T., Ringrose, J., Milne, B., & Mendes, K. (2023). #MeToo in British schools: Gendered differences in teenagers' awareness of sexual violence. *European Journal of Cultural Studies, 0*(0). https://doi.org/10.1177/13675494231191490

Jermyn, D. (2006). *Crime watching: Investigating real crime TV*. I.B.Tauris.

Jermyn, D. (2023). 'Everything you need to embrace the change': The 'menopausal turn' in contemporary UK culture. *Journal of Aging Studies, 64*, 1–8. https://doi.org/10.1016/j.jaging.2023.101114

Jones, B. (2023). Forensic fandom: True crime, citizen investigation and social media. In G. S. Larke-Walsh (Ed.), *True Crime in American Media* (pp. 163–179). Routledge. https://doi.org/10.4324/9781003225638-11

Keaney, E. (2023, May 9). Necessity and proportionality: questions police must ask when considering sharing personal information with the public. *Information Commissioner's Office (ICO Blog).* Retrieved February 24, 2024, from https://ico.org.uk/about-the-ico/media-centre/news-and-blogs/2023/05/necessity-and-proportionality-blog/

Kendall, T. (2021). From binge-watching to binge-scrolling: TikTok and the Rhythms of #LockdownLife. *Film Quarterly., 75*(1), 41–46. https://doi.org/10.1525/fq.2021.75.1.41

Krishnan, M. (2021, September 21). Gabby Petito's case got attention. Many Indigenous and Black Cases Do Not. *Vice News*, https://www.vice.com/en/article/z3xae3/gabby-petito-case-indigenous-and-black-cases

Lazaro, R. (2023, February 5). Nicola Bulley: Witness comes forward in search for missing mum, *BBC News,* https://www.bbc.co.uk/news/uk-england-lancashire-64526426

Lecheler, S., & Kruikemeier, S. (2016). Re-evaluating journalistic routines in a digital age: A review of research on the use of online sources. *New Media & Society, 18*, 156–171.

Mahon, L. (2023, January 5). Critics slam coverage for missing black women and girls after police appeal 10 months after schoolgirl vanished. *The Voice.* https://www.voice-online.co.uk/news/uk-news/2023/01/05/critics-slam-coverage-for-missing-black-women-and-girls-after-police-appeal-10-months-after-schoolgirl-vanished/

Marshall, M. (2023, February 16) Denise Welch slams 'disgraceful' comments about missing Nicola Bulley's 'alcohol issues'. *The Express.* https://www.express.co.uk/celebrity-news/1735563/denise-welch-nicola-bulley-missing-alcohol-struggles

McAthy, R. (2012, June 21). Study: 75% of UK journalists source news from known social media contacts. *Journalism.co.uk.* https://www.journalism.co.uk/news/study-75-percent-journalists-source-news-from-known-contacts-on-social-media/s2/a549652/

McDonagh, M. (2021, October 11). Asos menopause leave? Honestly, I would rather not. *The Evening Standard.* https://www.standard.co.uk/comment/paid-menopause-leave-women-asos-would-rather-not-b959838.html

Mendes, K., Milne, B., Ringrose, J., & Horeck, T. (2021, March 18). Lockdown, violence, and understanding women's anger. *The Conversation.* https://theconversation.com/lockdown-violence-and-understanding-womens-anger-157180

Mills, E. (2022, October 16). Menopause is having a moment but for many women it's still in the shadows. *The Guardian.* https://www.theguardian.com/commentisfree/2022/oct/16/menopause-is-having-a-moment-but-for-many-women-its-still-in-the-shadows

Mills, K. (2023, February 8). Nicola Bulley: Everything we know about devoted mum—From family ties to loving dog owner. *The Mirror.* https://www.mirror.co.uk/news/uk-news/nicola-bulley-everything-know-devoted-29162126

Monroe, R. (2021, September 23). We're not posting for Gabby Petito. We're posting for ourselves. *Washington Post.* https://www.washingtonpost.com/opinions/2021/09/23/gabby-petito-justice-instagram-tiktok-investigation/

Moon, S. J., & Hadley, P. (2014). Routinizing a new technology in the newsroom: Twitter as a news source in mainstream media. *Journal of Broadcasting & Electronic Media, 58*, 289–305.

Musial, J. (2024). Pregnant and Disappeared: The Missing White Women Syndrome in magazines. In K. Boyle & S. Berridge (Eds.), *The routledge companion to gender, media and violence* (pp. 271–280). Routledge.

NHS UK. (2022). Definition of 'menopause'. Retrieved February 26, 2024, from https://www.nhs.uk/conditions/menopause/

Nichols, B. (2017). *Introduction to Documentary* (3rd ed.). Indiana University Press.

Noble, S. (2018). *Algorithms of oppression: How search engines reinforce Racism.* New York University Press.

Noyce, E. (2023, February 21). Missing dog walker Nicola Bulley's final text before she disappeared revealed. *The Independent*, https://www.independent.co.uk/news/uk/home-news/nicola-bulley-final-text-b2286210.html

Oppenheim, M. (2023, February 16). Police in Nicola Bulley case accused of stereotyping women as 'crazy' after revealing menopause struggles. *The Independent*. https://www.independent.co.uk/news/uk/home-news/nicola-bulley-menopause-alcohol-criticism-b2283843.html

Paasonen, S., Hillis, K., & Petit, M. (2015). Introduction: networks of transmission: Intensity, sensation, value. In K. Hillis, S. Passonen, & M. Petit (Eds.), *Networked Affect* (pp. 1–24). The MIT Press.

Papacharissi, Z. (2015). *Affective publics: Sentiment, technology, and politics.* Oxford University Press.

Perz, J., & Ussher, J. M. (2008). "The horror of this living decay": Women's negotiation and resistance of medical discourses around menopause and midlife. *Women's Studies International Forum., 31*, 293–299.

Platell, A. (2023, February 16). *Tweet message.* https://twitter.com/amandajplatell/status/1626149567971446792

Purnell, D. (2021, September 29). The 'Missing White Woman Syndrome' still plagues America. *The Guardian.* https://www.theguardian.com/commentisfree/2021/sep/29/the-missing-white-woman-syndrome-still-plagues-america

Robinson, M., & Tingle. R. (2023, February 3). Nicola Bulley fell into the river, police believe: Officers hold press conference to say they think missing mother's disappearance was an accident but they have found no trace of her—As they try to piece together crucial "10 minute window". *Mail Online.* https://www.dailymail.co.uk/news/article-11710399/Nicola-Bulley-fell-river-police-believe.html

Slakoff, D. (2020). The representation of women and girls of color in United States crime newss. *Sociology Compass, 14*(1), 1–13.

Spring, M. (2023, February 18). Why TikTok sleuths descended on Nicola Bulley's village. *BBC News*, https://www.bbc.co.uk/news/uk-64677595

Steffan, B. (2022, October 14.) *Menopause awareness; A double-edged sword.* University of Edinburgh Business School. Retrieved February 24, 2024, from https://www.business-school.ed.ac.uk/about/news/menopause-awareness-a-double-edged-sword

Swann, J. (2022, April 18). A Murder Solved in DMs When Daisy De La O was killed, friends looked to social media for the man they suspected had done it. They found him, *The Cut*, https://www.thecut.com/2022/04/daisy-de-la-o-murder-suspect-instagram-tiktok.html

Turner, J. (2023, January 25). Don't turn menopause into a tragic female flaw. *The Times*. https://www.thetimes.co.uk/article/dont-turn-menopause-into-a-tragic-female-flaw-5n5hf2x3p

Tweed, L. (2023, February 15). Police say missing mum Nicola Bulley had 'significant alcohol issues' linked to menopause as search continues. *Manchester Evening News*. https://www.manchestereveningnews.co.uk/news/uk-news/police-say-missing-mum-nicola-26249544

UN Women. The Shadow Pandemic: Violence against women during COVID-19 (ND) Retrieved March 13, 2024, from https://www.unwomen.org/en/news/in-focus/in-focus-gender-equality-in-covid-19-response/violence-against-women-during-covid-19

Veljanovski, L. (2023, February 21). How TikTok turned hunt for mum Nicola Bulley into "vile circus of cruelty". *Daily Mail*, https://www.mirror.co.uk/news/uk-news/tiktok-turned-missing-mum-nicola-29277429

Wanzo, R. (2008). The era of lost (White) girls: On body and event. *Differences: A Journal of Feminist Cultural Studies, 19*(2), 99–126.

Watson, S. (2022). Investigating the role of social media abuse in gender-based violence: The experiences of women police officers. *Criminology and Criminal Justice, 23*(5) https://doi.org/10.1177/17488958221087487

Whelan, L. (2023, February 9). Nicola Bulley photos show her celebrating birthday with 'cheeky prosecco' before vanishing. *The Express*, https://www.express.co.uk/news/uk/1732533/nicola-bulley-birthday-photos-facebook-missing-river-wyre

Wyatt, P. (2023, February 18). *Tweet message*. https://twitter.com/PetronellaWyatt/status/1626893496933138432024)

7

Playing Their Own Private Detectives: Digital witnessing, Forensic Fandom and True Crime Narratives

Bethan Jones and Steff El Madawi

Introduction

On 27 January 2023 mother of two Nicola Bulley disappeared while walking her dog near the river Wyre not far from her home in St Michael's on the Wyre, a small town in Lancashire. She had dropped her children off at school before emailing her employer, texting a friend to arrange a get together for their children later that week, and joining a work Teams call on her mobile phone. Thirty minutes later, at 09:33, her phone was discovered by a passer-by, still connected to Teams, on a bench near the river. Her dog, still dry, was near the bench with her harness lying on the ground. Nicola was reported missing to Lancashire Police at 11am on the 27th, with a major missing person's operation

B. Jones (✉)
Cardiff University, Cardiff, UK
e-mail: jonesbv5@cardiff.ac.uk

S. El Madawi
Huddersfield, UK

L. Gies (ed.), *Trial by Media*, Palgrave Studies in Crime, Media and Culture,
https://doi.org/10.1007/978-3-031-80593-6_7

being launched by the force the following day. A formal appeal for information was also issued on the 28th and a police press conference, in which Nicola was referred to as a 'high risk' missing person, was held on February 15. On February 19 Nicola's body was found in the river approximately a mile from where she went missing. The inquest into her death began on 26 June and was concluded the following day, a verdict of accidental death as a result of drowning being recorded.

Data from the UK's National Crime Agency for 2021/2022 reveals that there were a total of 151,845 missing persons reported to police forces in England and Wales that year[1]; of which 65,445 (43.1%) were women (National Crime Agency, 2022). While fatal outcomes were reported for 1,037 of the missing persons, 99.3% of all reported cases resulted in no harm being done.[2] On the face of it, then, there was no need to suspect initially that any harm had come to Nicola; it was possible that she had decided to leave her family with no warning. Yet as soon as details of her disappearance were made public the following day, websleuths and armchair detectives began investigating. What piqued their interest was Nicola's phone, still connected to Teams, and the dog, running around on her own. These were—for social media users—indicative of foul play and were compounded by the police subsequently releasing details about a previous visit made by police and healthcare officials to the address Nicola shared with her partner on 10 January 2023, as well as details about Nicola's health, including her 'significant issues' with alcohol as a result of her struggles with the menopause (see Jermyn and Horeck in this volume). This chapter uses the case of Nicola's disappearance to examine the intersections between digital witnessing, websleuthing and fan practices in the post-pandemic popular culture landscape. We argue that social media users co-opted Lancashire police's appeal for information as a form of proxy digital witnessing, positioning Nicola as a protagonist within a true crime story and using intelligence they 'uncovered' to craft a narrative in which they also played central parts. Drawing on content posted to social media platforms

---

[1] Missing persons data is recorded differently in Scotland and Northern Ireland so these numbers are excluded from the total.

[2] No data on gender was available in relation to fatal outcomes.

including TikTok, Reddit and YouTube we argue that when proxy digital witnessing is coupled with forensic fandom (Jones, 2023), as in this case, it not only interferes with the resolution of the case but becomes a parasitic perpetuation of a true crime narrative which does not actually exist as a crime was not committed, and which extends sometimes months or years beyond the actual event.

Witnessing and Websleuthing

To witness something means to be an observer, witnessing an event as it happens, however in practice the concept is more ambiguous. John Durham Peters notes that 'As a noun, *witness* is intricate. The term involves all three points of a basic communication triangle: (1) the agent who bears witness, (2) the utterance or text itself, (3) the audience who witnesses' (2001, p. 709, emphasis in the original). Witnesses are thus the person who observes the event and the audience who view the text describing the event. Witnessing is predicated on an invitation that institutes an ethical 'pact' and empathy structure, much like those discussed in theories of autobiography and testimony (El Madawi, 2020). The role of the witness (the agent in Peters' definition) was traditionally assumed by individuals believed to be morally unflawed and thus has typically been filled by victims, activists or dissidents (Frosh & Pinchevski, 2009; Mortensen, 2022; Wagner-Pacifici, 2015). Witnessing in this expression takes on a testimonial form, instilling 'a documentary, activist and commemorative politics around bearing witness' (Gilmore, 2017, p. 307). As Stefanie El Madawi points out, the recent #BlackLivesMatter and #MeToo movements have brought testimonial discourse to the forefront of public consciousness and reframed both 'the experiences of marginalised others, and their ability to attest to that experience […] bringing to the fore the intersectional ethics of engagement that testimonial witnessing entails' (2020, p. 9). Testimonial texts typically position the subject as a self-witness who testifies to their own experiential truth, requiring a receiver or witness to accept the testimony and bear witness to it. In traditional media witnessing testimonial texts have typically constituted of photographs, videos, recollections, court hearings and traditional journalistic reporting. Yet with the emergence of the internet and the growth of platforms such as Facebook, Instagram, YouTube and TikTok, media witnessing has to be recontextualised. The term digital witnessing may be more accurate to describe this twenty-first-century form of witnessing. For Jon Benedik Bunquin and Fatima Gaw digital witnessing can be described 'as forms of mediated witnessing emerging from the interactions and intersections of assemblages of actors, texts, and technologies governed by the affordances and logics of digital media' (2021, p. 24). As smartphone technology becomes more commonplace multiple users are able to witness and share testimony through content posted online after the fact, or livestreamed (Allan, 2013; Chouliaraki, 2010; Mortensen, 2022). Multiple audiences are also able to bear witness to this testimony and interpret it based on their own experiences, beliefs and knowledge. This is particularly the case when considering witnessing in relation to true crime—or suspected true crime—when the witness (or agent) is not in a position to share testimony.

In the Nicola Bulley case there is no first-hand account to engage with as the subject—Nicola—was missing prior to any testimony being shared. However, the invitation to bear witness (by proxy) is issued by the family and authorities in an attempt to reconstruct and/or resolve the subject's experiential truth. This initial invitation was made on 28 January 2023, when Superintendent Sally Riley issued an appeal for information from anyone who may have been in the vicinity at the time of Nicola's disappearance:

> We appeal for anyone who may have been driving through the village of St Michael's last Friday morning at about 9.15am or who may have dashcam footage that could be of use to us or people who may have been dog-walking in the area or on the towpath, to come forward. they can ring 101, or if they have a sighting of Nicola, 999. (quoted in McGee, 2023)

The Lancashire Police appeal can be seen as the issuing of a f*ormal and recognisable* invitation for information pertaining to the circumstances of Nicola's disappearance. However, we argue that it formed a request for testimony, *not* an invitation for those unconnected to, or without first-hand knowledge of, the circumstances to engage in public speculation or undertake their own investigations. In considering the communication triangle, then, we see the agent who witnesses being replaced by the agent who invites objective testimony (i.e. testimony discussing the missing subject—Nicola) and the utterance or text being replaced by the appeal for information.

Of course, police appeals for information are not uncommon. Shows like *Crimewatch* (1984–2017) reconstruct crimes in an effort to appeal to viewers who may have witnessed something and police forces around the country regularly request information via a range of means, including social media channels. The growth of networked technologies have, however, 'enhanced opportunities not only for people to consume cases but to participate in collective investigations and create their own representations' (Yardley et al., 2018, p. 85). So-called citizen investigations have taken place around a range of cases, perhaps most notably Reddit users' investigation into the perpetrator of the 2013 Boston Marathon bomber. Converging on the social media platform, users shared their collective knowledge and resources to assist the police in their investigation, including one member who claimed to have a background in military forensics and another who was a radio-controlled (RC) car enthusiast, who was able to help identify the triggering mechanism (Nhan et al., 2017). Johnny Nhan et al. suggest that 'It was the first time online communities were actively involved in conducting their own investigation into a terrorist attack concurrently with the official police investigation' (2017, p. 357) but it would not be the last. As social media platforms increased and advances in technology gave the public the means to create and share their own content, amateur detectives became involved in investigating both cold and active cases.

Elizabeth Yardley et al., argue that 'Websleuthing is the embodiment of participatory media, where the lines between the producer, consumer and subject are blurred [and] there are fewer restrictions in relation to time and space' (2018, p. 82). The 2014 premiere of the Netflix documentary *Making a Murderer* demonstrates this: focused on the 2005 trial and imprisonment of Steven Avery and Brendan Dassey for the murder of Teresa Halbach in Manitowoc, Wisconsin, the series resulted in scores of viewers taking to social media to investigate a potential miscarriage of justice. As Greg Stratton points out, websleuths responded to the documentary 'by presenting arguments, debates, and evidence that may help resolve the debates around the convictions of Avery and Dassey' (2019, p. 188). From detailed analysis of the documentary, media statements and court documents to recreating physical movements on Google maps from the period, viewers performed a literal form of forensic fandom (Mittell, 2007, 2009a, 2009b, 2009c, 2012, 2015), where fannish behaviour as mobilised via digital witnessing platforms creates communities of websleuths—what we refer to as proxy witnesses.

This has become an increasingly common phenomenon, perhaps most famously seen in the 2022 disappearance of Gabby Petito (Jones, 2023), but also visible in other true crime cases popularised by *Serial*, *Making a Murderer* and so on. Jason Mittell points out that 'fan cultures have long demonstrated intense engagement in storyworlds, policing backstory consistency, character unity, and internal logic' (2006, p. 38) and argues that programmes such as *Lost* focus this detailed dissection onto complex questions of plotting and enigmatic events in addition to storyworld and characters. This has the effect of 'convert[ing] many viewers into amateur narratologists, noting patterns and violations of convention, chronicling chronologies, and highlighting both inconsistencies and continuities across episodes and even series' (Mittell, 2015, p. 52). For Mittell, forensic fandom takes place around texts which require viewers to engage with narrative complexity—texts such as *Lost* or *Battlestar Galactica*, which add layer upon layer to the overarching narrative and often span multiple media forms, including webisodes and websites. Mittell offers the example of the fan website Lostpedia as a form of forensic fandom: 'LostPedians come together to decode episodes, theorize possible explanations, play paratextual games, and draw connections across the scope of the program and external references' (2009b). These forensic efforts enable fans to connect the narrative dots, a practice increasingly demanded by mainstream network programmes. Bethan Jones argues that this can also be applied to true crime, where viewers enact a literal form of forensic fandom. In true crime, the fan practices Mittell describes as forensic fandom are applied to real-life cases, such as the murder of Hae Lee Min, the focus of the first season of the *Serial* podcast, and the imprisonment of Steven Avery, subject of *Making a Murderer*, evidence forensic fandom. Jones argues that 'These texts are not fictional but the producers still demand the audience pay attention and, by asking questions, encourage them to join the narrative dots' (2023, p. 167). Audiences join the dots by analysing interviews, Google maps data, court transcripts and legal documents, and using digital technology to discuss the cases and share theories. Of course, both *Serial* and *Making A Murderer* were completed texts by the time audiences discovered them. In this respect the forensic fandom enacted aligns more closely with Mittell's definition. In forensic fandom as related to *ongoing* true crime events, however, audiences are not necessarily fans of the text in the way we might consider them in relation to superhero films or novels. Rather, they may be fans of the true crime genre, or followers of a specific case. It is perhaps no surprise that these forensic fandom practices spread beyond the borders of the text, especially when it comes to an ongoing case. Seeing the success these investigations can result in in cold cases it would be logical to assume they might also prove useful in real-time. And this is what we see with social media users in relation to the Nicola Bulley case.

Forensic Fandom on TikTok

We have argued that the communication triangle of witnesses proposed by Peters is recontextualised in true crime or suspected true crime cases as: (1) the agent who invites testimony and (2) the appeal for information. We now make the case that the third point of the triangle, the audience who witnesses, becomes the audience who *investigates* and therefore the audience that becomes a proxy witness. As evidenced in other cases of true crime and citizen investigation, posts, videos and communities were created on a range of platforms to discuss Nicola's disappearance. Three subreddits were created on Reddit, the largest with 6.4 members (identified as investigators in the subreddit description on the mobile app) created on the 3 February 2023. Between 27 to 30 January three tweets using the hashtag #NicolaBulley were circulated on Twitter, the number increasing from the 31 January as news of her disappearance spread. Several Nicola Bulley discussion groups were also created on Facebook during February 2023, the largest with 27,000 members at the time of writing created on 2 February, with others, including a group calling for a second inquest, created later in the year. In this chapter, however, we focus on TikTok content, partly because TikTok has been highlighted as playing a role in other cases (Aguilar et al., 2021; Barrett, 2022; Jones, 2023) but also because of the role the platform was afforded in media discourse surrounding Nicola's disappearance (Dalton, 2024; Faulkner, 2023; Sinclair, 2023; Vaughan, 2024).

TikTok allows users to create and share videos of up to 10 minutes in length and offers a range of features including the ability to 'duet' other creators' content, add voiceovers and filters, and include green screen content—the user appearing in front of content such as news reports. TikTok provides users with the opportunity to like, favourite and share videos, as well as follow other users, but unlike sites like X (formerly known as Twitter) and Facebook TikTok presents users with an endless list of algorithmically recommended content on their 'For You' page. The algorithm keeps track of users' likes, dislikes, follows, search terms, viewing duration and comments posted to curate a highly personalised experience. This, as Aguilar et al. (2021) suggest, positions criminal investigation, by way of true crime TikTok, as an *affordance* of the platform. The first TikTok videos related to Nicola's disappearance were posted between 29 and 31 January 2023 and included content from the @ghrnews and @skynews accounts. The 2-minute 15-second long Greatest Hits Radio News video featured an interview with Lancashire Police Superintendent Sally Riley offering an update on the case. The video is a standard news interview, the focus on the interviewee rather than the interviewer although the GHR-branded mic is visible in shot. The interviewer asks several questions about the search, including whether certain sections of the path should be closed and whether the search had narrowed following the weekend. The Sky News video follows a similar pattern, featuring interviews with two of Nicola's friends, one of whom describes the search that the community had organised and invites viewers to join the search and share any information they might have—functioning as a second invitation to bear witness. From the beginning comments speculated about Nicola's disappearance, suggesting that she had not simply fallen into the river as police believed. Among the 617 comments replying to the GHR News video were many suggesting that something had happened to Nicola. The most liked comment on the video states 'I cannot believe they are not treating this as a crime!!!! What!!! Are we missing something?! 🤷‍♀️😳' leading another user to respond with 'They're investigating. They have to keep an open mind and not jump to conclusions. Unlike people on the internet 😳'. The most liked comment on the Sky News video, also suggested that Nicola had been abducted, with the second most liked (151 compared to 588) suggesting that Nicola had fallen in the river while trying to rescue her dog. In the comments to both of these videos theories are introduced and discussed based on the users' understanding of the news story. The first is that Nicola has been taken; the second that she fell into the river (which was also the theory proposed by the police); and the third that she had chosen to run away. These continued to be debated with other users joining in and adding comments based on their own experiences, including how quickly their dogs' fur dries after getting wet.

While some users discussed the case based on the physical evidence—or lack thereof—at the site of Nicola's disappearance others began to look further afield. One user, commenting on the GHR News TikTok, wrote 'You should be checking her husband movements I mean just in case' while another commented on body language: 'His body language the fact he laughs no sadness whatsoever'. Similar comments were made on the various true crime accounts that began sharing the news about Nicola's disappearance. @crimeanalystpod, an account run by a Criminal Behavioural Analyst and former member of New Scotland Yard, posted a 59-second TikTok on 31 January 2023 detailing the facts of Nicola's disappearance before saying 'police have said it's not a crime enquiry but it certainly sounds like one to me'. She expands on her reasoning for this in the video's description:

> Police said they were not initially treating this as a 'crime inquiry.' I don't know why they said this. All Nicola's family and friends are worried as hell. She has two daughters who she took to school & her dog, Willow,

> was found without it's harness. Her phone was found on a bench. It seems highly unlikely she took herself off. Women don't just disappear into thin air and leave their children. More urgency is needed when women disappear. Call 101 if you have any information or 999 if you have seen Nicola #NicolaBulley #Missing #CanYouHelp #CrimeAnalyst #Expert #WomenMatter #Crime #TrueCrime #Podcast #CrimeTok

This video moves the case from a story about a missing woman to that of a potential crime, not simply because of its content or the hashtags used, but because of the person behind the account. The positioning of @crimeanalystpod as an expert through the inclusion of her degrees (a BSc and MSc), what appears to be her job title and her prior work experience gives her an air of authority that comes with a suggestion of expertise. A similar perception is afforded to many of the true crime accounts on the platform: @hantruecrime, who was also active in posting about the Gabby Petito case, posted a 55-second video providing context on the case including a comment Nicola had made online previously about how the footpath can become foggy and she finds it 'spooky'. Although comments were turned off for the post the hashtags in the description included #truecrimeTikTok, #truecrimecommunity, #crimeTikTok and #crimetok, and the music used was an instrumental piece titled 'Suspense, horror, piano and music box'. A similar soundtrack was used by a video posted by @truecrimecaitlyn. In the video, which runs to 4 minutes 29 seconds, Caitlyn discusses Nicola's father's statement that there is no evidence of Nicola slipping into the river and his question of whether someone could have taken her. She adds 'for me this [Nicola's actions and behaviour prior to her disappearance] doesn't really reflect someone who would up and leave their family, so I don't really know what could have happened to Nicola'. She ends the video by asking followers to contact the police if they have any information and stating that she will keep them up to date as the case progresses. While several commenters to the video suggest that there is something 'more' going on—that Nicola had been abducted or that her partner was somehow involved—Caitlyn refuses to be drawn on those speculations, yet the hashtags she used in the video description included #truecrime, #truecrimecommunity and #truecrimeuk. This merging of true crime with a missing person case begins to blur the boundaries between fact and fiction. While the three accounts discussed may have intended the video simply to raise awareness, the inclusion of specific hashtags suggests to viewers that it may be something more nefarious and encourages speculation in the comments.

Digital Witnessing Technologies and Trial by (Social) Media

This speculation soon began to spread to videos created by others, however, as TikTok users began using 'the digital tools that have enabled fans to collectively apply and share their forensic efforts' (Mitell, 2009, n.p.) to interrogate what they believed to be the 'key facts' in the case. These tools included software that could slow down videos in order for them to be analysed in further detail, mobile phone GPS, and wearable technology such as Nicola's Fitbit. TikTok user @thepsycologybehindit posted a video of Nicola's partner, Paul Ansell, which they had slowed down to better observe his micro expressions (see Fig. 7.1). Responding to a comment querying the point of the video they write 'If you understand micro expressions, you will see quite a few indicators of fear and deception in the clip', before expanding on their reasoning as follows:

> Eye direction is one indicator during dialogue for truth or deception. Eye direction is in relation to which part of the brain is being used…… Facial mannerisms also show us truth from lies. A verbal truth will always be congruent with the face, a lie will be incongruent So for a basic eg: if someone says yes, but shakes their head no. It's a possibility of deception.

Several users added their thoughts to the thread, agreeing that Paul's body language suggested that he had something to hide:

> that's what I noticed, his eyes are everywhere like he's searching for the right thing to say
> the weirsest one is when he looks to the far right like hes looking where nikkis body is. wonder wer he was standing

Fig. 7.1 Video posted by @thepsycologybehindit of a slowed-down interview with Paul Ansell

Comments had been made on other videos, including the GHR News and Sky News videos discussed earlier, but these technologies allowed for 'proof' to be offered by TikTok users engaging in forensic fan practices to develop their own narrative theories. These videos, circulating and recirculating on online platforms, also served to function as a trial by (social) media, accusing and convicting Nicola's partner, in particular, of being involved in her disappearance (Fig. 7.1).

The concept of trial by media is not new. Nikitha Sureshi and Lucy Sara George points out that the phrase found popularity in the late twentieth and early twenty-first centuries to 'describe the impact of television and newspaper coverage on a person's reputation by creating a widespread perception of guilt or innocence before, or after, a verdict in a court of law' (2021, p. 269). Notable examples of media influencing public opinion, and in some cases affecting the outcome of a case, include Michael and Lindy Chamberlain, who maintained that their daughter's 1982 disappearance was as a result of a dingo; Hugh Grant, who was arrested while cheating on his then-partner Liz Hurley with a prostitute in 1995; and Kate and Gerry McCann, whose daughter went missing in 2007 after they left her and her siblings alone while they went for dinner with friends. Chris Greer and Eugene McLaughlin define trial by media as:

> a dynamic, impact-driven, news media-led process by which individuals—who may or may not be publicly known—are tried and sentenced in the 'court of public opinion'. The targets and processes of 'trial by media' can be diverse, and may range from pre-judging the outcome of formal criminal proceedings against 'unknowns' to the relentless pursuit of high-profile celebrity personalities and public figures deemed to have offended in some way against an assumed common morality. (2011, p. 27)

Indeed, much of the discourse surrounding trial by media foregrounds press involvement. Yet as digital technologies enable more users to create and share their own content the concept needs to be expanded. We include the word social in the subheading for this section as sites like TikTok played a much larger role in accusing Paul Ansell than any news media, yet we bracket it because social media is ultimately part of a broader media landscape and must be considered as such, particularly in relation to real-life events.

Furthermore, it is in these forensic fan practices that we can see parallels and equivalencies in shuttle reading—that is the oscillation between text and context or subject, their testimony and the contextual framing of it—and the role that these practices play in trial by (social) media. For Felman and Laub, shuttle reading is the 'necessary work of textualization of the context' that must complement 'the very basic and critical demand for contextualization of the text' (1992, p. xv; emphasis in the original); they further contend that.

> this shuttle movement [...] – the *very tension between textualization and contextualization* – might yield new avenues of insight, both into the texts at stake and into their context – the political, historical, and biographical realities with which the texts are dynamically involved and within which their particular creative possibilities are themselves inscribed. (ibid.; emphasis in the original)

Where the autobiographical reading practices of emersion and testimonial shuttle reading overlap is in their acknowledgement of the world outside the text, the world in which the subject's experience occurred, and in which the subject does—or did—exist beyond the text. For self-referential narratives such as autobiography and testimony, the text and the context of its production are intrinsically linked, and therefore must be read in tandem. Forensic fandom does the same thing, digging into the personal lives of victims/subjects, drawing their own relational conclusions and ultimately accusations based on their findings. As discussed, the affordances of TikTok as a platform allow for this kind of reading and contribute to the trial by media which those suspected by websleuths underwent. Another video, posted by the @cometcrime account, undertakes a close reading of interview and CCTV footage to make the case that the CCTV footage showing the morning of 27 January 2023 was actually Nicola's friend Emma White (see Fig. 7.2). This feeds the theory circulating online that Paul and Emma were having an affair and murdered Nicola.

Fig. 7.2 @cometcrime video analysing interview and CCTV footage

While digital witnessing technologies were largely thought of as CCTV or even phone records a decade or two ago, they have now been expanded to include elective platforms of self-witnessing like social media and passive self-witnessing technology like GPS tracking in phones and smart watches or metadata in shared photos. Fitbit data was also analysed by TikTok users, including @crimeanalystpod. In a 2-minute video she discusses a police statement in which they stated they do not believe Nicola left the area, and notes that Nicola was wearing a Fitbit which might contain the data that corroborates the police statement. However she also adds that 'just because her Fitbit might be in that area or body of water it doesn't necessarily doesn't mean to say that Nicola is'. She then discusses the timeline of Nicola's disappearance and states that abductions can take place within seconds, clearly suggesting that she doesn't believe Nicola is in the river and that she has been taken by someone.

These developments in digital witnessing cause issues as the boundaries between fact and fiction become blurred. As Frosh and Pinchevski (2009) point out, contemporary developments in media technologies and audience participation, including mobile phones, social media content, camera phones and YouTube make media witnessing an extremely complex issue, particularly given the fact that these technologies are utilised by ordinary media users who do not have the experience, skills or training to investigate cases like Nicola's in an ethical way. Indeed, some social media users took it upon themselves to physically investigate Nicola's disappearance, a fact that some locals blamed TikTok for:

> This TikTok stuff is ridiculous. It's a lot of people playing armchair detectives and speculating about things they don't know anything about. it's not helping the police at all. These videos just attract more people who haven't got anything to contribute but just want to be part of it [...] There's even people filming themselves digging in some of the woods nearby. It's shocking. (Jon, a local dog walker, quoted in Rachman, 2023)

What Jon the dog walker describes is what Hobbs and Hoffman call 'a cultural moment dominated by stories of abuse, murder and societal despair' (2022, p. 35). These proxy witnesses feed into speculation and co-opt allegedly benign, if tragic, stories as potential true crimes awaiting discovery, exposure, investigation and ultimately resolution. Tanya Horeck argues that in the twenty-first-century true crime has become 'a multimodal entertainment 'experience'' (2019, p. 1) in which neither producers nor fans are content to bear witness in a passive way as consumers of these narratives. Rather, interactivity is solicited on both sides of the digital screen and affective reactions and responses are mobilised as a call to action. The growing popularity of the hybridisation of true crime narratives (Hobbs & Hoffman, 2022) coupled with the pervasiveness (or perverseness) of monetised social media platforms has fed into the phenomenon of forensic fandom in a 'live' and 'proactive' context—as opposed to the retrospective (and sometimes corrective) evaluation seen in cases like *Making A Murderer*.

From Proxy Witness to Proximate Witness

Unlike the content creators who serve as secondary witnesses by sharing and bearing witness while acknowledging their unique position via sensitivity statements and acknowledgements of their own outsider perspective—often referencing surviving family members and/or the need to name and humanise victims to mediate or ameliorate any potential harm—the proxy witnesses we discuss in this chapter take part in a relational (and often parasitic) bid to become part of the narrative in real time. Several newspapers reported on the attention the village was receiving, with security firms being employed to provide 'reassurance' to residents (Edrich et al., 2023). Spencer Sutcliffe, owner of one of those firms, detailed how websleuths had entered a house that overlooked the river, one of the buildings that had been searched after Nicola's disappearance, and discovered that 'the owner was actually camping in his car to stop people coming on' adding that 'We've even had people come down from Kilmarnock in Scotland, just to have a look round and take videos' (quoted in Dalton et al., 2024). At least two of those who visited the village and took videos shared them online as part of their own 'investigations'. The two best-known creators sharing content of their investigations were Explorer Danny and Curtis Media. Although

Explorer Danny has a TikTok account his main platform is YouTube, where he styles as a full-time YouTuber, explorer, paranormal investigator and debunker. He posted several videos of himself 'investigating' Nicola's disappearance including a 12 minute video which interspersed news footage with himself and his dog wandering around St Michael's on Wyre at night (see Fig. 7.3).[3] At one point in the video he tells his dog to 'find her'—in reference to Nicola—despite his dog not being trained in search and rescue or cadaver recovery; at another he breaks into an abandoned building which he believes might be where Nicola is being held with no concern for preserving the crime scene (Fig. 7.3).

Explorer Danny is obviously neither affiliated with nor trained in law enforcement or investigation but his videos received scores of comments from people commenting on how brave he was for searching for Nicola and how important his work is. This mediatisation and increased visibility leads to 'witnessing performed *in*, *by*, and *through* the media' (Frosh & Pinchevski, 2009, p. 1) and feeds not just a need to know (what Nichols (1991) calls 'epistephilia') but in extreme cases, a need to *be near to know more.*

Another example of this epistephilia can be found in Curtis Media's videos. Curtis Media drove from his home in Kidderminster to Lancashire on several occasions in order to investigate Nicola's disappearance. On one occasion he filmed a man digging in the woods near to where Nicola disappeared; on the last occasion he was able to get past

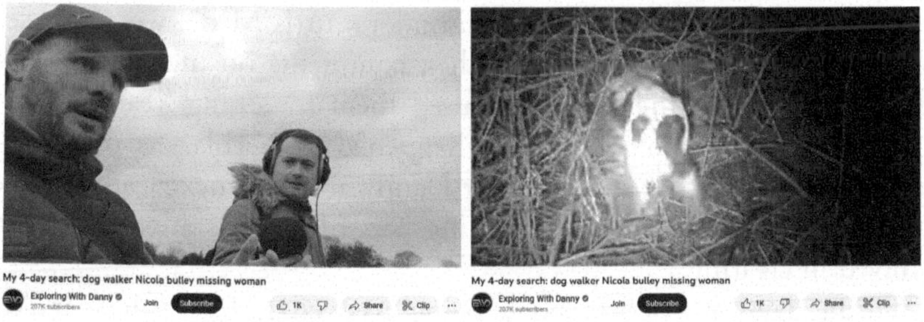

Fig. 7.3 Stills from an Explorer Danny video investigating Nicola's disappearance

[3] Explorer Danny's account has since been removed from YouTube.

a police cordon which was in place as the river was being searched by telling them he had parked his car inside it before the police arrived. He then captured video of police retrieving Nicola's body from the river Wyre and shared it on TikTok and YouTube.[4] We argue that Explorer Danny and Curtis Media are proxy witnesses who become *proximate* witnesses by inserting themselves into the narrative, not just digitally, but physically. They also perpetuate the metanarrative of Nicola's disappearance being a result of a crime beyond the digital to the physical—literally inserting themselves into the broader scope of the case and formal investigation—as part of it. Both creators were arrested due to their involvement in the investigation. Curtis Media was arrested on suspicion of malicious communications offences and perverting the course of justice after he uploaded the video of Nicola's body being recovered and was forbidden from posting, sharing or uploading content related to the case. He was subsequently re-arrested on suspicion of stalking after being banned from Lancashire as part of his previous bail conditions. Explorer Danny was detained on a public order offence and forced to pay a £90 fine under Section 4 of the Public Order Act: Fear/Provocation of Violence. Explorer Danny filmed his arrest and posted it to his YouTube channel, saying 'Hi guys, I'm being arrested on a public order offence. They've had an allegation. As you all know I was in search to find the missing woman Nicola but this is what this country's turning into. No freedom of speech' (Duffy, 2023). Unlike Paul Ansell, who underwent a trial by media because of his theoretical involvement in Nicola's disappearance, neither Explorer Danny nor Curtis Media were exposed to the court of public opinion. Rather, comments on their videos and news articles about their arrests praised them for doing 'real' work in attempting to discover what really happened to Nicola. As proximate witnesses Curtis Media and Explorer Danny are now inextricably linked with Nicola's disappearance, becoming part of the narrative they were involved in creating.

Within days of Nicola's body being recovered, Lancashire's Police and Crime Commissioner Andrew Snowden announced an independent review to understand how the force 'lost control of the narrative'.

[4] Curtis Media's channels have also been removed from both YouTube and TikTok.

He noted that 'TikTok, in particular, [saw] online amateur detectives pushing conspiracy theories out, which resulted in vile abuse towards Nicola's family and friends. How did that get so out of hand?' (quoted in Dalton, 2024). There are several reasons for this, including Lancashire police's initial response. As Deborah Jermyn and Tanya Horeck point out in this volume, a pathologisation of menopause occurred in the case which, coupled with the police force revealing information about previous calls to the Bulley/Ansell residence and Nicola's struggles with alcohol, led to a lack of trust in the official investigation. In addition Peter Faulding, the underwater search expert who joined the search, made several comments in the media criticising the police's 'low-tech' diving equipment which 'had a significant impact on the investigation and public confidence' (quoted in Cobham, 2023). This true crime narrative continued beyond the immediate circumstances surrounding Nicola's disappearance and the recovery of her body. Rather than accepting the formal account offered by the police and the coroner (which we argue is a secondary testimony—informed though impossible to confirm), fans continue to bear digital witness, appealing to their communities and questioning the so-called facts of the case. This was compounded by digital witnessing technology bearing false witness in the form of Nicola's Fitbit recording additional heart rate activity beyond her alleged time of death which fuelled further speculation, resuscitating doubt and reinvigorating websleuths in their search for the 'truth' of what happened to Nicola.

Conclusion

The inquest into Nicola's death concluded in June 2023, after which the family were forced to speak publicly about the ongoing impact of the forensic fandom practices, speculation and insistence on pursuing a true crime narrative. As willing witnesses, audiences agree to engage with narratives of subjective experience *as* truth, but absent the subject—in this case, the missing Nicola—and the secondary witnessing structure becomes skewed, tainted or co-opted by those who feel compelled to define that truth for themselves (whether based on facts or not). The proxy witnesses in Nicola's case didn't wait for an invitation—in fact they were actively disinvited from witnessing—and they disregarded multiple direct requests to stop. Discussing violent events Lilie Chouliaraki (2015) argues that the rise in ordinary media users as digital witnesses has had at least two implications for the issue of truth. Firstly, the monopoly of journalists as the only legitimate producers of media witnessing has been broken, democratising the process. Secondly, questions around ordinary media users' truthfulness as witnesses merge. Chouliaraki argues that this relates both to users' motivations (TikTok allows creators to monetise content and indeed, Curtis Media earned almost £1,000 from his video of Nicola's body being recovered), the use of everyday digital technologies like mobile phone cameras and the immediate circulation of evidence online as these tools can 'dehumaniz[e] the process of witnessing and the victims to whose suffering they provide witness [...] concealing more truth than they reveal' (2015, p. 1365). We would also argue, however, that this rise in ordinary media users as digital witnesses also lays the ground for more instances of trial by social media. Even when ordinary users make clear they are not experts in the field, they can help fuel the fires of speculation and significantly raise their online profile as a result.

Over a year after Nicola's death and new theories continue to be discussed online regarding her disappearance. TikTok user @armchairdetective posted a video in November 2023 in which they claimed the crime scene was faked while the sudden death of the Assistant Chief Constable Peter Lawson, who was involved in the investigation, was deemed suspicious by many. The disappearance of two other women—Gaynor Lord and Lucy Charles—near rivers in late 2023 and early 2024 led to speculation that a serial killer was actively targeting women and @cometcrime posted a video suggesting that Nicola's death was related to a drugs operation carried out in Blackpool and Lancashire between 2016 and 2018. While none of these users have—thus far—moved beyond the digital their content nevertheless fuels those that do. Jermyn and Horeck note that 'there is indeed violence in this case, but it is located in the collective fantasies that are spun around Bulley as a simultaneously idealised and tarnished lost white woman, which spilled out into the physical world and caused harm to her family and the community in which she lived' (2023, n.p.) Proxy witnesses find like-minded others online, forming a tribal 'digital mob' which engages in 'collective fantasy' and creates a true crime narrative out of neither truth nor crime, undertaking a trial by social media which continues even after the 'crime' has been solved.

Competing Interests The author has no conflict of interests to declare that are relevant to the content of this chapter.

References

@armchairdetective. (2023, November 25). Peter Faulding 'Man in black faked Nicola Bulley crime scene'? *TikTok*. https://www.TikTok.com/@thearmchairdetective/video/7305303181993528609

@cometcrime. (2023, April 23). Was the cctv actually Emma White? *TikTok*. https://www.TikTok.com/@cometcrime/video/7225271858881383686

@cometcrime. (2023, January 1). WTAF!!!! *TikTok*. https://www.TikTok.com/@cometcrime/video/7322449987831467297

@crimeanalystpod. (2023, January 31). Can you help? *TikTok*. https://www.TikTok.com/@crimeanalystpod/video/7194886308047703339

@crimeanalystpod. (2023, February 3). Update: One Week Ago Today Nicola Bulley Was Last Seen Walking Her Dog. *TikTok*. https://www.TikTok.com/@crimeanalystpod/video/7196055747896151338

@ghrnews. (2023, January 30). 45-year-old mum of two Nicola Bulley disappeared while walking her dog. *TikTok*. https://www.TikTok.com/@ghrnews/video/7194507524874259717

@hantruecrime. (2023, February 1). MISSING Nicola Bulley. *TikTok*. https://www.TikTok.com/@hantruecrime/video/7195175629120179461

@skynews. (2023, January 31). We are trying to hold onto hope that Nicola will be found. *TikTok*. https://www.TikTok.com/@skynews/video/7194915692716592389

@skynews. (2023, February 2). Sky News speaks to family of missing woman Nicola Bulley. *TikTok*. https://www.TikTok.com/@skynews/video/7195581713865624837

@thepsychologybehindit. (2023, February 3). Nicola Bulley partner interview. *TikTok*. https://www.TikTok.com/@thepsychologybehindit/video/7196003642820824326

@truecrimecaitlyn. (2023, February 2). This is all the information i could find at the time of this recording. *TikTok*. https://www.TikTok.com/@truecrimecaitlyn/video/7195629002743205125

Aguilar, G., Ompolasvili, S. Garcia Amaya, L., & Kerstens, S. (2021). True crime TikTok: Affording criminal investigation and media visibility in the Gabby Petito case. *Masters of Media*, 29.

Allan, S. (2013). *Citizen witnessing: Revisioning journalism in times of crisis*. Polity Press.

Barrett, N. (2022). Justice online: TikTok, platform properties and the fight for familial conviction. *Revenant Journal, 8*, 264–298.

Bunquin, J. B., & Gaw, F. (2021). Digital witnessing in a Pandemic: An assemblage analysis of the twitter hashtag network #MassTestingPH. *Southeast Asian Media Studies Journal, 3*(1), 23–52.

Chouliaraki, L. (2010). Ordinary witnessing in post-television news: Towards a new moral imagination. *Critical Discourse Studies, 7*(4), 305–319.

Chouliaraki, L. (2015). Digital witnessing in conflict zones: The politics of remediation. *Information, Communication & Society, 18*(11), 1362–1377.

Cobham, T. (2023, November 21). Nicola Bulley: Underwater search expert criticised in review of missing mother case. *The Independent*. https://www.independent.co.uk/news/uk/home-news/nicola-bulley-peter-faulding-diver-b2450949.html

Dalton, N. (2024, January 27). Exclusive: Nicola Bulley's disappearance and amateur TikTok 'detectives'—what's changed one year later? *The Mirror*. https://www.mirror.co.uk/news/uk-news/nicola-bulleys-disappearance-amateur-TikTok-31912951

Dalton, N., Smith, R., Newton, S. & Walker, A. (2024, January 27). 'The idiots won't go away': A year since Nicola Bulley's tragedy tore a community apart. *Manchester Evening News*. https://www.manchestereveningnews.co.uk/news/greater-manchester-news/the-idiots-wont-go-away-28524713

Edrich, P., Newton, S., & Fiorillo, C. (2023, February 11). Security patrols area where Nicola Bulley vanished to warn off 'TikTokers and YouTubers'. *The Mirror*. https://www.mirror.co.uk/news/uk-news/security-patrols-area-nicola-bulley-29191353

El Madawi, S. (2020). *Approaching Contemporary Cinematic I-Witnessing* (Doctoral thesis). University of Huddersfield.

Faulkner, P. (2023, May 23). Nicola Bulley: 'It was amateur TikTok detectives who were the problem'. *Lancashire Telegraph*. https://www.lancashiretelegraph.co.uk/news/23540755.nicola-bulley-it-amateur-TikTok-detectives-problem/

Felman, S., & Laub, D. (1992). *Testimony: Crises of witnessing in literature, psychoanalysis, and history*. Routledge.
Frosh, P., & Pincheski, A. (2009). Why media witnessing? Why now? In P. Frosh & A. Pincheski (Eds.), *Media witnessing: testimony in the age of mass communication* (pp. 1–19). Palgrave Macmillan.
Suresh, N., & George, L. S. (2021). Trial by media: An overview. *International Journal of Law Management and Humanities, 4*(2), 267–272.
Gilmore, L. (2017). *Testimony. a/b: Auto/biography Studies, 32*(2), 307–309.
Greer, C., & McLaughlin, E. (2011). Trial by media': Policing, the 24–7 news mediasphere and the 'politics of outrage. *Theoretical Criminology, 15*(1), 23–46.
Hobbs, S., & Hoffman, M. (2022). 'True crime and...': The hybridisation of true crime narratives on YouTube. *Crime Fiction Studies, 3*(1), 26–42.
Horeck, T. (2019). *Justice on demand: True crime in the digital streaming era*. Wayne State University Press.
Jermyn, D., & Horeck, T. (2023, June 30). *Nicola Bulley and the TikTok detectives: Missing white woman syndrome in the social media era*. Paper presented at the New Perspectives on Trial by Media Workshop. Online.
Jones, B. (2023). Forensic Fandom: True crime, citizen investigation and social media. In G. Lake-Walsh (Ed.), *True crime in American media* (pp. 163–179). Routledge.
McGee, S. (2023, January 31). Nicola Bulley: Partner of missing dog walker speaks out. *Lancashire Telegraph*, https://www.lancashiretelegraph.co.uk/news/23287531.nicola-bulley-partner-missing-dog-walker-speaks/
Mittell, J. (2006). Narrative complexity in contemporary American television. *Velvet Light Trap, 58*, 29–40.
Mittell, J. (2007, October 23). Lost in a great story. *Just TV*. https://justtv.wordpress.com/2007/10/23/lost-in-a-great-story/
Mittell, J. (2009a). 'Sites of participation: Wiki fandom and the case of Lostpedia.' *Transformative Works and Cultures, 3*. http://journal.transformativeworks.org/index.php/twc/article/view/118/117
Mittell, J. (2009b, February 25). To Spread or To Drill? *Just TV*. https://justtv.wordpress.com/2009/02/25/to-spread-or-to-drill/
Mittell, J. (2009c). Lost in a great story: Evaluation in narrative television (and television studies). In R. Pearson (Ed.), *Reading 'lost': perspectives on a hit television show* (pp. 119–138). I. B. Tauris.
Mittell, J. (2012, December 17). Forensic fandom and the drillable text. *Spreadable Media*. https://spreadablemedia.org/essays/mittell/index.html

Mittell, J. (2015). *Complex TV: The poetics of contemporary television storytelling*. NYU Press.

Mortensen, M. (2022). Perpetrator witnessing: Testing the norms and forms of witnessing through livestreaming terror attacks. *Journalism, 23*(3), 690–707.

National Crime Agency. (2022). *UK Missing Persons Unit Missing Persons Data Report 2021/22*. https://missingpersons.police.uk/en-gb/resources/downloads/download/128

Nhan, J., Huey, L., & Broll, R. (2017). Digilantism: An analysis of crowdsourcing and the Boston marathon bombings. *The British Journal of Criminology, 57*(2), 341–361.

Nichols, B. (1991). *Representing reality: Issues and concepts in documentary*. Indiana University Press.

O'Neill, M., & Fyfe, N. R. (2017). Plural policing in Europe: Relationships and governance in contemporary security systems. *Policing and Society, 27*(1), 1–5.

Peters, J. D. (2001). Witnessing. *Media, Culture & Society, 23*(6), 707–723.

Rachman, J. (2023, February 19). TikTok detectives dig up woodland near where Nicola Bulley vanished. *The Independent*. https://www.independent.co.uk/news/uk/home-news/nicola-bulley-disappearance-TikTok-detective-b2285189.html

Sinclair, H. (2023, September 22). Nicola Bulley TikTok sleuth says its 'easy to fall down a conspiracy hole'. *yahoo!news*. https://uk.news.yahoo.com/nicola-bulley-TikTok-sleuth-says-its-easy-to-fall-down-a-conspiracy-hole-132820537.html

Stratton, G. (2019). Wrongful conviction, pop culture, and achieving justice in the digital age. In D. Akrivos & A. K. Antonioupp (Eds.), *Crime, deviance and popular culture international and multidisciplinary perspectives* (pp. 177–201). Palgrave Macmillan.

Sumiala, J. (2019). Agony at a distance: Investigating digital witnessing on YouTube. In T. Eberwein, M. Karmasin, F. Krotz, & M. Rath (Eds.), *Responsibility and resistance: Ethics in mediatized worlds* (pp. 131–145). Springer VS.

Sumiala, J., Tikka, M., & Valaskivi, K. (2020). Just a 'Stupid Reflex'? Digital witnessing of the Charlie Hebdo Attacks and the Mediation of Conflict. In P. Budka & B. Bräuchler (Eds.), *Theorising media and conflict anthropology of media* (no. 10). Berghahn Books.

Vaughan, H. (2024, March 31). How 'TikTok idiots' and 'wild' conspiracy theories are disrupting police investigations. *Sky News.* https://news.sky.com/story/how-conspiracy-theorists-TikTok-sleuths-and-armchair-detectives-are-impacting-police-investigations-13103720

Wagner-Pacifici, R. (2015). Dilemmas of the witness. In M. D. Jacobs & N. W. Hanrahan (Eds.), *The Blackwell companion to the sociology of culture* (pp. 302–313). Blackwell Publishing.

Yardley, E., Lynes, A. G. T., Wilson, D., & Kelly, E. (2018). What's the deal with 'websleuthing'? News media representations of amateur detectives in networked spaces. *Crime, Media, Culture, 14*(1), 81–109.

Part III

Media Campaigns for Justice

8

'How We Brought Down a War Criminal': Defamation Cases as an Alternative Space for Justice

Maria Rae

Introduction

'How we brought down a war criminal' (Robinson, 2017) were not words the Australian police, the military or the government declared. It was a journalist who described how they had tracked down Captain Dragan Vasiljković to an Australian golf course from a tip-off he had committed horrific human rights abuses in the early 1990s while running a paramilitary unit in the former Yugoslavia. Vasiljković, an Australian citizen and Serbian commander, was involved in mass killings, torture and rape before moving back to Australia in 2004 (Aarons, 2020). In 2005, *The Australian* newspaper's journalists Natasha Robinson and Paige Taylor found and interviewed him, then published a series of articles about the war crimes allegations, which sparked an extradition notice from Croatia three months after the publication (Aarons, 2020). He was arrested and imprisoned during which time Vasiljković launched 13

M. Rae (✉)
Deakin University, Geelong, VIC, Australia
e-mail: maria.rae@deakin.edu.au

L. Gies (ed.), *Trial by Media*, Palgrave Studies in Crime, Media and Culture, https://doi.org/10.1007/978-3-031-80593-6_8

Federal Court actions attempting to halt his extradition, and two High Court appeals of Full Federal Court decisions (Aarons, 2020). The Full Federal Court ruled his extradition would be unjust but in 2009 the High Court overturned the decision and Vasiljković fled from justice (Aarons, 2020). He was found, extradited and, in 2017, he was finally convicted for war crimes and sentenced to prison for 15 years.

The extraordinary aspect of this case is that, in the meantime, Vasiljković launched a defamation case against *The Australian* newspaper and this civil trial preceded the criminal court proceedings. As Aarons (2020, p. 39, my emphasis) writes:

> The paper vigorously defended the case, spending considerable amounts on both legal costs and on gathering evidence from cyewitnesses in Croatia and bringing some of those whose testimony was especially powerful. Although conducted under civil, not criminal, law *the case was in effect the only successful war crimes trial ever held in Australia.*

This was because the judge ruled that the imputations against Vasiljković were substantially true, to a civil standard of proof, and ordered him to pay $1.5 million to the newspaper to cover some of its legal costs, but this money was never recovered (Aarons, 2020). It is worth quoting Aarons (2020) extensively again to demonstrate the uniqueness of this case study:

> Vasiljković's defamation case demonstrated that with determination war crimes trials could be successfully conducted in Australian courts...But the array of eyewitnesses brought from Croatia by *The Australian* underlined the federal government's dereliction of its duty to apprehend accused war criminals and try them in either our own justice system or extradite them to a country where the crimes were allegedly committed. This, of course relies upon our government having the investigative tools and political will to bring war criminals to justice, not leaving it to the media to make the case and expend considerable resources to carry out the government's role.

This case study raises questions of the media's role as an alternative space for justice for holding perpetrators accountable for war crimes. On the one hand, this defamation case could be considered a trial by media as it can subvert procedural justice, invert the principle of innocent until proven guilty and cause reputational damage to further the commercial and ideological agendas of corporate news organisations (Greer & McLaughlin, 2012). However, given its successful defence of truth, this case may be conceived as 'media justice' (Greer & McLaughlin, 2012, p. 413) which can 'sometimes exercise parallel functions of justice, potentially fulfilling in the eyes of the public a role that lies beyond the capacity of institutional justice' (Machado & Santos, 2009, p. 147). This chapter questions how we can conceptualise 'trial by media' and the role of investigative journalism in the context of defamation cases. Firstly, this chapter examines the complex intersection of Australia's legal framework for prosecuting war crimes, the concentrated media landscape and how this impacts investigative journalism, and defamation laws to establish the research problem of why a defamation case became the first successful war crimes trial. It then analyses the media coverage of this case to determine how the main actors viewed *The Australian* newspaper's role in its reportage. Firstly, it finds that defamatory reporting can be conceptualised as a trial by media due to its capacity for reputational damage. Secondly, that if a news organisation successfully defends its reporting it can be conceptualised as media justice. It should be noted that if a media company is unsuccessful in defending its reportage as truth, then this could be conceived inversely as a form of defamatory injustice. Finally, it argues that the role of investigative journalism is critical in pursuing media justice and institutional accountability for war crimes. However, it argues this role is seriously challenged by the financial costs and states must take the lead role in investigating and prosecuting human rights abuses in formal legal proceedings. Subsequently, a 'trial by media' in the form of media justice holds the potential to expose crimes in the public interest and be an alternative space for justice that brings attention to the shortcomings of legal proceedings and the protection of human rights.

War Crimes and Trial by Media

War Crimes Prosecutions in Australia

Australia has a poor track record of holding perpetrators accountable for war crimes through legal prosecutions. The country had initially demonstrated its commitment to accountability for human rights abuses when it signed up to the Genocide Convention Act in 1949. However, the case of Nulyarimma v Thompson in 1999 exposed how there was no domestic law of criminalising and prosecuting genocide in Australian courts (Guilfoyle, 2001; Mitchell, 2000). Subsequently, the passing of the International Criminal Court (Consequential Amendments) Act in 2002 created offences for genocide, war crimes and crimes against humanity. Despite this, there is still no legal framework for prosecuting war crimes before 2002 (Boas, 2004) and Australia has yet to prosecute any perpetrators 'arguably reflecting both disinterest and a lack of clear policy' (Boas & Chifflet, 2016).

A lack of media and public discourse has also been blamed for Australia's inertia when it comes to addressing human rights abuses. Boas and Chifflet (2016) argue that the public view war crimes as distant conflicts that are dealt with overseas in institutions such as the Hague. As they write,

> From time to time, an ageing Nazi or runaway Serb appears in the headlines of the popular press. However, these are aberrations, absent from the experience of most Australians. Popular discourse surrounding Australian participation in armed conflict very rarely considers the laws of war or war crimes. The consequence is that there is no electoral capital to be made on the issue from the broad majority of voters. (Boas & Chifflet, 2016, p. 77)

Scott (2004) agrees that genocide is considered a distant problem, which in the broader context of human rights discourse pits the Global South evil savage against the good Western saviour such as the United Nations (Mutua, 2001). However, Scott (2004) goes even further in arguing that the media actively worked against policy moves to investigate war crimes perpetrators, citing the unsuccessful trials in the 1980s of three Nazis who became Australian residents (Aarons, 2020). As she argues, 'controversy surrounded the cases, in part because of a lack of political will to cover the necessary financial costs and in part due to the media supported impression of victimising old men for events that had occurred a long time ago' (Scott, 2004, p. 169). In this example, the media represented alleged war criminals as victims of an overzealous legal system. This case study also illustrates the economic costs for states pursuing justice for human rights abuses.

Despite the challenges of holding war criminals accountable, there seems to be a recent shift in Australian policy. In 2016, the Inspector-General of the Australian Defence Force was tasked with investigating allegations that soldiers had committed human rights abuses while serving in Afghanistan. The subsequent report found 'credible evidence' that elite soldiers unlawfully killed 39 people in Afghanistan (IGADF, 2020, pp. 40–41). A critical analysis of the inquiry report argues that significant reforms are possible through such investigations, however, they can also fail to address lawful harm that might be unethical, can exceptionalise illegal behaviour rather than see it as a systemic problem and can reproduce problematic assumptions about toxic military cultures (MacKenzie et al., 2023). Since the report was handed down, a former special forces veteran Oliver Schulz was the first Australian soldier to be charged with a war crime and is awaiting trial (McKinell, 2023). In a case very similar to the Vasiljković defamation trial, Australia's most decorated soldier Ben Roberts-Smith has also been found in a civil court to have been complicit in the murder of four Afghan men (Housden & Turnbull, 2023). The ruling came after Roberts-Smith sued three Australian newspapers for defamation after they reported he had committed war crimes. At the time of writing this chapter, he has appealed the finding and there have been no criminal charges against Roberts-Smith. It appears that a shift in media and public discourse may prompt stronger policy action from governments. As Boas and Chifflet (2016, p. 77) note, 'in the past, Australia's war crimes policy has been shaped by the need for governments to avoid scandalous injustice'. Likewise, McCormack and Simpson (1994) state that prosecutions 'have tended to be highly controversial, and occasionally embarrassing, attempts by national governments to respond to the prevailing public mood'. Therefore, the media's coverage of war crimes seems to be somewhat influential in documenting and making visible atrocities to the public, which may have an impact on public policy.

Media, Investigative Journalism and Defamation Law in Australia

Australia's media ownership is among the most concentrated in the developed world. Reporters Without Borders (2024) has highlighted the concerning way in which Australia's media resemble an oligarchy, with little diversity of sources and has ranked the country 39th in the world for press freedom. A recent report found Australia has the second-highest media concentration in the world and the newspaper sector is dominated by four companies who control 84% of the market (Flew et al., 2024). There are also almost 200 small, independently owned commercial publications, in local and regional areas, however, the COVID-19 pandemic has taken a devastating toll on the press with more than 150 newsrooms closing (Hess, 2020; Meade, 2020). The internet has facilitated new digital-only entrants to the market, but none of these have challenged the dominance of incumbent legacy media (Wake, 2020). Furthermore, the rapid transition from print to digital media has precipitated an ongoing crisis in funding for journalism in Australia where publishers are 'not earning enough from digital revenues to abandon print, yet digital subscriptions are cannibalising print subscription revenue' (Carson, 2015, p. 1037). The situation is somewhat better for broadcast media but even so, Australia is placed 13th out of 18 Western countries for per capita public funding of radio and television (Nordicity, 2020). As Bennett and Rae (2021) argue, government subsidies, such as those in Nordic countries, could improve and strengthen Australia's media landscape, particularly in adopting the view that journalism is a public good.

In a liberal democracy like Australia, the media should be considered a public good as it informs citizens to make political choices, such as when voting, while supporting scrutiny of powerful and elite figures and institutions (McNair, 2000). The media's main roles are to: inform citizens; educate the public on the facts; provide a platform for political discourse; play a watchdog role to hold power accountable and serve as a channel for the advocacy of political viewpoints (McNair, 2017). However, this ideal normative role has been challenged to the point of being a crisis of public communication (Blumler & Gurevitch, 2002). This has been blamed on the growth of public relations (Habermas, 1989), an ideological bias due to increased media ownership (Curran, 2002; Herman & Chomsky, 1988; McChesney, 2016) and the use of media power to distort or influence the public agenda; 'for example, in the ways that the press outlets of Rupert Murdoch's News Corp have sought to influence electoral outcomes and policy-making processes in several countries, including Australia, the UK and the US' (McKnight & McNair, 2012). *The Australian* newspaper, the only daily national broadsheet and owned by News Corp, has a relatively small audience, which is skewed towards older, wealthier, university-educated men in professional jobs (Young, 2011, p. 44). It is also widely read by the elite political class, is an active player in influencing politics and sometimes shows overt political bias in its reporting (Manne, 2011; McKnight, 2012; Tiffen, 2014). For example, *The Australian* actively campaigned against a press council and other media accountability mechanisms (Young, 2015).

Despite these challenges, investigative journalism is the form of media that is most likely to uphold this ideal role of holding power to account. As Schudson (2008) argues, it not only exposes abuses of power but serves as a deterrent to wrongdoing. Carson (2019, p. 92) identifies five essential features of investigative journalism:

> The story must be exclusive or revelatory in a way that sets the news agenda rather than follows it; the revelation belongs in the public domain and it is in the public's interest to know about it; and the story (or story series) contains evidence of serious efforts to verify information rather than simply compile competing perspectives. Investigative stories also show evidence of active reporting and are not the result of a press release

or passive observation such as a court report. Lastly, through the examination of the investigative series or story, it is apparent that it took time and effort by the journalist to produce.

Other functions include identifying 'victims and villains', investigating a breach of public trust, pursuing a suppressed truth in the public interest and implying a moral standard (Carson, 2019, p. 92).

However, investigative journalism is expensive to produce as journalists need time and resources, such as travel and legal costs, to find and defend a story (Birnbauer, 2012, p. 83). This means a media company's profit-making motives can result in neglect of costly investigative journalism (Curran, 2002, p. 225). Despite this, scholars find that 'the public interest function of journalism and its economic imperatives do not have to be mutually exclusive' (Carson & Farhall, 2018). This is because investigative journalism is both normatively and economically valuable (Hamilton, 2016) and it 'can drive audiences to a news outlet if it is quality reporting' (Carson, 2019, p. 226). Furthermore, digital media can provide opportunities for funding and support reporting practices such as news companies collaborating on investigative stories (Carson & Farhall, 2018). So as Carson (2014) found, although Australian newspaper revenues and circulations have declined, the amount of investigative reporting (with the exception of corporate stories) had not, in part, because it is beneficial for a news company's reputation as it sets the agenda. However, the threat of defamation is another challenge for investigative journalism.

Australia has been called the 'defamation capital of the world' with laws that impede reporting on matters of public interest (Lim, 2019). In a survey by Australia's journalist union, '89% of respondents believed that Australia's defamation laws made reporting more difficult. Some 32% of respondents said that in the previous 12 months they had a news story "spiked" or dropped because of fears of a defamation action' (MEAA, 2021). As Lim (2019) argues, 'Australia's unique legal situation arises out of its lack of a Bill of Rights or any explicit constitutional guarantee of freedom of speech. Against this backdrop, Australia's defamation law tends to privilege the right to reputation over freedom of expression. Defending an action is often far costlier than settling, making the law especially punitive for media companies'. Scholars have also found that 'defamation law is perceived to have a more direct, and potentially chilling, effect in Australia' than in the USA (Kenyon & Marjoribanks, 2003). This research found that newsrooms manage defamation through reliance on the experience and judgement of senior journalists and there is active negotiation of these laws between media organisations and legal advisers (Kenyon & Marjoribanks, 2003). In Australia, 'the plaintiff needs to prove three things: the defendant published material, which identified the plaintiff, and which would harm the plaintiff's reputation. Once these elements are established, the material must be defended by truth, comment, qualified privilege or other defences' (Kenyon & Marjoribanks, 2003, p. 34). In 2021, the defence of public interest was introduced in reforms, which will help traditional media fend off defamation cases through demonstrating the integrity of their sources and balanced reporting, however, this defence can succeed even if the media company used malice (Douglas, 2020). Defamation can be considered an outcome of trial by media because it can cause reputational damage through sensational reporting and preceding any formal legal proceedings.

Trial by Media and Alternative Spaces of Justice

Greer and McLaughlin (2017, p. 120) provide a comprehensive definition of trial by media as 'a market-driven form of populist justice in which individuals and institutions are accused, prosecuted, judged, sentenced and permanently stigmatized in the "court of public opinion"'. There are dangers a trial by media will subvert procedural justice, invert the principle of innocent until proven guilty and cause reputational damage that can further the commercial and ideological agendas of corporate news organisations (Greer & McLaughlin, 2012). Specifically, Greer and McLaughlin (2011, p. 27) have identified how a trial by media can undermine legal processes:

> Due process and journalistic objectivity can give way to sensationalist, moralizing speculation about the actions and motives of those who

> stand accused in the news media spotlight. Judicial scrutiny of 'hard evidence' yields ground to 'real time' dissemination of disclosures from paid informants, user-generated content, and hearsay and conjecture from 'well-placed sources'. Since the news media substitute for the prosecution, judge and jury, the target may find themselves rendered defenceless.

However, scholars have begun to consider the benefits that a trial by media might have in cases of injustice. Machado and Santos (2009, p. 148) describe it as 'the media frenzy following the discovery of a crime and which precedes the court trial. The media engage in a search to find the 'truth' and uphold the public interest'. Such 'media justice' (Greer & McLaughlin, 2012) can potentially hold powerful figures and states to account. In some cases, the media can 'exercise parallel functions of justice, potentially fulfilling in the eyes of the public a role that lies beyond the capacity of institutional justice' (Machado & Santos, 2009, p. 147). Similarly, Karniel (2014, p. 117) contends that the media has developed into 'a parallel forum where the contest between the prosecution and the defence over the guilt or innocence of an accused is carried out. The media also moulds the public's opinion about the legal institutions and has a great impact on the public's faith in these institutions'.

There is the possibility for institutional accountability, which is often difficult to achieve in legal processes which focus on individual culpability. As Greer and McLaughlin (2017, p. 123) note, when scandal implicates the state as the responsible authority, it is forced to act. In this sense, a trial by media can be political and challenge the establishment and elites (Greer & McLaughlin, 2017, p. 121), thereby becoming 'alternative platforms for delivering "justice" to victims who for decades may have been denied legal recourse by institutional and state cover-up' (Greer & McLaughlin, 2017, p. 129). Karniel (2014, p. 188) has shown in his analysis of public figures on trial for human rights abuses that the media has the potential to produce a public judgement that is better than a court outcome. As Greer and McLaughlin (2017) argue:

> The news media have always been a key site where justice is seen to be done. Today, however, UK newspaper corporations are redefining

> what justice is, and how it can and should be achieved. Victim-centred campaigns are exposing the scandalous institutional failure of the UK criminal justice system to provide public protection. In a context of heightened crime consciousness and declining confidence in the effectiveness of contemporary governance, trial by media is creating and delivering an alternative and highly distinctive form of justice.

Greer and McLaughlin (2012, p. 397) have also discussed how a trial by media 'reclaims 'justice' from the courts and returns it to a networked citizenry' in such a way that can lead to formal prosecutions, and they argue, 'in that sense its democratic potential should not be overlooked'. It 'may function as a discursive flashpoint, upon which moral boundaries may be formed and reformed', can influence police investigations and provide a forum for restorative justice (Chagnon & Chesney-Lind, 2015, p. 2). Those from subordinated groups, such as women, have used social media to make claims of sexual assault and violence with the potential to create online counter-publics that challenge the dominant discourse on gendered crimes (Powell, 2015; Salter, 2013). Likewise, detained asylum seekers and refugees employ social media and new digital technology to make justice claims and expose human rights abuses (Rae et al., 2017, 2019). Although highly problematic, a trial by media has the potential to address injustice when the public or victims perceive the legal system to be failing or constrained in certain functions. Indeed, war crimes survivors and those who advocate for justice after conflict perceive the media's key functions are to expose crimes, bear witness to crimes, name perpetrators, influence public opinion and apply pressure on legal and political institutions to respond to human rights abuses (Rae, 2020). However, they also recognise the media is limited in delivering justice and, therefore, a trial by media could be conceived of more as an accountability mechanism that has the capacity to draw attention to the shortcomings of official legal responses and processes (Rae, 2020). Simply put, it cannot deliver justice through a formal judgement in a court of law to a higher legal standard of proof. Another key aspect of the media's limitations is whether a news organisation is willing to risk the time and resources to pursue justice for human rights abuses. As Greer and McLaughlin (2017) argue:

> Newspaper corporations must only be convinced that it is sufficiently compelling to justify the risk of libel action. Those who deny the charges and attempt to fight back through public statements or legal retaliation risk intensified scrutiny aimed at uncovering further evidence of their guilt. Media justice is a parallel and, at times, more visible, easily intelligible, and immediately impactful justice paradigm than that represented by the increasingly dysfunctional criminal justice process. Its core mechanisms—trial by media and institutional scandal hunting—form the basis of a business model that has been adopted by all UK newspaper corporations system.

In the following case study, I examine how the key actors perceive *The Australian* newspaper's role in reporting on war crimes to analyse how this aligns with the current conceptualisations of a trial by media.

Captain Dragan on Trial and Media Justice

This section analyses the media coverage of Dragan Vasiljković, his legal proceedings and the defamation case. An initial search on the Newsbank database using his name 'Dragan Vasiljković' resulted in 923 results from the first story on 7 August 1991 when he was still living in Belgrade. The articles that mentioned the case briefly in the context of other topics were excluded. Once this was done, a thematic analysis was conducted on the remaining data. Thematic analysis is a method for identifying, organising, analysing and reporting patterns found within a data set (Braun & Clarke, 2006). It is also a powerful tool for understanding thoughts, experiences and behaviours across a data set (Braun & Clarke, 2012). The data was analysed for themes that corresponded to the literature on Australia's war crimes legal framework, trial by media and investigative journalism. Firstly, it found that defamation trials can be conceptualised as a trial by media due to its capacity for sensational reporting and reputational damage. Secondly, that if a news organisation successfully defends its reporting it can be conceptualised as media justice. Finally, it argues that the role of investigative journalism is critical in pursuing media justice and accountability for war crimes. However, it argues this role is seriously challenged by the financial costs and states must take the lead role in investigating and prosecuting human rights abuses in formal legal proceedings.

Defamatory Reporting as a Trial by Media

The exact term 'trial by media' was never used in the news coverage of the Dragan Vasiljković case study. However, there are corresponding terms used in the reporting of the case that align with conceptualisations of this phenomenon such as when individuals are accused in the media and the court of public opinion (Greer & McLaughlin, 2017, p. 120). In response to *The Australian's* first story, Vasiljković said, 'this is just part of [war] propaganda…what surprises me is that they are making *accusations*, specific *accusations* like killing, rape, murder. I mean, when you put that next to someone's name you had better come up with some evidence. [The article] has not been checked, it has not been cross-checked. It says I led the troops which participated in organised rape of women and children – that's a very, very serious *accusation*' (Quinlan, 2005, my emphasis). From this perspective, an individual is accused and stigmatised of being a killer, rapist and murder in the 'court of public opinion' without evidence. There are also dangers a trial by media can undermine legal processes when reporting is sensationalist (Greer & McLaughlin, 2011, p. 27). This aligns with Vasiljković's suing of *The Australian* over an article that he says 'sensationally portrayed him as someone who had authorised and condoned murder, torture and rape' (Madden, 2009a, 2009b, 2009c, 2009d, p. 3). A group called Serbs for Justice and Democracy also issued a press release condemning the 'scandalous allegations that have been circulating against [Mr Vasiljković]' (Madden, 2009a, 2009b, 2009c, 2009d, p. 3). From this perspective, it appears that Vasiljković and his supporters view the reporting as a sensational accusation akin to conceptualisations of a 'trial by media'.

Greer and McLaughlin (2012) also argue that a trial by media can subvert procedural justice. Vasiljković, when in court said that, 'your witnesses you have brought here to pervert the course of justice have holes which can be found in two hours' (Milavanovic, 2009, p. 5). In other court evidence, a friend of the complainant said 'Vasiljković had often told him how "very upset" he was by the September 2005 article in *The Australian*, because it had "started the whole, unjust [extradition] process"' (Madden, 2009a, 2009b, 2009c, 2009d, p. 7). In this example, Vasiljković calls the reportage of his crimes a perversion of justice that started an unjust legal proceeding. Perhaps the most critical connection between defamation cases and trial by media is the harm to reputation. Australian defamation law states that the plaintiff needs to prove the published material would harm the plaintiff's reputation (Kenyon & Marjoribanks, 2003, p. 34). And one danger of a trial by media is that it can cause reputational damage (Greer & McLaughlin, 2012). In this case, Vasiljković told the Supreme Court, 'I think every Serb on the planet of the earth - or at least 90% of them - considers me as a hero' (Madden, 2009a, 2009b, 2009c, 2009d, p. 3). This suggests that he would suffer great reputational damage due to the allegations. Moreover, Greer and McLaughlin (2011, p. 27) argue that, 'since the news media substitute for the prosecution, judge and jury, the target may find themselves rendered defenceless'. This appears to be how Vasiljković perceived the accusations as he was quoted saying, 'the trial had been a 'sham': and likened it to a 'David and Goliath' contest, given the resources of Nationwide News as part of the News Corporation group, as well as the involvement of the Croatian government. 'It was David and Goliath, only David was handcuffed too', he said. 'How could I get a fair trial with all these forces working against me?' (Warne-Smith, 2009, p. 1). In this example, Vasiljković sees himself as rendered defenceless to protect his reputation against the media organisation and the state. Although, as commentator (Goldberg, 2009, p. 18) wrote, 'the evidence now emerging in the legal action may well be more damaging to Captain Dragan's reputation than the original article'.

Finally, this defamation case aligns the conceptualisation of a trial by media as 'the media frenzy following the discovery of a crime and which precedes the court trial' (Machado & Santos, 2009, p. 148). There was no mechanism to delay the defamation trial although there were pending criminal proceedings. A defamation lawyer Leanne Norman was quoted as saying, 'I definitely think the criminal proceedings should go first…The criminal justice system is more important than people's civil rights and it must take priority' (Merritt, 2017, p. 1). Similarly, the

Australian Press Council chairman Ken McKinnon said he 'did not see how it would help justice to permit the issue of defamation to supersede the question of whether war crimes had taken place. "It's a subsidiary issue. It's crazy"' (Merritt, 2017, p. 1). Therefore, defamatory reporting can be considered an outcome of trial by media because it can cause reputational damage through sensationalism and preceding any formal legal proceedings. Defamation actions can be seen as a response to defending oneself against trial by media. The next section will consider to what extent, if any, this case can be conceptualised as media justice.

Defamation Cases as Media Justice

The Australian newspaper's coverage of Dragan Vailjkovic obviously set the agenda on exposing the war criminal and subsequent legal proceedings. This was actively acknowledged and promoted in the newspaper with quotes such as '*The Australian* has played a central role in Dragan Vasiljković's apparently imminent departure, revealing in 2005 that he had returned to Australia to work as a golf instructor in Perth' (Ferguson, 2015, p. 3), 'the Oz's journos are Dragan slayers...We couldn't be prouder of our present and past Oz colleagues who pursued this butcher' (The Australian, 2017b, p. 13) and 'it was a dogged, difficult and important legal battle of which we are extremely proud. Justice, at least to some degree, appears to have been done. This newspaper and its reporters have played a vital role' (The Australian, 2017a, p. 13). As *The Australian*'s editor Paul Whittaker said, 'We were forced to effectively run a war crimes trial in the NSW Supreme Court' (Merritt, 2017, p. 1).

This positioning of the newspaper as a central player aligns with the notion of 'media justice' (Greer & McLaughlin, 2012), which can hold powerful figures, such as war commanders in this case, to account. The editor's assertion that the media effectively ran a war crimes trial can also be seen as exercising parallel forums for justice (Karniel 2014, p. 117; Machado & Santos, 2009, p. 147). As discussed earlier, the lack of media and public discourse about Australia's legal framework on war crimes has led to a passive policy position often shaped by governments avoiding scandal, controversy or embarrassment (Boas & Chifflet,

2016, p. 77; McCormack & Simpson, 1994). As Greer and McLaughlin (2017, p. 123) note, when scandal implicates the state as the responsible authority, it is forced to act. In this case, the media's coverage of Vasiljković's crimes prompted Croatia's extradition order, which meant the Australian government had to act.

The Australian's news coverage and subsequent defamation case may also be considered media justice in the sense that it gave a voice to victims. The story was initiated from a tip-off from the community, as journalist Natasha Robinson (2017) recounts, 'I had heard from contacts in both the Serbian and Croatian diasporas in Australia that Vasiljković, who was born in Belgrade and emigrated to Australia aged 14, was back in his adopted country'. This sparked the investigation and, in that way, 'reclaims 'justice' from the courts and returns it to a networked citizenry' in such a way that can lead to formal prosecutions (Greer & McLaughlin, 2012, p. 397). *The Australian* also told the stories of those Vasiljković had tortured and raped, so effectively served as an 'alternative platform for delivering "justice" to victims who for decades may have been denied legal recourse by institutional and state cover-up' (Greer & McLaughlin, 2017, p. 129). One woman, who Vasiljković raped, had told her story to *The Australian* before it was heard in the defamation trial. When asked 'how she felt when she saw the news about the arrest of Mr Vasiljković, "I was stunned because [I thought] he was out of reach of our law. At last … I was really happy that he was captured"' (Madden, 2009a, 2009b, 2009c, 2009d, p. 3). These victims then gave evidence directly to the courts in the defamation trial. Importantly, these allegations of war crimes were heard in a court of law and believed. As Judge Latham wrote in her judgement, 'It was obvious to anyone in the courtroom that the memory of her experience was still painful and distressing' (NSW Supreme Court, 2009, para. 145). The widow of a journalist who Vasiljković had murdered was present at his sentencing in Croatia and said 'I will always be grateful to all the people who helped to find justice in this case. I am especially grateful to *The Australian* and its reporter Natasha Robinson, who found Dragan Vasiljković in Australia' (Schloetzer-Scotland, 2017, p. 10) As *The Australian* newspaper (2017b, p. 13) wrote, 'Justice at last for Dragan Vasiljković's dozens of victims during the 1990s conflict… *The Australian* did not stop fighting for them'. Despite this fight for media justice, there are obvious limitations to what role a news organisation and its investigative journalists can play as an accountability mechanism for war crimes.

The Role of Investigative Journalism in Media Justice and Its Limitations

The Australian newspaper's coverage falls under the definition of investigative journalism, according to Carson's (2019, p. 92) five essential features of this distinct form of news reporting. *The Australian* stories fulfil those features as it was an exclusive story that set the agenda in the public interest to expose war criminals. The story took time, effort and active reporting to verify facts and track down Vasiljković to a golf course where one of the journalists confronted and interviewed him:

> I had no leads on where he was living, so I drew up a list of places we might start to look. I knew he sailed yachts. I knew he played golf. I knew he'd been raising money via the Serbian community for his Belgrade-based charitable foundation. I set about calling marinas, Serbian community organisations and golf clubs. When the trail started pointing us to Perth, Paige made a phone call to a Serbian community centre in Maddington which happened to have a golf course attached. (Robinson, 2017)

The series of stories identified the victims and Vasiljković as the villain, implied a moral standard that war crimes were wrong and pursued the suppressed truth of his human rights abuses. As one of the investigative journalists Natasha Robinson wrote on social media when Vasiljković was sentenced to jail: 'What journalism can do. An investigation, a paper that backed the story, now 15 years in a Croatian prison' (*The Australian*, 2017b, p. 13). This also aligns with the notion of media justice 'in a search to find the 'truth' and uphold the public interest' Machado and Santos (2009, p. 148). *The Australian* newspaper also used the defence of truth in its defamation case.

However, investigative journalism is expensive to produce as journalists need time and resources, such as travel and legal costs, to find and defend a story (Birnbauer, 2012, p. 83). The newspaper's editor Paul Whittaker said a team of lawyers went to former Yugoslavia to gather evidence for the defamation case at enormous cost to the media company. As he said:

> We undertook work normally left to the criminal courts or The Hague, albeit with a less onerous burden of proof. That we were compelled to take this course of action should concern anyone with a commitment to justice, press freedom and the public's right to know. It would have been easier - and cheaper - to settle but we had strong evidence to back a story that we believed was manifestly in the public interest. Mainstream media outlets, like our own, accept the ethical responsibility to pursue issues in the public interest. It is our core business to reveal stories such as that of Captain Dragan. (*The Australian*, 2009, p. 13)

These comments align with Greer and McLaughlin's (2017) argument that newspapers must be convinced that the risk of libel action is justified and that media justice and trial by media form the basis of a business model for press organisations. Similarly, it further shows that 'the public interest function of journalism and its economic imperatives do not have to be mutually exclusive' (Carson & Farhall, 2018). However, the editor's comments also echo the concerns about an ongoing crisis in journalism funding (Carson, 2015). As *The Australian* (Merritt, 2017, p. 1) commentary notes:

> There might once have been a time when media outlets could simply absorb that sort of cost. But not anymore. Hundreds of jobs in newspapers have disappeared and they are not coming back. Paul Whittaker, editor-in-chief of *The Australian*, believes this case shows that the justice system is out of step with the financial reality confronting the media industry. On one level, the justice system — here and in Croatia — has vindicated this newspaper. But the Australian aspect of the Captain Dragan case has set a dreadful precedent. Who will risk exposing the next war criminal?

As Schudson (2008) argues, investigative journalism not only exposes abuses of power but serves as a deterrent to wrongdoing. Therefore, this case also provides evidence that the threat of defamation is another critical challenge for investigative journalism (MEAA, 2020; Lim, 2019; Kenyon & Marjoribanks, 2003). These comments are also highly critical of the passive role that the state took in investigating these war crimes, leaving the burden to the newspaper. As Scott (2004, p. 169) argues, governments can be reluctant to do so precisely 'because of a lack of political will to cover the necessary financial costs'. This defamation case was not only successful in defending the truth of these war crimes but in leading to successful criminal prosecutions. However, it is limited in holding institutions to account such as the Australian government for its passive war crimes policy. This case has provided further evidence of how the legal framework failed to address human rights abuses.

Conclusion

This chapter has contributed to an expansion of how we can understand a trial by media and the role of investigative journalism in the context of defamation cases. It finds that defamatory reporting can be conceptualised as a trial by media due to its capacity for reputational damage. However, if a news organisation successfully defends its reporting as truth or in the public interest it can be conceptualised as media justice, which can be defined as a corrective to institutional failures of the legislature and criminal justice system. It demonstrates how the role of investigative journalism is critical in pursuing media justice and accountability for war crimes. Finally, it argues this role is seriously challenged by the financial costs and states must take the lead role in investigating and prosecuting human rights abuses in formal legal proceedings.

Subsequently, a 'trial by media' in the form of media justice holds the potential to expose crimes in the public interest and be an alternative space for justice that brings attention to the shortcomings of legal proceedings and the protection of human rights. Despite the challenges of a concentrated media landscape and financial pressures on the business model of journalism, this case shows how the Australian press still have a capacity to act in the public interest and scrutinise powerful figures. But there is that the potential that such media justice exposes the state's failure to do the same and can lead to a mistrust of formal legal institutions.

This chapter has established an empirical case study to explore these tensions between formal and media justice. However, this could be further extended to examine other defamation cases, as a comparative analysis, to gauge how often the truth defence is used successfully or whether there is greater sensational reputational damage inflicted in these trials by media. This case study has also focused on legacy media's role in investigative journalism and media justice. What becomes complicated is if we also consider how citizen journalists may contribute through social media to expose such wrongdoing. Future research could apply the five essential features of investigative journalism (Carson, 2019) to these online armchair detectives as one way to assess if this is also a legitimate form of media justice.

Competing Interests The author has no conflict of interests to declare that are relevant to the content of this chapter.

References

Aarons, M. (2020). *War criminals welcome: Australia, a sanctuary for fugitive war criminals since 1945*. Black Inc.

The Australian. (2009, December 19). Free press comes at a price. *Weekend Australian*, p.13

The Australian. (2017a, September 28). Tenacity exposes war criminal. *The Australian*, p. 13.

The Australian. (2017b, September 28). The Oz's journos are Dragan slayers with Serb war criminal jailed after years of scoops. *The Australian*, p. 13.

Bennett, E., & Rae, M. (2021). Towards a more diverse media and stronger public broadcasting. In A. Scott & R. Campbell (Eds.), *The Nordic edge: Policy possibilities for Australia* (pp.168–186). Melbourne University Publishing.

Birnbauer, B. (2012). The power of investigative journalism and why it is needed more than ever. In M. Ricketson (Ed.), *Australian journalism today* (pp. 78–91). Palgrave Macmillan.

Blumler, J., & Gurevitch, M. (2002). *The crisis of public communication.* Routledge.

Boas, G. (2004). An overview of implementation by Australia of the statute of the International Criminal Court. *Journal of International Criminal Justice, 2*, 179.

Boas, G., & Chifflet, P. (2016). Suspected war criminals in Australia: Law and policy. *Melbourne University Law Review, 40*(1), 46–86.

Braun, V., & Clarke, V. (2006). Using thematic analysis in psychology. *Qualitative Research in Psychology, 3*(2), 77–101.

Carson, A. (2014). The political economy of the print media and the decline of corporate investigative journalism in Australia. *Australian Journal of Political Science, 49*(4), 726–742.

Carson, A. (2015). Behind the newspaper paywall—Lessons in charging for online content: A comparative analysis of why Australian newspapers are stuck in the purgatorial space between digital and print. *Media, Culture & Society, 37*(7), 1022–1041.

Carson, A., & Farhall, F. (2018). Understanding collaborative investigative journalism in a "post-truth" age. *Journalism Studies, 19*(13), 1899–1911.

Carson, A. (2019). *Investigative journalism, democracy and the digital age.* Routledge.

Chagnon, N., & Chesney-Lind, M. (2015). 'Someone's been in the house': A tale of burglary and trial by media. *Crime, Media, Culture, 11*(1), 41–60.

Curran, J. (2002). *Media and Power*. Routledge.

Douglas, M. (2020, July 28). Australia's 'outdated' defamation laws are changing—But there's no 'revolution' yet. *The Conversation*. https://theconversation.com/australias-outdated-defamation-laws-are-changing-but-theres-no-revolution-yet-143532

Ferguson, J. (2015, May 16). Captain charted a defamation course—and lost. *Weekend Australian*, p. 3.

Flew, T., Fitzgerald, S., McTernan, C. & Nicholls, R. (2024). Media and internet concentration in Australia, 2019–2022. *Global Media and Internet Concentration Project*. https://doi.org/10.22215/gmicp/2024.9

Goldberg, J. (2009, May 11). Defamation and your reputation. *The Advertiser*, p. 18.

Greer, C., & McLaughlin, E. (2011). Trial by media': Policing, the 24–7 news mediasphere and the 'politics of outrage.' *Theoretical Criminology, 15*(1), 23–46.

Greer, C., & McLaughlin, E. (2012). Media justice: Madeleine McCann, intermediatization and 'trial by media' in the British press. *Theoretical Criminology, 16*(4), 395–416.

Greer, C., & McLaughlin, E. (2017). News Power, Crime and Media Justice. In A. Liebling et al. (Eds.), *Oxford handbook of criminology*, (6th ed., pp. 260–283). Oxford University Press.

Guilfoyle, D. (2001). Nulyarimma v Thompson: Is genocide a crime at common law in Australia? *Federal Law Review, 29*(1), 1–36.

Habermas, J. (1989). *Jurgen Habermas on society and politics: A reader.* Beacon Press.

Hamilton, J. (2016). *Democracy's detectives: The economics of investigative journalism.* Harvard University Press.

Herman, E. S., & Chomsky, N. (1988). *Manufacturing consent: The political economy of the mass media.* Random House.

Hess, K. (2020, March 28). Another savage blow to regional media spells disaster for the communities they serve. *The Conversation.* https://theconversation.com/another-savage-blow-to-regional-media-spells-disaster-for-the-communities-they-serve-139559

Housden, T., & Turnbull, T. (2023, June 2) Ben Roberts-Smith case: Will Australia see a war crimes reckoning? *British Broadcasting Corporation.* https://www.bbc.com/news/world-australia-65774434

IGADF. (2020). *Inspector-General of the Australian Defence Force Afghanistan Inquiry Report, (Brereton Report).* Retrieved April 9, 2024 from www.defence.gov.au/about/reviews-inquiries/afghanistan-inquiry

Karniel, Y. (2014). Who needs the sub judice rule? Israel as a test case in the relationship between law and media. *Journal of Media Law, 6*(1), 94–120.

Kenyon, A. T., & Marjoribanks, T. (2003). Negotiating news: Journalistic practice and defamation law in Australia and the US. *Australian Journalism Review, 25*(2), 31–49.

Lim, L. (2019, March 8). How Australia became the defamation capital of the world, *New York Times*, https://www.nytimes.com/2019/03/05/opinion/australia-defamation-laws.html

Manne, R. (2011). Bad news: Murdoch's Australian and the shaping of the nation. *Quarterly essay*, (43), 1–119.

McChesney, R. W. (2016). *Rich media, poor democracy: Communication politics in dubious times.* New Press.

McCormack, T., & Simpson, G. (1994). The International Law Commission's draft code of crimes against the peace and security of mankind: An appraisal of the substantive provisions. *Criminal Law Forum, 1*, 9.

Machado, H., & Santos, F. (2009). The disappearance of Madeleine McCann: Public drama and trial by media in the Portuguese press. *Crime, Media, Culture, 5*(2), 146–167.

MacKenzie, M., Gregory, T., Sarwary, B., & Razack, S. (2023). Australian war crimes in Afghanistan: Race, gender and responsibility. *Australian Journal of Political Science, 58*(3), 247–255.

McKnight, D. (2012). *Rupert Murdoch: An investigation of political power.* Allen & Unwin.

McKinell, J. (2023, March 23) Former SAS soldier Oliver Schulz charged with war crime granted Bail. *Australian Broadcasting Corporation,* https://www.abc.net.au/news/2023-03-28/former-sas-soldier-oliver-schulz-granted-bail-war-crime-trial/102153756

McKnight, D., & McNair, B. (2012). The empire goes to war: News Corporation and Iraq. *Australian Journalism Review, 34*(2), 7–17.

McNair, B. (2000). *Journalism and democracy: A qualitative evaluation of the political public sphere.* Routledge.

McNair, B. (2017). *An introduction to political communication.* Routledge.

Madden, J. (2009, April 21). 'Serb hero' feared extradition. *The Australian,* p. 3.

Madden, J. (2009, April 22). Court implicated accused war criminal in 2007—Dragan link to violence. *The Australian,* p. 7.

Madden, J. (2009, May 1). 'I never forgot image of Dragan'. *The Australian,* p. 3.

Madden, J. (2009, May 7). I'm a war hero, says Captain Dragan. *The Australian,* p.3.

MEAA. (2021, February 12). *Defamation outcomes chill public interest journalism,* Retrieved April 10 from https://www.meaa.org/mediaroom/defamation-outcomes-chill-public-interest-journalism-meaa/

Meade, A. (2020, May 18) More than 150 Australian newsrooms shut since January 2019 as COVID-19 deepens media crisis, *The Guardian,* https://www.theguardian.com/media/2020/may/18/more-than-150-australian-newsrooms-shut-since-january-2019-as-covid-19-deepens-media-crisis

Merritt, C. (2017, September 30). Paper that exposed Dragan paid a big price for its pains. *Weekend Australian,* p. 16.

Milovanovic, S. (2009, May 7). Ex-Serb soldier claims to be hero. *The Age,* p. 5

Mitchell, A. D. (2000). *Is genocide a crime unknown to Australian law?* (pp. 362–383). Yearbook of International Humanitarian Law, TMC Asser Press, The Hague.

Mutua, M. (2001). Savages, victims, and saviors: The metaphor of human rights. *Harvard International Law Journal, 42*(1), 201–245.

New South Wales Supreme Court. (2009). Snedden v Nationwide News, *NSWSC*, p. 1446

Nordicity. (2020). *International Comparison of Public Funding for Public Service Broadcasting, 2018, for Canadian Broadcasting Corporation.* https://site-cbc.radio-canada.ca/documents/vision/strategy/latest-studies/Nordicity-analysis-of-government-support-for-public-service-broadcasting-april-2020.pdf

Powell, A. (2015). Seeking rape justice: Formal and informal responses to sexual violence through technosocial counter-publics. *Theoretical Criminology, 19*(4), 571–588.

Quinlan, H. (2005, September 8). Perth golf teacher denies war crime allegations. *Australian Associated Press.*

Rae, M. (2020). Trial by media: Why victims and activists seek a parallel justice forum for war crimes. *Crime, Media, Culture, 16*(3), 359–374.

Rae, M., Holman, R., & Nethery, A. (2017). Self-represented witnessing: The use of social media by asylum seekers in Australia's offshore immigration detention centres. *Media, Culture and Society, 40*(4), 479–495.

Rae, M., Russell, E., & Nethery, A. (2019). Earwitnessing detention: Carceral secrecy, affecting voices, and political listening in the messenger podcast. *International Journal of Communication, 13.*

Reporters without Borders. (2024). *Australia.* https://rsf.org/en/country/australia

Robinson, N. (2017, September 27). 'Captain Dragan' Vasiljković: How we brought down a war criminal. *Australian Broadcasting Corporation.* https://www.abc.net.au/news/2017-09-27/captain-dragan-vasiljkov-story-of-egon-scotland/8992726

Salter, M. (2013). Justice and revenge in online counter-publics: Emerging responses to sexual violence in the age of social media. *Crime Media Culture, 9*(3), 225–242.

Scott, S. (2004). Why wasn't genocide a crime in Australia? Accounting for the Half Century Delay in Australia Implementing the Genocide Convention. *Australian Journal of Human Rights, 10*(1), 159–178.

Schloetzer-Scotland, C. (2017, September 30). Justice is necessary for those on both sides. *Weekend Australian*, p. 10.

Schudson, M. (2008). *Why democracies need an unlovable press*. Polity Press.

Tiffen, R. (2014). *Rupert Murdoch: A reassessment*. UNSW Press.

Wake, A. (2020, May 14) 9 reasons you should be worried about the closure of BuzzFeed News in Australia, *The Conversation*, https://theconversation.com/9-reasons-you-should-be-worried-about-the-closure-ofbuzzfeed-news-in-australia-138610

Warne-Smith, D. (2009, December 19). Captain Dragan 'committed torture and rape. *Weekend Australian*, p. 1.

Young, S. (2011). *How Australia decides: Election reporting and the media.* Cambridge University Press.

Young, S. (2015). Sending a message: The Australian's reporting of media policy. *Media International Australia, 157*(1), 79–90.

9

The Paradox of True Crime Podcasting: Advocacy, Prejudice, and the Pursuit of Justice

Katrina Clifford

Introduction

In the digital age, the allure of true crime stories has not only persisted, but intensified. True crime podcasts, especially those produced by professional journalists and media organisations, represent a transformative shift in true crime storytelling. These podcasts offer an immersive experience that traditional media formats cannot always match, engaging listeners through multiple episodes, often with real-time updates and interactive elements. This deep engagement fosters a unique relationship between content creators and their audiences, transforming listeners into active participants in the narrative, who discuss and sometimes even influence the outcomes of cases. Such engagement carries significant implications for the judicial system, reshaping how justice is perceived and interacted with by the public. In particular, true crime podcasts are the latest media forms to challenge the judiciary's ability to uphold the

K. Clifford (✉)
Deakin University, Melbourne, Australia
e-mail: katrina.clifford@deakin.edu.au

L. Gies (ed.), *Trial by Media*, Palgrave Studies in Crime, Media and Culture, https://doi.org/10.1007/978-3-031-80593-6_9

right to a fair trial. This is not a novel phenomenon; as data compiled by Reuters Legal shows, between 1999 and 2010 in the United States, at least 90 verdicts faced challenges due to alleged juror misconduct, often linked to inappropriate internet and social media use during court proceedings (Grow, 2010; see also Barnset al., 2019; Bartels & Lee, 2013; Johnston et al., 2013). However, true crime podcasts differentiate themselves in several key respects.

These media texts can shape and sometimes skew public perceptions of justice, legality, and morality with their distinctive approach to storytelling, often featuring elements of suspense and drama that 'have the potential to reach into a new emotional space and engage audiences in new ways' (Yardley et al., 2019, p. 508). Consequently, popular true crime podcasts often cultivate a dedicated and engaged audience that follows the series over time. This fosters a community of listeners who may remain deeply invested in the case, continuing their discussions and investigations on social media long after the series ends (see Jones, 2023; Horeck, 2019; Stratton, 2019). This detailed exploration of the case can amplify biases and create echo chambers that reinforce listener preconceptions, potentially shifting 'where the presumption of innocence starts' (Ruyters cited in Schwarz, 2019, p. 42). Moreover, the publicity generated by these podcasts can propel the cases they cover into broader public discourse, extending their reach beyond the original podcast audience. Cases featured in true crime podcasts, especially those produced by professional journalists, can gain new life in other media, including news reports and social networks, thus broadening their influence on public perceptions and demonstrating the complex pathways through which serialised true crime podcasts can impact the administration of justice.

Of course, it is important to acknowledge that the demographic of true crime podcast listeners may not entirely overlap with the pool of potential jurors for a criminal trial, who are typically drawn from a broad and diverse cross-section of society. Moreover, the judicial system has mechanisms in place to mitigate such biases and ensure fairness. This includes rigorous juror screening and instructions to avoid media coverage related to the cases they are involved in. Judges also have the authority to take remedial actions, such as declaring mistrials, approving judge-alone trials, or changing the venue to reduce the risk of prejudice. Despite these measures, the potential for serialised true crime podcasts to influence public perceptions of the criminal justice system, as well as assessments of guilt and innocence, cannot be ignored—especially where these media forms appear to pre-emptively judge a person before any formal adjudication has occurred. Such a situation flirts with the prospect of 'trial by media', creating a scenario whereby the accused is 'tried and sentenced in the "court of public opinion"' before facing a court of law (Greer & McLaughlin, 2011, p. 27). This is particularly problematic given that, for many listeners, these true crime podcasts may be their sole source of information about such matters (McNair, 1994). As research shows, public knowledge of crime, criminality, and criminal justice is often shaped by media rather than direct or personal experience (Clifford & White, 2017).

In the case of journalistic investigations, existing regulations such as contempt laws provide clear boundaries for reporting, especially when charges have been laid or courtroom proceedings are in motion. These laws are designed to prevent prejudicial media publicity that could influence trial outcomes, safeguarding the accused's right to a fair trial. However, true crime podcasts often delve into cold cases, operating in a domain where traditional legal guidelines offer less clarity. In their quest to shed light on these cases, journalists may introduce theories, speculate on potential suspects, or present new evidence that, while lawful at the time of the podcast's production, could later be deemed prejudicial if legal proceedings are initiated. The temporal gap between the podcast's release and the possible reopening of a case creates a legal grey area: statements that were considered lawful and non-prejudicial when originally published may acquire a different significance if the case progresses to court. The enduring nature of digital content, coupled with the deep engagement of audiences with these serialised narratives, means that the influence of true crime podcasts can persist and potentially prejudice cases yet to enter the legal system. Unlike other forms of conventional media, where reporting is often temporally bound to active legal cases, true crime podcasts can pre-emptively shape public perceptions of individuals and events, complicating subsequent judicial efforts to ensure impartiality. This introduces a critical tension between upholding the sacrosanct principle of a fair trial—enshrined in instruments like Article 14 of the International Covenant on Civil and Political Rights—and the freedom of expression of the press, as safeguarded by Article 19 of the same covenant. Consequently, a delicate balancing act is produced between upholding an accused's rights and the media's imperative to inform, especially where the issue is deemed to be in the public interest, such as when the functioning of the criminal justice system is perceived as fallible or flawed.

This further calls into question the adequacy of existing legal protections against prejudicial media content, especially in the context of cold cases that may later transition into active legal proceedings. While achieving justice may remain paramount, the journey to it—and the potential compromise of such foundational principles—warrants critical reflection and evaluation. As true crime podcasts increasingly blur the lines between public interest and the sanctity of the courtroom, a renewed emphasis on preserving the integrity of the judicial process, as well as the ethical and legal boundaries to which journalists are accountable, becomes imperative. While responsibility for remedial measures to balance the media's freedom of expression with the imperative to maintain the integrity of the judicial process has traditionally fallen to the judiciary and lawmakers, this chapter asks what of media responsibility and accountability for their approach to seeking justice?

To explore this and the implications of serialised true crime podcasts on both investigative journalism and the criminal justice system, this chapter examines the case study of *The Teacher's Pet*, an award-winning true crime podcast produced by *The Australian* newspaper. The trial of Chris Dawson, a former schoolteacher and Australian professional rugby league footballer accused of murdering his then-wife Lynette in 1982, serves as the focal point. The trial's delay, largely attributed to the 'unrestrained and uncensored public commentary' generated by *The Teacher's Pet*, ignited fresh debate about the potential threat to a person's right to a fair trial resulting from the public attention engendered by a mediated crime narrative (*R v Dawson [2020] NSWSC 1221*, par 443). While concerns about the consequences of prejudicial pre-trial publicity are not without precedent in judicial history—for example, *Sheppard v Maxwell* in the United States—the Dawson case marks the first instance in Australian legal history where a serialised podcast has been cited as the primary reason for an application for a permanent stay of criminal proceedings. The chapter argues that the underlying logic of serialised true crime podcasts can therefore be problematic, sometimes obscuring the inherent tension that exists between public conceptions of 'truth' and 'justice' and their application within legal standards and contexts. Ultimately, the chapter poses a crucial question: If justice is the outcome, can we overlook the path we took to get there? More to the point, is justice truly served if the path taken risks compromising fundamental human rights, such as the right to a fair trial and the presumption of innocence until proven guilty according to law?

The Rise of True Crime Podcasts and Their Impact on Justice-Seeking

A decade ago, Greer and McLaughlin (2012, p. 413) observed that networked news sites were becoming 'an increasingly important forum for crime and justice debates' and an 'influential player in establishing the parameters of those debates'. The same observation now arguably holds true in relation to journalist-produced serialised true crime podcasts, which have increasingly captivated Australian audiences. According to the Australian Broadcasting Corporation (ABC)'s podcast survey, the popularity of true crime podcasts has surged, with 44% of people claiming to have listened to one in the month preceding the survey (September–October 2018), up from 30% the previous year (ABC, 2019). Although Sherrill (2022, p. 1490) suggests this was 'arguably the height of the true crime podcast boom', continued growth in listenership has been observed more broadly.

The *Infinite Dial Australia* study found that, in 2022, Australia had officially overtaken the United States as the largest podcast-listening nation on the planet, with listeners actively engaged with an average of seven episodes in a week (Edison Research, 2022). While podcasting dates back to the 1980s, it arguably did not take hold in its current form until the portable digital boom of the 2000s. It was not until another decade later, following the runaway success of *Serial* in 2014, that true crime became the media darling of the podcast scene it is now. A podcast co-produced and hosted by American journalist Sarah Koenig, *Serial* captivated millions with its week-by-week investigation into the 1999 murder of Hae Min Lee and the conviction of her ex-boyfriend Adnan Syed, reinvigorating interest in long-form journalistic narratives in audio format. This breakthrough set the stage for what is now known as the '*Serial* effect' (Vogt, 2016), describing the surge in popularity of true crime media narratives. Since then, there has been 'an absolute glut of [true crime] content to churn through, across basically every medium we have at our collective disposal' (Hennessy, 2018). True crime podcasts, in particular, have consistently ranked within the top ten on platforms like Apple Podcasts and Spotify.

The allure of these media texts lies in the uniqueness of their stories—the horror of the crime, the weight of injustice, the unresolved nature of the case, and the quest for answers. As Simpson (2017) points out, true crime podcasts are 'often at their best when they're covering stories that are still in need of answers, or where justice may not have been done'. Sherrill (2023, p. 15) adds that these podcasts represent 'a new breed of true crime' predicated on the belief that fans without training in the law can impact the criminal justice system. Their narratives, she writes, are 'goal-oriented, often focusing on victims, desired outcomes, or mobilization for specific causes' (Sherrill, 2023, p. 15). They follow the tradition of long-form journalism, providing in-depth analysis, the building of complex arguments, and correction of mistakes (Sherrill, 2023).

There are certainly virtues to what serialised true crime podcasts can achieve as 'a corrective justice tool' (Williams, 2018, p. 204). Through the medium of podcasting, journalists can 'drive real change in the criminal justice system by shedding light on the wrongly convicted, exposing faults or failures by people in powerful positions, and engaging the public in crime stories they are not familiar with' (Boling, 2019, p. 161). For instance, *Phoebe's Fall*, an investigative podcast by *The Age* newspaper, led to legal reforms in the Australian state of Victoria after it brought attention to questionable coronial findings related to the mysterious death of Phoebe Handsjuk (Baker & Bachelard, 2018). Similarly, the ABC's *Trace* podcast prompted the reopening of the cold case of Maria James, murdered in 1980, demonstrating the potential of podcasts to breathe new life into unsolved cases. At the time, former detective Ron Iddles observed, 'when a podcast gets more than three million downloads, that is a new initiative that needs to be seriously looked at as a way of solving unsolved cases' (cited in Brown, 2018). Greer and McLaughlin (2012, p. 397) describe this phenomenon as the media's ability to reclaim 'justice' from the courts and return it to 'a networked citizenry'. In podcasting, this is achieved through the use of a number of 'authenticating devices' that generate a sense of 'authentic insight into closed institutions and private experiences' (Vitis & Ryan, 2023, p. 296).

Like radio, podcasting creates 'an intimate medium that can powerfully convey emotion' (McHugh, 2017), which aligns perfectly with the more recent 'affective turn' in professional journalism (Wahl-Jorgensen, 2019). Rather than outsourcing emotions to their news subjects, however, a journalist's emotions are often very obviously on display in serialised true crime podcasts, serving as a central feature of the story. In this way, the medium has the potential to augment the credibility of journalists, precisely because it strips away their 'veneer of polished authority' (Mead, 2018), allowing listeners to hear the uncertainty and vulnerabilities of the reporter, their sympathies and frustrations, their tormented indecision over what to believe, and their desire to come to some sort of resolution and understanding. The podcast is often as much the story of the journalist's investigation of the case and its aftermath as it is the story of the crime itself (Buozis, 2017).

However, Rebecca Mead (2018), writing for *The New Yorker*, questions whether the intimacy afforded by podcasting verges on the manipulative. She points to the 'unapologetically invasive', exploitative, and disrespectful tactics sometimes used to construct a podcast's audio narrative, and the negative side effects this can have on listeners, who feel satiated by the podcast's narrative 'because it is beguiling, not because it is true'. This raises broader questions about the ethos that underpins how journalists decide *whose* story is worth investigating. Similar concerns about the ethics and equity of media selectivity have previously been raised in relation to crime news more generally, with Greer (2007, p. 23) identifying a 'pecking order of sorts', which positions 'ideal victims'—those perceived as vulnerable, defenceless, innocent, and worthy of sympathy and compassion—as the preferred subjects of journalistic investigation and reporting. But if only the most compelling or captivating cases—or 'ideal victims'—are chosen to be the subjects of true crime podcasts, where does this leave those considered insufficiently engaging for commercial success? Must we accept that justice might be delayed or denied altogether for these cases due to a lack of media attention? Does this place an undue burden or expectation on journalist-produced true crime podcasts to serve as instruments of justice, a role traditionally reserved for the legal system? Does it overrate the capacity of serialised true crime podcasts to even be able to deliver these outcomes?

Expanding on these concerns, objections have been raised as to how serialised true crime podcasts often present assumptions of guilt and innocence that, while plausible, are infrequently supported by hard evidence, but especially evidence that would satisfy legal standards. 'The obvious upside to this kind of investigative journalism', writes Marshall (2018), 'is the chance that new, meaningful evidence could be found that will help get a conviction. But that has to be balanced very carefully against the risk involved in broadcasting information that is prejudicial and unlikely to be admissible as evidence in court'. Matters that make it to trial are obviously 'constrained by rules of evidence… and the (justifiably) high standard of proof for a finding of guilt' (Stratton, Sigamoney, & Bartle, 2022). True crime entertainment is not beholden to these same standards, as exemplified by critiques of the way in which true crime podcasts often encourage amateurism over professional investigation and cultivate ethically questionable relationships between journalists and their subjects. The creators of these media forms, argue Stratton, Sigamoney, and Bartle (2022), need to accept that 'a compelling narrative is not the same as a solid case'. True crime podcasts may otherwise inadvertently reinforce pre-existing misconceptions, affecting public trust in police investigations and the criminal justice system—although, as some would counter, the job of an investigative journalist-come-podcast producer is 'not to uphold confidence in these institutions' (Thomas, 2023, p. 463).

While the 'interactive nature of digital true crime' opens up the potential for 'closer public engagement with crime and legal process' (Horeck, 2019, p. 9)—be it constructive or otherwise—this interactivity has been identified by mainstream media organisations as a means of binding audiences more tightly to their commercial products. Michael Bachelard, one of the journalists who worked on *Phoebe's Fall*, notes that serialised true crime podcasts have offered a lifeline to mainstream media organisations savvy enough, and with the resources at their disposal, to capitalise on the armchair detective or 'websleuthing' phenomenon (cited in Ward, 2016; see also Soothill, 1998; Walsh, 2024; Yardley et al., 2018). Indeed, in Australia, news publishers are well represented as creators within the true crime genre. In the 2023 Australian Podcast Awards' 'True Crime' category, for example, contenders included podcasts originating from established newsrooms like *The Australian*, Nine News, and the ABC (Australian Podcast Awards, 2023).

Since *Serial*, advertisers have also started to take a more serious look at these podcasts as valuable storytelling and branding platforms, proving in the process that 'journalism is alive and well', according to Bachelard (cited in Ward, 2016), despite ongoing speculation to the contrary. Bachelard is not alone in his thinking. Following the launch of *The Teacher's Pet*, *The Australian*'s editor-in-chief Paul Whittaker (cited in Brook, 2018) observed that the series had given the newspaper 'a new platform, a new audience and a reach beyond the written word'. This is, of course, until a podcast goes behind a paywall, as happened after the conviction of Chris Dawson when *The Teacher's Pet* became available only to subscribers, prompting criticism: 'It was free, and now it's famous you're charging to make money? Off the life of a dead woman? The Australian newspaper should be ashamed for charging for this now' (Apple Podcasts review, Nickdavid16, 7 February 2023).

The Teacher's Pet and the Reopening of a Cold Case

Published by *The Australian,* a national news brand produced by News Corp Australia, *The Teacher's Pet* delves into the then-unsolved case of Lynette Dawson (née Simms), a mother of two who disappeared from the northern beaches of Sydney in 1982. Her body, at the time of writing, has never been found nor have any reliable sightings of her ever been recorded. *The Teacher's Pet* was credited with bringing about significant developments in the case, reigniting public interest in Dawson's disappearance which had already been the subject of hundreds of newspaper, television, and radio stories. In particular, the podcast claimed to offer new interviews and evidence that highlighted potential police and institutional failings in the original investigation and handling of Lynette Dawson's disappearance.

Successive episodes of the 16-part podcast series, available on platforms such as Apple Podcasts, Google Podcasts, Spotify, and *The Australian*'s website, aired between May and August 2018, with the final two episodes broadcast in November and December of that same year. A 'Special Update Episode', announcing the takedown of the series in preparation for the impending murder trial, was released on 5 April 2019. By 2020, the podcast had reached nearly 30 million downloads globally, topping charts in Australia, the UK, Canada, and New Zealand (Connery, 2022). Several prominent public officials with substantive roles in the criminal justice system participated in the podcast series, including former New South Wales (NSW) deputy state coroner Carl Milanovich and the then-NSW Commissioner of Police, Michael Fuller. Fuller's involvement, which 'in addition to giving an interview' included arranging 'extensive media access to the ongoing police investigation' (Nelson, 2024, p. 89), signalled an arguably unprecedented level of engagement between law enforcement and media during an ongoing investigation.

The Teacher's Pet not only focused on Lynette Dawson's mysterious disappearance; it also drew attention to allegations of sexual assaults and inappropriate teacher-student relationships at Northern Beaches' high schools in the 1970s and 1980s. This aspect of the podcast led to a police investigation under Strike Force Southwood, culminating in charges against several former teachers. However, these developments were overshadowed by the more controversial claims of the podcast's co-producer and presenter, journalist Hedley Thomas, who alleged that Lynette Dawson was deceased and that her husband, former schoolteacher and professional rugby player Chris Dawson, had murdered and disposed of her body.

Thomas's interest in the case had preceded the production of the podcast, dating back to 2001 when he was writing features for the *Courier Mail* newspaper in Brisbane, Queensland (Prendergast, 2018). As a journalist, he had covered both the 2001 and 2003 coronial inquests into Lynette Dawson's disappearance. At the time, both inquiries had recommended that a 'known person' be prosecuted for her murder. In each instance, however, the Director of Public Prosecutions (DPP) refused to lay charges against Chris Dawson, citing insufficient evidence. Thomas (2022) has publicly acknowledged that he saw *The Teacher's Pet* podcast series as 'a final push for justice for Lyn'. The publicity generated by the podcast has been widely attributed as a catalyst for Chris Dawson's eventual arrest and subsequent conviction in 2022 for Lynette's murder (Tufvesson, 2022). In June 2024, Dawson lost a bid to have his conviction overturned, when his appeal was unanimously dismissed by a panel of three judges in the NSW Court of Criminal Appeal, citing 'no substantial miscarriage of justice' had occurred (*Dawson v R [2024] NSWCCA 98*, par 413). The year prior, Hedley Thomas (2023) had released *The Teacher's Pet*, the book, providing a 'blow-by-blow account' of the case and his podcast investigation (see Fig. 9.1).

According to court documents, Lynette Dawson went missing in January 1982, leaving behind two daughters, aged two and four. Her husband Chris did not report her missing until six weeks later, claiming she had abandoned her children and the family home, leaving behind all her personal belongings, to join a religious group and to take some time to 'sort herself out' following marital problems (*R v Dawson [2022] NSWSC 1131*). In the meantime, the family's babysitter, JC, a student at the high school where Chris Dawson taught, was invited by Dawson to move into the family home. Dawson had formed a sexual relationship with JC in the two years prior to Lynette's disappearance. The Crown's case during the subsequent murder trial alleged that Dawson had been 'motivated to kill his wife' in order to be able to enter into 'an unfettered relationship with JC' (*R v Dawson [2022] NSWSC 1131*, par 9). Dawson and JC married in 1984, had a daughter together, and divorced in 1990. JC later told police and friends that she had feared for her life due to violence allegedly endured during her relationship with Dawson (*R v Dawson [2020] NSWSC 1221*).

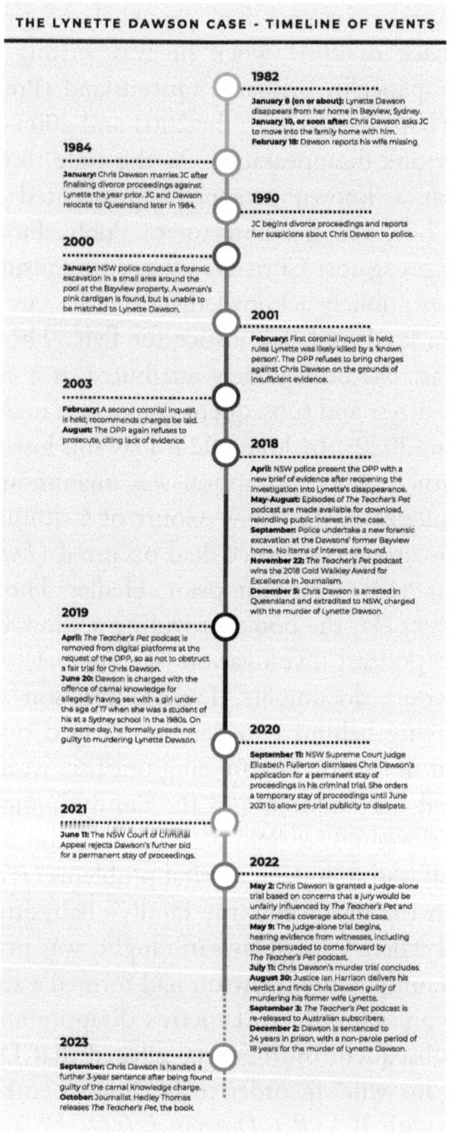

Fig. 9.1 The Lynette Dawson case: Timeline of events

In 2023, Dawson was found guilty of past unlawful sexual activity with a then-teenage student, receiving a three-year prison sentence for the offence. At the time of the verdict, he was already serving a sentence of 24 years, with a non-parole period of 18 years, for the murder of Lynette, having been arrested by police at his Queensland home and extradited to NSW in December 2018 (McGowan, 2018). Just two weeks earlier, Thomas and his co-producer, Slade Gibson, had won the highest accolade in Australian journalism, the Gold Walkley Award, for *The Teacher's Pet.* The Walkley Foundation's judges called the podcast 'a masterclass in investigative journalism' (The Walkley Foundation, 2018). However, among the legal fraternity, *The Teacher's Pet* was not seen in such glowing terms. NSW Chief Justice Tom Bathurst wrote that he regarded its objective 'to incite prejudice against [Chris Dawson] in a sensationalist fashion with a view to convincing listeners of his guilt and the need for him to be prosecuted', supported by 'apparently reputable members of the community' who 'should not have participated' in the podcast (*Dawson v R [2021] NSWCCA 117*, par 9). Justice Harrison, who presided over Dawson's murder trial, noted that the podcast had presented him with challenges in reaching a verdict. 'These challenges', he explained during his five-hour judgement on the case, which was live-streamed, 'were often based upon the proposition that particular witnesses were irrevocably compromised by the influence upon them of the Teacher's Pet podcast, either because they have developed a predisposition against Mr Dawson as a result of listening to it or participating in it, or because their memories have otherwise been corrupted or supplanted by the publicity that it has generated' (*R v Dawson [2022] NSWSC 1131*, par 448).

Following the verdict, Hedley Thomas claimed the public response to *The Teacher's Pet* had influenced the DPP's decision to prosecute (Samios, 2022), prompting the DPP to issue a public statement of correction (ODPP NSW, 2022). Nonetheless, Thomas (2023, p. 434) maintains that the system was 'shamed into action by the ensuing public outcry' generated by the podcast series. News reports about the verdict endorsed Thomas' claims with headlines such as 'How The Teacher's Pet podcast helped catch and jail a killer' (Turnbull, 2022). Some speculated that Thomas might even be in line for the A$200,000 reward the NSW state government had previously posted for new information leading to the arrest and conviction of those responsible for Lynette's disappearance and presumed murder (Airs, 2022). Chris Merritt, the vice-president of the Rule of Law Institute of Australia—and a former chief of staff at *The Australian*—argued in an editorial written for the newspaper that the case had shown 'the law provides plenty of room' for journalists 'to expose wrongdoing without interfering with the duty of the courts to provide a fair trial', concluding that Dawson's conviction 'would not have happened without the Teacher's Pet podcast' (Merritt, 2022a, p. 2). While it is unlikely that the podcast series alone prompted a murder trial, as Gans (2022) observes, 'neither did it stop one', despite some critics arguing it should have.

Pre-trial Publicity and the Legal Landscape

In response to the extensive publicity generated by *The Teacher's Pet*, Chris Dawson's legal team filed an application prior to the murder trial for a permanent stay of criminal proceedings, arguing that the unrestrained public commentary about the case had irrevocably compromised Dawson's ability to receive a fair trial. They claimed the podcast had portrayed Dawson in a guilty light before the commencement of legal proceedings, thereby prejudicing public opinion to such an extent that an impartial jury could not be assembled. By this stage, *The Teacher's Pet* had been removed from digital platforms at the request of the DPP. Within days of the conclusion of the trial, *The Australian* had re-released the podcast, with edits, to Australian subscribers.

In handing down a decision, Justice Fullerton granted a temporary stay of proceedings, allowing the case to proceed to trial but not before June 2021 to allow time for the publicity to subside (*R v Dawson [2020] NSWSC 1221*, par 443). Her decision was underscored by the legal principle that a 'trial according to law' must prevail over a 'trial by media' (citing Brennan J, *R v Dawson [2020] NSWSC 1221*, par 361), highlighting the necessity of maintaining legal processes, grounded in law and courtroom evidence, despite external pressures from public sentiment and the media. Ruling in favour of a permanent stay of proceedings on the grounds of prejudicial pre-trial publicity would have arguably undermined trust in the judicial system's capacity to deliver justice. As Williams (cited in Tufvesson, 2022) explains: 'There's potential for faith in the justice system to be diminished if the legal processes used to mitigate the impacts of intense pre-trial publicity and protect the integrity and fairness of the trial are seen to be a barrier to justice instead of a protection of it'. In other words, the public should be able to rely on the law's ability (e.g. through judicial directions) to safeguard the integrity of the criminal justice process and protect against the adverse effects of prejudice and pre-judgement—precipitated by pre-trial media publicity and public commentary—on the sworn duty of jurors to determine a case.

Kurz (2018) had foreshadowed the risks of potential jurors being exposed to a partisan version of events, even before Dawson's arrest and extradition, noting that:

> A journalist is, at the end of at the day, a story teller. Hedley Thomas has told a ripping and compelling yarn but there are times, despite his best intentions, where questions of admissibility are left by the wayside. Of course a juror will only hear evidence which is admissible. They will not hear scores of opinions offered by concerned neighbours or hearsay conversations. Rules of evidence exist to recognise the danger and unreliability of such evidence. A journalist need not make such a distinction. By populating the podcast with so much innuendo and opinion, which makes for great listening, there is a risk that any potential juror who has followed the podcast or accessed related news content may be exposed to evidence which is ultimately unable to be led at trial. This can lead the juror to base their decision on matters which are not relevant to the case.

In the Sydney region, where the jury pool for Dawson's trial was presumed to be sourced, *The Teacher's Pet* had been downloaded over 1 million times before Nationwide News Pty Ltd 'took down' the podcast from *The Australian*'s website (*R v Dawson [2020] NSWSC 1221*, par 18). Justice Fullerton acknowledged that, had *The Teacher's Pet* been published *after* Dawson had been charged with the murder of his former wife, 'a number of individuals and publishers would inevitably have been liable and likely convicted of a criminal contempt' (*R v Dawson [2020] NSWSC 1221*, par 443).

While the application for a stay of proceedings highlighted the challenges of managing pre-trial publicity in the digital age, it also prompted broader discussions about the responsibilities of content creators towards the subjects of their investigations and, in particular, where 'the craft [of journalism] is even permitted to tread in the context of the law' (Condon cited in Thomas, 2023, p. 463). Under Australian law, from the time somebody is arrested, charged or a warrant is issued up to the moment when the court finishes dealing with it, the case is said to be *sub judice* or 'under judgement'. Only details of what is happening officially within the legal process can be reported. The rationale is to avoid a 'trial by media' by 'prohibiting the publication of material which might prejudge issues at stake in particular proceedings' (Victorian Government Solicitor's Office, 2009). In deciding whether material is prejudicial, 'the court will attempt to balance the public interest in free speech with the public interest in ensuring a fair trial' (Victorian Government Solicitor's Office, 2009).

True crime podcasts are 'no different' in this respect 'to any other form of publication, in that they carry the same legal risks about things like defamation, contempt of court and sub judice rules' (Sunderland cited Crampton, 2020). It would be fair to assume that, so too, they should carry the same ethical responsibilities. Courts are a place of authority. True crime podcasts often question this authority—but what do they offer in terms of interpretations of journalistic authority in the process? As the Media, Entertainment, and Arts Alliance (MEAA) code of ethics for Australian journalists reminds us, while public interest journalism serves to scrutinise power, it also wields it. Journalists should therefore exercise their own power responsibly (MEAA, 2018). After all, as Foreman (2021) explains, 'true crime is not just entertainment. These are real stories of real people in really terrible moments—and that comes with real consequences'.

From an Australian perspective, contempt laws are not the only legal mechanism for dealing with prejudicial pre-trial publicity or restricting the publication of information. Parties to a case can also apply in advance to a judge for a ban on the reporting of information they feel will unfairly prejudice the case. But for non-publication orders to be effective in the context of podcasts, not only the podcast itself but all associated media coverage would need to be removed or access blocked. By this stage of the proceedings, the podcast and its surrounding media coverage would have likely been in circulation for some time, meaning any non-publication order would have limiting effect. As Williams (2018, p. 228) perceptively puts it: 'Courts cannot enforce a 'collective forgetting' of information in the public domain'. For this reason, the Victorian Law Reform Commission (2020, p. 141) suggests that existing legal mechanisms may be inadequate for controlling 'the risks of prejudice' in the digital era, highlighting a need for new procedures that address the contemporary media landscape.

Despite numerous judges involved in the Dawson case denouncing *The Teacher's Pet*, no steps were taken to prosecute its producers. This is because liability for sub judice contempt is influenced by what stage of proceedings a matter has reached when publication occurs. In NSW, where the Dawson case was prosecuted, penalties can only be imposed on media for conduct relating to 'proceedings *currently before the court*' (emphasis added, Judicial Commission of New South Wales, 2007, p. 35). As Merritt (2022b, p. 24) explains: 'This means the courts are restricted to imposing penalties on the media for conduct that takes place once criminal proceedings are pending. They cannot reach back in time and retrospectively penalise journalists for publishing information that covers the same ground as a later criminal prosecution'. In other words, regardless of one's opinion of how it was delivered, 'Thomas's assessment of Dawson [as guilty] was lawful' at the time *The Teacher's Pet* was published as no formal charges had yet been laid against him (Merritt, 2022b, p. 24).

This was acknowledged by Chief Justice Bathurst, one of the judges responsible for dismissing Dawson's appeal for a permanent stay of proceedings. He noted that, while the pre-trial publicity and delays in the case were serious, 'a fair trial is not necessarily a perfect trial' (*Dawson v R [2021] NSWCCA 117*, par 6). While fairness to the accused is one consideration, Bathurst noted, so is 'the substantial public interest of the community in bringing those charged with serious criminal offences (of which murder is the most serious) to trial' (*Dawson v R [2021] NSWCCA*

117, par 7). But, arguably, the fact that Dawson's trial proceeded before a judge rather than a jury, due to fears the latter would be more easily prejudiced by the intense media attention, says something about both the confidence in the courts to counteract 'trial by media' in this case and the impact of *The Teacher's Pet* podcast.

Conclusion

The trial of Chris Dawson highlights the complex challenges the criminal justice system faces in an era dominated by digital and social media and heightened public scrutiny. It serves as a poignant reminder of the way in which serialised true crime podcasts, such as *The Teacher's Pet*, can resurrect public interest in cold cases—potentially aiding in solving them—while at the same time they can risk prejudicing legal outcomes by virtue of their very production. Put simply, in the pursuit of justice, true crime podcasts can be troubling as much as they can be useful.

The Teacher's Pet may have captivated public interest, but it also ventured perilously close to undermining and even obstructing the very justice it sought to serve. Journalist Hedley Thomas's decision to proceed with the podcast, despite knowing the legal reconsiderations being made of the case, highlights a critical tension between journalistic freedom and the ethical responsibilities that many within the legal fraternity would argue should govern such investigations. As part of his testimony to the court, Thomas revealed that he knew the DPP was reconsidering the Lynette Dawson case, and the sufficiency of evidence to support a prosecution of Chris Dawson for murder, but that he pushed ahead with *The Teacher's Pet* nonetheless to 'flush out new witnesses or evidence that might make the difference' (Thomas cited in McPhee, 2022, p. 3). He also accepted that he had shared his own opinion of the case with witnesses; specifically, his belief that Dawson had gotten away with murder (Genders, 2022). While this may have been a plausible conclusion, as Gans (2018) points out, at the time, there was 'hardly any evidence to support it'.

Such admissions from Thomas suggest that he and his creative team must have known how 'perilously close' *The Teacher's Pet* was straying to being 'so prejudicial' as to prevent a possible trial from ever proceeding (Sarre, 2022), raising questions about the motivations for the podcast's production in the first place and possible tensions between journalist-driven justice-seeking and the commercial realities of mainstream media practice. Rebecca Hazel, the lawyer who collaborated with Thomas for parts of *The Teacher's Pet*, told the court that Thomas' journalistic style—in which he commenced his interviews by openly disclosing he thought Chris Dawson was the killer—made her uncomfortable as she became 'alive to the risk' that potential witnesses could be influenced by this view, thereby threatening the impartiality and fairness of any future legal proceedings (*R v Dawson [2020] NSWSC 1221*, par 230). Justice Fullerton was more forthright in her assessment of the situation, describing *The Teacher's Pet* as 'the most egregious example of media interference' witnessed by the court (*R v Dawson [2020] NSWSC 1221*, par 443). She lamented that, even after days on the witness stand, Thomas 'gave no indication that he had gained any insight into the damage he has done... and no obvious awakening of his ethical role as a journalist' (*R v Dawson [2020] NSWSC 1221*, par 331).

Hedley Thomas has publicly denied that he tried to incite prejudice against Chris Dawson with *The Teacher's Pet* podcast, and disputes suggestions that journalists should not investigate or report because a cold case is being reconsidered, saying that, to do so, would 'represent a chilling restraint on journalists' (Baker, 2022, p. 4). While this may be so, one might argue that it does not excuse professional journalists from being mindful of the potential impacts of their reporting; avoiding speculation, or presenting unverified information to mitigate the risk of obstructing justice by prejudicing any future trial that may arise if new evidence emerges and the case is reopened. While an unbridled desire to uncover the truth and to achieve justice is commendable, media practitioners must still be acutely aware of the potential legal and ethical boundaries they may encounter, or even unintentionally cross, in their reporting. As McQuail (2003, p. 299) contends, 'human rights, especially as codified, of all those affected by communication should be respected'.

This is not to say that reflective and ethically minded podcast content creators do not exist or that the intentions of journalists who set out to right wrongs through their podcast investigations are not beneficently oriented. But from a media criminology perspective (see Clifford & White, 2017), it is important to not let the commercial or entertainment value of true crime podcasts overshadow or subvert ongoing critical conversations about the ethics of podcasting, the gaps between representation and reality, and the framing effects that such series can produce. As with any representation of law and order, the mediated view of reality presented by serialised true crime podcasts warrants scrutiny for the normative expectations it can establish and promote about crime, criminality, and the criminal justice system; definitions of justice; and the roles, responsibilities, and limits of journalistic storytelling in relation to wrongful convictions and cold case investigations. At stake here, as McQuail (2003, p. 139) highlights, is 'a larger issue that concerns the appropriate attitude of media communicators and publishers to the consequences of their activities'.

There are also broader implications for the criminal justice system. In an era where jurors can easily access a plethora of information, the traditional concept of an unbiased jury is increasingly under threat. Discussions about the potential shift towards more frequent judge-alone trials reflect concerns over a jury's ability to remain impartial in high-profile cases, potentially altering the dynamics of the justice system itself. The podcast as a form of digital media represents a new challenge to legal safeguards against prejudicial pre-trial publicity, and the traditional boundaries between and responsibilities of courts and media (see Waller & Clifford, 2022). The instantaneous and pervasive nature of digital media could be argued to necessitate a re-evaluation of the measures needed to protect the right to a fair trial, particularly where cold cases are concerned, as well as the media's roles and responsibilities in seeking justice while respecting the rights of individuals involved. The case of Chris Dawson and *The Teacher's Pet* serves as a crucial reference point for these ongoing discussions and the roles and responsibilities of media in legal contexts (and vice versa).

Competing Interests The author has no conflict of interests to declare that are relevant to the content of this chapter.

References

ABC. (2019). *ABC Podcast Research 2019.* Australian Broadcasting Corporation. http://www.abc.net.au/cm/lb/11563738/data/download-2019-abc-podcast-research-pdf-data.pdf

Airs, K. (2022, August 30). How Australia's first-ever smash hit podcast – listened to by 30MILLION – helped bring a killer to justice – as the host delivers a compelling statement about the disgraceful circumstances leading to a murderer spending most of his life a free man, *The Daily Mail*. https://www.dailymail.co.uk/news/article-11159369/How-Teachers-Pet-podcast-Hedley-Thomas-brought-justice-Lynette-Dawson-murder.html

Australian Podcast Awards. (2023). *Results 2023: Congratulations to all of our finalists and winners!* https://www.australianpodcastawards.com/results-2023

Baker, J. (2022, June 13). Walking a Thin Blue Line: Top police and the 'pet' podcast. *The Sydney Morning Herald*, p. 4.

Baker, R., & Bachelard, M. (2018, June 21). Coronial findings, cold case investigations may be re-opened under new laws. *The Age*. https://www.theage.com.au/national/victoria/coronial-findings-cold-case-investigations-may-be-re-opened-under-new-laws-20180621-p4zms8.html

Barns, G., Yew, J., & Lloyd, R. (2019, August 20). Juries and Social Media: Problems Arising from Jurors' Social Media Use [Paper presentation]. Carroll & O'Dea Lawyers, Sydney. https://www.codea.com.au/sub-publication/7531/

Bartels, L., & Lee, J. (2013). Jurors using social media in our courts: Challenges and responses. *Journal of Judicial Administration, 23*(1), 35–57.

Boling, K. S. (2019). True crime podcasting: Journalism, justice or entertainment? *Radio Journal: International Studies in Broadcast & Audio Media, 17*(2), 161–178.

Brook, S. (2018, June 27). The Australian's Teacher's Pet podcast hits million downloads. *The Australian Business Review*. https://www.theaustralian.com.au/business/media/the-australians-teachers-pet-podcast-hits-million-downloads/news-story/78860ab0476c9d76fcc28eb047d128e4

Brown, R. (2018, November 30). Trace podcast subject Maria James's murder case reopened by Victorian coroner. *ABC News*. https://www.abc.net.au/news/2018-11-30/trace-podcast-subject-maria-james-murder-case-to-re-opened/10569792

Buozis, M. (2017). Giving voice to the accused: *Serial* and the critical potential of true crime. *Communication and Critical/Cultural Studies, 14*(3), 254–270. https://doi.org/10.1080/14791420.2017.1287410
Clifford, K., & White, R. (2017). *Media and Crime: Content, Context and Consequence*. Oxford University Press.
Connery, T. (2022, August 30). Chris Dawson, subject of The Teacher's Pet podcast, found guilty. *Mediaweek*. https://www.mediaweek.com.au/chris-dawson-subject-of-the-teachers-pet-podcast-found-guilty
Crampton, C. (2020, October 6). How a podcast held up a murder trial. *Hot Pod*. https://hotpodnews.com/how-a-podcast-held-up-a-murder-trial/
Edison Research. (2022). *The Infinite Dial Australia 2022 study*. http://www.radioalive.com.au/Research-Insights/Major-Research/Infinite-Dial-Australia/2022
Foreman, A. (2021, September 8). Untangling true crime: Inside the ethics of Hollywood's greatest guilty pleasure. *Mashable*. https://mashable.com/feature/ethics-of-true-crime
Gans, J. (2018, November 26). The media's pet. *Inside Story*. https://insidestory.org.au/the-medias-pet/
Gans, J. (2022, September 4). The podcast's trial. *Inside Story*. https://insidestory.org.au/the-podcasts-trial/
Genders, T. (2022, June 27). Creator of hit Teacher's Pet podcast denies he led a campaign against Chris Dawson. *Nine News*. https://www.9news.com.au/national/chris-dawson-trial-journalist-hedley-thomas-teachers-pet-takes-the-stand/557444b9-5e54-45fe-87b8-3b6deaa5378d
Greer, C. (2007). News media, victims and crime. In P. Davies, P. Francis, & C. Greer (Eds.), *Victims, Crime and Society* (pp. 20–49). SAGE Publications.
Greer, C., & McLaughlin, E. (2012). Media justice: Madeleine McCann, intermediatization and 'trial by media' in the British press. *Theoretical Criminology, 16*(4), 395–416. https://doi.org/10.1177/1362480612454559
Greer, C., & McLaughlin, E. (2011). 'Trial by media': Policing, the 24–7 news mediasphere and the 'politics of outrage'. *Theoretical Criminology, 15*(1), 23–46. https://doi.org/10.1177/1362480610387461
Grow, B. (2010, December 8). As jurors go online, U.S. trials go off track. *Reuters*. https://www.reuters.com/article/idUSTRE6B74Z8/
Hennessy, J. R. (2018, November 16). Our insatiable appetite for true crime leaves behind a moral hangover. *The Guardian*. https://www.theguardian.com/commentisfree/2018/nov/16/our-insatiable-appetite-for-true-crime-leaves-behind-a-moral-hangover

Horeck, T. (2019). *Justice on demand: True crime in the digital streaming era.* Wayne State University Press.

Johnston, J., Keyzer, P., Holland, G., Pearson, M., Rodrick, S., & Wallace, A. (2013). *Juries and Social Media: A report prepared for the Victorian Department of Justice*. Standing Council on Law and Justice.

Jones, B. (2023). Forensic fandom: True crime, citizen investigation and social media. In G. S. Larke-Walsh (Ed.), *True crime in American media* (pp. 163–179). Routledge. https://doi.org/10.4324/9781003225638-11.

Judicial Commission of New South Wales. (2007). *Criminal Trial Courts Bench Book*, section 1–250. https://jirs.judcom.nsw.gov.au/public/assets/benchbooks/criminal

Kurz, R. (2018, September 29). The Teacher's Pet: Do viral podcasts have the ability to taint a jury pool?. *Robertson O'Gorman Solicitors Criminal Law Blog*. https://www.robertsonogorman.com.au/2018/october/03/the-teachers-pet-do-viral-podcasts-have-the-ability-to-taint-a-jury-pool/

Marshall, H. (2018, September 16). A fair trial catch-22: The problem with the teacher's pet podcast. *New Matilda.* https://newmatilda.com/2018/09/16/fair-trial-catch-22-problem-teachers-pet-podcast/

McGowan, M. (2018, December 5). Chris Dawson arrested and expected to be charged with murder of Lyn Dawson. *The Guardian.* https://www.theguardian.com/australia-news/2018/dec/05/chris-dawson-arrested-and-expected-to-be-charged-with-of-lyn-dawson

McHugh, S. (2017, August 31). Truth to power: how podcasts are getting political. *The Conversation.* https://theconversation.com/truth-to-power-how-podcasts-are-getting-political-81185

McNair, B. (1994). *News and journalism in the UK*. Routledge.

McPhee, S. (2022, June 28). Journalist sought 'only clues, not prosecution'. *The Sydney Morning Herald*, p. 3.

McQuail, D. (2003). *Media accountability and freedom of publication.* Oxford University Press.

MEAA. (2018). *MEAA journalist code of ethics.* https://www.meaa.org/download/meaa-code-of-ethics/

Mead, R. (2018, November 12). How podcasts became a seductive – and sometimes slippery – mode of storytelling. *The New Yorker*. https://www.newyorker.com/magazine/2018/11/19/how-podcasts-became-a-seductive-and-sometimes-slippery-mode-of-storytelling

Merritt, C. (2022a, August 31). Result a victory for media and justice: The system worked. *The Australian*, p. 2.

Merritt, C. (2022b, September 2). Teacher's Pet criticism from judges misplaced. *The Australian*, p. 24.

Nelson, C. (2024). The 'most maligned' witness in the Christopher Dawson case: Gender, power, media and legal culture in the digitally distributed live-streamed court. *Crime Media Culture, 20*(1), 83–106. https://doi.org/10.1177/17416590231168330

ODPP NSW. (2022, September 1). *Matter of Christopher Dawson: Statement from the Office of the Director of Public Prosecutions (ODPP) NSW* [Press release]. https://www.odpp.nsw.gov.au/sites/default/files/2022-09/Media%20Statement%20-%20Christopher%20Dawson%201%20September%202022.pdf

Prendergast, K. (2018, June 13). 'Why haven't they found this stuff?': An interview with The Teacher's Pet host Hedley Thomas. *The Walkley Magazine*. https://medium.com/the-walkley-magazine/why-havent-they-found-this-stuff-an-interview-with-the-teacher-s-pet-host-hedley-thomas-d86e6412a490

Samios, Z. (2022, August 31). Teacher's Pet journalist 'doubles down' on cold case investigations after Dawson trial. *The Sydney Morning Herald*. https://www.smh.com.au/business/companies/teacher-s-pet-journalist-doubles-down-on-cold-case-investigations-after-dawson-trial-20220831-p5be7n.html

Sarre, R. (2022, August 30). 'A clear victory for dogged investigative journalism': Chris Dawson found guilty of murdering wife Lynette in 1982. *The Conversation*. https://theconversation.com/a-clear-victory-for-dogged-investigative-journalism-chris-dawson-found-guilty-of-murdering-wife-lynette-in-1982-189625

Schwarz, K. (2019). Trial by media: Our true crime obsession. *LSJ: Law Society of NSW Journal, 54*(April), 40–43.

Sherrill, L. A. (2023). Beyond entertainment: Podcasting and the criminal justice reform 'Niche'. In G. S. Larke-Walsh (Ed.), *True crime in American media* (pp. 14–31). Routledge. https://doi.org/10.4324/9781003225638-2

Sherrill, L. A. (2022). The 'serial effect' and the true crime podcast ecosystem. *Journalism Practice, 16*(7), 1473–1494. https://doi.org/10.1177/21533687231199271

Simpson, S. (2017, October 14). The unlikely role of true crime podcasts in criminal justice reform. *Quartz*. https://qz.com/1101889/the-unlikely-role-of-true-crime-podcasts-in-criminal-justice-reform/

Soothill, K. (1998). Armchair detectives and armchair thieves. *Police Journal, 71*, 155–159.

Stratton, G. (2019). Wrongful conviction, pop culture, and achieving justice in the digital age. In D. Akrivos & A. K. Antoniou (Eds.), *Crime, deviance and popular culture: International and multidisciplinary perspectives* (pp. 177–201). Palgrave Macmillan.

Stratton, G., Sigamoney, A., & Bartle, J. (2022, September 6). True crime entertainment like The Teacher's Pet can shine a light on cold cases – but does it help or hinder justice being served? *The Conversation.* https://theconversation.com/true-crime-entertainment-like-the-teachers-pet-can-shine-a-light-on-cold-cases-but-does-it-help-or-hinder-justice-being-served-189787

The Walkley Foundation. (2018, November 22). *Hit podcast The Teacher's Pet wins the 2018 Gold Walkley Award* [Press release]. https://www.walkleys.com/hit-podcast-the-teachers-pet-wins-the-2018-gold-walkley-award/

Thomas, H. (2023). *The Teacher's Pet*. Pan Macmillan Australia.

Thomas, H. (2022, June 29). Email that sparked a journalism-led pursuit of justice. *The Australian.* https://www.theaustralian.com.au/commentary/email-that-sparked-a-journalismled-pursuit-of-justice/news-story/7bca209294831edc8c6c067eaea76e54

Tufvesson, A. (2022, November 14). Probing the legacy of The Teacher's Pet. *LSJ Online: Law Society of NSW Journal*. https://lsj.com.au/articles/probing-the-legacy-of-the-teachers-pet

Turnbull, T. (2022, August 31). Chris Dawson: How The Teacher's Pet podcast helped catch and jail a killer. *BBC News*. https://www.bbc.com/news/world-australia-62735339

Victorian Government Solicitor's Office. (2009, June). *Managing the Risk of Sub Judice Contempt* [Client newsletter]. https://www.vgso.vic.gov.au/node/331

Victorian Law Reform Commission. (2020). *Contempt of Court: Report*. Victorian Law Reform Commission, Melbourne. https://www.lawreform.vic.gov.au/wp-content/uploads/2021/07/VLRC_Contempt_of_Court_report_forWeb.pdf

Vitis, L., & Ryan, V. (2023). True crime podcasts in Australia: Examining listening patterns and listener perceptions. *Journal of Radio & Audio Media, 30*(1), 291–314. https://doi.org/10.1080/19376529.2021.1974446

Vogt, N. (2016). *State of the news media 2016. Podcasting: Fact sheet*. Pew Research Center. http://www.journalism.org/2016/06/15/podcasting-fact-sheet/

Wahl-Jorgensen, K. (2019). *Emotions*. Polity Press.

Waller, L., & Clifford, K. (2022). Courts and the media. In M. Camilleri & A. Harkness (Eds.), *Australian courts: Controversies, challenges and change* (pp. 73–89). Palgrave Macmillan.

Walsh, J. P. (2024). Digitally networked sleuthing: Online platforms, netizen detectives, and bottom-up investigations. In E. Pica, D. Ross, & J. Pozzulo (Eds.), *The impact of technology on the criminal justice system: A psychological overview* (pp. 304–329). Routledge.

Ward, M. (2016, September 24). Fairfax's first investigative podcast series proof that 'journalism is alive and well'. *Mumbrella.* https://mumbrella.com.au/fairfaxs-first-investigative-podcast-series-proof-journalism-alive-well-397565

Williams, H. (2018). 'Serial' concerns: The rise of 'new true crime' journalism in the United States, and corresponding legal impediments in Australia. *Media and Arts Law Review, 22*(2), 201–243.

Yardley, E., Kelly, E., & Robinson-Edwards, S. (2019). Forever trapped in the imaginary late capitalism? The serialized true crime podcast as a wake-up call in times of criminological slumber. *Crime Media Culture, 15*(3), 503–521. https://doi.org/10.1177/1741659018799375

Yardley, E., Lynes, A. G. T., Wilson, D., & Kelly, E. (2018). What's the deal with 'websleuthing'? News media representations of amateur detectives in networked spaces. *Crime Media Culture, 14*(1), 81–109.

Cases

Dawson v R [2024] NSWCCA 98.

Dawson v R [2021] NSWCCA 117.

R v Dawson [2022] NSWSC 1131.

R v Dawson [2020] NSWSC 1221.

10

When Is Trial by Media *Not* Trial by Media?: Seeking Justice for Sanda Dia in Post-Dutroux Belgium

Lieve Gies

Introduction

When is trial by media *not* trial by media? Establishing what constitutes legitimate media scrutiny requires granular knowledge of the specific harms associated with the mediatisation of the judicial process. At present, such granularity is lacking because much of the literature is focused on the excesses of trial by media to the exclusion of more complicated and ambiguous cases. The interests of victims, offenders and society at large are ill-served if 'trial by media' is used as an all-purpose label to delegitimise media scrutiny and discourage public debate. A key argument of this chapter is that a highly mediatised trial does not preclude the pursuit of legitimate aims. Assessing trial by media claims requires the type of the balancing exercise which is often conducted when there are tensions between the media's freedom to report and the public's right

L. Gies (✉)
University of Leicester, Leicester, UK
e-mail: lg149@leicester.ac.uk

L. Gies (ed.), *Trial by Media*, Palgrave Studies in Crime, Media and Culture,
https://doi.org/10.1007/978-3-031-80593-6_10

to know, on the one hand, and countervailing interests, such as an individual's right to privacy, on the other. Indeed, an important example of such balancing exercise is contained in the routine application of article 10 of the European Convention on Human Rights (1950).

The case study at the heart of this chapter concerns the fatal student hazing of Sanda Dia. Sanda was a minority-ethnic Belgian student studying at Leuven University who lost his life in 2018 during an extreme hazing initiation held by Reuzegom, an elite, predominantly white student fraternity with racist views and far-right sympathies. He was subjected to a series of humiliating challenges over a two-day period during which he was goaded into consuming excessive amounts of alcohol, denied access to water and made to drink large quantities of fish sauce, resulting in fatal levels of salt in his body. Most of the eighteen accused came from very wealthy and influential families. At trial, judges ruled that the defendants did not intentionally administer harmful substances. The defendants were sentenced to community service and a fine. These sentences were criticised for being unduly lenient, causing an outcry on social media and triggering street protests. The Reuzegom case[1] attracted intense media interest, bolstered by the active campaigning of Sanda's family and friends. The hashtag #justiceforsanda would go on to gain more than 6.5 m views on TikTok (Davies, 2023), making it an example of what Wood et al. (2019) term 'viral justice'. Defence lawyers, by contrast, voiced concerns that their clients were subjected to trial by media and denounced the media treatment of the case. Whether the media campaign should be classed as a legitimate form of justice seeking or as a 'witch-hunt' became a bone of contention.

Against this backdrop, I argue that the case displays several characteristics which place the media attention it garnered in the category of legitimate media scrutiny. Firstly, despite attempts to out the accused on social media, their anonymity was largely preserved in legacy media, meaning that there was not the kind of intrusion into privacy and reputational damage typically observed in trial by media cases. Instead, media reporting in the Reuzegom case balanced the question of individual

[1] I will refer to the case as the 'Reuzegom case' in this chapter out of respect for the Dia family's wishes that Sanda's name should not be continually associated with the degrading treatment that cost him his life.

culpability—rendered abstract by the anonymity policy—with broader concerns about privilege and power. Secondly, a generic 'trial by media' label often assumes a uniform media output, overlooking potential diversity and divergence in media reporting. In this case, there were not only different issues on 'trial' in different media platforms, but social media commentators also diverged from dominant media discourse by actively questioning the restraint shown by mainstream media in their reporting of the case. Thirdly, the Reuzegom perpetrators were not tried by an easily influenced lay jury but by a panel of professional judges, offering safeguards which reduced the risk of media publicity harming the defendants' prospect of a fair trial. Finally—and crucially—the Reuzegom case has to be understood against the historical backdrop of low public confidence in the Belgian criminal justice system, more specifically the long shadow cast by the notorious 1990s case of the serial child sexual offender Marc Dutroux which was dominated by allegations of an institutional cover-up. Accusations that institutional racism and the perpetrators' powerful connections had thwarted the Dia family's search for justice inevitably reactivated concerns that the establishment was once again seeking to protect its own interests.

In what follows, I will first offer an account of Sanda's fatal hazing and its aftermath, including the actions taken against the perpetrators by both university authorities and the criminal justice system. Readers should be warned that they may find some details triggering and upsetting. Next, I will discuss how media interest in the Reuzegom case developed and evolved over time and across different media outlets. In the third section, I analyse the features of media reporting in more detail to explain why media reporting in the Reuzegom case did not meet the threshold of trial by media.

Sanda Dia's Fatal Hazing

Initiation rituals for freshers wishing to join a student society are an established feature of student life in Belgium where the tradition is widely known as a 'student baptism'. Extreme iterations in the form of hazing occur relatively frequently, despite attempts by university authorities to regulate baptisms. Hazing, which exists in several other organisations including the army and other workplaces (Thomas et al., 2021), involves the extensive humiliation of aspiring members. It carries the risk of significant emotional and physical harm and even in some cases death. Hazing can be defined as 'any activity expected of someone joining or participating in a group (such as a student club, organization, or team) that humiliates, degrades, abuses, or endangers regardless of a person's willingness to participate' (Hoover & Pollard 1999 cited in Allan et al., 2019, p. 32). As Allan et al. (2019) observe, victims of hazing are typically forced to drink excessive amounts of alcohol and to obey the commands issued by group leaders. Moreover, hazing is usually performed in front of other group members, augmenting its humiliating effect, and it is strongly associated with the display of masculinity and heteronormativity.

Sanda Dia was rather unusual in wishing to join the elite fraternity Reuzegom because he was not a fresher but a third-year student in civil engineering at the Catholic University Leuven (Katholieke Universiteit Leuven, hereafter KU Leuven). According to his family and friends, Sanda, as a working-class minority-ethnic student, wanted to join the fraternity to network and enhance his career prospects. Reuzegom was a very selective male-only club with many well-connected members who would often follow in the footsteps of their parents by pursuing careers as lawyers, judges, medical doctors and CEOs. The fraternity has been compared to the notoriously elitist Bullingdon Club to which the likes of David Cameron, Boris Johnson and George Osborne, all very senior former members of the UK Government, belonged in their student days at Oxford University (Huyberechts, 2023). Reuzegom exclusively recruited members who hailed from the Antwerp region.[2] The fraternity was co-founded in 1946 by an Antwerp student who went on the become a high-profile Flemish politician. Gaining membership of Reuzengom involved a lengthy process and required elaborate heats, with hazing as its final and most extreme endurance test. The fraternity is associated with

[2] 'Reuzegom' refers to wooden puppets which were popular as an eighteenth century fairground attraction in Borgerhout, a suburb of the city of Antwerp. 'Reuzegom' also features in the lyrics of the folk song *Reuzenlied* ('Giant's Song'), the tune of which is played every 15 minutes by the belfry of the university library of the KU Leuven.

a notoriously racist chant celebrating Belgium's brutal colonial past in The Congo (De Coninck, 2022). The student leader in charge of hazing in the year when Sanda died referred in his pitch to be elected to 'our good friend Hitler', adding that he wanted hazing to be 'really brutal' and 'insanely brutal' (De Coninck, 2022, p. 15). In 2013, an animal welfare charity took legal action against Reuzegom over its treatment of animals during its hazing rituals. Alongside the degrading treatment of aspiring members, animal abuse appeared to have been a routine feature of Reuzegom's baptism rituals. Reuzegom steadfastly refused to sign up to the KU Leuven's code of conduct for student baptisms aimed at regulating hazing and curb its excesses.

Sanda's fatal hazing took place over two days in December 2018. The ordeal began on 4th December with a challenge involving the selling of roses to passers-by. Sanda was punished for selling the least number of roses by being made to ingest several unsavoury substances, along with copious amount of alcohol. This challenge was followed by a quiz; for each wrong answer, Sanda and two other applicants were punished by being made to drink alcohol. This continued until they passed out. At that point, they were urinated on by Reuzegom members, as was 'tradition' at the club. Sanda and the other two students were taken back to his student accommodation for the night. All three were prevented from drinking water by Reuzegom members who had sealed off all the taps. The following day, the three were transferred by car to a remote site in the woods which was rented out by the local Scouts association. A witness who saw Sanda in Leuven that day would later testify that he looked very unwell, but when she challenged Reuzegom members about his welfare, they managed to convince her that he was fine. They also gave her false reassurances that the hazing event had ended and falsely claimed to be medically qualified. On their arrival in the woods, the three aspiring members were made to dig a pit in which they had to sit for several hours in freezing cold water. To keep them 'warm', they would once again be urinated on repeatedly by Reuzegom members. There is also video evidence that an unidentified victim was defecated on (Huyberechts, 2023, p. 13). The applicants were forced to ingest a mouse (which had been torn to shreds alive in a blender), pet food and fish oil containing very high concentrations of salt. They were also challenged to swallow a live goldfish and vomit it back up alive. As Sanda failed in the challenge, he was made to swallow a second live goldfish and drink more fish oil. By the evening, the other two student undergoing the hazing noticed that Sanda had become unresponsive and severely undercooled. They were eventually instructed by Reuzegom members to remove him from the pit and leave him to warm up by a campfire, but he remained unresponsive. After a considerable period of delay during which Reuzegom members dithered over whether Sanda required medical attention, he was finally taken to hospital by car late in the evening. He was unconscious and was suffering from severe hypothermia. He also suffered a cardiac arrest and tests revealed extremely toxic levels of salt in his blood. Sanda was transferred to a larger university hospital where he died on 7 December 2018 of a swelling on the brain, following his family's decision to take him off life support. The two other hazing victims were also hospitalised with less severe symptoms of salt poisoning which they both survived.

In the intervening time, panicking Reuzegom members who had participated in the fatal hazing attempted to destroy evidence by eliminating all traces at the site and deleting their messages on social media, actions which would later be portrayed in the media as aggravating factors amounting to an admission of guilt. They also took down Reuzegom's official website so as to protect the identities of the club's members. Sanda's death triggered two separate investigations: one by the criminal justice authorities and one by university authorities. The former involved a long and complex procedural journey which would eventually see 18 members of Reuzegom convicted in May 2023 of several offences including involuntary manslaughter, degrading treatment, culpable negligence and animal cruelty. In keeping with Belgian law, Sanda's father joined the criminal trial as a civil party, along with the two surviving victims of Sanda's fatal hazing. Significantly, much to the distress of the Dia family, the defendants have never revealed who administered the fatal amount of fish oil to Sanda. While their excessive consumption of alcohol may account to some extent for their failure to recollect specific events (yet they were apparently sober enough to rid the site of the hazing of potentially incriminating forensic evidence), their silence was interpreted as yet another form of closing ranks.

The four-year long criminal justice process to bring the defendants to justice involved several twists and turns. The trial, which was originally scheduled to be held in the Antwerp criminal court, was transferred to a different part of the country following a successful appeal by the Dia family's legal team arguing there was a risk of bias in the Antwerp court where the parent of one of the accused was a judicial office holder. Another judge had to recuse themselves over links with the KU Leuven. Not long after the start of the trial in April 2022 in the city of Hasselt, the presiding judge declared that judges could only consider what had occurred on the final day of the hazing in the woods to the exclusion of events leading up to this final stage. Narrowing the scope of the trial in this manner would have meant that only a lesser charge carrying a less severe sentence could be brought against the defendants. The judge's declaration triggered a further appeal before the Antwerp Appeal Court which eventually resulted in the guilty verdicts, with the Reuzegom defendants sentenced to community service and a fine of €400. They were also ordered to pay compensation to the Dia family. Their sentences meant that defendants were not given a criminal record and were free to resume their lives and careers unburdened by their past. As for the KU Leuven, the disciplinary measures taken against the Reuzegom participants were initially limited to a community task and the writing of a paper. They were all allowed to continue with their university studies. In 2020, twenty staff members of the University wrote an open letter to the head of the university demanding heavier sanctions and, in 2021, following a new disciplinary procedure, seven of the Reuzegom participants who were still students at the University were expelled, some permanently (Verstraete, 2021). Reuzegom itself was disbanded shortly after Sanda's death in December 2018.

Media Coverage and the Social Media Campaign for Justice

Pieter Huyberechts, a Belgian investigative journalist who extensively investigated the circumstances of Sanda's fatal hazing, published a detailed account charting the media's interest in the case (Huyberechts,

2023). In his book, he describes how journalists were already contacting Reuzegom members when Sanda was critically ill in hospital and there was a still a glimmer of hope that he would survive. Aware of the seriousness of the situation, he claims that the club decided to close ranks and remain tight-lipped about the precise nature of their involvement in Sanda's death (Huyberechts, 2023). 'We have stay out of the media', one of their leaders wrote on the club's WhatsApp group which would subsequently be deleted, along with all other forms of Reuzegom's online presence (Huyberechts, 2023, p. 309). The news of Sanda's passing was published on news websites at exactly 17:41 local time on 7 December 2018 (Huyberechts, 2023, p. 312). Three days later, Huyberechts published an interview with the Dia family in which they criticised the complete silence of the Reuzegom fraternity and expressed concern that the privileged backgrounds of its members would mean that the full truth about Sanda's death might never see the light of day (Huyberechts & Van Damme, 2018). Meanwhile, public indignation was taking hold in social media. The KU Leuven and the Minister for Education issued public condemnations of Reuzegom's hazing practices.

Yet, in the first 18 months, news coverage of the story was limited as there was relatively little information to report: there was an ongoing criminal investigation and official information was extremely scant, something which Huyberechts attributes in part to the defendants' successful strategy to maintain complete silence. However, it should also be noted that maintaining secrecy in a criminal investigation during its preparatory stage is commonplace in inquisitorial systems (Resta, 2008; Stoyanova in this volume). The family and friends of Sanda, by contrast, actively engaged with the media, for example, cooperating with a television reconstruction of Sanda's fatal hazing on the Flemish current affairs show *Telefacts* revealing disturbing details not just about the hazing ritual but also about the toxic culture of humiliation, racism and far-right sympathies at the heart of Reuzegom. The programme was broadcast in July 2020. Huyberechts would also publish his own reconstruction in his newspaper *Het Nieuwsblad* in July 2020. He describes how it took him a year and a half to unearth details about the case: 'the culture of silence made it seem like [I was] digging with a small spoon' (Huyberechts, 2023, p. 23). He was repeatedly told that he could not have access because the criminal investigation was still ongoing, before eventually obtaining the intelligence required: 'How? I can't reveal [that], but from different well-informed sources comes tangible information' (Huyberechts, 2023, p. 335).

Summer 2020 proved a turning point in terms of media interest in the case. It coincided with the height of the COVID-19 pandemic but also, importantly, with the Black Lives Matter protests in the US following the death of George Floyd at the hands of police. Campaigners and protesters seeking justice for Sanda drew inspiration from the Black Lives Matter movement. Racism became a prominent media frame, although as I discuss below, it resonated much more strongly in social media than it did in mainstream media. Racial and class bias in the criminal justice system and fears about an institutional cover-up all featured in the media coverage. Sanda's friends launched an online campaign for justice under the hashtag #justiceforsanda, gaining more than 6.5 m views on TikTok. International media also began paying attention to the case. In October 2020, the *New York Times* published a blistering report blaming Sanda's death on racist, anti-immigrant and far-right politics in Flanders, Belgium's Flemish-speaking northern region (Apuzzo & Erlanger, 2020). Anti-racism campaigners started mobilising online and offline, culminating in widespread protests in several cities in Belgium and The Netherlands after the 2023 Reuzegom trial. The Dia family also gained celebrity support from the Belgian film star Matthias Schoenaerts who produced a graffiti artwork in honour of Sanda, generating widespread online publicity (Anonymous, 2022). Not all publicity was welcomed by the Dia family. A television station showed the harrowing final images of a dying Sanda at his hazing in the run-up to the aborted 2022 trial, much to the distress of his relatives who had not been warned that the footage would be broadcast (Huyberechts, 2023, p. 401).

Reuzegom defendants and their family members were personally targeted online and offline as a result of the growing publicity. The dentist parent of one of the defendants received fake online reviews warning that patients at the practice were being made 'to rinse their mouths with fish oil' (Huyberechts, 2023, p. 444). While Reuzegom has always remained anonymous in mainstream news media where they are systematically referred to by their Reuzegom nicknames (the club had a tradition of assigning often puerile monikers such as ‘shit fly’, ‘fart pit’ and ‘cry baby’ to aspiring members who successfully underwent the hazing process), their identities were circulating online. In September 2020, Reuzegom defence lawyers voiced concerns that their clients had become victims of trial by media. Lawyers made media appearances to discuss their fear that media publicity was depriving their clients of the prospect of a fair trial (Heymans, 2020). Some were threatening legal action against the media. The trial by media claim would also be used by the defence at the appeal trial of the Reuzegom defendants in the Spring of 2023 (Anonymous, 2023).

The 2023 trial took place in a febrile atmosphere which was reflected by intense media attention and public anger in social media. The defendants hid their faces as they entered and left the court building so as to avoid being filmed or photographed. The Dia family, as a civil party in the trial proceedings, was represented by the high-profile criminal lawyer Sven Mary who had already gained much media coverage for his legal work (Gijs & Moens, 2023). In contrast with the Reuzegom defence lawyers, he was not averse to tapping into the growing media interest in the case. He spoke frequently—and continues to speak—with the media and he did not shy away from commenting on the criminal investigation and subsequent trials. Mary also demanded in court that the identities of the defendants be made public, arguing that full disclosure was in the public interest.

The verdicts from the 2023 trial, handing down what were perceived to be relatively light sentences for all defendants, were met with considerable public anger. Protest marches, graffiti displaying the names of the offenders and more fake negative online reviews targeting businesses with Reuzegom links followed. The most eye-catching intervention came from the young Belgian YouTube influencer Acid who in June 2023 following the Reuzegom appeal trial posted a video in which he named and shamed four Reuzegom members. A Michelin starred restaurant owned by the family of a former Reuzegom member who was not involved in Sanda’s hazing had to temporarily close as a result of the negative publicity. In an unusual legal move, Acid was subsequently criminally prosecuted by the aggrieved party for disclosing their identity (Decré, 2023). In February 2024, he received a three-month suspended prison sentence and a €800 fine. He was also ordered to pay €20,000 in damages (Anonymous, 2024b). The fact that he received a larger penalty than the Reuzegom accused did attracted further public indignation in social media. Remarkably, the crowd funding appeal to help Acid pay the fine and damages yielded more than €125,000 within just a day of being launched (Anonymous, 2024a), far exceeding the amount required. At the time of writing, it is still possible to find the (alleged) names of Reuzegom defendants and other personal identifiers online; however, mainstream legacy media are continuing to uphold their anonymity. As I discuss in the next section, this ongoing preservation of anonymity challenges the argument that the defendants received a trial by media, but at the same time it has also been grist to the mill of critics who claim that mainstream media have been complicit in an establishment cover-up.

Trial by Media or Not?

When Reuzegom defence lawyers complained that their clients were being treated unfairly in the media, it was striking that they resorted to using the English term 'trial by media'. The absence of an equivalent Dutch (Flemish) term or suitable translation from English underlines that that the terminology is an import from a very different legal system. Indeed, the literature is almost exclusively preoccupied with the way in which trial by media tends to play out in US and UK media. Indiscriminately transplanting the concept of trial by media across different legal and media systems is problematic (Resta, 2008). This is not to say that the general thrust of trial by media does not apply in a wide range of settings and circumstances. After all, at its heart, trial by media is about the question of whether media coverage oversteps the mark of legitimate scrutiny and journalistic inquiry with adverse consequences for those who are accused of serious wrongdoing. Media coverage of the Reuzegom case undoubtedly displayed some elements of trial by media. However, as I explain below, there were also several factors which point to a legitimate form of public scrutiny and justice seeking. Thus, the bulk of the media coverage was focused on the privileged position of the Reuzegom fraternity collectively, rather than on the accused individually who remained anonymous throughout in mainstream media. Unlike typical trial by media cases whereby different media channels and platforms promote largely similar and often simplistic narratives of guilt, different media pursued different agendas in the Reuzegom case, with, for example, the racism frame being much more resonant in social media. Furthermore, there is no immediate evidence that the media publicity had any detrimental impact on the outcome of the court process which was conducted before a panel of professional judges. Finally, historic precedent in the form of the notorious Dutroux affair justified robust and intense media probing in the Reuzegom case to ensure transparency and maintain public confidence.

Anonymity and Focus on Power and Class Privilege

The most recognisable scenario of trial by media involves media coverage featuring an intensely personal focus on the conduct, character and often also appearance of named individuals, usually suspects in a criminal investigation. Personalisation is the hallmark of tabloid justice characterised by baseless rumours, sensationalism, ad-hominem attacks and character assassination, often accompanied by the full identification of individuals through the publication of their names, photographs and other personal information which is repeatedly and routinely included in the reporting across a wide range of media outlets. An insightful example is the comprehensive vilification in the British tabloid press of the American exchange student Amanda Knox who was initially convicted and later exonerated for the murder of her British flatmate and fellow exchange student Meredith Kercher in Perugia in 2007 (Gibson, 2012; Gies & Bortoluzzi, 2016). In the Reuzegom case, the Belgian media's treatment of the student suspects was of a very different nature, helped to a large extent by the absence of a tabloid press. Despite (contained) Internet leaks of personal information, mainstream media have consistently adopted a blanket policy of protecting the identity of the suspects. In fact, the Reuzegom offenders have enjoyed greater anonymity in Belgian media than do many other suspects who are usually identified in run-of-the-mill crime reporting by their first name and the initial of their surname. Full anonymity is normally reserved for vulnerable suspects such as minors, but this did not apply to the Reuzegom accused who were all already adults when they committed the offences.

It was the unnamed suspects along with their well-connected but equally anonymous families and the illustrious membership of the Reuzegom society at large who all found themselves collectively at the heart of the media storm. In other words, it is a question of *what* rather than *who* was on trial in the media: in this instance, it was a system and a culture of privilege and entitlement which resulted in fatal and near-fatal outcomes for three of the elite student society's aspiring members. Reuzegom's elite character and record of impunity (evident from previous legal action over the club's animal abuse and the fact that Reuzegom had steadfastly refused to sign up to the university student baptism code of conduct) gave journalists and commentators cause to investigate issues such as the KU Leuven's mild disciplinary sanctions against Reuzegom students following its initial inquiry and the appearance of judicial bias in the criminal case. These questions turned out to be all the more legitimate considering that the case was taken away from the Antwerp criminal court, the recusal of one particular trial judge with connections with the KU Leuven and also the KU Leuven's decision to conduct a second inquiry resulting in harsher penalties for Reuzegom members. Moreover, as I discuss further below, historic failings of the Belgian criminal justice system and recriminations of establishment cover-ups further increase the legitimacy of the nature of the journalistic inquiry into the Reuzegom case. Overall, this kind of media scrutiny is a world away from the treatment befalling the individual suspect whose name and image are gratuitously exposed in the tabloid press for no apparent reason other than that scandal and clickbait sell.

Social Media Versus Legacy Media

An obvious pitfall of the generic 'trial by media' label is that it may obscure relevant distinctions between different types of media forms and contents. While the effects of trial by media may be greatly amplified when a large number of media outlets reproduce very similar, often simplistic, narratives of guilt and innocence, it is also important to be aware of diverging narratives in the reporting (Middleweek, 2017). Trial by media can take on different forms within the context of the same case. One of the most fascinating aspects of the Reuzegom case is how a young generation of TikTok, Instagram and YouTube users—broadly speaking contemporaries of both Sanda and the Reuzegom fraternity—utilised the online media space to demand justice. Social media acted as a counterpublic (Wood et al., 2019) targeting not just criminal justice agencies but also other forms of power, including media power. Social media commentators expressed deep unhappiness with the anonymity granted to the Reuzegom accused in mainstream media which they saw as a sign of journalists' complicity in a cover-up. YouTuber Acid's much talked about June 2023 video in which he decided to publicly expose Reuzegom members is a case in point. However, it was not just anonymity that was a bone of contention between mainstream and social media. There was much more outspoken anger about the injustice of Sanda's death in social media than there was in mainstream media still dominated by professional journalistic accounts. The absence of professional journalistic standards of balance and objectivity afforded a space for a deeply affective response in social media (Papacharissi, 2014). Huyberechts observes in his account: 'it is incredibly striking: as soon as one of their [Reuzegom accused's] lawyers makes a public statement, the digital knife is out' (Huyberechts, 2023, p. 362).[3]

Social media accusations of racism and 'class justice' (referring to class bias in the criminal justice system) were explicitly targeted at the Reuzegom fraternity but they were also aimed at Belgian society more broadly, indicting higher education, criminal justice and the broader political system. By contrast, mainstream media outlets showed restraint and also denial. Huyberechts in his memoir is categorical that throughout his investigations he did not find a single shred of evidence that Sanda had been treated more harshly during the hazing on account

[3] I should add that he makes this observation about a Reuzegom lawyer's very controversial and offensive statement defending the Reuzegom accused decision to immediately clear up the scene of Sanda's fatal hazing by arguing 'that it is only normal for a party's organisers to have a clear up when the party is over' (Heymans, 2020).

of his skin colour. Moreover, the journalist is very critical of *The New York Times* article which blamed Sanda's death and the authorities' response on institutional racism in Flemish society, calling its accusations 'more than an exaggeration' (Huyberechts, 2023, p. 350). Yet, despite his reluctance to accept that racism played a material role, his book repeatedly quotes Sanda's friends and relatives as saying that racism and class bias were both factors not just in Sanda's tragic death but also in the failure of the criminal justice system and university authorities to impose appropriate sanctions. The journalist also acknowledges past racist conduct by Reuzegom members which included verbally abusing Sanda with the N-word. Huyberechts, who undoubtedly shows great empathy towards the Dia family, recognises the existence of unconscious bias, but he nonetheless fails to explore its impact in the case. His criticism was predominantly targeted at the wall of silence he encountered as a journalist and his lack of access to the criminal investigation, which points to a very different agenda from that pursued by social media activists demanding radical social change under the hashtag #justiceforsanda.

Impact and Outcomes of Media Publicity

The concept of trial by media is largely predicated on the idea that media trials have an inherently harmful impact. Not only does such an interpretation ignore the possibility that intense media attention may be beneficial; it also overlooks the possibility that it may make no significant difference to the outcome of a legal trial. Extreme case scenarios in terms of legal outcomes include the possibility that the defendant is deprived of a fair hearing, that a trial is aborted because of extraneous media influences on jurors and witnesses and that trial by media gives grounds for a legal appeal. These scenarios are largely tailored to an adversarial system with a tradition of jury trials and cross-examination (e.g. Gabriel, 2000; Geragos, 2006), but they are not particularly relevant to the Reuzegom case which was tried by a panel of professional judges in the context of an inquisitorial system (Resta, 2008).[4] One Reuzegom defence lawyer

[4] In the Belgian legal system, only the most serious offences are tried by jury and this did not apply to the Reuzegom case.

countered the argument that professional judges are perfectly capable of rising above what is said in the media by pointing out that 'judges were only human'. The sentences that were eventually handed down to the Reuzegom accused appear to suggest that judges were not excessively punitive. Whether they may have been more lenient in view of the intense media interest is a separate matter: one of the defence lawyers pleaded in court for the charges against their client to be dropped on the basis that he had been the victim of trial by media, but this was not given any effect. As far as the direct outcome of the legal trial was concerned, there is no immediate evidence that media reporting had much influence.

The greatest impact as far as the accused are concerned is to be found outside of the courtroom: defence lawyers bristled that the KU Leuven was pandering to the pressure of public opinion when it decided to impose harsher disciplinary sanctions following its second inquiry into Sanda's hazing. The University strenuously denied this, saying that new facts had come to light warranting more severe sanctions. There is also the economic harm flowing from the fake online reviews targeting businesses owned by the families of Reuzegom members. Additionally, there is the potential harm associated with long-term digital exposure. The Internet is often referred to as the medium that never forgets, although this must be qualified because of the right to have personal data erased under the EU's GDPR law. Other harms flowing from the intense media interest, such as the invasion of privacy and the psychological distress suffered by the accused but also by their families and members of the Reuzegom fraternity who had no involvement in Sanda's death, should not be dismissed either. The most unsettling aspect of Reuzegom's toxic culture is that it involved a vicious circle whereby past victims of hazing would be expected to perpetrate the same violence against incoming recruits in subsequent years. Each of the Reuzegom perpetrators was therefore also a victim. Nevertheless, any such harmful effects must be balanced against the benefits of widespread public discussion of the case and enhanced scrutiny of the criminal justice system, the relevance of which I detail below.

Context and Historical Antecedent

In 1996, the Belgian criminal justice system was engulfed by a crisis causing widespread public protest and unprecedented levels of media attention. Its impact included substantial reforms of the police service and aspects of the judicial system. The crisis centred on Marc Dutroux who in the mid-1990s abducted six young girls, hid them in a dungeon in his home and killed four of his young victims. Despite a string of previous convictions and the existence of strong intelligence pointing to Dutroux as the main suspect, the police and judicial authorities failed to intervene and squandered several opportunities to save the lives of the four young victims (Punch, 2003). Dutroux and his accomplices were eventually apprehended and arrested in the summer of 1996 when two victims were rescued alive from his basement. The subsequent public inquiry would be broadened to other missing persons cases, including the unsolved murders of the young siblings Kim and Ken Heyrman. Rumours of organised criminal activity by a paedophile ring providing children on demand to the rich and powerful formed the focus of much speculation, but they have never been proven (Frenkiel, 2002), although they would resurface as part of the 2010 Wikileaks dossier (Charter, 2010). A profound public clamouring for justice and transparency gave the Dutroux case its social and political significance (Punch, 2003), resulting in a lengthy parliamentary inquiry and subsequent institutional reforms inaugurating 'a new political culture' (Staelraeve, 2004).

There are some striking parallels between the affair Dutroux and the Reuzegom case. One obvious similarity is the raw pain of grieving parents who felt misled and badly let down by the authorities and who feared that an institutional cover-up would prevent them from getting justice (Punch, 2003). In both instances, the parents would co-opt the media as allies and would use the media spotlight as an alternative path to justice. A complex 'puzzle' (Walgrave & Varone, 2008, p. 365) underpinned the catalogue of failings in the Dutroux case. This included considerable impropriety in the form of interference with the judicial process by the establishment, including politicians. In what Punch (2003) terms 'the Belgian disease', he describes how 'a culture of deals', cover-ups, favouritism—the custom of seeking favours from influential and powerful individuals—and nepotism gave rise to an incompetent, unfeeling and corrupt criminal justice system. Strikingly, the Reuzegom investigation would be plagued by very similar accusations, with the fraternity portrayed in the media as the epitome of nepotism and favouritism in modern-day Belgium. Allegations of a coordinated cover-up in favour of Reuzegom members and their powerful families were once again rife. The notion of impunity for the powerful and well-connected became an all too familiar refrain, given the broader historical context. Just as in the Dutroux case, class bias, along with racist attitudes, was thought to have obstructed the Dia family's search for justice. Large-scale public protests ensued, although the so-called White March of protesters which saw 1 in 30 Belgians take to the streets (300,000 in total) in the Dutroux case remains a historical record in terms of mass mobilisation in Belgium (Lippens, 1998). On the other hand, justice campaigners in the Reuzegom case benefited from the reach of social media to congregate and mobilise, providing various platforms where users could generate their own commentary.

When a crime exposes systemic problems which transcend the question of individual guilt, we should be very wary to dismiss the media attention as trial by media. The Dutroux precedent gave the Reuzegom case special social and political significance which warranted a very high level of media scrutiny. While it may be difficult at times to distinguish between personal attacks and intense criticism of institutional processes, it is paramount that there can be maximum publicity when fundamental issues of legitimacy and public trust are at stake. Just as during the affair Dutroux, the politico-legal system found itself on trial in the Reuzegom case, albeit with less intensity. To restrict or curb such scrutiny may lead to even greater suspicions of a cover-up: the effect of the blanket anonymity police of mainstream news media in the Reuzegom case was to fuel conspiracy theories that public broadcasters and newspapers were 'too scared' to reveal any names. Comparable to the Dutroux case—again, admittedly on a lesser scale—the intense media spotlight in the Reuzegom case came with a clamouring for social justice. Moreover, precisely because of specific historic antecedents, the publicity in the Reuzegom case was a way of stress-testing the police and judicial reforms that followed in the wake of the Dutroux affair.

Conclusion

Trial by media occurs when media coverage manifestly exceeds the limits of ethical reporting. Cases usually involve a high degree of personalisation in the form of attention on individual actors—typically suspects and victims—who are personally vilified by targeting their conduct, character, physical appearance, race, sexuality, gender and other characteristics in building a narrative of deviance. As a form of infotainment, the coverage is inflammatory and frequently revolves around lurid details, unfounded rumours, speculation and insinuation. While popular, tabloid media are most prone to trial by media, the effects are magnified when other platforms reproduce a very similar set of narratives, even when these are more moderate in tone and language. The media feeding frenzy typically engulfs the entire media ecology, with social media acting as an especially fertile ground. Individuals caught up in trial by media are found guilty before the judicial process has been concluded and, in some cases, suspicions may linger even after a formal legal trial has exonerated the defendant. The most extreme manifestation of trial by media is when it compromises a defendant's right to a fair hearing, a scenario which reporting restrictions (e.g. through contempt of court laws) aim to prevent. The gratuitous nature of trial by media coverage is often exacerbated by the limited public interest in extensive or prolonged media coverage of a particular case. Such is the level of personalisation that broader issues pertaining to societal, political or institutional failings or responsibilities (e.g. the impact of social deprivation) are ignored or barely acknowledged. Trial by media is typically devoid of a social justice agenda.

Media reporting does not need to be completely free from these features to pursue legitimate aims. In a complex and rich media ecology, there are bound to be elements of media discourse which both stimulate and inhibit a trial by media scenario. This was amply demonstrated in the Reuzegom case. Inhibiting factors included the anonymity granted to the accused in mainstream media and the absence of UK-style tabloid media. There was vehement criticism of the culture, practices and privileged backgrounds of the Reuzegom fraternity, but the sting was removed because the individual suspects remained anonymous. Individuals caught up in a typical trial by media often become household names against their will. By contrast, while Reuzegom collectively undoubtedly gained infamy and notoriety, individual members were not readily identifiable. Some social media users, as counterpublic, took it upon themselves to name Reuzegom members, but the pressure to out these individuals was not sufficient to rob them of their anonymity. Social media were vectors of public anger and resistance directed at the establishment, criminal justice agencies and also mainstream media. The social media campaign is a textbook example of viral justice with its grassroots, bottom-up dynamics aimed at contesting deeply entrenched power structures (Wood et al., 2019). Compared to mainstream media reporting, social media discourse was more affective and more vocal about the role which racism played in Sanda's death and the response of criminal justice and university authorities. The impact of the publicity on suspects was limited because they were tried by a panel of professional judges, with no evidence that they received a harsher sentence because of the media coverage. However, in a few isolated cases, naming and shaming on social media inflicted direct damage affecting not just the defendants but also third parties. On balance, however, media interest in the case was justified by a strong public interest element because of the specific historical precedent of the Dutroux affair with which there are some clear parallels. The Reuzegom case acquired a relevance which went beyond the shocking and distressing circumstances which resulted in a young person of colour losing his life in a hazing event organised by a white, elite student fraternity. Much of the coverage was inspired by a social justice agenda. Intense media scrutiny of the decisions taken by different agencies in the Reuzegom case was therefore rendered proportionate by the gravity of allegations of potential racism and class bias, but also by the need to stress-test the robustness of the reformed criminal justice system after the Dutroux scandal.

Competing Interests

The author has no conflicts of interest to declare that are relevant to the content of this chapter.

References

Allan, E. J., Kerschner, D., & Payne, J. M. (2019). College student hazing experiences, attitudes, and perceptions: Implications for prevention. *Journal of Student Affairs Research and Practice, 56*(1), 32–48. https://doi.org/10.1080/19496591.2018.1490303

Anonymous. (2022, May 18). Matthias Schoenaerts maakt graffitikunstwerk van Sanda Dia op festivalweide Rock Werchter: 'Zwart op wit. #justiceforsanda'. *DeMorgen.* graffitikunstwerk-van-sanda-dia-op-festivalweide-rock-werchter-zwart-op-wit-justiceforsanda~b051b3bd/

Anonymous. (2023, March 6). Advocaat van 'Protput': "Waar is de KU Leuven? De ouders hebben hun kinderen aan de universiteit toevertrouwd". *Het Nieuwsblad.* https://www.nieuwsblad.be/cnt/dmf20230316_93564546

Anonymous. (2024a, February 23). Crowdfunding Belgische youtuber voor Sanda Dia-zaak levert ruim 125.000 euro op. *NOS Nieuws.* https://nos.nl/artikel/2510055-crowdfunding-belgische-youtuber-voor-sanda-dia-zaak-levert-ruim-125-000-euro-op

Anonymous. (2024b, February 22). Sanda Dia death: Suspended sentence for influencer Acid after naming (former) Reuzegom fraternity members on YouTube. *VRTnws.*https://www.vrt.be/vrtnws/en/2024/02/22/acid-nathan-vandergunst-reuzegom-fraternity-court-case-hazing-sa/.

Apuzzo, M., & Erlanger, S. (2020, October 5). A black Belgian student saw a white fraternity as his ticket. It was his death. *The New York Times.* https://www.nytimes.com/2020/10/04/world/europe/belgium-racism-sanda-dia.html

Charter, D. (2010, August 27). WikiLeaks attacked over Belgian child murder files. *The Times.* https://www.thetimes.co.uk/article/wikileaks-provokes-protest-by-publishing-child-abuse-files-k85fmm86cqq

Davies, A. (2023, June 3). Sanda Dia-Belgium reckons with verdict over black student's hazing death'. *BBC News.* https://www.bbc.co.uk/news/world-europe-65767457.

Decré, H. (2023, September 7). YouTuber acid versus ex-Reuzegommer: zaak wordt pas gepleit op 18 januari. *VRTnws*. https://www.vrt.be/vrtnws/nl/2023/09/07/acid-versus-reuzegommer-zaak-meteen-uitgesteld-naar-18-januari/

De Coninck, D. (2022). *Ontmenselijkt: Achter de schermen bij studentenclub Reuzegom*. Pelckmans.

De Coninck, D. (2020, July 31). Alexander G., 'schachtentemmer' bij Reuzegom, wilde er 'een gestoord bruut jaar van maken'. *DeMorgen*. https://www.demorgen.be/nieuws/alexander-g-schachtentemmer-bij-reuzegom-wilde-er-een-gestoord-bruut-jaar-van-maken~b59fab51/

Frenkiel, O. (2002, May 5). Belgium's silent heart of darkness. *The Guardian*. https://www.theguardian.com/world/2002/may/05/dutroux.featuresreview.

Gabriel, R. (2000). This case is brought to you by..: how high-profile media trials affect juries. *Loyola of Los Angeles Law Review, 33*(2), 725–736.

Geragos, M. J. (2006). The thirteenth juror: Media coverage of supersized trials. *Loyola of Los Angeles Law Review, 39*(4), 1167–1196.

Gibson, J. C. (2012). *Judges, tabloids and trial by media*. Union Internationale des Avocats: 56th Annual Congress, Dresden. https://districtcourt.nsw.gov.au/download.html/documents/Trial%20by%20media%20-%20Judges%20and%20the%20tabloid%20intrusion%20into%20the%20court%20process.pdf

Gies, L., & Bortoluzzi, M. (2016). *Transmedia crime stories: The trial of Amanda Knox and Raffaele Sollecito in the Globalised Media Sphere*. Palgrave.

Gijs, C., & Moens, B. (2023, February 13). Lawyer for Paris bomber takes over MEP Eva Kaili's defense in Qatargate probe. *Politico*. https://www.politico.eu/article/paris-bomber-lawyer-sven-mary-takes-over-eva-kailis-qatar-corruption-defense-qatargate-probe/

Heymans, P. (2020, September 7). Advocaat Reuzegommer: "Druk op rechters is zo groot, dat ik hoop dat ze nog onafhankelijk kunnen oordelen". *VRTnws*. https://www.vrt.be/vrtnws/nl/2020/09/07/advocaten-reuzegom

Huyberechts, P. (2023). *De doop die leidde to the dood*. Dasmag (third edition).

Huyberechts, P., & Van Damme, D. (2018, December 10). Familie student die stierf na doop hoopt op gerechtigheid: "Dit verhaal mag niet in de doofpot belanden". *Het Nieuwsblad*. https://www.nieuwsblad.be/cnt/dmf20181210_04021901

Lippens, R. (1998). The white march as a Belgian body without organs: On dissipative structures, strange attractions and empty signifiers. *Crime, Law and Social Change, 29*, 49–65.

Middleweek, B. (2017). Dingo media? The persistence of the "trial by media" frame in popular, media, and academic evaluations of the Azaria Chamberlain case. *Feminist Media Studies, 17*(3), 392–411. https://doi.org/10.1080/14680777.2016.1235054

Papacharissi, Z. (2014). *Affective publics: Sentiment, technology, and politics.* Oxford University Press.

Punch, M. (2003). Rotten orchards: 'pestilence', police misconduct and system failure. *Policing and Society, 13*(2), 171–196. https://doi.org/10.1080/10439460308026

Resta, G. (2008). Trying cases in the media: Comparative overview. *Law and Contemporary Problems, 71*(4), 31–66.

Staelraeve, S. (2004). De zaak-Dutroux: lessen over parlementair onderzoek en controle. *Samenleving en Politiek, 11*(7), 22–30. https://www.sampol.be/2004/09/de-zaak-dutroux-lessen-over-parlementair-onderzoek-en-controle

Thomas, B. J., Cimino, A., & Meglich, P. (2021). Workplace hazing: Toward an organizational science of a cryptic group practice. *Group and Organization Management, 46*(2), 286–326.

Verstraete, A. (2021, February 5). Advocaat Reuzegommer die weggestuurd wordt van de KU Leuven is ontgoocheld: "Wat bereikt Universiteit Hiermee?". *VRTnws.* https://www.vrt.be/vrtnws/nl/2021/02/04/reuzegom-fup/

Walgrave, S., & Varone, F. (2008). Punctuated equilibrium and agenda-setting: Bringing parties back in—Policy change after the Dutroux crisis in Belgium. *Governance, 21*(3), 365–395. https://doi.org/10.1111/j.1468-0491.2008.00404.x

Wood, M., Rose, E., & Thompson, C. (2019). Viral justice? Online justice-seeking, intimate partner violence and affective contagion. *Theoretical Criminology, 23*(3), 375–393. https://doi.org/10.1177/1362480617750507

Part IV

Impacts of Trial by Media

11

The Impact of Media Publicity on the Presumption of Innocence

Maria Stoyanova

Introduction

In a democratic society, both media freedom and the impartial administration of justice are paramount. On the one hand, it is undeniable that the media plays a crucial role in modern society by disseminating information, shaping public opinion, and serving as a watchdog over governmental and institutional actions. It facilitates the flow of information, ensuring transparency and accountability, while also influencing societal norms and values through its portrayal of events and issues. From a human rights and criminal law perspective, media outlets are indispensable in enabling the public to exercise their right to information. Public access to information about the criminal justice system adheres to the principle of open justice and is essential for maintaining public awareness and trust in the judiciary. Nonetheless, the relationship between justice and the media is typically turbulent (Synodinou, 2012). Media

M. Stoyanova (✉)
Center for the Study of Democracy, Sofia, Bulgaria
e-mail: maria.stoyanova@csd.eu

L. Gies (ed.), *Trial by Media*, Palgrave Studies in Crime, Media and Culture,
https://doi.org/10.1007/978-3-031-80593-6_11

coverage of criminal cases frequently serves as a battleground for these two pillars of democracy to clash. Media interference in legal proceedings is a well-documented phenomenon, often referred to as 'trial by media,' a term coined in the late twentieth century (Krishnan, 2018). The delicate balance between reporting what is in the public interest and what attracts public curiosity is easily disrupted (Stoyanova, 2021).

In their quest to satisfy public curiosity, which is typically heightened vis-à-vis crime news, media outlets often resort to practices that imply guilt during pre-trial and trial proceedings. Consequently, while journalists and media exercise their right to freedom of expression, they often carelessly infringe upon several rights of the defendants, including the right to a fair trial and respect for private and family life. Achieving an equilibrium between these conflicting rights remains a persistent challenge in the realm of human rights protection and media coverage of criminal proceedings.

The disregard for the presumption of innocence and the privacy of defendants is problematic from both legal and societal perspectives. From a legal perspective, there has been a wide debate about the role of the media in legal decision-making (Mensah, 2024). Excessive media coverage of pending penal cases is known to affect due judicial process and influence the impartiality of the judges, jury and ultimately the case outcome. Judges' decisions, prosecutors' and lawyers' tactics may be influenced by public scrutiny and may seek to fit in with the prevailing media narratives. The generated pressure can lead them to prioritise the public's opinion over the rules of justice that require concentrating only on the merits of the case (Mensah, 2024). From a societal perspective, media can generate hype among the public according to the way in which the cases are depicted in news materials, thereby influencing public sentiment. Depending on the narrative chosen to describe the crime story, the media can sway the public opinion towards guilt or innocence, creating expectations for a particular judgment. Furthermore, the crime story presented in the news can emphasize certain personal characteristics of the offender and inflame sensitive issues that tend to polarise society such as migration, racism and discrimination.

This chapter strives to bring to attention the harmful consequences of media publicity on the presumption of innocence of suspects and accused individuals. To achieve this goal, it presents case studies scrutinised to discover commonalities among the malpractices employed by media outlets and public officials in their reporting of information regarding criminal trials. They are examined through the prism of the existing legal and non-legal standards for ethical journalism.

The present chapter is inspired by the results of research conducted under the JUSTICE project called ARISA-2: Assessing the Risk of Isolation of Suspects and Accused: The Role of the Media. The research shed light on the damaging consequences that occur in the personal lives of defendants. The negative impact also affects family members and people close to the suspect or accused person. The work introduces the term 'extra punishment' to describe the traumatising experiences of thousands of people suspected or accused of a crime that attracts intense media coverage.

First, the author provides an overview of the evolution of the scope and meaning of the presumption of innocence as a legal principle. It is followed by a brief examination of the legal framework and soft-law norms regulating the disclosure and dissemination of information about criminal cases. Against this regulatory environment, the next section presents the media malpractices identified through analysis of case studies. In particular, Sect. 11.3 presents the case studies of criminal cases from Italy, Bulgaria, Greece and Spain.

Several considerations determined the selection of these countries for the research. First, all of them are European Union members located in Southern Europe, resulting in regulatory and cultural similarities, as well as interrelated political and social processes and issues. These national similarities facilitated the comparative analysis. At the same time, there is a division between Eastern and Western European countries, with the latter traditionally boasting robust media environments and ranking high in international indexes, such as the World Press Freedom Index by Reporters Without Borders. From 2021 to 2024, Spain and Italy maintained positions approximately around the 30th and 40th places (out of 180 countries), respectively. In contrast, Greece and Bulgaria consistently held the last place in Europe.

The analysis identifies patterns and common misconducts by news media and public officials that often endanger the presumption of innocence and privacy of the defendants. Hence, this chapter summarises the media toolbox that jeopardises the right to be presumed innocent until proven guilty and crystallises the negative implication of 'trial by media' at the individual, familial and societal levels.

Legal Protections and Boundaries of the Presumption of Innocence in International Law

Over the decades, the presumption of innocence has evolved into a fundamental legal principle in criminal justice systems worldwide. Often referred to as a human right itself (Ho, 2012), or a fundamental right not to be wrongly sentenced (Ashworth, 2006), it aims to protect individuals from the highest injustice of convicting an innocent person. It is also intended to safeguard individuals from arbitrary treatment by authorities such as unfounded or malicious accusations. As an integral part of the right to a fair trial, it ensures that any person facing a trial is presumed innocent until proven guilty through a fair and due trial process.

Initially, the presumption of innocence has been established as a legal principle placing the burden of proof in criminal cases on the prosecution and prohibiting the punishment of defendants without their guilt being proved according to law. Over time, the scope of the presumption of innocence has gradually expanded. The modern human rights system has broadened its interpretation to encompass issues concerning the public presentation of the defendants. In light of the latter, measuring the scope of the presumption of innocence inevitably leads to issues such as prejudicial public references to guilt, the provision or divulgence of information to the media, and its role in shaping public perceptions about suspects and accused persons (Doichinova et al., 2021).

A broader understanding of the scope and meaning of the presumption of innocence is particularly prevalent in the European legal systems. As Ashworth claims, in the realm of European human rights law, the presumption appears to operate at two different levels—one is the criminal trial and the other is the criminal process in general. Within the criminal trial, he argues, the original and almost universally accepted narrow conception of the principle applies, providing that when a person is charged with a criminal offence, the prosecution bears the burden of proving the guilt of that offence. The second aspect discussed by Ashworth supports a wider interpretation of the presumption of innocence, grasping issues such as public presentation and claiming that pre-trial and trial procedures should be conducted as if the defendant were innocent (Ashworth, 2006). Importantly, the fact that an accused individual had confessed to the crime does not remove the protection of the presumption of innocence.

Similar assumptions are asserted by European human rights bodies. The European Union Agency of Fundamental Rights (FRA) examines the presumption of innocence as a two-sided issue that has an internal and external dimension. The internal aspect relates to the criminal procedure. This encompasses how the actors directly engaged in the criminal proceedings, such as judges, prosecutors, police officers and lawyers, perceive and treat the defendant and how this affects their daily work. The external aspect deals with the presentation of the defendant to the public, which is shaped by the media to a large extent. Furthermore, the distinction between these two aspects is conditional as media is able to affect not only the external audience but also to reinforce biases of professionals directly engaged in the proceedings (European Union Agency for Fundamental Rights, 2021). In other words, FRA recognises that authorities are not immune to the cognitive influence of media.

The European Court of Human Rights (ECtHR) further elaborates our understanding of the protection of the right to presumption of innocence through its extensive case law tackling Article 6(2) of the ECHR. The ECtHR's case law provides us with a deeper understanding of the scope and meaning of the presumption of innocence in practice.

For example, in the *Natsvlishvili and Togonidze v. Georgia* judgment for alleged violation of Article 6(2), the ECtHR specified that the presumption of innocence is breached if any public official, including prosecutors, gives a public statement that reflects an opinion that a person charged with a criminal offence is guilty, even if this reflection is implied only by the choice of phrasing (*Natsvlishvili & Togonidze v. Georgia*, 2014). In the case of *Daktaras v. Lithuania*, the ECtHR also made a clear distinction between public statements reflecting the opinion of a suspect or accused person being guilty before conviction and statements that describe 'a state of suspicion', the latter not being prohibited (Daktaras v. Lithuania, 2000).

In the case of *Allen v. The United Kingdom*, the ECtHR made a distinction between two aspects of the presumption of innocence: firstly, as a procedural right within the trial, and secondly, as a protection for the personal reputation of the defendant. Specifically, the ECtHR assessed that the first aspect concerns the manifestation of the presumption of innocence as a procedural right in the context of a criminal trial, which is linked to issues such as the allocation of the burden of proof, the right to remain silent and prevent self-incrimination, rules of pretrial publicity, and premature expressions about the defendant's guilt made by the court or by other public officials. The second aspect concerns 'the person's reputation and how that person is perceived by the public' (Allen v. The United Kingdom, 2013).

ECtHR underlined that a press campaign can adversely affect the fairness of a trial by influencing public opinion and violating the defendant's rights. Consequently, the press must not overstep certain boundaries, particularly regarding the privacy of accused persons and the presumption of innocence. For instance, the publication of photographs does not automatically mean a breach of the presumption of innocence itself but accompanying the suspect's images with sensationalist text is a prerequisite for a violation (Bédat v. Switzerland, 2013). For that reason, in all cases, the journalists reporting on criminal cases should consider the harmful effects that the disclosure of information, enabling the identification of suspects, accused or convicted persons, or other parties to criminal proceedings, may have on these persons (Council of Europe, 2003).

Historically, the major focus of ECtHR case law has been on the impact of traditional media on the presumption of innocence, but its conclusions are also applicable to digital newspapers. However, the ongoing shift to online changed the media scene dramatically. Complicated by the democratisation of content production allowing regular citizens to take the role of journalist and freely disseminate news content online, including about criminal cases, this process has raised regulatory and accountability concerns of how to respond to illegal or harmful public digital content.

Rules on Publicity of Criminal Cases at National and Supranational Levels in the EU

Despite the international legal framework, different approaches to the protection of the presumption of innocence exist at regional and national levels. As outlined in the previous section, the European system, composed predominantly of democratic countries, has established and upholds higher standards for the protection of the rights of defendants, including the presumption of innocence, by employing a broader and multifaceted understanding of its scope and meaning.

In the European Union (EU) legal order, this protection is elevated to an even higher level. The supranational EU ensures the harmonisation of national laws in the field of criminal justice and the establishment of standards that all Member States shall comply with. Hence, EU Directive 2016/343 comprehensively addresses this principle of presumption of innocence. It encompasses a broad range of matters concerning the right not to be portrayed as guilty by public authorities before a final judgment, the public presentation of suspects and accused individuals, the requirement that the burden of proof lies with the prosecution, and the right to remain silent and avoid self-incrimination.

In terms of publicity endangering the presumption of innocence, the Directive stipulates that authorities may publicly disclose information on criminal proceedings at the pre-trial stage only when it is essential for the criminal investigation (e.g., releasing video footage to seek public assistance in identifying an alleged perpetrator) or for public interest reasons (e.g., for safety reasons when informing residents of an area affected by an alleged environmental crime, or when authorities provide information to prevent public disorder). Furthermore, the Directive dictates that suspects or accused persons must not be presented as guilty in court or in public through the use of physical restraints, namely handcuffs, glass boxes, cages and leg irons (European Parliament & Council, 2016).

EU law is a prerequisite for similarities of the approaches among Member States. At the same time, domestic legal traditions in criminal justice vary, including regulations on the publicity of criminal cases.

Similarities and Differences of Publicity Rules at the Pre-Trial and Trial Stages in Bulgaria, Greece, Italy and Spain

Publicity rules differ depending on the stage of the criminal proceedings. As a general rule, the pretrial phase is closed to the public. In contrast, the principle of publicity prevails during the trial phase. In principle, the public and media have the right to access information throughout the criminal proceedings, but this right can be limited in certain situations to ensure the effective administration of justice.

Typically, the pre-trial stage encompasses the period of crime reporting, arrest, and investigation until the pressing of charges provided that the prosecution or other competent authorities gather sufficient evidence. During the pre-trial stage, confidentiality is paramount, serving as a prerequisite for the proper conduct of the investigation. Consequently, the disclosure of information is generally forbidden, with certain exceptions defined by law. The secrecy of the investigation mandates the prohibition of revealing the identity of suspects and publishing pre-trial records, images, collected evidence, and other materials and documents obtained or produced as part of the investigation.

Exceptions to the confidentiality rule are permitted only when they pursue a legitimate aim and are proportional to the pursued goal. Such exceptions are typically reserved for high-profile crimes or those of significant public interest, such as the misuse of public funds, environmental crimes, threats to national security, or other offences that may have widespread consequences for the population. The principle of confidentiality during investigations is enshrined in the penal laws of all four countries under scrutiny, notwithstanding minor variations in their regulations.

In practice, during the initial stage of criminal proceedings, information about the criminal act is most limited while public interest is at its peak. At this point, speculative versions and potential suspects are often publicly discussed despite the scarcity of definitive information. Hence, media coverage poses risks of premature and potentially wrongful accusations, exposing the private lives of those involved as suspects or victims, and jeopardising the following stages of the investigation (Doichinova & Stoyanova, 2022). It is precisely at this stage that most misconduct and uncontrolled disclosure of information occurs, particularly by rapidly circulating information on online and social media, putting the presumption of innocence of suspects at significant risk.

In contrast, publicity is the dominant principle during the trial phase. Public hearings before the court are a key legal principle that is a necessary condition for carrying out a fair trial. Publicity of criminal trials is an important opportunity for the media to exercise the right to information, and, ideally, to serve as a watchdog for miscarriages of justice. Media coverage of court proceedings is also essential for upholding the principle of open justice (Townend & Welsch, 2023). However, reaching the trial phase implies that the pre-trial investigation has been completed and sufficient evidence has been collected to support the indictment. As noted, this often leads to intensified speculation and premature references to the defendant's guilt, frequently accompanied by compelling images of individuals in handcuffs or seated in the defence area, sometimes in plastic cages. Such visuals are powerful and may convey a perception of guilt.

Essentially, a public trial means that ordinary citizens and journalists can attend the courtroom during hearings, take notes and disseminate information from the proceedings, all of which is ensured in the criminal procedural law of all four countries under examination. The examined national legislation established limitations in terms of recording as a measure to protect the public status and reputation of the defendants and the victims. Thus, the legal systems of Bulgaria, Greece, Italy and Spain provide that the use of technical means for broadcasting and recording videos, photographs and audio is generally forbidden in the courtroom, unless allowed and justified by the presiding judge. Regulations regarding the capture of audio and visual in courtrooms vary across the four countries and exhibit distinct differences. In Bulgaria, participants in the hearing (defendants, witnesses, and other attendees) may appear in audio and video recordings only with the approval of the panel of judges provided the attendants have not lodged an objection (Country Report Bulgaria, 2020). In contrast, under Italian law, the judge may authorise the recording of hearings even without the consent of the attending parties provided the existence of a significant social interest in the community to have access to the hearing (Country Report Italy, 2020). In addition to the courtroom, Greek law prohibits the recording or photographing of defendants on the court premises, as they are escorted to the hearing by judicial authorities or police (Country Report Greece, 2020).

In all four countries, similar exceptions exist to the publicity rule during trial. Normally, the judge may issue a decision to hold the hearing behind closed doors, meaning that the media and the public are not allowed in the courtroom. They might be granted access to wait outside or in front of the court building, or at designated places. A common exception to the principle of public trial concerns the protection of minors, protected witnesses and other vulnerable parties, as relevant provisions are found in all four countries.

Notably, at the trial phase, the identity of defendants is usually disclosed, which the media often uses to delve into their personal lives, backgrounds, and even families, publishing information unrelated to the criminal proceedings, all while appealing to the audience's curiosity and enriching the story. Hence, journalistic activity can move beyond the legitimate provision of factual information to the illicit practice of creating parallel judgments on a criminal case. In Spain, the term 'parallel judgments' has been used to explain the process of intentional collection of information and news, accompanied by an explicit opinion on the matter of guilt, which is disseminated throughout media publications at any phase of the proceedings (Espín Templado, 1999 as cited in Country Report Spain, 2020). Parallel judgment is formed through communication by journalists who attribute the role of defence lawyers, public prosecutors or judges. This determines the selection and presentation of case-related information, which construct a biased narrative. Hereby, a valued opinion is formed over time that influences the public perception of justice and the judicial process (Country Report Spain, 2020). Such phenomenon are not strictly regulated by law, although they can significantly damage the public perception of the defendant and undermine the presumption of innocence in the eyes of the public and jurors.

Therefore, media coverage of criminal cases is typically not strictly regulated by law. In the countries examined, there are no specific legal provisions governing media reporting on criminal cases beyond the general provisions outlined above. At the institutional level, internal rules on public relations are usually established by the court, prosecution office, or law enforcement department to manage their interactions with the media and journalists. These administrative rules, however, are adopted by the respective body of the judiciary or executive branch and are not usually codified into law.

Legislation that holds the press liable for causing moral damages to individuals, which defendants can invoke in civil cases for compensation, does exist. Additionally, criminal proceedings may be initiated for offences such as insult, defamation, libel, breach of confidentiality, and violation of data protection regulations. In practice, however, defendants rarely pursue civil or criminal proceedings for damages to their presumption of innocence or reputation caused by media coverage of a criminal case, unless they are a public figure such as a politician or celebrity. Despite the laws on defamation and personal data protection, the defendants in criminal proceedings are not sufficiently protected by disproportionate media coverage and the effect it has on their personal sphere.

Media Self-Regulation and International Soft-Law Norms

Media is known for its self-regulation, which is essential for preserving editorial freedom, minimising state interference, enhancing the quality of journalism, ensuring media accountability, and facilitating audience access to media products (Haraszti, 2008). Consequently, the media largely operates under self-regulatory rules enshrined in ethical codes that are non-mandatory in legal terms. In the absence of an international legal framework mandating rules for media practitioners on reporting criminal proceedings, most transnational standards are found in ethical codes developed by international organisations and journalist associations. Notable among these international instruments are the Global Charter of Ethics for Journalists (GCEJ) from 2019 by the International Federation of Journalists, the Code of Ethics by the Society of Professional Journalists (SPJ), and the Council of Europe's Resolution on Ethics of Journalism. The GCEJ, which builds on the 1954 Declaration of Principles on the Conduct of Journalists, is grounded in key international legal texts, particularly the Universal Declaration of Human Rights. The SPJ Code of Ethics, dating back to 1926, was last updated in 2014. Both codes embody enduring ethical standards revised to reflect modern media practices. In addition, the Resolution on Ethics of Journalism adopted by the Council of Europe emphasizes that the media must respect the presumption of innocence, especially in ongoing cases, and avoid premature judgments.

These soft-law and quasi universal standards for media coverage of criminal proceedings can be summarised as the following duties:

- A suspect's right to a fair trial should be balanced with the public's right to know. Journalists must consider the implications of identifying criminal suspects before they face legal charges.
- The distortion of facts, slander, libel, defamation, and unfounded accusations are considered serious professional misconducts.
- A clear distinction must be drawn between news and opinions, making it impossible for the reader to confuse them (i.e., news is information about facts and data, while opinions convey thoughts, ideas, beliefs or value judgments on the part of media companies, publishers or journalists).
- The provision of information or opinion on criminal cases should not contribute to hatred or prejudice in society.
- Information shall be reported in a non-discriminatory manner.
- Published information found to be inaccurate shall be rectified and corrected in a timely, explicit, complete, and transparent manner. A

new article should acknowledge the mistake, correct the erroneous information, and be equally disseminated.

'Extra Punishment' by Media to Suspects and Accused Individuals

This section examines criminal cases from Bulgaria, Italy, Greece, and Spain to identify media behaviour patterns and highlight common malpractices that news media outlets, journalists, and public authorities employ when reporting on criminal proceedings. It is based on the findings of an extensive examination of fourteen case studies conducted under the ARISA-2 project. The evidence was gathered through online media monitoring and content analysis, mainly from online newspapers, complemented by additional sources such as publications by public officials or non-governmental organisations. The content sources include traditional media outlets, such as TV and news media outlets in their digital format, as well as entirely online media that either produce original content or serve as a platform for re-sharing journalistic content. Due to the limitations of this chapter, it includes a sample of four cases chosen to present repeating media malpractices observed in multiple contexts, and to represent a case from each country included in the study.

The evaluation of (mal-)practices is based on the legal and non-legal norms presented in the previous section. They may undermine the presumption of innocence and result in various harmful consequences for the private lives and rights of suspects and accused individuals, which can be considered as 'extra punishment' caused by the media. The conclusions presented in the final subsection reflect the findings from the examination of all fourteen case studies in Stoyanova's comparative case studies analysis (Stoyanova, 2021).

Case Studies Sample

The Sotirya Murder

The murder of a six-year-old girl in the village of Sotirya, Bulgaria, in August 2019, led to the arrest and subsequent conviction of M.T. After his arrest, the suspect confessed to committing the crime and was subsequently charged with rape and homicide. This tragic case highlights significant issues regarding media coverage and its impact on the defendant's rights to the presumption of innocence and privacy.

From the onset, the media coverage was intense and sensationalist. The suspect, M.T., was arrested shortly after the crime and immediately became the subject of extensive media scrutiny. The coverage included detailed accounts of the crime and the suspect's arrest, often accompanied by personal data, photos, graphic descriptions and speculative commentary. The media's portrayal of M.T. as guilty, reinforced by official statements, created a public perception that he was the perpetrator long before the court had rendered a verdict. For instance, the Secretary General of the Ministry of Interior described him as the perpetrator of the crime in a television interview, effectively convicting him in the eyes of the public before the trial had even begun (e.g., Nova TV, 2019).

The right to privacy was grossly violated by the media. The suspect's name and age were disclosed immediately after the crime was reported) Atanasova, 2019a, 2019b). The disclosure of the suspect's identity at such an early stage practically prevented any subsequent efforts to respect his privacy. Furthermore, reports delved deeply into his personal history, exposing details that were irrelevant to the case but served to vilify him further. Information about his family background, financial struggles, and previous minor offences was published extensively. Online media outlets frequently referred to him by his full name and often used derogatory terms such as 'monster', 'freak' and 'the perverted Roma' (e.g., Atanasova, 2019a, 2019b; Blitz.bg, 2019). Media outlets also aired footage and photographs of M.T. This immediate and biased portrayal significantly undermined M.T.'s presumption of innocence and privacy.

The case provoked a strong public reaction, leading to protest rallies and calls for legislative changes that eventually were passed in the parliament. Specifically, although the accused man was sentenced to life imprisonment without parole, the Bulgarian Penal Code at that time envisioned a hypothesis for the reduction of the sentence to thirty years in case of confession. The victim's family, supported by the community, campaigned on for harsher penalties and organised a public manifestation, and a petition urging for amendments to the Penal Code that would eliminate this opportunity for people charged with intentional murder (Tsvetanova, 2019). The petition gained popularity and was supported by ministers and Members of Parliament who later adopted the bill. It is very likely that the media's portrayal of the crime and the accused inflamed public outcry. Far-right politicians also seized upon the case, with some linking the crime to broader social issues such as the integration of the Roma community (e.g., Nova, 2019). This politicisation of the case further complicated the public discourse and detracted from the objective legal proceedings, demonstrating the power of media in shaping public opinion and influencing policy (Case 1, 2021).

The Francofonte Murder

The criminal proceedings for the murder of Antonino Barbaro in November 2014, a sixty-seven-year-old pensioner found dead with multiple stab wounds in the countryside near Francofonte, Italy, highlight the significant negative impact of media coverage on the rights and lives of the suspects. Italian Carabinieri carried out investigations without success for nearly two years. On September 20, 2016, the owners of the building where the victim lived, the brothers A.G. and G.G. were arrested and consequently detained for 130 days.

The suspects' arrest was captured by national TV cameras and broadcast live. The initial investigation against the brothers was based on weak circumstantial evidence, including tire tracks and ambiguous testimonies. Still, media coverage of the arrest portrayed it as the resolution of the case and pronounced that the brothers were guilty of the offence. Media outlets reported the story with definitive and accusatory tones, presenting the suspected brothers as murderers without substantial evidence. Headlines such as ‘Syracuse, they killed defaulting tenant with 27 stab wounds, two brothers arrested’ (La Republicca, 2016) and ‘Francofonte, they killed a 67-year-old man with 27 stab wounds for 700 euros: Carabinieri arrest the perpetrators of the murder’ (SiracusaNews, 2016) were indicative of the prejudiced media narrative. The publication of their names, photographs, and reports delving into their personal lives included details that were not pertinent to the case but served to vilify them further.

The portrayal of the brothers as greedy and violent landlords exacerbated this assault, contributing to a narrative that tarnished their reputations irreparably. For instance, a report on the murder was featured in a popular Italian TV show. The episode began with the presenter posing the question, ‘Can one be killed for unpaid rent?’, framing the narrative around a dramatic conflict. The segment portrayed the brothers as greedy landlords who murdered an elderly man over a debt of 700 euros. The show emphasized a dichotomy between the ‘inhuman perpetrators’ and the ‘human victim,’ reinforcing a biased narrative against the suspects. Throughout the episode, the brothers were depicted in a negative light, with the reporter asking leading and provocative questions during an interview with A.G. The interview painted the brothers as violent and unscrupulous, despite the lack of conclusive evidence at the time (Videonews, 2016).

When further investigations revealed the insufficiency of the evidence, the suspects were eventually released and the case was subsequently dismissed without a hearing. The media failed to rectify their previous reports, leaving the public with a distorted perception of the brothers’ guilt.

The biased media coverage provoked strong public reactions, cementing a negative perception of the brothers in their small local community of only 12,000 inhabitants and across the country. The immediate vilification and continued neglect to rectify the narrative contributed to their social marginalisation. The brothers and their families faced significant distress, social isolation, and stigmatisation as a result of the media’s premature and biased reporting (Case 8, 2021).

The HIV-Positive Women

In April 2012, Greek authorities launched a police operation in Athens that targeted women suspected of being illegal sex workers and potential carriers of HIV. This operation resulted in the mandatory HIV testing of ninety-six women, leading to the arrest of eleven women, including K., who tested positive. The operation was publicly justified by authorities as a necessary measure to combat the rise of HIV infections, allegedly attributed to illegal prostitution and immigration, although this claim was not supported by evidence. K., along with the other women apprehended, was prosecuted on felony charges without legal representation and was remanded in pretrial detention for nearly a year.

The media played a pivotal role in amplifying the details surrounding this case. Following a prosecutor's order, the Hellenic Police released photographs and personal information of the arrested women, including their names, ages, places of residence, and their HIV-positive status. The authorities justified the disclosure of this sensitive information as necessary to protect public health. This information was quickly disseminated by TV channels, newspapers, and online platforms, with sensationalist headlines such as 'Health Bomb: The Prostitutes Infected with AIDS' (Karlatira, 2012) and 'The 16 HIV Positive Prostitutes Remained in Custody' (Karamanoli, 2012) dehumanising the women and portraying them as public threats. Publications called them 'the health bombs prostitutes infected with AIDS' who caused 'terror for 700 men clients' (Madata.gr, 2012).

By portraying these women as criminals and health hazards before any legal proceedings took place, the media essentially prejudged their guilt, undermining the fundamental legal principle that individuals are innocent until proven guilty. Furthermore, the public exposure egregiously compromised the women's right to privacy. The disclosure of their HIV status and personal information constituted a serious breach of medical confidentiality and data protection laws. This exposure not only stigmatised the women but also subjected them to public ridicule, discrimination, and social ostracization.

The relentless media scrutiny and public shaming significantly impacted their personal lives. One of them, K., experienced a relapse in drug use after her release and tragically committed suicide in November 2014. Her suicide letter highlighted the perpetual harm and stigma inflicted by public exposure. The repercussions for the family members of K. and the other women were equally devastating. In interviews after the end of the trial, some of the accused women shared that K.'s father attempted suicide and subsequently lost his job following her arrest. Another woman reported that her daughter was subjected to HIV testing at school in front of her peers. The women recounted experiences of social ostracism, with neighbours and relatives severing contact with them and their families, particularly in smaller communities. One woman noted that her siblings were dismissed from their jobs and her child was expelled from school.

In 2016, the trial ended with the acquittal of all accused women for all charges pressed against them. It was followed by a campaign of public support for them and an application to ECtHR for the illegal detention (Case 6, 2021).

The Murder in Hortichuelas

On 27 February 2018, in the small village of Las Hortichuelas in southern Spain, a nine-year-old boy went missing. From the moment the boy disappeared, the case attracted significant public attention. The search operation involved over 3000 volunteers and 2000 members of the security forces. The arrest of his stepmother, A.J.Q., a woman from the Dominican Republic, caught driving the victim's body in her car, further intensified the media scrutiny. Subsequently, the accused woman confessed to having killed the victim but claimed that it had been an accident.

The publicity of the case, including media coverage and authorities' statements, portrayed A.J.Q. as a cold-blooded murderer. Coupled with the extensive dissemination of her private life details and focus on her foreign descent, a public narrative of guilt overshadowed the legal proceedings. Following A.J.Q.'s arrest, her image was circulated by online media through non-anonymised photos and videos. The news articles delved deeply into her personal life, exposing numerous details that were not directly relevant to the crime, including interviews with her relatives residing in the Dominic Republic. Journalists unearthed and published information about her previous romantic relationships, her occupations, and her past, including the tragic death of her daughter in 1996 and sowed doubts about the accidental nature of the incident (Cadeira, 2019).

An interesting detail in this case study is that the media campaign digging into the suspect's private life was based on data disclosed by the police authorities in a press conference. The Spanish Guardia Civil held a press conference narrating the search process and the investigations leading to A.J.Q.'s arrest. During this conference, the officer in charge mentioned that they suspected her due to her 'past in Burgos,' although no further details were provided at the time. In the following weeks, the press published that the suspect had worked as a prostitute in the early 1990s and that one of her daughters had died in 1996 after falling out of a window. When questioned by the press, one of the Guardia Civil commanders described the suspect as 'extremely cold,' 'quite manipulative', and a person 'with economic ambition' (El Independiente, 2018). This press conference was broadcast live by several media outlets such as the Spanish public television (El Independiente, 2019). A.J.Q.'s foreign descent was another focal point of the media coverage, significantly affecting public perception. As a black woman from the Dominican Republic, her ethnicity and nationality were frequently emphasized in publications, at times with racist undertones (SOS Racismo Madrid, 2018).

This information, often sensationalised, painted A.J.Q. in a highly negative light and contributed to a public perception of guilt before the legal process could conclude. The media coverage provoked strong public reactions, leading to petitions demanding severe punishment for the defendant and her deportation to the Dominican Republic 'as she would be comfortable in any of Spain's prisons' (Antena3, 2018). Social media amplified these sentiments, with xenophobic and racist comments proliferating (Case 12, 2021).

Media Toolbox that Jeopardises the Presumption of Innocence

Case studies revealed that suspects and accused persons are frequently presented negatively since the moment of their arrest and become subject to defamation and premature accusations in the press. Their public presentation is frequently characterised by biased comments and offensive terms. Moreover, disproportionate disclosure of information and sensationalist language may prevail over objective reporting of facts particularly in cases that catch the public attention. The analysis identified common malpractices occurring across all examined countries and types of media, including:

- Use of derogatory language to describe the suspects or accused individuals.
- Publication of private information that is unrelated to the case.
- Publication of non-anonymised photos or videos showing the face of the suspect or accused person when it is not necessary for the investigation.
- Publication of data allowing the identification of suspects when it is not necessary for the investigation.
- Prejudiced headlines and journalist opinions implying guilt, often in articles that lack authorship.
- Negligence in rectifying published information that later proves to be incorrect.

The combination of these practices constitutes the toolbox utilised by the media to increase their audience at the expense of the presumption of innocence. Media research has extensively examined the relationship between emotion and media selection, particularly the effects of media messages on emotional arousal, and the subsequent cognitive and behavioural outcomes in society (e.g. Nabi, 2009). In the context of media coverage of criminal cases, case studies show that conceiving a perception of guilt can be either a targeted action, for example, by drafting headlines directly naming the suspect or accused person as the perpetrator, or indirectly through the utilisation of cognitive manipulation techniques used to engineer public opinion. The latter is achieved by crafting a narrative built on a hypothesis of guilt, intentionally supported by the selection of expressions, drawing parallels and connections between selected facts, and visual materials that present the defendant as a criminal, such as recordings from the arrest. Emphasizing certain personal characteristics of the defendant that intentionally or unintentionally evoke deeply embedded emotions, such as anger or fear, can significantly increase viewership by provoking an emotional reaction within a substantial segment of the audience. However, this practice also reinforces bias and hatred perpetuating the perception of an individual or certain group as inherently criminal.

The harmful implications of excessive media coverage of criminal cases occur at three levels—individual, family, and society. The individual suffers from the long-lasting effects of a compromised reputation and the potential risk of a biased outcome of the judicial trial. In addition, delving into their background exposes the individual to unnecessary scrutiny, as the media often wrongfully suggests that the arrest or the pressing of charges against a person automatically permits unlimited divulsion of their personal life. It is likely that this leads to implications for family members, who may bear the consequences of being related to a suspect or accused and can become subject to unwanted media attention. Associated with the negative portrayal of their arrested relative, they experience isolation within their communities. Ultimately, the malicious media practices outlined above can be detrimental to broader democratic values and structures. This is demonstrated in cases where the suspect or accused individual belongs to a marginalised social group, such as migrants or ethnic minorities. Journalists frequently exploit this aspect, stressing these personal characteristics in their storytelling to leverage existing emotive tensions against these groups. This dichotomy between 'us, the victims' and 'them, the perpetrators' can severely impede the long-term integration of these marginalised communities and reinforce existing stereotypes and polarisation in society. Evidently, media-generated hype among the general public may lead to interference in and politicisation of the judicial process. The case studies involving petitions for more severe punishments for the defendants demonstrate how the public can put pressure on the court and practically question its ability to adjudicate cases fairly. Nonetheless, the limitations of this study should be recognized. Further research is needed to measure the impact of news media coverage, with a specific focus on online and new types of media, of criminal cases on the lives of suspects and the accused, their families, communities, and society as a whole. Such findings are essential for addressing (self-)regulatory gaps and imperfections, raising awareness, and promoting changes in media behaviour that, although often unintentional, prove to be harmful.

Conclusion

The contemporary understanding of the scope of the presumption of innocence, which evolved from a purely procedural right in the court to a right to preserve one's public image and reputation in society, requires robust regulation of media exposure of defendants and stricter compliance with the rules of ethical journalism. The case studies demonstrated that media malpractices are consistent even in the European context, which is typically known to maintain a high level of human rights protection.

The cases examined in this chapter illustrate the potentially profound and often devastating impact of disproportionate media coverage on the lives and rights of suspects and accused individuals, although further research is needed to examine the extent of the impact. The case studies underscore the need for stricter ethical standards and self-regulation in journalism. By adhering to higher standards of reporting and ensuring that the presumption of innocence is respected, the media can contribute to a more just and fair society. This includes refraining from publishing unverified and prejudicial information, ensuring anonymity where appropriate, and correcting misinformation promptly and prominently. Ethical journalism is crucial not only for the protection of individual rights but also for the integrity of the justice system as a whole.

Competing Interests

The author has no conflicts of interest to declare that are relevant to the content of this chapter.

References

Ashworth, A. (2006). Four threats to the presumption of innocence. *The International Journal of Evidence & Proof, 10*(4), 241–279.

Atanasova, M. (2019a). Смразяващи подробности за убийството на малката Кристи. *Fakti.bg.*

Atanasova, M. (2019b). Извергът от Сотиря е прострелян в крака. *Fakti.bg.*

Bédat v. Switzerland, Application No. 56925/08, European Court of Human Rights, 2013.

Blitz.bg (21, August, 2019). Проблемите на жестокия убиец от Сотиря стават все по-сериозни.

Cadeira, B. (September, 8. 2019). Judit, la otra víctima que Ana Julia dejó en Burgos: 'Mi madre nunca me dijo que me quería'. *El Español.*

Case 1: The Sotirya murder. Arisa. (2021, May 26).

Case 6: Katerina, one of the cases of HIV positive women. Arisa. (2021, May 26).

Case 8: The murder of Antonino Barbaro. Arisa. (2021, May 26).

Case 12: Gabriel Cruz Case. Arisa. (2021, May 26).

Council of Europe. (1993). *Resolution 1003 (1993) Ethics of journalism.*

Council of Europe. (2003). *Recommendation Rec(2003)13 of the Committee of Ministers to member states on the provision of information through the media in relation to criminal proceedings.*

Daktaras v. Lithuania, Application No. 42095/98, European Court of Human Rights (2000).

Disclosure of information and media coverage of criminal cases: Country report Bulgaria. Arisa. (July 31, 2020).

Disclosure of information and media coverage of criminal cases: Country report Italy. Arisa. (July 21, 2020).

Disclosure of information and media coverage of criminal cases: Country report Greece. Arisa. (July 21, 2020).

Disclosure of information and media coverage of criminal cases: Country report Spain. Arisa. (July 21, 2020).

Doichinova, M., Edzie, J., Dorak, O., Martello, C., Kasapi, Z., Mousmouti, M., Legato, M., & Aguerri, J. (2021). *The presumption of innocence and the media coverage of criminal cases* (pp. 6–8). Center for the Study of Democracy.

Doichinova, M., & Stoyanova, M. (2022). *Disclosing information on criminal cases: Guidebook for criminal justice and media professionals*. Center for the Study of Democracy.

El Independiente (Ed.). (2018, March 15). *Ana Julia Quezada es una persona de 'Frialdad Máxima', según La Guardia Civil*. [Video]. YouTube.

El Independiente (Ed.). (2019, September 10). *'Le tapé la boca y ya no respiraba': Ana Julia Quezada admite que mató al niño Gabriel*. [Video]. YouTube.

European Parliament and Council. (2016). Directive (EU) 2016/343 of the European Parliament and of the Council of 9 March 2016 on the strengthening of certain aspects of the presumption of innocence and of the right to be present at the trial in criminal proceedings. *Official Journal of the European Union, L65*, 1–11.

European Union Agency for Fundamental Rights. (2021) *Presumption of innocence and related rights*. Publications Office of the European Union.

Espín Templado, E. (1999), Número especial XVII: Justicia, información y opinión pública. Cited in *Disclosure of information and media coverage of criminal cases: Country report Spain*. Arisa. (July 31, 2020).

Haraszti, M. (2008). The merits of media self-regulation. Balancing rights and responsibilities. In *The media self-regulation guidebook*. Chapter (pp. 7–18), Organization for Security and Co-operation in Europe.

Ho, H. L. (2012). The presumption of innocence as a human right. In P. Roberts & J. Hunter (Eds.), *Criminal evidence and human rights: Reimagining common law procedural traditions* (pp. 259–282). Hart Publishing. Bloomsbury Collections.

International Federation of Journalists. (2019). Global charter of ethics for journalists.

Каракачанов за убийството в Сотиря: Да се приеме концепцията за несоциализираните общности. *Nova*. (August, 17, 2019).

Karamanoli, E. (2012, May 5). Προφυλακιστέες κρίθηκαν οι 16 οροθετικές ιερόδουλες). *Kathimerini*.

Karlatira, P. (2012, May 1). «Υγειονομική βόμβα» οι μολυσμένες με AIDS πόρνες. *Protothema*.

Krishnan, S. (2018). Trial by media: Concept and phenomenon. *International Journal of Advanced Research, 6*(3), 889–901.

La indignación en las redes sociales deriva en una cadena de peticiones en Change.org tras la muerte de Gabriel Cruz. (2018, 12 March). *Antena3.*
Mensah, E. K. (2024). Assessing the role of media influence and public perception in legal decision-making. *SSRN Electronic Journal.*
Nabi, R. (2009) Emotion and media effects. In R. Nabi & M. Oliver (Eds.), *The SAGE Handbook of Media Processes and Effects* (pp. 205–222). Sage.
Natsvlishvili & Togonidze v. Georgia, Application No. 9043/05, European Court of Human Rights (2014).
Siracusa, uccisero affittuario moroso con 27 coltellate: arrestati due Fratelli. (September, 21, 2016). *La Repubblica.*
SOS Racismo Madrid. (2018, November 15), *Comunicado ante los hechos derivados por el caso de Gabriel Cruz.*
Society of Professional Journalists. (2014). Code of ethics.
Stoyanova, M. (2021). *The presumption of innocence and the media coverage of criminal cases: Case studies analysis.* Center for the Study of Democracy.
Synodinou, T. (2012). The media coverage of court proceedings in Europe: Striking a balance between freedom of expression and fair process. *Computer Law & Security Review, 28*(2), 208–219.
Τρόμος στις πιάτσες με το AIDS. Έκκλησεις ΚΕΛΠΝΟ. *Madata.gr* (2012, May 12).
Townend, J., & Welsh, L. (2023). The role of the public and media in observing justice. In *Observing justice: Digital transparency, openness and accountability in criminal courts* (pp. 65–92). Chapter, Bristol University Press.
Tsvetanova, K. (2019, September 18). Почернени роднини на протест: Искаме строги наказания!. *Dnes.bg*
United Nations. (1966). International covenant on civil and political rights.
Videonews (Producer). (September, 23, 2016). Quarto Grado (Episode 4) [TV show episode].

12

The Critical-Forensic Linguistic Interface and the Spectrum of Trial by Media: Media-Made Sexual Assault in the Courtroom

Simon Statham

Introduction: Crime in the Media

Coverage of crime is a prominent feature of the media and the media plays a significant role in constructing and reinforcing conceptualisations of crime and deviance for the public. Statistics from the British Crime Survey, for example, have suggested that 75% of the public's information about crime is obtained from the media (Levenson, 2001). The contemporary mediascape is comprised of discourses of the so-called 'new media'—including social media and other platforms such as podcasts, often focused on the 'true crime' genre that has exploded in recent years—as well as traditional media such as television and radio broadcasts and newspapers. The mass media also includes portrayals of criminal justice as an entertainment commodity through factual, fictional and 'factional' portrayals of crime and deviance. These portrayals of crime

S. Statham (✉)
Queens University Belfast, Belfast, UK
e-mail: s.staham@qub.ac.uk

L. Gies (ed.), *Trial by Media*, Palgrave Studies in Crime, Media and Culture,
https://doi.org/10.1007/978-3-031-80593 6_12

are not neutral reflectors of society but rather they operate to ideologically construct the social world and the role of crime and criminality within it. As Mayr and Machin (2013, p.1) put it, '[Mass media images of crime and deviance] are both entertaining, due to their dramatic nature and appeal to morbid curiosity about the worst in human nature, and compelling, as they appear to tell us about features of our society that best characterise our sense of insecurity and impermanence'. As compelling as media representations of crime inevitably are, for critical scholars working in areas like linguistics, criminology, sociology and psychology they are also deeply problematic. Media constructions often individualise crime for example, root causes such as poverty and marginalisation are rarely scrutinised in detail whilst certain types of crime, such as white collar and corporate crime, which adhere less to values of newsworthiness (Galtung & Ruge, 1965; Jewkes, 2011) that are important institutional factors in determining the content of the news media, are disproportionately absent from the press. Media content addresses the most serious and violent crimes, often through a narrative framework of law and order (Schlesinger & Tumber, 1994), and often through linguistic constructions that do not tally with legal definitions of crime (Statham, 2016) but that do find a correlation with the perceptions of different types of crime possessed by the general public (Smith, 1993). From a trial by media perspective, it is particularly noteworthy that the general public that forms the readership of the news media and are the consumers of mass media representations of crime and deviance are the same group of people from which juries are selected in Common Law jurisdictions such as the United Kingdom, the United States and Australia.

The Spectrum of Trial by Media that will be outlined and applied in this chapter notes that Common Law juries represent the 'infusing of community values into the operation of the criminal law [which] engages some of our deepest and most strongly held moral sentiments' (Brown & Neal, 1988, p. 131). In recognising that much of the public's information about crime comes through interaction with media discourse, it is argued that these 'community values' and 'moral sentiments' are filtered through the ideological parameters by which the media constructs crime for the general public. This direct relationship between the media and the criminal trial is enhanced by the linguistic composition of the trial itself and may be reinforced by the linguistic strategies utilised by courtroom advocates, demonstrating the extent to which trial by media can be perceived as routine and ongoing rather than just sensationalist and high-profile. This chapter will consider the crime of sexual assault, constructed by the media through a series of conventional 'rape myths' (Dowler, 2006; O'Hara, 2012; Soothill, 2004). Franiuk et al. (2008) note that 65% of media representations include at least one of these myths, which often relate to the sexual history and/or the behaviour of alleged victims. When the same myths that mark the media's construction of sexual assault play a role in the legal processes through which rape is investigated and prosecuted, trial by media can be said to be in operation.

Sexual Assault in the Media

In the UK rape is a statutory offence under the Sexual Offences Act 2003, which defines the act as non-consensual penetration and other types of non-consensual sexual assault. In the United States, where rape legislation is codified by individual states with some small variations, the key defining factor is also consent. In many jury trials the defence may therefore pursue a 'redefinition strategy' (Bennett & Feldman, 1981) ultimately aimed at recasting the claim of the prosecution that non-consensual sex has taken place as an occurrence of consensual sex, where the defendant can be shown to 'reasonably believe' that consent is present. In Common Law jurisdictions the burden of proof is on the prosecution, who must prove the absence of consent beyond a reasonable doubt. Pursuing a 'redefinition strategy' rather than a 'challenge strategy', which would be to deny the interaction happened at all, can also negate physical or forensic evidence given that the defence is not disputing physical contact between alleged perpetrator and victim but rather disputing the nature of this contact.

The construction of a defence narrative in which the alleged perpetrator of rape or sexual assault reasonably believes that consent is present often involves several strategies that assess and characterise the complainant. In so doing 'legal professionals can utilise societal expectations which are essentially prejudicial towards certain characteristics in victims of alleged sexual assault' (Statham, 2016, p. 222). Olsen-Fulero (1997, p. 407) states that 'rape, unlike other crimes, involves not only victimisation but also attitudes towards sex-role behaviour and sexuality' whilst Burt and Albin (1991, p. 213), who also conducted groundbreaking research into the operation of 'rape myths' (Burt, 1980), refer to the 'ideological baggage' of attitudes to rape. Through interviews conducted with barristers involved in hundreds of rape trials in Britain, Temkin (2000) provides an in-depth insight into the operation of this ideological baggage in the courtroom. Barristers interviewed for this study refer to the 'central strategy in the defence armoury' (Temkin, 2000, p. 231) as 'discrediting the complainant' through three main tactics. 'Maligning the victim's behaviour' therefore 'dwells on the foolishness of the complainant's behaviour with the message that she had brought what happened upon herself and had only herself to blame' with one barrister commenting that 'if a woman puts herself in a compromising position, I don't think juries are ready to convict' (Temkin, 2000, p. 232). 'Maligning the victim's clothes' is essentially an extension of the 'brought it on herself' theme and a defending barrister comments that 'I don't think young girls realise the effect of their appearance on men. Guys get turned on if they can see through the women's clothes. Dress is significant' (Temkin, 2000, p. 233). The third tactic to discredit the victim is 'maligning the victim's sexual character', which is not immediately permissible at trial but which is often admitted following an application by the defence who aim to show that 'a woman who has had sexual experience and, particularly varied and a lot of sexual experience, is frankly more likely to consent to sexual experience with someone new that someone who hasn't'. One barrister states that 'there are lots of women who make complaints of rape who would sleep with the local donkey [and] if she sleeps with nine out of ten men why is it that she wouldn't sleep with this one' (Temkin, 2000, p. 234). Whilst deeply uncomfortable, particularly in terms of victim-blaming, the qualitative insights provided by this study confirm that factors are in operation at trial that far exceed the legal definition of a crime. As another barrister interviewed by Temkin (2000, p. 232) puts it in terms of rape, 'There is a difficulty in properly presenting women with a right to decline sexual intercourse despite the fact that they may have been drunk or acted in a sexually explicit way towards the man. It goes down to a number of attitudes that are ingrained in people. There plainly is a perception that women should act in a certain way'.

For scholars investigating the operation of trial by media, particularly from the perspective of Critical Discourse Analysis (CDA) which views the institutional discourse of the media as actively constructing and reinforcing the principles of the social world, what is of pivotal interest is how attitudes that are 'ingrained in people' are ingrained by the media, as it were. When media-made conceptualisations play so significant and so routine a role in the courtroom, especially when these constructs far exceed the legal definition of a crime, it is clear that trial by media is taking place. Soothill (1991) notes that the media is instrumental in shaping public opinion about rape and Soothill and Walby (1991, p. 22) refer to a 'soft pornography appeal' that often marks media portrayals of sexual assault. Whilst rape is a violent and controlling crime and '"sexual" is the means to an end not the end itself' (Kitzinger & Thomas, 1995, p. 45), media portrayals of rape often focus disproportionately on the sexual aspects of the crime. Other dominant rape myths in the media often refer to the alleged victim's failure to adhere to stereotypical expectations of 'feminine' behaviour such as the choice of a woman to visit the home of her alleged attacker or the role of alcohol in an alleged rape incident, which operates to mitigate the perpetrator but to blame the victim. Mooney (2007, p. 206) notes that the 'effect of alcohol on a woman in a rape scenario is to make her culpable' despite the much-generalised presence of drinking culture in contemporary society. Meyers (1997) states that many of the representations of rape in the media are routinely connected to patriarchal assumptions about the 'appropriate behaviour' of women, assumptions that prevail in the construction of both victim and perpetrator.

Clark (1992) establishes that an important dichotomy prevails in the media that legitimises some victims of rape over others and further notes that even when victims are constructed in the press as legitimate, perpetrators are still represented through ideological frameworks that mitigate the patriarchal organisation of society. Through a systemic-functional analysis that applies the transitivity framework (Halliday, 1994) to the actions of participants and examines linguistic strategies in the naming of these participants in the construction of rape in the tabloid press, Clark (1992, p. 211) finds that 'names seem to relate to sexual availability: 'fiends' attack 'unavailable' females (wives, mothers and girls) whilst 'non-fiends' attack 'available' females (unmarried mothers, blondes and sexually available girls)'. The close linguistic analysis of the tabloid press yields a dichotomy of victim-blaming in which 'respectable' and 'unavailable' women are raped by 'fiends' rather than 'men' and when victims are 'unrespectable' and hence 'sexually available', they themselves are complicit in and culpable for the attacks. Rape myths that prevail in the media and which are reproduced in courtroom tactics to 'discredit the complainant' all contribute to characterising an alleged victim as 'unrespectable'. Subsequent and more contemporary linguistic research (Meyer, 2010; Statham, 2016) demonstrates that frameworks of 'respectable/sexually unavailable' and 'unrespectable/sexually available' continue to mark media constructions of rape. Women whose behaviour can be characterised as 'unrespectable', who are promiscuous or provocative, for example, are constructed as 'vamps' in the popular press whilst those who are 'respectable', whose behaviour is marked by maternity and sobriety, for example, are represented as 'virgins' (Benedict, 1992; O'Hara, 2012). For defence attorneys, a focus on behaviour that characterises an alleged victim as an unrespectable, sexually available vamp can delegitimise claims that an alleged sexual interaction was non-consensual. Given that these frameworks are media-made and not theoretically relevant to the consent-centred legal definition of these crimes, the process of trial by media is reinforced when advocates utilise 'maligning' strategies drawn from attitudes ingrained in members of the jury through their role as consumers of media discourse.

Whilst victims are represented through features of respectability and availability, media constructions of rape also ideologically represent perpetrators. Examples of the 'fiend naming' investigated by Clark (1992) and others are names like *beast*, *predator*, *sicko*, *sadist*, *pervert*, *brute* or *monster*. This 'monsterisation' others rapists as monsters rather than men, they are literally not 'of this world' and therefore cannot be deemed representative of the organisation of society. The acts that are carried out by depraved monsters are by definition not those of 'normal men' so that even when vulnerable 'virgins' are attacked, no close scrutiny of patriarchal privilege or stereotypical expectations of 'feminine' behaviour emerges in social discourse. The neo-Gothic naming strategies that characterise rapists as monsters also imply that the onus should be upon women to protect themselves and that they are to blame for putting themselves in dangerous situations that result in rape if they fail to undertake appropriate precautions. Mayr and Machin (2013, p. 2) note that constructions of crime in the press are important for powerful groups as 'they distract from their own responsibilities to create safe and supportive societies'. If 'monsters' rape 'respectable' women and 'unrespectable' women are complicit in the attacks upon them, there is little room remaining for the complex scrutiny of the structure of society and the responsibilities of those in whose service the structures of society are maintained.

One particularly significant misrepresentation of 'legitimate rape' perpetrated by the media concerns the resistance of the victim to her attacker. What Tiersma (2007, p. 88) has called the 'notorious resistance requirement', the legal requirement that a victim physically resists an attack, is no longer present in rape legislation, however it still plays a significant role in classifying the perceived legitimacy of an attack in both the media and at trial. Sexually unavailable women in media portrayals of rape, which are often violent and carried out by a stranger, physically resist their attackers so that if a defence barrister can establish the absence of physical resistance, the attack is less likely to be defined as non-consensual by a jury. Tiersma (2007, p. 95) elucidates on the fact that the matter of resistance is particularly complicated because consent is essentially a mental state, therefore readers and jurors must draw inferences about whether or not it is present. Unless the mental absence of consent is manifested by material resistance, 'jurors are conditioned by social discourses to assume that victims have consented' (Statham, 2016, p. 217). Larcombe (2002, p. 132) states that a 'case is more likely to have success if it is clearly interpretable as violence: if the assailant is a stranger, if a weapon is used, if the victim/survivor's resistance is overt and physical injury is sustained and documented'. These criteria are not required by law but they account for the expectations of a jury whose definition of rape is driven by media constructions of crime. The burden of proof means that the prosecution is faced with the difficult task at trial of proving a negative, they must establish that a mental state was not present. There have been calls by victims groups and campaigners to recast rape legislation so that the defence would have to prove the presence of consent, however central tenets of justice such as the presumption of innocence may be undermined by such moves, whilst their impact on the 'ideological baggage' of 'attitudes that are ingrained in people' is highly uncertain in any case.

Rape myths in the media also perpetuate the notion that most rapes are so-called 'stranger rapes'. In the media women are raped by Gothic monsters who drag them down secluded alleyways in heavily sexualised and even fetishised encounters. In reality the vast majority of rapes are 'simple rapes', a not entirely comfortable label that refers to the fact that most rapists are known to their victims. According to the National Crime Victimization Survey (2006) in the United States, 73% of assailants are known to the victim, Greenwood (1997) states that 60% of rapes occur in the home of the victim or of a family member or friend. The British Crime Survey (2011) finds that only 17% of rapes are 'stranger rapes' and a joint report by the Home Office, Office of National Statistics and the Ministry of Justice (2013) found that 90% of rape victims know their attackers. Despite these compelling statistics, the media continue to reinforce a prominence of 'stranger rape' so that victims who can be shown to be acquainted with their attacker in court may be viewed by the jury as an illegitimate or unlikely victim. When this is further contextualised by the fact that in scenarios where victims do not know their attackers or accompany them to their homes, for example, they can be also characterised as 'unrespectable' and complicit in an attack, the infamous difficulty of securing prosecutions in rape cases is placed into even sharper focus. Du Mont et al. (2003) suggest that victims are less likely to report attacks at all if they know their attacker. Given that this knowledge is representative of the vast majority of rapes but stands in direct contrast to media-made rape, somewhat ironically trial by media can also be said to be manifest when there is no trial at all.

When media-made constructions of sexual crimes are appropriated by legal professionals in court a correlation can be drawn between the media and the trial process. In this way trial by media is routine and consistent rather than limited to high-profile proceedings. The Spectrum of Trial by Media, outlined in the "Spectrum of Trial by Media" section, can be applied to specific cases but is ultimately intended to demonstrate that trial by media is pervasive and routine rather than incidental.

Spectrum of Trial by Media

The Spectrum of Trial by Media is comprised of three interrelated dimensions and addresses the role of the jury and the strategies of attorneys in criminal trials in Common Law jurisdictions. Based on the critical-forensic linguistic interface, which applies a range of models in critical, cognitive and forensic linguistics to both the media and the courtroom, the Spectrum aims to determine how ideological constructions of different types of crime play an active role in the criminal trial. Owing to the pivotal role played by the jury in these cases, both as the triers of fact and as the main audience of courtroom attorneys, this interface refers to the most serious crimes in society. Driven perhaps by the focus of the media and broadcast entertainment on trials by jury, there is an abiding public perception that those accused of crime will eventually be judged by a jury of their peers. In reality, as noted by Duff and Findlay (1997, p. 363), 'the proportion of cases heard before a jury is astonishingly low given the significance with which the institution is usually vested and the community confidence which it generates'. In Common Law legal systems most cases are discharged by either a plea bargain or a guilty plea and no jury is ever involved. Many other so-called 'lesser crimes' are heard in lower courts. In the three-tiered British legal system, for example, 95% of cases are heard in Magistrates' Courts, where there is no jury, whilst so-called Indictable Only and some 'triable either way' offences are heard by a jury in a Crown Court. In the United States, where Margolis (2009) reports that 90% of the world's jury proceedings take place, many minor offences no longer require a jury trial whilst most cases are the subject of pre-trial plea bargain arrangements. That said, it is very important to remember that the institution of the jury is not retained so that governments can peddle merely an impression of justice or due process.

Current UK Government figures (gov.uk, 2024) remind us that 400,000 British people are called for jury service every year and there are 28,000 cases heard in the Crown Court. According to the National Center for State Courts (NCSC), 8 million Americans report for jury duty annually. Jury trials address crimes like rape, murder, kidnap, robbery and serious assaults. Whilst viewing trials by jury as representative of the legal system, an impression itself constructed to a significant degree by the media, may be somewhat misleading, the importance of the institution of the jury remains unassailable. Certainly the context in which jury trials operate in the US, UK and other Common Law countries is more complicated and less idealistic than being 'the lamp that shows that freedom lives', as Lord Devlin (Devlin, 1956, p. 164) once famously described the jury system, but jury trials themselves retain an utmost importance, not least because it is the most heinous crimes in society that are judged by juries. By being focused on trials by jury, the Spectrum of Trial by Media is also focused on the role of the media in trying the most serious crimes in society. The crime of rape operates across the three dimensions of the Spectrum owing to the conscious utilisation of media-made rape myths by attorneys at trial.

The critical-forensic linguistic interface applies models from critical, cognitive and forensic linguistics. Critical Discourse Analysis (CDA) is applied to routine representations of a range of crimes across the media, Statham (2016) specifically examines the media construction of murder, assault, robbery and burglary and demonstrates how the linguistic representation of these crimes in the media overlaps with mock jury research that analyses the different conceptualisations of crime possessed by jurors and legal professionals (Smith, 1993). For example, conventionally held conceptualisations of murder are often incorrectly defined by the public as being premeditated and planned by a perpetrator who is armed with a weapon. Cognitive linguistic modelling, particularly the structures of 'dynamic memory' (Schank, 1982) and 'idealised cognitive models' (Lakoff, 1987), is used to construct the mental structures for each type of crime that are developed by readers through their routine and consistent interaction with media discourse. For example, the Memory

Organization Packet (MOP) for the crime of murder includes scripts for premeditation and armed perpetrators. Schank (1982, p. 129) defines a script as 'primarily a set of expectations about what will happen in a given situation'. As most jurors acquire their information about different types of crime through their role as readers of news and consumers of media, the scripts that comprise their MOPs—essentially the high-level mental schemata through which people understand and learn—for different crimes are media-made. When attorneys, who possess mental schemata comprised of scripts affected by their professional knowledge of the law, such as being aware of the fact that murder should be intentional but does not have to be premeditated, put the media-made scripts they know to be possessed by juries at the forefront of their trial strategies, they are reinforcing trial by media. In rape cases, where juries possess scripts that define a victim as 'sexually available' or 'unavailable' and 'unrespectable' or 'respectable', as a 'vamp' or a 'virgin', and in which attorneys construct their rhetorical strategies around these scripts, despite their irrelevance to the legal requirement of consent, trial by media is routinely reinforced.

The first dimension of the Spectrum of Trial by Media is known as 'direct trial by media' and refers to the fact that juries, as consistent interactants with the discourse of the media, carry pre-trial, media-made conceptualisations of types of crime 'directly' into the courtroom. 'Media-made' in this sense refers to the diverse types of contemporary media discussed in the "Introduction: Crime in the Media" section. For example, the MOP for rape is comprised of scripts that define 'sexual un/availability', related, for example to alcohol, resistance or sexual history. The jury system upholds the principle that someone accused of a crime will be judged by their fellow citizens. As representative of society at large, the jury system ensures that the 'common sense, popular knowledge of a group of ordinary citizens' (Findlay, 1988, p. 163) is used to assess the guilt of someone on trial. For critical linguists, psychologists, criminologists and sociologists of the law, this 'common sense, popular knowledge' is not organic or atomistic but rather it is constructed by the institutions of society itself. For crime and deviance generally and types of crime specifically, most of the 'popular knowledge' of jurors is acquired through interaction with the media (Levenson, 2001). Despite all of us being subject to the law, most members of the public have only limited direct contact with the legal system but have routine and consistent contact with the media so that their MOPs of different types of crime are comprised of scripts primarily constructed by the press, entertainment, infotainment and other media.

The legal system and the institutions of the law do not attempt to deny the importance of the 'common sense, popular knowledge' of members of the jury, indeed the 'community values' (Brown & Neal, 1988, p. 131) of jurors are prized by legal professionals exactly because they can be seen to uphold the very concept of justice itself. Legal rules and conventions do not attempt to assess the 'ideological baggage' of this popular knowledge, to engage in the critical linguistic analysis of crime in the press, for example, and certainly this is not an undertaking that we would expect. Nonetheless, the involvement of the press in court is regulated by both statute and convention. In Britain the Contempt of Court Act 1981 regulates publications that represent a 'substantial risk that the course of justice in the proceedings in question will be seriously impeded or prejudiced' (Contempt of Court Act 1981 Chapter 49, Section 2.2). There is no parallel Contempt legislation in the United States owing to the 'freedom of the press' enshrined in the First Amendment, however across the Common Law certain conventions and legal positions also aim to regulate the role of the media at trial. The so-called fade factor holds that the effect of pre-trial publicity of a case on the jury will be overtaken by the immediacy of courtroom proceedings and the 'facts' offered in evidence at trial. From a cognitive linguistic perspective, legislation and conventions like the Contempt of Court Act and the fade factor fail to recognise the memory-based nature of cognition. Additionally the view of the legal system on trial by media is that it is a matter for high-profile, individual cases whilst the Spectrum of Trial by Media on the other hand holds that it is in the routine representation of types of crime across the media that consistently construct and reinforce the mental schemata of readers and jurors where trial by media can really be situated. Of course we acknowledge that the legal system is somewhat hamstrung on the issue of trial by media. Should the definition and understanding of trial by media evolve to recognise trial by media as routine instead of infrequent and high-profile, the process of justice itself would be undermined. Corker and Young (2003, p. 249) state rightly that 'public confidence in the criminal justice system would surely be undermined if notorious defendants accused of horrific crimes could escape justice, not even stand trial because of adverse publicity'. To be legitimate, justice must be seen to be done after all.

One area in which the pursuit of some reform might be a more plausible endeavour is in the linguistic composition of the criminal trial itself. This is where second dimension of the Spectrum of Trial by Media—'enhanced trial by media'—addresses the 'forensic' end of the critical-forensic linguistic interface. Enhanced trial by media contends that the linguistic structure of the trial, rather than draw jurors into the immediate context of the proceedings, actually leads to a further isolation that enhances their reliance on the media-made conceptualisations of crime that mark the direct trial by media dimension of the Spectrum. A prevailing principle of the Common Law courtroom is the 'law/facts distinction', the arrangement that defines the jury as the 'triers of fact' and the judge as the 'trier of the law'. Juries cannot be expected to enter the trial process as legal experts, they are required to bring their knowledge of society rather than a knowledge of the law. In principle it 'falls on the trial lawyers and the judges both to convey to the jury clearly and effectively the legal elements of their decision-making task' (Heffer, 2008, p. 47). The jury applies their 'common sense, popular knowledge'—which comes to a large degree from the media in terms of crime—to the facts of a case and then should filter this evaluation through an understanding of the law that is given by legal professionals in court. However, the enhanced trial by media dimension of the Spectrum offers a comprehensive examination of the criminal trial by jury that suggests that the linguistic composition of the trial is an impediment to the courtroom conversion jurors are supposed to undergo in court.

For example, the comprehensibility of the instructions given by judges to the jury has been the longstanding subject of research in forensic linguistics (Dumas, 2000; Heffer, 2002, 2006, 2008; Tiersma, 1999). In a pioneering study that is still seminal in linguistic analyses of judicial instructions, Charrow and Charrow (1979) demonstrate that instructions are 'not well understood by the average juror' and that 'linguistic constructions' are responsible for this limited comprehension (Charrow & Charrow, 1979, p. 1309). Amongst these linguistic features are whiz deletion, multiple negations, difficult lexical items, poor discourse structure, embedding, nominalisation and passivisation. As well as forming part of 'instruction isolator 1', these features also mark a 'technical language isolator' that inhibits jury comprehensibility of the courtroom trial. These 'isolators' are two of six—the others being the isolator of silence, evidential isolator, narrative structure isolator and instruction isolator 2 (language of the burden and standard of proof)—that make up the 'framework of jury isolation' (Statham, 2016, p. 89). This framework operates across the jury trial and demonstrates by forensic linguistic analysis that the theoretical conversion that juries go through at trial is heavily curtailed by the linguistic composition of the trial itself. It is not possible here to expand on each of the isolators individually but Fig. 12.1 illustrates their effect on the comprehensibility of jurors. Enhanced trial by media suggests therefore that this linguistically-driven limitation of jury comprehensibility causes jurors to have enhanced reliance on the media-made conceptualisations of crime that accompany them into court. In turn this suggests that improvements to the linguistic composition of the trial would improve jury comprehensibility and potentially affect the consistency of trial by media as envisioned here. Reinforced trial by media, the third dimension of the Spectrum, is when lawyers, who Temkin (2000) has demonstrated are fully aware of attitudes possessed by jurors, structure their narratives to appeal to these schemata and scripts.

Reinforced Trial by Media: Sexual Assault in the Courtroom

At trial the complainant's version of events is elicited through direct examination during the presentation of the case for the prosecution, where the public prosecutor questions the alleged victim. The complainant is then cross-examined by the representative for the alleged perpetrator. As discussed in the "Sexual Assault in the Media" section, major tactics of cross-examining lawyers are to malign the character of

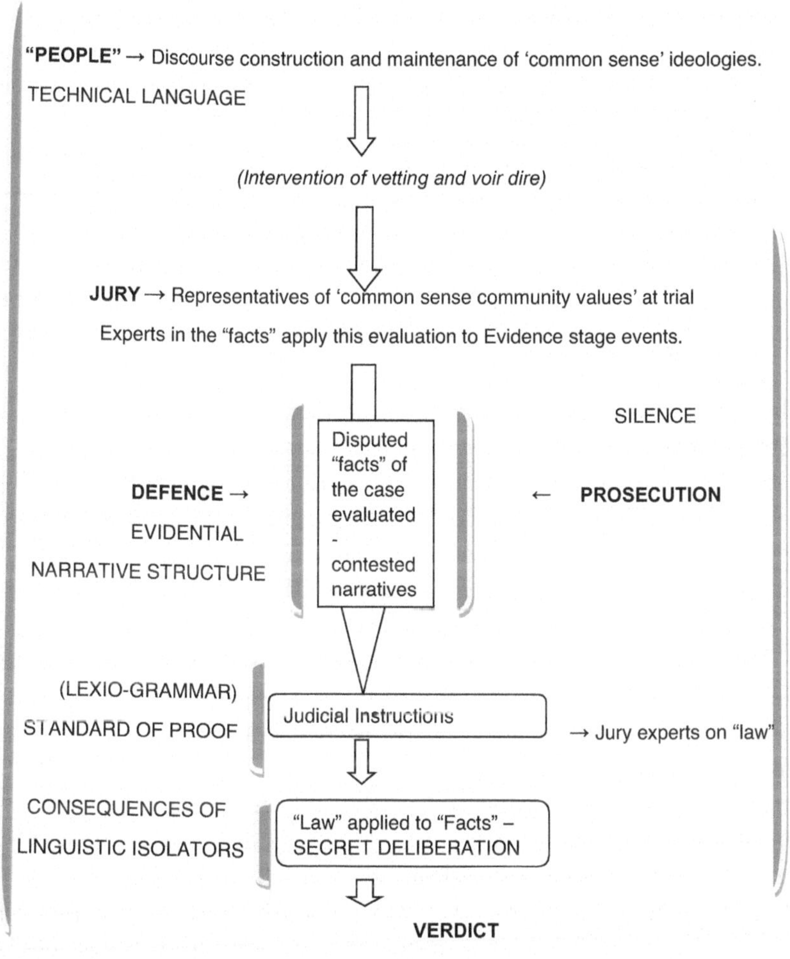

Fig. 12.1 Framework of jury isolation (after Statham, 2016, p. 89)

the alleged victim and her version of events. Owing to the primary significance of consent for sexual relations over the occurrence of sex itself in rape cases and noting the comparative absence of eyewitness accounts and of forensic evidence, the evidence given by the alleged victim is usually the main, if not the only site for the defence to discredit her account (Johnson et al., 2012).

Figure 12.2 comprises a transcript from the cross-examination of a woman who alleged she was raped at a party in Britain in 2019. The defendant was acquitted at trial in 2022 after the jury found that sexual relations were consensual.

The defence attorney in this case recasts the rape narrative previously proffered by the Crown Prosecutor as an instance of consensual sex, which ultimately casts sufficient doubt for the defendant to be found 'not guilty' at trial. In the account given by the defence, the alleged victim is presented as the instigator of contact with the defendant; 'flirting' outside a pub and then going to a 'house party' refer to behaviour that is 'unrespectable' and which recalls two sub-narratives—'party girl' and 'chooses not to go home'—noted by Statham (2016) that are used by defence advocates to construct a master narrative of consent in a rape trial. The alleged victim's role as the instigator in this version is solidified by her 'suggest[ing] that you could both go and sleep together in a room upstairs'. These actions do not legally make the defendant less culpable if sex itself is non-consensual but they are not the actions of a 'virgin' who is 'sexually unavailable' and 'respectable'.

The complainant's status as 'vamp' is constructed further in the subsequent sequence of questions in which she instigates arousing physical contact—'rubbing your body against his'—and undertakes actions that will be defined as sexual and consensual by the jury—'kissing with him in the bed', 'removing your underwear' and 'being on top of him'. In terms of the transitivity framework (Halliday, 1994), the complainant is the Actor in a range of material processes in which the defendant is the Goal, the acted-upon participant. Linguistically many of the questions of the defence attorney here incorporate a presupposition trigger known as a 'factive'. Presupposition is when a speaker embeds the assumed truth of an action into a subordinated part of a clause whilst matrix verbs—in this case 'remember'—restrict the ability of a respondent to deny the truth of a proposition which is presupposed as fact. For example, in 'Do you remember removing your underwear?' the proposition that 'you removed your underwear' is embedded as a fact, the question is about whether or not you 'remember' it. By answering 'no', this 'factive' status of the action is not compromised, it is only your memory of the act that is denied. The number of presupposed questions here emphatically

Defence barrister: Were you flirting with [the defendant] outside the pub before going to the house party?
Alison: No.
Q: Did you suggest to [the defendant] that you could both go and sleep together in a room upstairs?
A: No.
Q: Are you saying you can't remember if that happened or not, or it didn't happen?
A: I don't think that happened, but I was, I don't remember anything that happened, as I stated in my video interview, I don't remember anything after the game in the kitchen.
Q: Do you remember cutting your head from falling on the shower thing, if I use the words "on the shower thing"?
A: No, I don't remember that.
Q: In regards to what happened in the room, do you remember lying with your back towards [the defendant] and rubbing your body against his?
A: No, I don't remember that.
Q: Do you remember kissing with him in the bed?
A: No, I don't remember that.
Q: Do you remember removing your underwear?
A: No, I don't remember that.
Q: And in regards to consensual intercourse with him, do you remember having sex with him?
A: No, I don't remember having sex with him.
Q: Do you remember being on top of him at some stage?
A: No, I don't remember that.
Q: If I suggest to you that you consented to sex with [the defendant], you took part in consensual sex with him, what would you say to that?
A: I would say that is not true.
Q: In your evidence, you're asked by the officer who's asking you questions to account for your position in the bed, [the defendant's] position in the bed, and you say 'it's all a blur'.
A: Well-
Q: Is that because your version of events didn't happen?
A: No, it's because I woke up and I was drunk and confused, and I didn't, I don't remember how I woke up this morning, let alone on that night.
Q: Did you, the following day, realise that [Alison's female friends] knew that you slept in the same room with [the defendant] and is that why you told them you were raped?
A: No.
Q: Because you were embarrassed about the night before.
A: No.
Q: Your Honour, those are my questions. Thank you.
[Redirect by Prosecution barrister]
Prosecution barrister: I'm concerned as to whether the defence really have put their whole case to the witness because in interview the defendant said various things, might I put those matters in, just to see what [Alison] says? They are matters raised in interview that haven't actually been put to her.
Q: It may be suggested that you were actually having consensual sex for 10 minutes, and were actually having an orgasm with [the defendant]. What do you say about that?
A: I'd say that's not true.
Q: And that you at one point actually put his penis into your vagina.
A: No, that's not true.
Q: And that you were making pleasurable noises that meant that someone came in and knocked on the door.
A: No, that's not true.
Q: So, when you woke up, how did you actually feel?
A: I was confused. I woke up to my head banging against the headboard, and I didn't really know where I was or who I was with or what was going on.

Fig. 12.2 Trial transcript

constructs a scenario in which a 'sexually available' woman 'took part in consensual sex'. The force of these denials is undermined by the fact that the attorney essentially ignores them. By not responding to or acknowledging the complainant's denials, the lawyer generates an implicature for the jury that they are untrue and that the defendant is unreliable and untrustworthy. Westera et al. (2016, p. 18) state that the prevalence of the defence's version of events in cross-examination means that the 'complainant's responses are virtually superfluous to proceedings'. This impression is reinforced by the linguistic structure of the questions and by their content as operating to construct a master narrative of consent in which the alleged victim can be characterised by media-made frameworks like 'vamp', 'sexually available' and 'unrespectable'.

Many of the questions here are also examples of closed questions—polar interrogatives that require a yes/no answer—and leading questions which comprise a declarative statement like 'you took part in consensual sex with him'. Whilst more open-ended questions are utilised in direct examination (Brewer & Stapleton, 2008), Kebbell et al. (2003) establish that closed and leading questions that restrict the response options of witnesses are much more common in cross-examination in general and in rape cases specifically. Whilst Westera et al. (2016) acknowledge that changes to questioning practices to improve witness recollection have been adopted in investigative contexts, such as by the police, these would not be beneficial for courtroom defence advocates whose primary responsibility is to act in the interests of their clients. Zydervelt et al. (2017) establish that questioning reliability, plausibility, credibility and consistency are core strategies of lawyers when cross-examining complainants in rape cases. Key tactics for reliability are memory fallibility, barriers to perception and alcohol/drug intoxication and each is present in the cross-examination of the complainant here. The witness consistently states, 'I don't remember' and she is 'drunk and confused' so that the reliability of her evidence is highly questionable. A particularly interesting part of this cross-examination is the segment of re-direct by the Crown Prosecutor, an attempt to limit the effectiveness of the defence's strategies. By asking 'what would you say about that?' and 'how did you actually feel?', the prosecution does not focus on the memory of the witness but asks open questions which permit more response control to the alleged victim. The prosecutor essentially implies here that the defence may have omitted certain explicit questions because they would be more difficult for the jury to believe. Essentially the defendant is given greater scope and opportunity for denial on the central issue of consent. It is difficult to establish the effectiveness of the re-direct here given that the prosecutor has activated conceptualisations of an explicit sexual nature but which nonetheless do not include scripts like resistance, violence or injury and at a point in the proceedings when the witness' reliability has already been undermined. Certainly 'I woke up to my head banging against the headboard' undermines any impression that the complainant has consented but her credibility and character have been significantly maligned at this stage in the questioning.

Zydervelt et al. (2017, p.552) point out that a number of legal reforms across Common Law jurisdictions have been introduced to attempt to mitigate the fact that 'rape victims still find cross-examination distressing, demeaning and humiliating'. In what he has called the 'interactional violence' of cross-examination, Matoesian (1993) has gone so far as to suggest that the trauma of rape is reproduced in the courtroom and scholars such as Kingi and Jordan (2009) and Wheatcroft et al. (2009) offer similar views on what Williams (1984) initially labelled as 'secondary victimization'. Legal reforms have included changes to the definition of rape, the removal of the resistance requirement and a number of so-called special measures, such as pre-recorded evidence, which is extensively available in Britain, for example. 'Rape shield' legislation theoretically prevents the introduction of a victim's sexual history, although the defence will often be successful in applications to include this information, and judges no longer point juries to be wary of rape instances that do not include injuries or evidence of physical violence. Despite the fact that many of these advancements were 'developed to prevent leveraging rape myths' (Zydervelt et al., 2017, p. 554), the format of cross-examination questions and the topics and themes they address has undergone almost no statistically significant changes since the 1950s (Westera et al., 2016; Zydervelt et al., 2017). Owing to an advocate's awareness of the importance of 'attitudes ingrained in people' on the jury, rape myths that are constructed in the media continue to play a routine role in criminal trials so that reinforced trial by media operates consistently and in sexual assault cases especially.

Conclusion

A 2023 report (Quilter & McNamara, 2023) of a study commissioned by the Department of Communities and Justice (NSW) finds that despite the successful operation of some special measures, rape myths and stereotypes persist at trial. Half of the trials addressed by the report permitted questioning on the complainant's sexual history whilst an even greater percentage of cross-examinations addressed the lack of resistance, memory fallibility and delayed reporting. Despite calls in this report to reform the adversarial nature of proceedings and the fact that the combative nature of cross-examination in rape cases is deeply uncomfortable, defendants are presumed innocent and have the fundamental right to a robust defence whilst 'defence lawyers have a duty to defend their clients by discrediting the evidence against them, whatever form that evidence takes' (Zydervelt et al., 2017, p. 553). Owing to the persistence of rape myths in the media and the success of defence lawyers in utilising these in court, despite how unpalatable these tactics are (Kebbell et al., 2007), there is very little incentive for defence lawyers with a duty to the version of events given by their client to change their tactics. This fact is what makes ongoing debates about prosecuting sexual assault so complex. Rape cases are notoriously difficult to prosecute, have significantly low attrition rates as they move through the legal process—resulting in very many being dropped by public prosecutors—and are significantly underreported. Each of these realities can be related to the prevalence of rape myths in the media and to their tactical and routine presence at trial. Zydervelt et al. (2017, p. 566) note that 'to the extent that putting rape myths in front of the jury has a good chance of creating reasonable doubt, it is likely that lawyers will continue to use them' and there is a range of evidence that juries respond to these myths (Ellison & Munro, 2010; Grubb & Turner, 2012). Temkin and Krahé (2008) suggest that criminal justice reforms—which Victim Commissioner for England and Wales, Dame Vera Baird, in her 2022 report referred to as merely 'tinkering round the edges'—are unlikely to affect trial strategies until social attitudes to rape have changed. Given that the influence of the media on these attitudes is more likely to grow than to diminish in the age of social media, perhaps the only likely context in which social attitudes to rape may change is in a more diverse and ethical media space such as that discussed by scholars like Couldry (2019) and Couldry et al. (2013, 2018). In addressing the role of the media in the 'struggle for social progress', Couldry et al. (2018, p. 188) suggest that, alongside areas relating to infrastructure and regulation of corporate media structures, 'to be able to make reasonable decisions in political, cultural and social areas' people are served by 'curated, credible, verified and contextualized information' provided by journalists. It is also acknowledged here (Couldry et al., 2018, p. 180) that profit has so far been the sole goal of media organisation whilst how the lexico-grammatical content of media could be regulated so that it represents socially responsible journalism is another matter that is very difficult to envision, it is the case that social attitudes to rape are unlikely to undergo drastic change in any other context and trial strategies that rely on rape myths will otherwise abide. After all juries are representative of these social attitudes and the Spectrum of Trial by Media demonstrates their prevalence in court. As these social attitudes are largely media-made, 'putting rape myths in front of a jury' is a clear and continuing pattern of reinforced trial by media.

Competing Interests The author has no conflicts of interest to declare that are relevant to the content of this chapter.

References

Benedict, H. (1992). *Virgin or vamp: How the press covers sex crimes.* Oxford University Press.

Bennett, W. L., & Feldman, S. F. (1981). *Reconstructing reality in the courtroom.* Tavistock.

Brewer, T., & Stapleton, T. (2008) Examination-in-chief. In J. B. Robertson, A. Beck, & S. Mount (Eds.), *Introduction to advocacy* (2nd ed., pp. 205–245). New Zealand Law Society.

Brown, D., & Neal, D. (1988). Show trials: The media and the gang of twelve. In M. Findlay & P. Duff (Eds.), *The jury under attack* (pp. 126–140). Butterworths.

Burt, M. (1980). Cultural myths and support for rape. *Journal of Personality & Social Psychology, 38*, 217–230.

Burt, M., & Albin, R. S. (1991). Rape myths, rape definitions and probability of conviction. *Journal of Applied Social Psychology, 11*, 212–230.

Charrow, R., & Charrow, V. (1979). Making legal language understandable: A psycho-linguistic study of jury instructions. *Columbia Law Review, 79*, 1306–1374.

Clark, K. (1992). The linguistics of blame. In M. Toolan (Ed.), *Language, text and context* (pp. 208–224). Routledge.

Corker, D., & Young, D. (2003). *Abuse of process in criminal proceedings*. Butterworths.

Couldry, N. (2019). *Media: Why it matters*. Polity.

Couldry, N., Rodriguez, C., Bolin, G., Cohen, J., Goggin, G., Kraidy, M., Iwabuchi, K., Lee, K. S., Qui, J., Volkmer, I., Wasserman, H., Zhao, Y., Koltsova, O., Rakhmani, I., Rincón, O., Magallanea-Blanco, C., & Thomas, P. (2018). Media, communication, and the struggle for social progress. *Global Media & Communication, 14*(2), 173–191.

Couldry, N., Madianou, M., & Pinchevski, A. (Eds.). (2013). *Ethics of media*. Palgrave Macmillan.

Devlin, The Hon. Sir Patrick. (1956). *Trial by jury*. Stevens.

Dowler, K. (2006). 'Sex, lies and videotape': The presentation of sex in local television news. *Journal of Criminal Justice, 34*, 383–392.

Duff, P., & Findlay, M. (1997). Jury reform: Of myths and moral panics. *International Journal of Sociology of Law, 25*, 363–384.

Dumas, B. K. (2000). US pattern jury instructions: Problems and proposals. *Forensic Linguistics, 7*(1), 49–71.

Du Mont, J., Miller, K. L., & Myhr, T. L. (2003). The role of 'real rape' and 'real victim' stereotype in the police reporting practices of sexually assaulted women. *Violence Against Women, 9*, 466–486.

Ellison, L., & Munro, V. (2010). Getting to (not) guilty: Examining jurors' deliberative processes in and beyond the context of a mock rape trial. *Legal Studies, 30*, 74–97.

Findlay, M. (1988). The role of the jury in a fair trial. In M. Findlay & P. Duff (Eds.), *The jury under attack* (pp. 161–172). Butterworths.

Franiuk, R., Seefelt, J., & Vandello, J. (2008). Prevalence of rape myths in headlines and their effect on attitudes towards rape. *Sex Roles, 58*, 790–801.

Galtung, J., & Ruge, M. H. (1965). The structure of foreign news. *Journal of International Peace Research, 1*, 64–90.

Greenwood, L. (1997). *Sex offenses and offenders*. US Government Printing Office.

Grubb, A., & Turner, E. (2012). Attribution of blame in rape cases. *Aggression & Violent Behaviour, 17*, 443–452.

Halliday, M. A. K. (1994). *Introduction to functional grammar* (2nd ed.). Arnold.

Heffer, C. (2002). If you were standing in Marks and Spencers: Narrativisation and comprehension in English summing-up. In J. Cotterill (Ed.), *Language in the legal process* (pp. 228–246). Palgrave.

Heffer, C. (2006). Beyond reasonable doubt: The criminal standard of proof instruction as communicative act. *Speech, Language & the Law, 13*(2), 159–188.

Heffer, C. (2008). The language and communication of jury instruction. In J. Gibbons & M. T. Turell (Eds.), *Dimensions of forensic linguistics* (pp. 47–67). John Benjamins.

Jewkes, Y. (2011). *Media and crime*. Sage.

Johnson, D., Peterson, J., Sommers, I., & Baskin, D. (2012). Use of forensic science in investigating crimes of sexual violence. *Violence against Women, 18*, 193–222.

Kebbell, M., Deprez, S., & Wagstaff, G. (2003). The direct and cross-examination of complainants and defendants in rape cases. *Psychology, Crime & Law, 9*(1), 49–59.

Kebbell, M., O'Kelley, C. M. E., & Gilchrist, E. L. (2007). Rape victims' experience of giving evidence in English courts. *Psychiatry, Psychology & Law, 14*, 111–119.

Kingi, V., & Jordan, J. (2009). *Responding to sexual violence: Pathways to recovery*. Ministry of Victims' Affairs.

Kitzinger, C., & Thomas, A. (1995). Sexual harassment: A discursive approach. In S. Wilkinson & C. Kitzinger (Eds.), *Feminism and discourse: Psychological perspective* (pp. 32–48). Sage.

Lakoff, G. (1987). *Women, fire and dangerous things*. University of Chicago Press.

Larcombe, W. (2002). The 'ideal' victim v. successful rape complainants. *Feminist Legal Studies, 10*(2), 131–148.
Levenson, J. (2001). Inside information: Prisons and the media. *Criminal Justice Matters, 43*, 14–15.
Margolis, J. (2009). Anatomy of a jury trial. *EJournalUSA, 14*(7).
Matoesian, G. M. (1993) *Reproducing rape: Domination through talk in the courtroom*. Polity.
Mayr, A., & Machin, D. (2013). *The language of crime and deviance*. Continuum.
Meyer, A. (2010). Evil monsters and cunning perverts: Representing and regulating the dangerous paedophile. In M. Deflem (Ed.), *Popular culture, crime and social control* (pp. 195–219). Emerald.
Meyers, M. (1997). *News coverage of violence against women*. Sage.
Mooney, A. (2007). When rape is (not quite) rape. In J. Cotterill (Ed.), *The language of sexual crime* (pp. 198–216). Palgrave.
O'Hara, S. (2012). Monsters, playboys, virgins and whores: Rape myths in the news media's coverage of sexual violence. *Language & Literature, 21*(3), 247–259.
Olsen-Fulero, L. (1997). Common sense rape judgements: An empathy-complexity theory of rape juror story making. *Psychology, Public Policy & Law, 3*(3), 403–427.
Quilter, J., & McNamara, L. (2023). Experience of complainants of adult sexual offences in the District Court of NSW: A trial transcript analysis. *Crime & Justice Bulletin, 259*, 1–46.
Schank, R. C. (1982). *Dynamic memory*. Cambridge University Press.
Schlesinger, P., & Tumber, H. (1994). *Reporting crime: The media politics of criminal justice*. Oxford University Press.
Smith, V. L. (1993). When prior knowledge and law collide: Helping jurors use the law. *Law & Human Behavior, 17*(5), 507–536.
Soothill, K. (1991). The changing face of rape. *British Journal of Criminology, 31*, 383–392.
Soothill, K. (2004). Editorial. *Sex, Crime & the Media, 14*, 227–230.
Soothill, K., & Walby, S. (1991). *Sex crimes in the news*. Routledge.
Statham, S. (2016). *Redefining trial by media*. John Benjamins.
Temkin, J. (2000). Prosecuting and defending rape: Perspectives from the Bar. *Journal of Law & Society, 27*(2), 219–248.
Temkin, J,. & Krahé, B. (2008). *Sexual assault and the justice gap*. Hart.
Tiersma, P. (1999). *Legal language*. University of Chicago Press.

Tiersma, P. (2007). The language of consent in rape law. In J. Cotterill (Ed.), *The language of sexual crime* (pp. 83–104). Palgrave.

Westera, N., Zydervelt, S., Kaladelfos, A., & Zajac, R. (2016). Sexual complainants on the stand: A historical comparison of courtroom questioning. *Psychology, Crime & Law, 23*(1), 15–31.

Wheatcroft, J. M., Wagstaff, G. F., & Moran, A. (2009). Revictimizing the victim? How rape victims experience the UK legal system. *Victims & Offenders, 4*, 265–284.

Williams, J. E. (1984). Secondary victimization: Confronting public attitudes about rape. *Victimology, 9*, 66–81.

Zydervelt, S., Zajac, R., Kaladelfos, A., & Westera, N. (2017) Lawyers' strategies for cross-examining rape complainants: Have we moved beyond the 1950s? *British Journal of Criminology, 57*, 551–569.

13

Publicity and Legitimacy of Public International Law: Trial by Media and Proceedings Before International Courts and Tribunals

Paolo Vargiu

Introduction

The term 'trial by media' is often viewed negatively within the legal community, as it is intended as describing the media's propensity to dramatize court proceedings overshadowing their legal, personal, and social implications (Rogers, 2022).[1] This sensationalization transforms such proceedings into public spectacles, without much attention to the significant impact of reporting and debating on the lives, livelihoods, and privacy of those involved (Morris, 2003). Especially in high-profile cases involving celebrities, the media's approach can obliterate the human

[1] See the cases at the European Court of Human Rights, Application no. 31411/07, *Mustafa Kamal Mustafa (Abu Hamza) (No. 1) v. the United Kingdom*, Decision as to the Admissibility, 18 January 2011, para. 18; *T. v. the United Kingdom*, Application no. 24724/94, Judgment, 16 December 1999, para. 74.

P. Vargiu (✉)
University of Leicester, Leicester, UK
e-mail: paolo.vargiu@le.ac.uk

L. Gies (ed.), *Trial by Media*, Palgrave Studies in Crime, Media and Culture, https://doi.org/10.1007/978-3-031-80593-6_13

aspect of the trials, using dramatic personal experiences as mere instruments of entertainment (Friedman, 2015; Johnson, 2003). This not only affects the public's perception and understanding of legal matters, but also exacerbates the trauma for victims and their families, who have to endure public scrutiny and speculation on issues that are ultimately personal and private. Defendants, regardless of their innocence or guilt, face the risk of being judged prematurely by the public, influenced by media narratives rather than facts, and have their lives and reputations affected regardless of the outcome of the proceedings. However, trial by media would not be as influential, were the public not interested in questions of justice and, in a way, morality too. The attention trials receive is not solely based on curiosity or entertainment, but also indicates the existence of a deeper engagement with the ethical and moral issues raised by these cases. Therefore, the public's interaction with such media coverage suggests that, notwithstanding its downsides, trial by media can also encourage meaningful debates on justice, ethics, and legal and moral principles.

While prominent in domestic contexts, trial by media is conspicuously less prevalent in international law (Farrell et al., 2019). Indeed, aside from a handful of cases that involve egregious breaches of global peace and security such as invasions, mass violations of human rights or attempts at genocide, disputes between states seldom capture the headlines or ignite a level of public engagement that mirrors the fervour of the parallel trials conducted across traditional and social media platforms. This disparity in media coverage and public interest between domestic trials and international proceedings may initially suggest a diminished relevance of the latter to the general public. However, this assumption underestimates the profound impact international disputes have on the lives of individuals as well as the global community. Indeed, the significance of international disputes extends far beyond the immediate parties involved, influencing global politics, economics, and security. Therefore, I argue that international legal disputes not only match the importance of domestic trials in their impact on the public, but also have more tangible effects in the long term. This underscores the necessity for such disputes to be reported with accuracy, and for reporters and commentators to have a foundational understanding of international law in order to stimulate an informed public debate.

In this chapter, I argue that trial by media, despite its drawbacks, could serve as an invaluable instrument to develop the general public's understanding and engagement with international law and relations. Presenting international disputes in a manner that is both accessible and engaging can raise awareness on the tangible effects of treaties and customary international law on global politics and justice and the lives of all humans. For trial by media to reach this potential, the coverage of international disputes must transcend the sensationalism that too often affects the reporting of domestic trials, offering instead a platform for informed discussions and transforming international law from an esoteric discipline reserved for lawyers and diplomats to a subject of global debate.

This chapter is structured as follows: Sect. "International Law and the Media: Reporting and Misconceptions" provides a brief overview of how matters of international law are commonly addressed in the media; Sect. "Trial by Media as a Mainly Domestic Matter" presents the reasons why trial by media is mainly a domestic phenomenon; Sect. "International Trial by Media?" addresses the advantages and disadvantages of trial by media in international law from a theoretical standpoint, leading to Sect. "The Case for International Trial by Media" in which I make the case for the development of an 'international' trial by media. Finally, Sect. "Concluding Remarks" of the chapter will draw the threads together and provide some final thoughts.

International Law and the Media: Reporting and Misconceptions

The disputes between sovereign states and between states and international organizations or private investors, that constitute the international case-law, tend to unfold without much attention from the public or media coverage. The proceedings before the International Court of

Justice (ICJ) arising out of the Russian invasion of Ukraine[2] and the attacks of Israel against Gaza[3] stand as outliers to this general trend—partly because the proceedings have begun relatively shortly after the outbreaks of the two conflicts, and partly because of their significance: the former marks the first noteworthy European conflict since the dissolution of former Yugoslavia (Klip & Freeland, 2022), and the latter represents a zenith of prolonged tensions, both notable for their severity and the implications for international relations in the present day. In contrast, many other international legal cases, such as The Gambia v. Myanmar, receive at best a cursory nod from the media notwithstanding the undeniable relevance of the facts at the heart of the case.[4]

This disparity in media attention between domestic trials and proceedings before international courts and tribunals is in fact comprehensible. Domestic legal disputes often revolve around matters that are directly relatable to lay audiences, as they are based on common occurrences or involve celebrities or commercial entities that are household names, thereby engendering the interest of the general public (Greer & McLaughlin, 2010). International disputes, by comparison, frequently involve areas such as tariff barriers, demarcation of territorial limits, and quite often mere questions of interpretation of rules of international law.[5] These subjects, while certainly significant at the diplomatic and economic levels, seldom capture the attention of lay audiences, as are

---

[2] International Court of Justice, *Allegations of Genocide under the Convention on the Prevention and Punishment of the Crime of Genocide (Ukraine v. Russian Federation)*, Judgment of 2 February 2024. https://www.icj-cij.org/sites/default/files/case-related/182/182-20240202-jud-01-00-en.pdf.

[3] International Court of Justice, *Application of the Convention on the Prevention and Punishment of the Crime of Genocide in the Gaza Strip (South Africa v. Israel)*, Order of 26 January 2024. https://www.icj-cij.org/sites/default/files/case-related/192/192-20240126-ord-01-00-en.pdf.

[4] International Court of Justice, *Application of the Convention on the Prevention and Punishment of the Crime of Genocide (The Gambia v. Myanmar)*. https://www.icj-cij.org/case/178.

[5] See, *e.g.*, International Court of Justice, *Legal Consequences of the Separation of the Chagos Archipelago from Mauritius in 1965*, Advisory Opinion of 25 February 2019. https://www.icj-cij.org/sites/default/files/case-related/169/169-20190225-ADV-01-00-EN.pdf; *Judgment No.2867 of the Administrative Tribunal of the International Labour Organization upon a Complaint Filed against the International Fund for Agricultural Development*, Advisory Opinion of 1 February 2012. https://www.icj-cij.org/sites/default/files/case-related/146/146-20120201-ADV-01-00-EN.pdf; *Accordance with international law of the unilateral declaration of independence in respect of Kosovo*, Advisory Opinion of 22 July 2010. https://www.icj-cij.org/sites/default/files/case-related/141/141-20100722-ADV-01-00-EN.pdf.

characteristically technical and remote from the daily concerns of the average person. Moreover, the legal frameworks governing these disputes are typically not within the ambit of public knowledge, making it difficult for media outlets to present these cases in a manner that engages the general viewer or reader. Consequently, such international legal proceedings are relegated to the specialized pages of academic journals and the occasional brief mention in mainstream news, and rarely become the focal points of extensive media scrutiny and public debate.

Additionally, mistakes frequently flaw the reporting of international disputes, such as the habitual merging of international judicial bodies and their case-law by journalists, or fundamental misunderstandings of international law. One example is the expression 'The Hague Court', often used ambiguously and referring indistinctly to the aforementioned ICJ, the International Criminal Court (ICC), or the International Criminal Tribunal for the former Yugoslavia (ICTY), among others (Antonijević, 2023; Jones, 2023)—not to speak of the common misrepresenting of the European Court of Human Rights (ECtHR) as an organ of the European Union (EU), or the confusion of the European Convention on Human Rights (ECHR)[6] with the UK Human Rights Act 1998 (HRA).[7] The geographical proximity of many courts and tribunals does little to clarify the distinct functions, jurisdictions, and purposes of these institutions, leading to a blurred public perception and, often, inaccuracies in reporting. However, the core issue in media coverage often stems from a lack of familiarity with the unique characteristics of international law itself. Among these, most prominent are the absence of a clear hierarchy among states, international organizations and courts, the lack of a coercive force to ensure compliance with international law, and the misunderstood roles of organizations such as the United Nations (UN) and the EU (Hameed, 2017). The UN, in particular, is frequently misconceived as a supranational entity wielding control over the behaviour of states, while the EU is often mistakenly regarded as a kind of *de facto* federal state with an authority that supersedes that of

[6] https://www.echr.coe.int/documents/d/echr/convention_ENG.

[7] https://www.legislation.gov.uk/ukpga/1998/42/contents.

national governments (Moravcsik, 2017; Tessitore, 2007). Such misconceptions too contribute to a poor quality of reporting, and subsequently a certain degree of confusion among the general public.

This confusion does not aid lay audiences in understanding international law. The complex and rather technical nature of international legal proceedings, the roles and relationships between different courts and organizations, and the mostly implicit balance of powers and jurisdictions in international law are often lost or oversimplified in media reports. As a result, lay audiences are left with an incomplete or inaccurate reporting of international legal proceedings, thus diminishing the public's understanding of the significance of international law and the basic aspects of its function in international relations. The public's limited awareness of international law, its actors and its bodies, and the often inaccurate reporting on treaties and disputes, have been used at times, especially by politicians and stakeholders in financial affairs, to portray an imbalanced perspective of international diplomatic interactions, often twisted by national, personal, or partial interests.[8] Moreover, there is a pronounced gap in public understanding regarding the significant financial compensations granted to foreign investors by arbitral tribunals operating under international legal frameworks.[9] The awards issued by investment tribunals can have profound implications for national economies and public finances, but the treaties and dispute settlement mechanisms operating in investor-state relationships remain largely unknown to the general public. The media's reticence in covering these proceedings, combined with the esoteric nature of international law itself, obstructs the input of comprehensible and accessible information

[8] The use of the term 'Europe' to refer to the European Union as well as the European Court of Human Rights is so widespread that the Council of Europe has had to include in its own website a disambiguatory page: https://www.coe.int/en/web/about-us/do-not-get-confused. On how such linguistic ambiguity has served political ambitions may I refer the reader to Arato (2016).

[9] See *ex multis* Dearden (2021), Nielsen (2022), and Limb (2022). A partial exception (which still labelled arbitral tribunals as 'secret courts', but properly reported how compensation works in investment treaties) is Sheffield (2016). For context, the case-law of the International Centre for Investment Disputes (ICSID), including pending cases, is publicly available at https://icsid.worldbank.org/cases/case-database.

to non-specialists (Hakimi, 2016). Consequently, this lack of engagement and understanding undermines the capacity of lay audiences to fully grasp the implications of international legal decisions on their lives and on the economic policies of their own countries. Such insufficient awareness also impedes the development of an informed public debate on international legal matters, leaving the field predominantly to experts, select politicians, and policymakers.

Trial by Media as a Mainly Domestic Matter

Domestic trials, as mentioned beforehand, tend to garner widespread public attention mainly due to the dynamics between celebrity culture, media coverage, and public interest. Indeed, trials involving high-profile individuals often transcend their legal confines, morphing into spectacles of public consumption. This transition is primarily fuelled by the public's fascination with celebrities, whose personal and professional lives are subjected to intense scrutiny chiefly for recreational purposes. The recent case of Johnny Depp and Amber Heard, which commenced with a civil lawsuit in the United Kingdom[10] and concluded with another in the United States,[11] exemplifies this trend. The case began with a lawsuit brought by Depp against the publisher of The Sun newspaper for libel in which the High Court in London ruled in favour of The Sun, finding that the majority of the alleged incidents of domestic violence had been proven to the civil law standard. Depp subsequently filed a $50 million defamation lawsuit against Amber Heard in US in response to an op-ed she wrote for The Washington Post in December 2018 (Heard, 2018). Heard countered with a counterclaim, accusing Depp of orchestrating a 'smear campaign' against her and describing his lawsuit as a continuation of abuse and harassment. The trial for the defamation case took place in 2022, and over the course of six weeks, the jury (and, via the media, the public) was presented with extensive evidence, testimony from both

[10] *Depp v News Group Newspapers Ltd* [2020] EWHC 2911 (QB).

[11] Fairfax County Civil Court, CL-2019-2911, *John C. Depp, II v. Amber Laura Heard*. All the documents of the case are available at https://www.fairfaxcounty.gov/circuit/high-profile-cases.

Depp and Heard, and witness statements from friends, employees, and experts. The jury found that Heard had defamed Depp in three instances cited in his lawsuit; Heard was however awarded compensatory damages for her counterclaim, finding that one of Depp's attorney's statements was defamatory.

Notwithstanding the complexity of the case—at least from a procedural standpoint—the trial became a narrative constructed and deconstructed in the public arena. Both Depp and Heard found their personal ordeal broadcasted globally, turning the trial into as much of a media phenomenon as a legal one: in fact, the public's interest in the trial was not merely about seeking justice or understanding the legal arguments presented in court, but rather about partaking in the drama that unfolded between two worldwide famous individuals. One may argue that this trial's extensive media coverage underscored the symbiotic relationship between celebrity culture and the media, rather than the legal issues at stake. News outlets, social media platforms, and online forums became all places where the minutiae of the trial (or rather of the parties' and witnesses' statements) were analysed, often blurring the lines between factual reporting and sensationalism. The coverage of the trial on the media effectively moulded the public perception of the individuals involved—including the witnesses, for lack of evidence about the impact on lawyers and judges—influencing opinions on what the outcome should have been before the court had issued a judgement.

Moreover, the Depp v. Heard trial shown how social media play different—and at times clashing—roles in the discourse surrounding high-profile legal cases. On the one hand, social media platforms enabled a democratization of opinion, allowing individuals to express their views, share information, and engage in discussions about the trial. On the other hand, these platforms also facilitated the spread of misinformation, unchecked speculation, and harassment, complicating the public's ability to discern the truth. Depp v. Heard thus became a battleground not just in legal terms but also in the court of public opinion, where narratives were as likely to be shaped by emotion and personal bias as by evidence and legal arguments. This engagement with the trial raised questions about the impact of such a comprehensive media coverage on the legal process itself. Courts are assumed to operate independently of public opinion, save for the unquestionable influence that local customs and culture have on judges and lawyers (Sherwood & Clark, 1981); however, the pervasive media attention and the ensuing public scrutiny can exert a further indirect influence on the proceedings. In the hearings of Depp v. Heard, the attorneys in particular were evidently aware of the media's watchful eye, and one may wonder to what extent their strategies and even their demeanour in the courtroom were influenced by the knowledge that their actions and words were being analysed and judged by an audience far beyond the jury and judge (Nelson, 2024; Stern, 2022; Terry, 2022). It is ultimately evident that the public's interest in domestic trials involving celebrities extends beyond a mere quest for entertainment and carries the risk of transforming a process meant to adjudicate court proceedings into a show that feeds public curiosity but may not always serve the cause of justice.

Domestic trial by media, however, is not limited to cases involving celebrities: the fascination of the public may also arise from the inherent details of the cases themselves—from the grisly nature of a crime to scandals involving well-known figures of the political arena. A particularly gruesome crime, for example, grips public attention due to its shock value and the underlying fear it instils in the community. The extremity of the act, especially when contrasted with the perceived normality of everyday life, allows the media to create narratives that the public is drawn to. Similarly, scandals involving public figures captivate the public due to the inherent contradiction they present. People placed in positions of power, whether in politics, entertainment, or other spheres, are often seen as role models or, at the very least, as individuals held to a higher standard of conduct. When these figures are involved in legal disputes, especially those involving criminal activity, it not only marks a fall from grace but also discloses vulnerabilities and imperfections hidden beneath their public personas. The public's interest in these cases often stems from a mix of disappointment, betrayal, and a keenness to understand how those who wield influence can be implicated in the same ills they are expected to stand against.

A good example of this is the trial of Amanda Knox and Raffaele Sollecito (whose largely diminished role in the trial by media did not mirror that in the proceedings in court) (Gies & Bortoluzzi, 2016).

Amanda Knox, an American citizen studying abroad in Italy, was charged with the murder of her British roommate, Meredith Kercher, in November 2007. Kercher was found dead in the apartment she shared with Knox, under circumstances that suggested a violent assault. The prosecution's case against Knox and her then-boyfriend, Raffaele Sollecito, was built on a combination of forensic evidence, disputed DNA findings, and their allegedly erratic behaviour following the discovery of Kercher's body. Another individual, Rudy Guede, was also implicated in the crime; his fingerprints and DNA were found at the scene, and he was subsequently convicted in a separate trial. The initial trial concluded in 2009 with Knox and Sollecito being found guilty of murder, leading to Knox receiving a 26-year prison sentence and Sollecito a 25-year one. The judgement was met with widespread media coverage and public debate worldwide, with many questioning the strength of the evidence against Knox and Sollecito. In 2011, an appeal led to a review of the forensic evidence, which highlighted significant flaws in the DNA analysis presented at the first trial. This review played a crucial role in the Court of Appeal's decision to overturn their convictions in 2011. However, in 2013, the *Corte di Cassazione* (Italy's highest court) annulled the acquittal, citing inadequacies in the appellate court's reasoning and ordered a new trial.[12] In 2014, a new trial reinstated the convictions, sentencing Knox to 28 years and six months in prison and Sollecito to 25 years. This decision was once again overturned in March 2015, when the *Corte di Cassazione* definitively acquitted Knox and Sollecito of the murder charges, citing a lack of evidence to sustain the convictions and criticizing the police investigation for its errors.[13]

While the precise influence of media on the outcomes of trials remains challenging to quantify, trial by media raises significant questions about the interaction of media narratives, public perception, and the judicial process. The media presents the facts, allegations, and developments of a trial, but often accompany them with a variable dose of speculation and sensationalism—and the attention is not always centred on the whole case, but rather on its more appealing (or the more salacious) aspects: it

[12] Cassazione Penale, Sez. I., 18 giugno 2013 (ud. 25 marzo 2013), n. 422.

[13] Cassazione Penale, Sez. V, 7 settembre 2015 (ud. 27 marzo 2015), n. 36080.

is quite telling that, even though the trial before the Italian courts had both Sollecito and Knox appearing as defendants, most of the attention in the media and in the public debate was always directed to Knox only. This coverage does not merely inform the public but also invites them to participate in the discourse, leading individuals to form and share their own opinions about the case. Social media platforms, in particular, have amplified this trend, allowing for the rapid dissemination of information, rumours, and personal viewpoints. As a result, a parallel narrative often develops alongside the legal proceedings, shaped by public opinion, social media campaigns, and sometimes even activism. As a consequence, the scrutiny and debate can shine a light on aspects of the legal system that may require reform or highlight cases that might otherwise have been overlooked; however, the pressure of public opinion and the potential for misinformation can also pose challenges to the principles of due process. Parties to a trial may find their rights to privacy and, especially in jury-based judicial systems, the presumption of innocence until proven guilty compromised by prejudicial coverage and public judgement.

Moreover, the involvement of the public in these trials, fuelled by media coverage, can lead to a phenomenon where the trial by media outlasts the actual court proceedings. Long after a verdict has been reached, discussions, debates, and analyses continue to proliferate on social media and in other forums. This sustained engagement can have lasting effects on the individuals involved, who may find themselves perpetually tried in the court of public opinion, regardless of the outcomes in the courts of law. Knox, in particular, is hardly portrayed in Italian media as a former defendant who was eventually acquitted, but rather as one who got away with the proverbial murder; and her recent conviction for slander against Patrick Lumumba has done little to change the tone of the reporting of news on her trials.[14]

---

[14] See for instance the reporting of the judgement by RAI—Italy's national public broadcasting company—at https://www.rainews.it/articoli/2024/06/amanda-knox-oggi-il-processo-per-calunnia-a-porte-chiuse-accusa-lumumba-9cb23603-0eb0-40d9-8b11-2058ba650bff.html. The Guardian offers a rather comprehensive chronicle of the media coverage of Amanda Knox's post-trial life, including commentary on the questionable and controversial Netflix series, and Knox's reaction to such continued attention, at https://www.theguardian.com/us-news/amanda-knox.

International Trial by Media?

The issue of trial by media, with regard to international legal proceedings, poses rather different questions. The phenomenon of limited public interest in cases pending before international courts and tribunals, such as the ICJ, contrasts sharply with the often fervent attention that domestic legal proceedings can attract. This disparity is due to several factors, from the nature of the cases themselves, to the media's role in shaping public perceptions, and broader engagement with international legal proceedings.

As stated beforehand, among the many cases brought before the ICJ, a mere few have managed to attract the general public's attention to a degree comparable with high-profile domestic trials. Recent examples include the aforementioned The Gambia v. Myanmar, Ukraine v. Russia, South Africa v. Israel and, to a lesser extent, Armenia v. Azerbaijan cases.[15] These cases stand out primarily due to their connection to universally recognized human rights issues and the involvement of state actors in disputes with significant geopolitical implications. However, the level of media attention and public scrutiny they receive pales in comparison to that of major domestic legal disputes involving famous individuals or rather gruesome crimes. It is worth reflecting on the reasons behind this difference.

First and foremost, it is necessary to consider the difference in terms of perceived significance of the issue at stake, and to what extent the matter can be personalized. Although any domestic case has, in fact, the same impact on an individual not involved in the dispute as a case involving two states—especially when neither of these states is the nationality of the individual in question—it is undeniable that domestic trials such as Depp v. Heard often involve issues or personalities that are already part of the public's everyday discourse, making them more accessible and immediately impactful in spite of the substantial disparities in lifestyle between these celebrities and ordinary people. In contrast, the matters

[15] International Court of Justice, *Application of the International Convention on the Elimination of All Forms of Racial Discrimination (Armenia v. Azerbaijan)*. https://www.icj-cij.org/case/180; *Application of the International Convention on the Elimination of All Forms of Racial Discrimination (Azerbaijan v. Armenia)*. https://www.icj-cij.org/case/181.

addressed by international courts, though undeniably significant, can seem distant or abstract to the average person, lacking a direct connection to their personal experiences or national context. Additionally, the complexity of international law and the procedural aspects of international courts and tribunals can be rather obscure for lay audiences (Dias Varela, 2013). These cases frequently involve detailed legal arguments and principles that require specialized knowledge to fully understand. The media often struggle to convey the content and apparent contradictions of the rules international law in an engaging and comprehensible manner. This problem is exacerbated by the tendency of news outlets to prioritize stories that promise immediate interest and high viewership or readership figures, which can lead to a lack of thorough and accurate coverage of proceedings before international courts and tribunals. Trial by media, therefore, is much less frequent in international proceedings, and this prevents the development of a level of engagement comparable to that stimulated by domestic proceedings. On the one hand, this undoubtedly alleviates the burdens that stakeholders might otherwise endure were their case be under more thorough public scrutiny; on the other hand, a consequence of this is that the general public is left less informed and less emotionally connected to these important but underrepresented issues.

One factor that likely contributes to the lack of fascination with international legal proceedings by the general public is its consent-based nature. International law lacks the sort of hierarchical distribution of coercive powers proper of domestic legal systems. Instead, it relies on the cooperation of the state parties; and the principle of *pacta sunt servanda*, upon which the fundamental trust necessary for a horizontal system like international law is built, is not a mere custom, but it is the very basis of peaceful and fruitful relationships among states (Falk, 1959). One can hardly think of a more fascinating system than international law, in which each participant is equal to all others, any decision that affects multiple states is taken jointly, and the dispute settlement mechanism is not based on hierarchy but rather voluntary acceptance of jurisdiction (Goldie, 1983; Rosenne, 1974; Tammes, 1971). Such fascination, however, tends to affect specialists and very select few others: mainstream opinions on international law fluctuate from confusing it with a form of politics or a glorified version of diplomatic relations, to questioning whether it is, in fact, law—given the common identification, by the lay person, of law with command and coercion (Ozaki, 1984). In the eyes of lay audiences, international legal proceedings are long and hardly spectacular: one can easily compare extracts of the Depp v. Heard trial and any submission before the ICJ to ascertain the differences in terms of general palatability. Moreover, most cases and not followed by very tangible outcomes: the consequences of an internationally wrongful act consist mainly in cessation, non-repetition, and reparation.[16] All of these aspects can contribute to a perception of inefficacy or detachment from the immediate concerns of justice and accountability; and the procedural delays and diplomatic considerations inherent in international law can frustrate public expectations for swift and decisive action, diminishing interest and confidence in the ability of international courts to address grievances and resolve conflicts. In fact it is not uncommon, when an international conflict outbreaks, for the media to state that 'international law is arbitrarily applied' (Malik, 2023) even before an international court has had the chance to apply such law, notwithstanding the fact that, for an international court or tribunal to act, it is necessary that a state actually brings a case before it.[17] In comparison, even those who are most critical as to the effectiveness of criminal law dare to question the very legal nature of criminal law upon the mere occurrence of a homicide or a robbery. Offences persist despite the existence of criminal law, just like wars and invasions continue to occur notwithstanding the establishment of the UN and the ratification of the UN Charter (albeit at a much lower rate than pre-WWII times).[18] While this misconception is mostly due, as previously mentioned, to a generally widespread lack of familiarity with what international law is and how it operates, positions like these reinforce the general public's perception of the alleged ineffectiveness of international law, and the misguided idea that international law is not, in fact, law (D'Amato, 1984).

---

[16] International Law Commission, *Draft Articles on Responsibility of States for Internationally Wrongful Acts*, Supplement No. 10 (A/56/10), Ch. IV.E.1, November 2001, Articles 30 and 31.

[17] United Nations, *Statute of the International Court of Justice*, 18 April 1946, Article 40.

[18] United Nations, Charter of the United Nations, 1 UNTS XVI, 24 October 1945.

However, a number of international legal proceedings, if properly reported and discussed in traditional and social media, would actually have potential to resonate with a wider audience. The question is not whether trial by media can have an influence on disputes between states, but rather what beneficial effects would the media bring—and what could be the disadvantages of trial by media in matters that, while less spectacular than a breakup of Hollywood stars, are in fact more influential on peoples' lives on a global scale.

The Case for International Trial by Media

A more extensive media coverage of cases pending before international courts and tribunals would be instrumental to highlight issues that might otherwise remain under the radar of the global public and to educate the public about international law, the acts being adjudicated, and the legal proceedings in place to address them. Such an increase in visibility would bring international law out of the academic and legal circles and develop a quality debate on the legal and moral questions raised by international relations. To a certain extent, trial by media could perhaps contribute to increasing the accountability of international courts and tribunals too. Similarly to its effect on domestic proceedings, the presence of a better-informed public eye can serve as a check on these institutions, ensuring that they adhere to their mandates and standards of fairness and justice. In instances where political or diplomatic pressures might threaten to sway judicial proceedings, public scrutiny can act as a counterbalance.

While these possible effects of trial by media may be considered mere wishful thinking—at least in light of the relative influence of public outrage and protests on ongoing conflicts (Vasi, 2006)—there are a few aspects in which trial by media might prove invaluable as an instrument of education and clarification of complex issues for lay audiences. Chief among this is the concept of rule of law. While the notion is not foreign to most people, for it is an expression that features in many non-specialist publications and communications, its definition, particularly in the context of international law, is not as widespread as it should. The principle of rule of law generally asserts that everyone, including individuals, organizations, public or private entities, and states, must be subject to laws that are openly declared, uniformly applied, and any disputes are impartially determined by courts. These laws must align with international norms and human rights standards (Bingham, 2010).[19] Extensive coverage by the media on international disputes would first and foremost ensure that this notion becomes a familiar one in the public debate, and allow the civil society to exert pressure on the actors of international law for their actions to always adhere to such a standard. The next logical step would be for the media to act as tremendously effective vehicles of awareness on human rights. The concept of human rights is another one of those that routinely feature in the public debate, although its actual content is often ignored, misunderstood, and occasionally misrepresented (usually for political purposes). While the concept is often invoked, indeed, human rights cases before international courts and tribunals that have the potential of clarifying the extent of individual rights (such as the ECtHR or the Human Rights Committee of the UN) are seldom reported properly due to either lack of interest or lack of understanding, let alone discussed at large in the media while pending. This is notwithstanding the fact that human rights cases—whether domestic or international—tend to be reported by the media far more often than most other international law cases; however, such attention too is fairly limited to those select few cases capable of stimulating discussion and possibly outrage, while those that are not prone to evoke indignation get ignored in spite of their actual significance for one's understanding of their own rights and freedoms. This leads to a widespread lack of awareness about the rights that pertain to each and any person, thus *de facto* frustrating the very objective of human rights instruments—namely, to provide agency to individuals against possible restrictions to their fundamental rights and liberties by the state parties to the international community (Goodman & Jinks, 2003; Sohn, 1982). Finally, it is extremely rare that cases between a multinational corporation and a foreign host state are reported in the media. It is true, as often

[19] The definition reported here refers to that of Kofi Annan, in United Nations Secretary-General (2004). *The Rule of Law and Transitional Justice in Conflict and Post-conflict Societies: Report of the Secretary-General*, 23 August 2004, UN Doc S/2004/616.

underscored in the specialized as well as the non-specialist literature, that these cases are tried before arbitral tribunals, the publicity of which is dramatically inferior to that of institutions designed to settle disputes between states (Lindseth, 2020; Waibel et al., 2010); at the same time, significant efforts have been made recently to increase the transparency and the publicity of disputes between foreign investors and host states, to the point that it is now quite rare for such a dispute to begin and unfold completely hidden from the possibility of public scrutiny.[20] Notwithstanding these efforts, these disputes are publicised in the adjudicating institutions' websites but usually not reported in the media, unless the resulting award is so sizable that it becomes a matter of public interest; and even in those cases, though, the details of the proceedings tend to remain confined to the legal quarters of practitioners and academics and, for the most part, very private due to a lack of interest by the media. Disputes involving foreign companies, which touch on the equilibrium between investor rights and the interests of host states and their citizens, are actually quite suited for examination in the courts of public opinion. This suitability stems from their inherently less formal character compared to traditional court proceedings, and the fact that the issues at stake tend to be more accessible and relevant to the general public than the typical disputes adjudicated by the ICJ (Cole, 2017). Trial by media, therefore, would be a much welcome sideshow to the arbitral proceedings, spreading awareness on the various ramifications of contemporary global capitalism.

It goes without saying that the possible disadvantages of trial by media in domestic settings would be amplified in case of international disputes. In particular, a certain tendency to simplify and sensationalize facts and judgements can lead to misrepresentations of the legal issues involved, potentially skewing public perception and understanding. This oversimplification risks reducing sophisticated legal arguments and considerations to emotionally charged narratives that may not accurately reflect

[20] The most recent development in this sense is constituted by the 2014 United Nations Commission on International Trade Law (UNCITRAL) *Rules on Transparency in Treaty-based Investor-State Arbitration*, at https://uncitral.un.org/sites/uncitral.un.org/files/media-documents/uncitral/en/rules-on-transparency-e.pdf; but see also Shaw and Guzman-Diaz (2022) and Papanastasiou (2021).

the scope and purpose of international law, however appropriate they may at times be to allow lay audiences to relate to the issues at stake. Furthermore, it remains to be seen what would be the effects of the pressure generated by widespread media coverage and public opinion on the proceedings of international courts and tribunals. While such pressure could motivate these bodies to act more diligently and transparently, there is also the risk that it could inadvertently influence judges who, in spite of their professional obligations to impartiality, are not immune to the broader socio-political environment. This external pressure could affect the integrity of the judicial process, potentially leading to decisions that are more reflective of public sentiment than of the legal merits of the case—as it happens, at times, in domestic courts. The impact of trial by media on the fairness of judgements in international courts also hinges on the diversity of media coverage and the perspectives presented. In a global context, where media outlets may have varying degrees of independence from political influences, the narrative around a case can be significantly shaped by the interests of those controlling the media and the relationship between the states involved in the disputes and those in which such disputes are reported.

Finally, one should not overlook the role of social media in amplifying the 'trial by media' phenomenon. Social media platforms enable the rapid dissemination of information, as well as the mobilization of public opinion on a scale previously unimaginable. The effect can be ambivalent: while social media allow for a more democratic participation in discussing and scrutinizing legal issues (including international ones), such a horizontal debate also opens the door for misinformation, unchecked speculation, and the viral spread of biased or inaccurate representations of cases. It is thus fundamental to conceive a form of trial by media aimed at increasing the legal literacy of the public, ensuring that people are better equipped to critically evaluate the information presented to them, accompanied by a culture of ethical journalism that prioritizes accuracy and depth of coverage over sensationalism. This would be an ideal form of trial by media—one that contributes positively to the understanding and resolution of disputes before international courts and tribunals.

Concluding Remarks

As stated at the very beginning of this chapter, the concept of 'trial by media' carries quite some negative connotations in legal circles. The media's tendency to sensationalize legal proceedings often overshadows the gravity of the situations at hand, and the expression 'trial by media' embodies a series of repercussions, the most notable being the transformation of legal proceedings into spectacles. Such transformation is problematic for several reasons, primarily because it involves matters that significantly impact individuals' lives, livelihoods, and privacy. The sensationalization of legal proceedings is particularly concerning due to the human elements at the core of these trials. In cases involving celebrities, there is a tendency among the public to overlook the fact that the subjects of these trials are, first and foremost, human beings. The media's portrayal of these events often strips away the humanity of those involved, reducing their experiences to mere entertainment for the masses. Similarly, in criminal trials, the sensationalist approach can lead to a public disconnect from the human suffering involved. Victims and their families, who are already dealing with trauma, are subjected to the additional burden of having their experiences dissected and speculated upon by the media and, by extension, the public. This relentless exposure can force them to relive their pain on a daily basis. Furthermore, the individuals on trial, who may be innocent or guilty, find their fate hanging in the balance not just in a court of law but also in the court of public opinion, where the legal aspects of guilt and innocence are often eclipsed by sensationalist narratives.

In spite of these significant drawbacks, it is undeniable that trial by media also reflects a certain degree of engagement with the concepts of justice and morality. It is evident that part of the interest in these trials stems from more than mere curiosity or a thirst for drama: ultimately, there is also a genuine engagement with the moral questions that these cases raise. This suggests that the public's engagement with legal proceedings through the media is not entirely devoid of substance. Indeed, the discussions generated by media coverage of trials show a certain attention, at least by a part of the public, on the morality of human actions and the principles of justice. There is, in other words, a relationship between public interest, media coverage, and the civil and criminal justice systems which is at the same time exploited and enhanced by the media; and the public's engagement has the potential to transcend sensationalism and raise fundamental ethical questions.

Comparing proceedings before international courts and tribunals with domestic trials reveals both similarities and differences. Like domestic trials, disputes between states are based on fundamental questions of justice, with morality and ethics frequently coming to the fore. However, since the subjects of these disputes are states rather than individuals, the dynamics of the proceedings—and the reporting of the hearings—are rather different. These differences notwithstanding, the potential for media coverage to engage the public in discussions of justice and morality remains. The absence of the same level of sensationalism that characterizes many high-profile domestic trials can actually serve as an advantage in the context of international disputes. Given that such disputes often lack the personal drama and celebrity involvement that fuel media spectacle, they present a less enticing target for sensationalist media coverage. This relative lack of glamour, however, does not diminish the importance or public interest in these disputes: on the contrary, the depersonalization of these proceedings offers an opportunity for media coverage to focus more on the substantive issues at stake and to facilitate a more informed public debate on matters of international justice and morality. In this context, the role of the media in extending the debate on international disputes to society at large becomes crucial. The media has the potential to build a bridge between the apparently abstract international law and the general public, making the themes of international justice and morality of state conduct accessible and relevant to a wider audience. By means of focusing on the substantive issues rather than the spectacular ones, media coverage can contribute to a more thorough public understanding of international disputes and the rules that govern the relationships among sovereign entities.

Media plays a central role in developing the public's perception and understanding of global affairs. It is thus imperative for reporters to acquaint themselves with the foundational principles of international law in order to ensure that their coverage ultimately constitutes an informed trial by media. This necessity arises from the fact that the reporting of international disputes does not merely consist in the dissemination of news: it can—and should—also educate the public, inform global discourses, and influence international relations. Reporting and debating based on a thorough understanding of legal principles turns trial by media from a potential source of misinformation into an informed and much needed platform for public debate. This would ensure that the public receives accurate information, free from sensationalism, about the proceedings as well as the content of international law, which is mostly unknown to lay audiences as well as non-specialized professionals. Moreover, trial by media in international law would lead the public to understand the legal framework within which states operate, the nature of their obligations, the consequences of their actions from the standpoint of international relations, and the remedies available to states and individuals affected by violations of international law—in short, to make the public understand the significance of international law in pursuing peace, security and justice worldwide.

Contrary to the prevalent view in legal circles that trial by media is a detrimental force, I would argue that trial by media is neither inherently negative nor positive. Much like other aspects of entertainment, the impact of trial by media is contingent on the manner of its execution. On the one hand, trial by media can be a vehicle for the sensationalization and depersonalization of disputes, reducing sophisticated and often controversial legal and ethical issues to mere spectacles for public consumption. On the other hand, when conducted with a commitment to accuracy and a thorough understanding of international law, trial by media can transform into an exceptional instrument for education and global growth, promote international integration, and serve as a vital channel for information.

Competing Interests

The author has no conflicts of interest to declare that are relevant to the content of this chapter.

References

Antonijević, M. (2023, November 24). Five Serbian radicals charged with contempt before Hague court. *Euractiv.* https://www.euractiv.com/section/politics/news/five-serbian-radicals-charged-with-contempt-before-hague-court/

Arato, K. (2016). Pros and cons in the Brexit campaign: What do they tell us about the European Union? *ELTE Law Journal, 1*, 49–72.

Bingham, T. (2010). *The rule of law.* Allen Lane.

Cole, S. (2017). The lost promise of arbitration. *SMU Law Review, 70*(4), 849–890.

D'Amato, A. (1984). Is international law really 'law'? *Northwestern University Law Review, 79*(5&6), 1293–1314.

Dearden, N. (2021, August 2). Corporate courts vs the environment. *Al Jazeera.* https://www.aljazeera.com/opinions/2021/8/2/corporate-courts-vs-the-environment

Dias Varela, M. (2013). Central aspects of the debate on the complexity of international law. *Emory International Law Review, 27*(1), 1–22.

Falk, R. (1959). International jurisdiction: Horizontal and Vertical conceptions of legal order. *Temple Law Quarterly, 32*(3), 295–321.

Farrell, M., Drywood, E., & Hughes, E. (Eds.). (2019). *Human rights in the media: Fear and fetish.* Routledge.

Friedman, L. (2015). *The big trial: Law as a public spectacle.* University Press of Kansas.

Gies, L., & Bortoluzzi, M. (Eds.). (2016). *Transmedia crime stories: The trial of Amanda Knox and Raffaele Sollecito in the globalized media sphere.* Palgrave Macmillan.

Goldie, L. (1983). International 'constitutionality': State sovereignty and the problem of consent. In A. R. Blackshield (Ed.), *Legal change: Essays in honour of Julius Stone* (pp. 316–333). Butterworth.

Goodman, R., & Jinks, D. (2003). Measuring the Effects of human rights treaties. *European Journal of International Law, 14*(1), 171–183.

Greer, C., & McLaughlin, E. (2010). 'Trial by media': Policing the 24–7 news mediasphere and the 'politics of outrage.' *Theoretical Criminology, 15*(1), 23–46.

Hakimi, M. (2016). The media as participants in the international legal process. *Duke Journal of Comparative & International Law, 16*(1), 1–34.

Hameed, A. (2017). Some misunderstandings about legislation and law Chinese. *Journal of International Law, 16*(3), 475–514.

Heard, A. (2018, December 18). I spoke up against sexual violence—And faced our culture's wrath. That has to change. *The Washington Post*. https://www.washingtonpost.com/opinions/ive-seen-how-institutions-protect-men-accused-of-abuse-heres-what-we-can-do/2018/12/18/71fd876a-02ed-11e9-b5df-5d3874f1ac36_story.html

Johnson, J. (2003). The entertainment value of a trial: How media access to the courtroom is changing the American judicial process. *Villanova Sports & Entertainment Law Journal, 10*(1), 131–152.

Jones, M. (2023, December 11). The Hague court wants to probe war crimes in Israel and Gaza. Where does Europe stand? *Euronews*. https://www.euronews.com/my-europe/2023/12/11/the-hague-court-wants-to-probe-war-crimes-in-israel-and-gaza-where-does-europe-stand

Klip, A., & Freeland, S. (Eds.). (2022). *Annotated leading cases of international criminal tribunals. Volume 69: The International Criminal Tribunal for the former Yugoslavia, International residual mechanism for criminal tribunals, 30 June 2016–29 November 2017*. Intersentia.

Limb, L. (2022, November 19). Inside the 'secretive' tribunals where fossil fuel companies 'steal' from developing countries. *Euronews*. https://www.euronews.com/green/2022/11/19/inside-the-secretive-tribunals-where-fossil-fuel-companies-steal-from-developing-countries

Lindseth, P. (2020). Theorizing backlash: Supranational governance and international investment law and arbitration in comparative perspective. *The Journal of World Investment & Trade, 21*(1), 34–70.

Malik N. (2023, November 27). The war in Gaza has been an intense lesson in western hypocrisy. It won't be forgotten. *The Guardian*. https://www.theguardian.com/commentisfree/2023/nov/27/war-gaza-lesson-western-hypocrisy-international-community

Moravcsik, A. (2017, April 13). Europe is still a superpower—And it's going to remain one for decades to come. *Foreign Policy*. https://foreignpolicy.com/2017/04/13/europe-is-still-a-superpower/

Morris, J. (2003). The anonymous accused: Protecting defendants' rights in high-profile criminal cases. *Boston College Law Review, 44*(3), 901–946.

Nelson, C. (2024). 'A public orgy of misogyny': Gender, power, media, and legal spectacle in Depp v Heard. *Feminist Media Studies*. https://doi.org/10.1080/14680777.2024.2304225

Nielsen A. (2022, November 14). Revealed: Secret courts that allow energy firms to sue for billions accused of 'bias' as governments exit. *The Guardian*.

https://www.theguardian.com/business/2022/nov/14/revealed-secret-courts-that-allow-energy-firms-to-sue-for-billions-accused-of-bias-as-governments-exit

Ozaki, S. (1984). International law and coercion. *Japanese Annual of International Law, 27*, 12–26.

Papanastasiou, A. (2021). Media wars: Transparency and aggravation in international investment arbitration. In K. Fach Gómez (Ed.), *Private actors in international investment law. European yearbook of international economic law* (pp. 191–207). Springer.

Rogers, B. (2022). The dangers of trial by social media. *The Law Society Gazette.* https://www.lawgazette.co.uk/commentary-and-opinion/the-dangers-of-trial-by-social-media/5111441.article

Rosenne, S. (1974). Consent and related words in the codified law of treaties. In *Mélanges offerts à Charles Rousseau: la communauté internationale* (pp. 229–248). Pedone.

Shaw, G., & Guzman-Diaz, L. (2022). Looking in on transparency: A 2020 review of states' reactions to the UNCITRAL rules on transparency and the Mauritius convention. *Yearbook on International Investment Law & Policy, 2020*, 349–383.

Sheffield, H. (2016, April 27). TTIP: UK Government found secret courts in trade deal have 'lots of risk and no benefit' in its only assessment. *The Independent.* https://www.independent.co.uk/news/business/news/ttip-uk-government-only-did-one-assessment-of-trade-deal-and-found-it-had-lots-of-risks-and-no-benefit-a6999646.html

Sherwood, D. R., & Clarke, M. A. (1981). Toward an understanding of local legal culture. *Justice System Journal, 6*(2), 200–217

Sohn, L. (1982). The new international law: Protection of the rights of individuals rather than states. *The American University Law Review, 32*(1), 1–64.

Stern, B. (2022). Social media's influence on the outcome of trials: State v. Casey Anthony & Depp v. Heard—How Florida can prevent a breakdown in the adversarial process. *Nova Law Review, 47*(1), 111–136.

Tammes, A. (1971). The status of consent in international law. *Netherlands Yearbook of International Law, 2*, 1–28.

Terry, A. (2022). The ethics of 'LawTube' after Depp v Heard. *Journal of the Legal Profession, 47*(1), 231–246.

Tessitore, J. (2007, January 11). *The UN at 60: Still misunderstood*. Carnegie Council for Ethics in International Affairs. https://www.carnegiecouncil.org/media/article/the-un-at-60-still-misunderstood

Vasi, I. (2006). The new anti-war protests and miscible mobilizations. *Social Movement Studies, 5*(2), 137–153.
Waibel, M., Kaushal, A., Chung, K., & Balchin, C. (Eds.). (2010). *The backlash against investment arbitration*. Kluwer Law International.

Index

L. Gies (ed.), *Trial by Media*, Palgrave Studies in Crime, Media and Culture,
https://doi.org/10.1007/978-3-031-80593-6

The manufacturer's authorised representative in the EU is Springer Nature Customer Service Centre GmbH, Europaplatz 3, 69115 Heidelberg, Germany. If you have any concerns regarding our products, please contact ProductSafety@springernature.com

Printed and bound by CPI Group (UK) Ltd, Croydon, CR0 4YY
01/10/2026
02225912-0016